John Keats

JOHN KEATS
A Thematic Reader

THE LETTERS OF JOHN KEATS 1814-1821,
edited by Hyder E. Rollins, Cambridge, Mass.:
Harvard University Press, 1958, by the President and
Harvard College, and used by permission of the

W. Carlos Williams, Pictures ...
ton, N.J.: [illegible], Octob ...

M. Wei ...
(part selec ...
Correl.

The ...
edi ...

E. Will ...
Fellow ...

Philosophical Librar ... 15, South ... on Avenue ...
York, N.Y., used ...
Printed in the United States of America

Joseph Sendry
The Catholic University of America

Richard Giannone
Fordham University

Key Editions
John C. Gerber, General Editor

Scott, Foresman and Company
Glenview, Illinois   London

PREFACE

Keats came into his own in the modern century. The nineteenth century held a view of Keats directly opposite to the one most widely held now. Gerard Manley Hopkins, in advance of his time on many other poetic issues, spoke for whole generations of past readers when in 1888 he took his forerunner to task for a statement that had offended many, delighted a few, but was taken by virtually all as the essential Keats: "O for a Life of Sensations rather than of Thoughts!" Hopkins decided that Keats lived "in mythology and fairyland the life of a dreamer." The last two generations, by contrast, have viewed Keats more complexly. Because dream and subjectivity have had a great deal to say to the modern mind, Keats's poetic myths have appeared more as ways into reality than as escape routes from it. We now see that if he was not (and he did not claim to be) a systematic philosopher, Keats did reflect with the deep, concrete insight of a poet on man's perennial dilemmas. Poetry for Keats was not an avoidance of truth; it was a way of rendering truth.

The catalyst for this shift in the public assessment of Keats was the letters. In reading the poems it is easy to be sidetracked by their richly patterned surfaces, but the letters bring us directly to Keats's major concerns. Here we glimpse the poet in his shirt-sleeves, his constantly active mind moving naturally between the everyday and the profound, covering the full range of experience from the private to the universal. In rapport with a sympathetic correspondent Keats confronted the old riddles, and the strategies he devised to unravel these endlessly tangled questions reveal how Keats's mind grew. To go from the letters to the poems is to discover a new Keats, the authentic Keats who believed that poetry helps man live, makes men men.

Accordingly, we give Keats's letters prominence. We establish an interdependence between the letters and the poetry that suggests

Keats's belief that art shapes life. And from the letters comes the uniquely Keatsian idea of "negative capability" and our understanding of the special sense that he gives to more widely used concepts such as the imagination and identity. In the pages that follow we provide an unusually generous sampling of Keats's work. Each entry is placed with the other of Keats's writings to which it is most nearly related in theme. In this way the letters and poems illuminate each other to best advantage.

The thematic groupings that we use express our reading of the whole of Keats's work, an interpretation indebted to the accumulated insights of recent scholarship. Yet much of what Keats wrote is so rich in meaning that it defies any rigid classification. A case could be made, for example, to place the whole or parts of *Endymion* under "negative capability," "imagination," "the moral dimension," or "identity," instead of where it is, as a case study in the composition of a poem. Our thought here was to emphasize an aspect which would be true to Keats's progress and which would elicit from the reader his own proposal for arranging this poet's work.

We present Keats in his wholeness also by including many little-known minor pieces in addition to the major ones, and a representative offering of inferior works with those of unquestioned merit. And though Keats is most celebrated for his shorter lyrics, notably the odes, we think that the longer narratives—especially *Endymion* and the two *Hyperions*—are needed to show the tendency toward expansiveness out of which Keats's celebrated intensity is distilled. Our presentation of *Endymion* has its own claim to distinction. We have allowed Keats himself to write the preface to this work: numerous statements in letters covering a year and a half trace the chronological development of *Endymion* from its inception to the first reviews. The result is an invaluable study as much in the self-education of the poet as in the making of the poem. The letters on *Otho the Great* and the text of that play, here given in its entirety, show Keats in an unusual (for him) and seldom-noticed role—that of aspiring commercial playwright trying to make it in the marketplace.

If our book can be said to have a single theme, it would be the growth of the poet himself. The selections in the first part, "The Poet and Reality," are arranged to present the most important motifs in Keats's thought. They show him moving from a formless, somewhat dogmatic skepticism through an eager quest for experience for its own sake to a complex moral vision. The second part of the book, "The Poet at His Craft," shows Keats at the work of creation. Here he discusses the practical problems of composition; he arrives at a breakthrough by discovering the importance of form and, in fact, the nature of form; he tells us what he thinks of his fellow poets, and in doing so, tells us about himself as artist.

We try to help the reader in several ways. The lead essay comprehends Keats's total effort as a poet, and it spells out a rationale for the arrangement of the selections that follow. A chronological outline sketches the main events in Keats's life, against which the individual letters (the dates for which appear before each entry) and the individual poems (their dates of composition appear after the selections) may be compared. Thumbnail biographies of the friends with whom Keats corresponded—to be found at the end of the anthology—will help readers catch nuances in the letters that might otherwise be missed. The endnotes to the poems will clarify difficult allusions within the text.

We have taken care to use authoritative texts of both poems and letters. For the poems we have gone to H. W. Garrod's Oxford Standard Authors edition, *Keats Poetical Works,* published in 1956 by Oxford and representative of the usual high quality of that series. Our selections from the letters are taken from Hyder E. Rollins' two-volume edition—widely recognized as a model of scholarly rigor—*The Letters of John Keats, 1814–1821,* published by Harvard University Press in 1958. We refer the reader to these editions (or to the Oxford English Texts edition, *The Poetical Works of John Keats,* ed. H. W. Garrod, 2nd ed. 1958) for poems and letters not included in this book.

We thank the Clarendon Press, Oxford, and the Harvard University Press for permission to use the editions named. Our thanks also to Professor John C. Gerber of the University of Iowa for his judicious suggestions, which led to the improvement of our editorial work; and to Mary Garvey for guidance in assembling the manuscript.

Joseph Sendry
Richard Giannone

New York City

A NOTE TO THE READER

In his edition of Keats's letters (from which we take our selections) Hyder E. Rollins reproduced as far as he was able the poet's own—sometimes eccentric—spelling, capitalization, and punctuation, carefully noting by a set of editorial symbols any alterations from the manuscript as well as choices among possible variant readings. The reader will find it helpful to know these symbols, for they occur often in the pages that follow. Square brackets [ ] enclose editorial insertions, generally. Such insertions would include corrections of misspelled words that the editor found it necessary to make so as to prevent serious confusion. Curly braces { } designate gaps caused by missing pieces of the letters, and shaped brackets ⟨ ⟩ indicate words canceled out by Keats but still decipherable. The dating for each letter is as given by Rollins; the place of origin is supplied in abbreviated form by the present editors. Since almost every selection included here is an excerpt, ellipses have usually been omitted at the beginning and end of each passage. The few letters presented in their entirety can be identified by the fact that they begin with Keats's salutation to his correspondent and end with his signature.

CHRONOLOGY

1795	October 31: John Keats is born to Thomas Keats and Frances Jennings Keats in the Finsbury section of London.
1797	February 28: George Keats, the poet's brother, is born.
1799	November 18: Tom Keats, another brother, is born.
1803	June 3: Frances (Fanny) Keats, the poet's sister, is born.
	Fall: John and George Keats enter Mr. Clarke's school at Enfield, where they are enrolled until the summer of 1811.
1804	April 16: Thomas Keats, the poet's father, dies suddenly after falling from his horse.
	June 27: Frances Jennings Keats, the poet's mother, remarries. The children go to live with their maternal grandparents, John and Alice Jennings.
1805	March 8: John Jennings, Keats's grandfather, dies.

1810	Mid-March: Keats's mother dies of tuberculosis. Within a few months thereafter Alice Jennings has two London businessmen, Richard Abbey and John Sandell, appointed as guardians and trustees to the Keats children.
1811	Summer: At Abbey's behest Keats leaves Clarke's School at Enfield and becomes apprenticed to Thomas Hammond, a surgeon practicing in Edmonton, the village where Keats's grandmother lived. During his apprenticeship, which lasted until 1815, Keats often revisited his old school at Enfield to discuss poetry with his former teacher, the master's son, Charles Cowden Clarke.
1813	February 3: Leigh Hunt, editor of the liberal newspaper, the *Examiner,* is sentenced to two years in prison for libeling the Prince Regent. Under the influence of young Clarke Keats embraces the imprisoned Hunt as a hero both for his poetry and his political views. Keats commemorates Hunt's release from prison on February 2, 1815, by writing a sonnet.
1814	Mid-December: Alice Jennings, Keats's grandmother, dies. Richard Abbey assumes full guardianship of the Keats children.
1815	October 1: Keats registers at Guy's Hospital in London to study surgery.
1816	May 5: The sonnet *O Solitude! . . . ,* Keats's first published work, appears in Leigh Hunt's *Examiner.*
	July 25: Keats passes the examination enabling him to practice as an apothecary and surgeon when he reaches legal age.
	October: The sonnet *On First Looking into Chapman's Homer,* Keats's first accomplished poem, is written. He meets Leigh Hunt and (through him) Benjamin Robert Haydon, painter, and John Hamilton Reynolds, poet.

October 31: Keats arrives at legal maturity (age 21) and soon after abandons the medical profession in which he has been trained.

November: The Keats brothers take up lodgings in Cheapside, London, the first time in their mature lives that they have been able to live together.

1817 Late February or March 1: Hunt and Keats crown each other with laurel.

March 1 or 3: Haydon takes Keats to see the Elgin Marbles.

March 3: *Poems,* Keats's first volume of verse, is published.

March 25: The poet and his brothers have moved to Well Walk, Hampstead.

April 14: Keats leaves Hampstead to begin work on *Endymion.* His trip takes him to the Isle of Wight, Margate, and Canterbury.

June 10: The poet is back in Hampstead, with Book 1 of *Endymion* complete.

Mid-August: Book 2 of *Endymion* is finished.

September: Keats visits Benjamin Bailey at Oxford, where he writes Book 3 of *Endymion.*

November 28: Book 4 of *Endymion* is completed at Burford Bridge.

Mid-December: George and Tom leave for Teignmouth in Devon on account of Tom's health.

December and January, 1818: Keats writes three drama reviews for the *Champion* in Reynolds' absence. He meets and becomes acquainted with Wordsworth.

1818 January–April: Final arrangements for the publication of *Endymion.*

March 4: Keats leaves Hampstead to join his brother Tom in Devon.

May 11: Keats is back in Hampstead with Tom.

May 19: *Endymion* is published.

May 28: George marries Georgiana Wylie.

June 23: The poet takes leave of George and

Georgiana Keats, who are about to sail for America, at Liverpool. He proceeds northward with Charles Armitage Brown on a walking tour of the Lake Country and Scotland.

August 8: Keats interrupts his walking tour because of a severe throat condition. He leaves Scotland.

August 18: Keats is back in Hampstead.

September: Attacks on *Endymion* appear in *Blackwood's* and the *Quarterly*. Keats begins *Hyperion*.

Fall: The poet meets Fanny Brawne.

December 1: Tom Keats dies of tuberculosis. The poet moves from Well Walk to share Wentworth Place—also in Hampstead—with Brown.

1819   January 18 or 19: Keats leaves Hampstead to visit Chichester and Bedhampton. On this trip he composes *The Eve of St. Agnes.*

February 1 or 2: The poet is back in Hampstead.

February 13–17: *The Eve of Saint Mark* is begun, left unfinished.

Early spring: Keats abandons *Hyperion.*

April 21: Keats records *La Belle Dame sans Merci* and his reflections on the world as a "vale of Soul-making" in a letter to the George Keatses.

Late April–May: The "great odes"—to Psyche and the Nightingale, on Melancholy and the Grecian Urn—are written.

June 27: Keats leaves Hampstead for the Isle of Wight with his friend James Rice, to be joined there by Brown on July 22. He proceeds with Brown to Winchester on August 12. During these two sojourns he writes *Lamia, Otho,* and *The Fall of Hyperion.*

September 19: The ode *To Autumn,* the fifth of the "great odes" and Keats's last important work, is written at Winchester.

October 8 or 9:   He returns to London from Winchester.

Fall: He becomes engaged to Fanny Brawne; negotiations to have *Otho* produced are unsuccessful.

1820   January: George briefly returns to London from America to raise money.

February 3:   Keats has a severe hemorrhage which marks the onset of his terminal illness, tuberculosis.

July 1 or 3:   Keats's third volume of poetry, *Lamia, Isabella, The Eve of St. Agnes, and Other Poems,* is published.

September 17:   Keats and his friend Joseph Severn, a young painter, embark for Italy, a warm climate offering Keats the last chance of surviving his tuberculosis.

November 15:   Keats and Severn arrive in Rome.

1821   February 23:   Keats dies in Rome.

CONTENTS

2   THE POET AT HIS CRAFT

Calling or Career

Vision and Revision: *Endymion* as a Test Case

An Experiment with Form: The Sonnet

A Commercial Venture: *Otho the Great*

Among the English Poets

INTRODUCTION

I. THE POET AND REALITY

"What is real? That is the question which preoccupied Keats throughout his life. Yet it is not so much a question to be answered directly as it is a point of departure, since to ask about the existence of things forces us to examine the way in which they are known. And if we agree that knowledge carries responsibility with it, another question is not long in coming: how do we act upon what we know? Every man deals with these issues in his special way; Keats worked through them by self-analysis. He asked why he or anyone should be a poet in the first place, what peculiar insight poetry offers about the nature of things, what value the poet could be to his fellowman.

To seize upon one idea of Keats as the key to his mind would be to make a false start. In a mind as complex as his, many ideas coexisted in uneasy suspension, sometimes in open conflict, but never at rest. The interaction among these ideas, not their chronology, is the truest guide to Keats's development. The richest embodiment of this complex interaction is the *Ode on a Grecian Urn*. The poem condenses so much that to comprehend its varied meanings we are impelled toward the whole body of the poet's writing.

One thought generates another and yet another—qualifying, contradicting, straining for some equilibrium large enough to embrace all parties to the struggle.

Though the Grecian urn would have been literally immobile, in Keats's description it acquires motion. The pastoral scenes decorating it come to life, as if to reflect the life of its observer. In the first view, men madly pursue maidens, then other tableaux come into view. Musicians play assorted pipes and hand drums. Trees luxuriate in full bloom. Beneath them one youth pipes a perpetual song and another reaches for a kiss he will never get. The scene then shifts from the secular to the sacred. A cortege of worshipers is leading a heifer to sacrifice on an outdoor altar. The procession prompts still another scene, this one in the mind of the poem's speaker as he speculates about the town emptied of inhabitants by the ceremonial march. He pictures an indefinite place, quiet and peaceful, which could be situated anywhere—on a river, a seashore, or a mountain.

The images on the urn, though unforgettable, are still imprecise, paradoxical, and finally mysterious. The erotic figures can be either men or gods; the locale, either Tempe or Arcadia; and the revels have no exact emotional definition. The religious quality of the spectacle is also baffling. The worshipers have no identity, nor has their rite any specific meaning. The grammatical form of the question insistently repeats itself to pace both the rhetoric and the meaning of the ode. Though the exact wording of each query varies, each unobtrusively poses the same question, the one which seeks to reach the very nature of reality: what is it? What is real?

The speaker's approach to the urn is eloquent in its assumptions about the nature of things and of our ability to know them. In the first place, he is tentative and open. He characteristically allows for alternative answers (these may be men or gods, in Tempe or Arcadia). Where there is no ground for closing the question with a definite answer, the matter is left unresolved. Wonder is the appropriate response in the face of such uncertainty. In the second place, the speaker is always active in this ode, shifting his attention, striving to penetrate further into the meaning of the urn before him. The eye's focus passes through a succession of scenes on the vase and pushes beyond what is seen to a final imaginative vision. By the end of the ode the physical world is momentarily left behind, and with it the uncertainties and imperfections that define it.

The urn's sudden declaration that "Beauty is truth, truth beauty" is so sweeping that to arrive at it the poet has to risk a great leap of the imagination. That leap is in a sense justified by the preceding lines of the poem. The speaker has known the beauty of the urn. His enthusiasm testifies to this as fact. The intensity of his delight in viewing the urn has convinced him that if nothing else is clear or definite or real, at least this one thing, beauty, is. That much is highly affirmative, but a sobering note in the next clause, "That is all / Ye know on earth," undercuts the optimism and saves the poem from facile overconfidence. The world of uncertainty and imperfection has not long been left behind.

Skepticism

The Critical Spirit of the Enlightenment

Keats had a great distance to travel intellectually before he could arrive at the bold affirmation spoken by the urn. He was a thorough-going skeptic who questioned the loyalties he lived by and the art that he practiced. He confessed to his brother George, "I am however young writing at random—straining at particles of light in the midst of a great darkness—without knowing the bearing of any one assertion of any one opinion." His longing for that bit of light amid the great darkness did not prevent him from examining an issue from opposite angles. Throughout his career he questioned, doubted, objected, proposed, retracted, and revised his position (just as he made several different approaches to the urn). And if we pay close attention, we can detect his fear that the light that he sought might not be found.

Although the fact is seldom mentioned—because scholars like to pigeonhole him as a Romantic—Keats grew up in the wake of the Enlightenment, that eighteenth-century movement that tested all established belief in the acid of rational criticism. When the poet's friend Leigh Hunt got onto such subjects in his liberal newspaper the *Examiner*, Keats was delighted. "The last Examiner was [a] Battering Ram against Christianity," he wrote to Hunt about the issue of May 4, 1817. Keats himself could be blasphemous enough to declare, "I feel confident I should have been a rebel

Angel had the opportunity been mine." In the sonnet *Written in Disgust of Vulgar Superstition* he implied that religion holds "the mind of man . . . closely bound / In some black spell" from which he must be extricated. It is particularly interesting to catch a glimpse of this rebel angel in the anomalous position of having to instruct his sister Fanny for confirmation. His letter on the occasion, dated March 31, 1819, is all that a fraternal letter should be. He dutifully answers the questions posed to him. But after giving the conventional responses, he cannot resist a final touch of self-mocking levity, and he signs himself "Your affectionate Parson."

This epistolary flourish is the more ironic in light of Keats's deep-seated and oft-professed anticlericalism. He had as little use for individual parsons as for their profession. "A Parson," he wrote to George, "is a Lamb in a drawing room and a lion in a Vestry. . . . He must be either a Knave or an Ideot." Bishops drew down even mightier indignation. When the bishop of Lincoln moved to prevent his friend Benjamin Bailey's ordination. Keats's reaction ranged from acerbity to wrath. He was shocked "to find in a sacred Profession such barefaced oppression and impertinence" and dismissed the prelate as "a smashed frog putrifying."

Keats also shared the political iconoclasm of the Enlightenment. Many of his friends (Hunt most notably) were liberals, and though politics could hardly be called one of his primary concerns, in his earlier days especially the poet took a stand with the rebels. The sonnet on Leigh Hunt's release from prison is indicative: it equates truth with individual vision ("immortal spirit"), falsehood with the political powers that be. Among the few political leaders that Keats championed was one genuine revolutionary, Thaddeus Kosciusko (1746–1817), the Polish patriot whose passion for freedom involved him in the affairs of America and France as well as those of his native Poland. In a sonnet Keats transports him "To where the great God lives for evermore."

Nothing in This World Is Proveable

Keats's skepticism was neither a defense for dealing with a hostile world nor a late symptom of adolescent defiance. It was a considered view of life. The world seemed irregular, complex, and confusing. "The more we know," Keats wrote, "the more inadequacy we discover in the world to satisfy us." He came to terms with that complexity by attempting to embrace it without any superimposition of order. He would accept neither religious nor philosophical systems simply because a system offered comfortable settlements. His mind was inhospitable to absolutes. In stating his position to Benjamin Bailey, Keats repeated what must have been an old theme in their discussions: "You know my ideas about Religion . . . . Nothing in this world is proveable." In this context Keats seemed to have taken proof to mean logical, unassailable argument. He was in the habit of saying that such "consequitive reasoning" was not his affair. Nor did he believe, as did many Romantics, that feeling alone is a valid approach to truth. So deep was his skepticism that he could doubt feeling as well as reason.

Lamia, a late poem, dramatizes the extent of Keats's disbelief. Apollonius the philosopher embodies "consequitive reasoning." When his mind works its will through abstract categories, nothing of the world's rich variety is left.

> *Philosophy will clip an Angel's wings,*
> *Conquer all mysteries by rule and line,*
> *Empty the haunted air, and gnomed mine—*
> *Unweave a rainbow, as it erewhile made*
> *The tender-person'd Lamia melt into a shade.*

Lamia, the heroine, represents feeling. She is not so "tender-person'd" after all. A snake-woman, unknown and ambiguous, her sensuality recommends itself as a life style; but that appeal is perhaps only her destructiveness turned inside out. Her balm can be toxic as well as soothing. Our puzzlement at the ending of Lamia is a demonstration of the poet's success in making his point that truth cannot be finally known.

In Lamia Keats deliberately leaves the issue unsettled in the reader's mind, and that uncertainty is the product of narrative structure. In the sonnet *"Read Me a Lesson, Muse . . ."* it is an encompassing mental state. Keats employs the opaque "mist and crag" that confine his view on the mountain top as a symbol of the mind's inability to penetrate beyond itself, a mental stance that could lead ultimately to despair. But Keats at other times would not be content with so little; his searching mind was always alert for something that he *might* be sure of. Thus, if he wrote to Bailey at one moment that "nothing in this world is proveable," he could allow himself an escape from this skepticism at another point: "I am certain of *nothing but* of the holiness of the Heart's affections and the truth of Imagination" (emphasis ours). In a sense this second declaration is a paraphrase of the last two lines of the *Ode on a Grecian Urn*. There the poet implied that we know *nothing but* the compellingly convincing experience of beauty, which is finally apprehended not by the reasoning mind but by the heart and the imagination.

Empiricism

Immediate Experience, the Standard of Truth

Keats's act of trust in the heart's affections and in the imagination opened a way out of the confinements of skepticism. Having turned his back on abstract categories, he had almost inevitably to take an opposite course in his struggle toward certitude, that of direct experience unmediated by classifications of the intellect. In some of the strongest utterances that the letters contain, Keats affirmed his conviction that immediate experience is one thing of which we are sure, and even more, the test of all truth. "Nothing ever becomes real till it is experienced—Even a Proverb is no proverb to you till your Life has illustrated it." And "axioms in philosophy are not axioms until they are proved upon our pulses." Pain and sickness, for example, would be mere words to anyone who had not endured them. As with pain, so with pleasure; in the abstract it offers "no lasting happiness." "Why did I laugh to-night?" Keats asks in a sonnet, and he goes on to say that neither God nor devil could answer the question for him. He must finally turn to his heart, the seat of his feelings, as the authority capable of informing him on the strange, private emotions that issue forth in sudden, irrational ways.

Negative Capability

Yet a world defined only by immediate experience is necessarily egocentric and solipsistic. Ideas not understood, people not met, emotions not felt: all must be relegated to meaninglessness if the actuality of the world is judged only by personal experience. "I have not felt" is no answer to "What is it?" Exclusion as an approach to the world is naïve, for it claims an unwarranted confidence in the face of natural complexity; equally false, it cuts nature to subjective specifications. Keats sensed all these difficulties. And just as he felt the need for knowledge too keenly to stay anchored in dogmatic skepticism, he was too fascinated by the world to cling to a rigorous empiricism that confined itself to his own experience.

Keats found a way out of the dilemma by extending, not curtailing, the principle that experience is the only way of knowing. He maintained, in effect, that just as the self has the appropriate means of knowing its own experience, it also has the means to know the experience of others. By an effort of the imagination we can identify with others, put ourselves in the other person's shoes, and learn indirectly what it is like to be that person. Keats coined the rather awkward phrase "negative capability" to designate this capacity of the mind to grasp how others feel and look at things. In this state, to take up the poet's terminology, a man is capable of negating or putting aside his moral and intellectual categories, "of being in uncertainties, Mysteries, doubts, without any irritable reaching after fact & reason." In short, he permits things to speak to him. And the word "speak" is right, for the negatively capable man would accord to all things the respectful attention that we ordinarily pay only to human beings. His willingness to accept and listen springs from sympathy and deepens into a creative cooperation of his mind with nature. Whereas egocentricity turns the world into a static mirror of itself, negative capability minimizes the self and allows it to participate in the diversity and variety of the world.

The model for Keats's negatively capable man was Shakespeare, for that dramatist could realize within himself every variety of human experience. He could create a villain as despicable as Iago and a heroine as virtuous as Imogen, and create each with an insight so profound that he seems to have lived their lives. The process that Keats used to explain these operations of Shakespeare's mind also served him to describe the workings of his own. In a letter, for example, the poet demonstrates negative capability when he imagines himself sharing the life of a common bird. "If a Sparrow come before my Window I take part in its existince and pick about the Gravel." When Keats made a mighty effort to open himself imaginatively to alien modes of life, as he did in the ode *To Autumn,* the results could be spectacular. There, he channels his awareness into union with the multiple forms of the season, ranging from a panoramic sweep over the landscape to a minutely focused gathering of swallows as they twitter in the evening sky.

The Truth of the Imagination

We said that "negative capability" is an awkward phrase. *Negative* misleads. It refers to an act of the mind that is negative in word only. The term actually describes a positive act, an act of purgation. In this state the mind opens itself hospitably to receive as many presences as possible from the outside world.

Negative capability has this limitation: passivity, no matter how open, does not adequately account for what happens in human knowing. The perceiving self is not a mere blankness on which stimuli impress themselves in duplicate form. The mind takes its own initiative, moving outward to discover and embrace the reality that lies beyond it. Keats recognized the fact of this activity and referred to it once as a "greeting," a term that nicely catches the required attitudes of goodwill and interest in the other. "Things semireal such as Love, the Clouds &c . . . require a greeting of the Spirit to make them wholly exist." "Wholly" in this observation hints at the next stage in the process. The mind greets but then makes whole the subject before it, bringing out the meaning that was there in nature all along. The relationship is mutually beneficial. Nature acquires completeness; man, knowledge. The world presents itself through physical appearance, its prose. Its poetry resides in the ideal that waits to be realized behind the appearance. By crossing into and revealing the ideational shape of things, the mind transforms the world.

Wallace Stevens, a modern American poet, took up many of the issues that engaged Keats, and it would be helpful to glance at one of his statements on this question in the poem *The Man with the Blue Guitar*. The guitar represents the inventive power of the imagination. The guitarist readily admits the accusation leveled by the literal-minded that his music alters the reality of which it sings: "Things as they are / Are changed upon the blue guitar." Keats made basically the same point in a letter to his artist friend Haydon. From personal struggle with his own art the poet described to the painter the "innumerable compositions and decompositions which take place between the intellect and its thousand materials before it arrives at that trembling delicate and snail-horn perception of Beauty." "Beauty" is of course the crucial word. It represents the final outcome of the creative process, the product of the interplay between the imagination and reality. Stevens is again helpful, if paradoxical. His guitarist plays "A tune upon the blue guitar / Of things exactly as they are." If instead of "exactly" a word like "ideally" or "perfectly" is introduced, Stevens' line effectively states Keats's point that some things "require a greeting of the Spirit to make them *wholly* exist." "Things as they are" in the world are changed by the imagination, made better, more complete, finally truer to themselves—in short, beautiful. It took a "greeting of the spirit," after all, to summon the full beauty of the Grecian urn.

Beyond The Sweet and Bitter World

With these speculations Keats advanced well beyond skepticism, which denies our ability to know anything finally as true, and beyond empiricism, which limits the truth we know to matters of direct experience. In a letter to his friend Bailey—who was then preparing to take orders in the Church of England—he went farther still: "What the imagination seizes as Beauty must be truth—whether it existed before or not." The assertion that truth can be known is here unequivocal. So much for skepticism. The phrase "whether it existed before or not" permits the discovery of truth not only beyond direct experience but even beyond the objective world. So much for empiricism. And if this sounds as if Keats has abandoned his intellectual rigor to claim that the mind can manufacture truth at will, the next comment in the same letter to Bailey is hardly likely to dispel the suspicion. "For I have the same Idea of all our Passions as of Love[.] they are all in their sublime, creative of essential Beauty."

Of course, modest interpretations of such statements are easy enough to make. For one, the beauty (and therefore truth) that our passions create could very well remain in the eye or mind of the beholder, true for him only, and therefore subjective. Or if such beauty should achieve objective existence, it could do so through artistic creation. Keats would have given due acknowledgment to both these notions, but he was also willing to risk a much bolder, more radical affirmation. The imagination, he would claim, can lead us to knowledge in its sphere just as validly as the senses do in theirs. The point is not that the imagination fabricates truths out of nothing, but rather that in its acute sensitivity it registers special degrees of awareness. The senses are organs of physical perception; the imagination would be to Keats an organ of spiritual perception.

Keats wanted to believe that there are more things in heaven and on earth than are dreamed of in the philosophies of skepticism and empiricism. To suggest how the mind might make the acquaintance of such things he devised a fable with two characters called the "material Cottager" and the "spiritual Cottager." The first is a man who never steps beyond the boundaries of his own small property. Yet this man, says Keats, "knows there are such places as france and Italy and the Andes and the Burning Mountains"—though he has not visited them. The material Cottager cannot think beyond physical geography. The spiritual Cottager is as much a stay-at-home as the other. When he goes forth, however, he visits countries that cannot be found on maps: "the spiritual Cottager has knowledge of the terra semi incognita of things unearthly."

Ironically, Keats's trust in the imagination led him to reaffirm on new grounds some of the beliefs that he seemed to put aside with his rejection of Christianity. For example, writing to Bailey again he hazards a claim for personal immortality, speculating that "we shall enjoy ourselves here after by having what we called happiness on Earth repeated in a finer tone." The nature of this afterlife, however, falls well outside the traditional notions, since it is designed for those like Keats "who delight in sensation" rather than those like Bailey who pursue an abstract ideal such as truth—or, for that matter, goodness. Even in his thoughts of heaven, Keats's characteristic preference for immediacy in experience asserts itself.

Needless to say, such belief in immortality would be inadmissible on empirical grounds, for (in the phrasing of the *Ode on a Grecian Urn*) "not a soul to tell" about that state of existence "can e'er return." There is, then, a point "beyond this sweet and bitter world" of experience where Keats is willing to proceed on faith. Not faith in a Church or a formal creed, but faith in our deepest feelings, which he sees as ultimately reliable, and in our imagination, which can give us intimations of such finer worlds. Given these premises, it is no wonder that Keats uses religious language when speaking of the imagination. Almost in defiance of Bailey's Christianity he proclaims to his friend "the holiness of the Heart's affections and the truth of the imagination."

Such Stuff as Dreams Are Made On

This belief, or hope, that man can through the imagination transcend this imperfect world and reach out toward a finer one is a favorite theme of Keats, and the dream is his favorite symbol for the imagination at work. To explain the matter he cited Adam's dream in *Paradise Lost*. In Milton's epic Adam falls asleep, dreams of Eve, and wakes to find that she actually exists. The hero of *Endymion* repeats the cycle. He meets his heavenly lover in dreams and discovers on waking that she is the Indian maiden whom he loves on earth. Madeline in *The Eve of St. Agnes* dreams of her ideal lover, and he is waiting to embrace her when she wakes. In each instance the work of imagination is the same: not to manufacture the object of love from nothing but to assist in bringing it to full realization. Beauty, at whose birth Imagination acts as midwife, turns out to be Truth.

As the religious believer well knows, the price of faith is often the pain of doubt. Keats's faith in the imagination exacts the same toll. Some of his most desolate cries mourn the failure of the imagination and, even worse, its treachery. Thus, the nightingale in the ode transports the speaker to a luxuriant forest where the bird's singing immerses him in almost unbearable delight. But the ecstasy is short-lived. In the last stanza the "finer tone" fades and the poet is stranded in uncertainty, complaining that "the fancy cannot cheat so well / As she is fam'd to do, deceiving elf." The moral of the story in *La Belle Dame sans Merci* is even grimmer. If the lady in that ballad is taken (as she has often been) to represent the imagination, the poem stands as a warning that this faculty may not only delude but destroy. On waking in the "elfin grot" to which she has led him, the knight discovers that the daylight world is a veritable nightmare, not the fulfillment of his "latest dream." Betrayed, deserted, emaciated, his last state is far worse than his first.

The Moral Dimension

The perils of the imagination have often been likened to the fate of Icarus, the figure in Greek mythology who fastened wings of wax to his back and managed in brief triumph to lift himself off the earth. But the sun quickly melted his wings and he plunged into the sea. By virtue of his feat Icarus momentarily left behind the afflictions of his fellowmen below, only to rejoin them abruptly in the inevitable: death. The story is instructive to anyone with thoughts of transcending human limitations.

Keats used the legend and would have appreciated its applicability to himself. The breadth of his claims for the imagination and for poetry, its proper expression, generated a dizzy uneasiness. If the imagination succeeded in its ecstatic flights, if the poet could record these flights in all their triumph, humanity would still suffer, struggle, and die below. At one point Keats felt compelled to say that he would reject the poet's traditional crown of laurel "on account of my dying day, and because women have Cancers." The death of his younger brother Tom especially sharpened Keats's sense of the tragedy of human experience. If men died, if women had cancer, wouldn't his place be to help them on earth? Had he any right to flights of poetic fancy?

Keats poses such questions in his letters, and he broached them in his poems. In the Icarus myth one figure fell from the heavens. In *Hyperion* an entire race falls. The fact that it is a race of gods, the Titans—who are defeated by a younger, more forceful breed, the Olympians—does not make the tale any less relevant. In their ruin the Titans learn for the first time what it is to undergo, not merely suffering, but all human feeling. Coelus, father of the whole dynasty, himself once overthrown by these his children, draws the appropriate moral:

> solemn, undisturb'd,
> Unruffled, like high Gods, ye liv'd and ruled:
> Now I behold you in fear, hope, and wrath;
> Actions of rage and passion; even as
> I see them, on the mortal world beneath,
> In men who die.

The Need to Know

Keats presents these vanquished gods with abundant pathos, but his implied moral indictment of them is unflinching. One of their number, Oceanus, explains their defeat by citing "Nature's law" that "first in beauty should be first in might." Beauty, however, emerges as a secondary consideration: the Titans' primary failing was their lack of insight. "The pain of truth," says Oceanus as bluntly as the blank verse will allow, is that supremacy is based on understanding, the capacity "to bear all naked truths, / And to envisage circumstance."

Of all the Titans, only Hyperion, god of the sun and of poetry, retains his power, but in the third book, which Keats never finished, even the sun god's defeat is in sight. The poem breaks off in midsentence just as Apollo, Hyperion's successor, has achieved his godhood. From a diffident figure handicapped by his "aching ignorance," Apollo realizes an instant transformation when he gazes on the face of Mnemosyne, the Titaness who represents memory. There he sees the accumulated history of the human race, the gods, and the cosmos: "Names, deeds, grey legends, dire events, rebellions, / Majesties, sovran voices, agonies, / Creations and destroyings." Apollo exclaims that these revelations "Pour into the wide hollows of my brain, / And deify me. . . . Knowledge enormous makes a God of me."

In writing *Hyperion* Keats was virtually penning a warning to himself. He had boasted to Bailey that he was one of those who delighted in sensation rather than in the pursuit of truth. In his sonnet *O Thou Whose Face Hath Felt* . . . he agrees with the bird's advice to "fret not after knowledge." Hyperion's fellow Titans had no knowledge and suffered stunning defeat, a fate that also awaited Hyperion. What about Keats himself? Particularly after his brother George's departure for America in June 1818, he felt increasingly at the mercy of events, and the fallen Titans represented with disconcerting accuracy what appeared to be his own predicament. As if to insure his psychic survival, Keats gradually formed a resolution to go the way of Apollo, for whom knowledge had secured godhood. He would learn all that he could. Writing to Reynolds, the poet argued that there is the widest difference between a life with knowledge and one without; instinctively, he resorted to the imagery that he used in *Hyperion,* now with reference to himself. Lacking knowledge, "we are falling continually ten thousand fathoms deep and being blown up again without wings and with all the horror of a bare shoulderd Creature." With knowledge, "our shoulders are fledged, and we go through the same air and space without fear." If it cannot provide us with the means for reaching heaven, knowledge can at least keep us from plunging into hell.

A Tragic Sense

But fear for himself was not all that tormented Keats. He saw how much suffering there was about him, and he felt compelled to do his share to alleviate it. Poetry seemed an evasion of the pressing realities of human pain. Learning, on the other hand, presented itself as a possible means of involvement on the side of humanity in the struggle for existence. More and more, knowledge (or "philosophy") and doing good linked themselves in his mind. He wrote to John Taylor, his publisher, "I find there is no worthy pursuit but the idea of doing some good for the world. . . . there is but one way for me—the road lies th[r]ough application study and thought."

Perhaps Keats never finished the first version of *Hyperion* because it was too much about himself and he could not sustain his narrative subject. In any event he began the project anew. Rather than Milton's epic, Dante's dream vision—*The Divine Comedy*— became his model, as he shifted the point of view from an omniscient narrator to a first-person participant in the action. Keats entitled this second attempt, also left unfinished, *The Fall of Hyperion,* though most of its 500-odd lines have nothing to do with the title character but with the lessons in moral awareness learned by the narrator. His teacher is Moneta, who in representing memory is much like Mnemosyne in the first version; but instead of instructing Apollo in the history of men and gods, she now schools the speaker in the reality of suffering and defeat. He looks upon her face and reads there the tragic story of the fallen Titans. By shifting the focus of his narrative from the making of a god to the education of a man, Keats brought the Hyperion myth in touch with the human tragedy that increasingly concerned him.

Moneta serves as her creator's spokesman, especially when she draws basic distinctions regarding the moral responsibility of men generally and of poets particularly. The goddess explains that the real benefactors of mankind, those already active in promoting human good, need no such vision as he is granted to make them aware of their duties. "They are no dreamers weak, / They seek no wonder but the human face" in which they perceive the same tragedy that must be magnified to literally titanic proportions before men like the speaker can understand it. In Keats, of course, the word "dream" inevitably suggests the imagination and poetry. The speaker chafes at the wholesale indictment of poetry that Moneta seems to imply, and he raises a reasonable objection. "Not all / Those melodies . . . Are useless: sure a poet is a sage; / A humanist, physician to all men." Moneta agrees, but she distinguishes sharply between the poet and the dreamer. "The one pours out a balm upon the World, / The other vexes it." The speaker understands immediately, and he makes his own distinction between true poets on one hand and "mock lyrists, large self worshipers / And careless Hectorers in proud bad verse" on the other. The first group reach out to mankind; the second remain enclosed within their own world of fantasy.

Because it points to the resolution of a major conflict in Keats's thought, this passage from *The Fall of Hyperion* is a milestone on the poet's road toward self-definition. He no longer states the issue as a question of either/or: a choice between poetry and human commitment. The two can be merged. The poet can bring to the imagination as a power of vision or of creation a sympathetic understanding of the ills that man is prey to; in fact, the poet's imaginative power is precisely what enables him to see deep into the human condition. In *The Fall of Hyperion* the antidote to the dreamer's envenoming self-centeredness is not a plunge into the troubles of ordinary life but a vision of Moneta's face, wherein those troubles appear condensed in symbolic richness. Isn't this a subtle way of paying tribute to the power of imaginative vision? For the poet must answer what he sees with "a greeting of the spirit." He offers a part of himself to the spectacle of misery that confronts him; thereupon, that spectacle becomes real to him, but even more remarkable, he finds his whole self transformed.

Identity

Apollo in *Hyperion* became a god through knowledge. The speaker in *The Fall of Hyperion* became a poet by acquiring a tragic view of existence. But Keats's strongest utterance on the transformation into selfhood occurs not in his poems but in his letters, specifically in the letter of April 21, 1819, to George Keats and his wife Georgiana, customarily spoken of as "the vale of soul-making letter." To appreciate the importance of this document in the poet's self-development, it will help to recall some of his earlier views. When he enunciated the doctrine of negative capability (principally in a letter to George and Tom Keats in December 1817), Keats affirmed that the poet has no identity: particularly on moral questions, he remains deliberately neutral in order to surrender himself to experience unhindered. Keats discovered that the very experience that earlier he had sought so enthusiastically could by its own dynamics form the self that experiences. Those encounters with life so educated him in the human tragedy that he came to make precisely the moral decisions that he had once ruled out for poets. Far from denying that an identity is desirable for a poet, he affirmed at length that the formation of identity was the very goal of human existence. Here lay his answer to the perennial problem of evil: evil has meaning because through our struggles with it we are transformed from mere receptacles for experience into souls, beings with complete selfhood, individual identity.

In the "vale of soul-making letter," Keats distinguishes "three grand materials" that enter into this process. The first is what he calls intelligence or mind, which is an "atom of perception" that comes into the world able to know and perceive, but having done neither. The second is the human heart, capable of feeling joy, pain, and—above all—love. The third is the world, which provides not only the stage upon which this drama is enacted but also the antagonist with whom the mind and the heart must struggle. From this struggle the mind learns to know itself through the world; it develops a distinct character as it interacts with the world and is guided by the heart's sensitivity to suffering and its demands for love. The final result is what Keats calls "soul," the individual moral being formed and transformed by the fullness of its human experience. To Keats the soul was godlike. He referred to the original "atoms of perception" as "sparks of the divinity," going so far as to say "they are pure, in short they are God." Even the phrase "vale of soul-making" is replete with religious implications. It was Keats's answer to that voice in traditional Christianity that called the world a "vale of tears." Leigh Hunt once taught Keats to scoff at the established religion; now, finally, Keats had arrived at a belief of his own.

The letter on soul-making marked a crucial point in Keats's career, for it generated the *Ode to Psyche*. Psyche is the goddess of the soul. In his ode Keats honors her as the one divinity in the whole Olympian hierarchy who is still vital, still worthy of his homage. (Ironically, it was the Olympians who replaced the Titans as the ruling race of gods, and Psyche holds the same position as Hyperion in being the sole survivor in a supplanted dynasty.) According to the ancient myth, Psyche attained godhood only after bitter trials on earth and intense conflict even with Cupid her beloved. To achieve her identity, Psyche had to undergo much the same sort of interaction with the world and the heart that Keats spoke of in his vale of soul-making letter. The result was glorious: she became divine.

In a matter of months after Keats sang his praises to the soul deified by moral experience, his career reached its end, cut off by illness and finally by death. But finality was never Keats's trademark, and the *Ode to Psyche* bears this out. Even after she is deified and securely installed in a splendid shrine within the poet's mind, she leaves the casement ajar, open to the world and to Cupid: that is, to love.

II. THE POET AT HIS CRAFT

The material gathered in the second part of this reader, dealing with the poet at his craft, dictates a more informal mode of organization than that used in the first part on the poet and reality. A poet's view of reality can be set forth consecutively because the elements of that view are of the same order: observations about experience refined to generality either through concept or through image. The question of the poet at his craft, however, involves different orders of things. General observation is, to be sure, one of them. The poet tries to explain to himself, as much as to others, what he is and what his art is. We have included, accordingly, in the section "Calling or Career" some of Keats's reflections on the nature of his art. Then, in the last section of the reader, "Among the English Poets," Keats implicitly describes the poet he wished to become by commenting explicitly on what other poets, past and present, are.

But such statements about poetry give an incomplete picture, for poetry is an act, the act of creation. To understand well what a poet is, we ought to observe him in the act of creating. Keats's letters catch him in that act, and we have allowed him to tell in his own words—with his works as exhibits—how he proceeded. In the section entitled "Vision and Revision: *Endymion* as a Test Case" his correspondence over a year and a half traces the progress of Keats's longest poem from its inception to the reviews. Keats had more to say about writing this one poem than about poetic form as such, but by placing together what he said about one form, his practical experiments with it, and the developments that led from it, we suggest in "An Experiment with Form: The Sonnet" how Keats came to apply this concept to splendid result in his creation. In the section, "A Commercial Venture: *Otho the Great,*" we glimpse Keats as the professional writer tailoring his material to the taste of his audience. Each of these sections shows the working artist in a different light; each contributes to our fuller understanding of how he matured in his craft.

Calling or Career

Traditionally, there have been two ways of viewing the poet. The loftier has shown him as inspired, called to his art almost despite himself by a mysterious force beyond him. The other attitude is down-to-earth, taking the poet as a craftsman whose skill is acquired through practice. The one is born a poet; the other is made such. Each promises something distinctive. Whereas the born poet deals in prophecy, the craftsman offers expertise.

Keats's thinking on his role as artist, like all of his thinking, matured steadily. To the degree that we can extract it from his writing, the young Keats's position on the nature of the poet comes down on the side of poetry as inspiration. The letters and poems grouped under "The Poet and His Muse" and "The Poet and His Public" record Keats's changing attitudes. Most of the selections in the first group were written before May 1817. This was the period highlighted by Keats's meeting in October 1816 with Leigh Hunt, his first major contact with the London literary world. As Hunt's protégé he joined a circle of artists and writers among whom were Benjamin Robert Haydon, a painter, and John Hamilton Reynolds, a poet—not to mention Percy Bysshe Shelley. In March 1817, with Hunt's help, Keats published his first book of verse. At this point he was rapturous about poetry. "I find that I cannot exist without poetry," he announced to Reynolds; and to Hunt, "What a thing to be in the Mouth of Fame."

The poems written to May 1817, and the work included in the volume of March, show that rapture. *Sleep and Poetry* is the best case in point. Its theme is the poet's dedication to his art, and its imagery defines the peculiar nature of that dedication. Religious images dominate. Pope and his school are dismissed as a "schism" from the authentic tradition of English verse; the "vast idea" of poetry is "manifest / As a large cross, some old cathedral's crest." Even the mythological material gathers religious force. Poetry is a divine visitant to earth, a charioteer descending from heaven. The allusion is to Apollo, the god of poetry, who as sun god drove his fiery chariot daily across the skies.

An episode at Leigh Hunt's points up the increasingly sober quality of Keats's dedication to his art as represented by Apollo. At the end of February 1817, immediately before the publication of his first book, Hunt crowned Keats with laurel ("Apollo's very leaves," to cite one of the young poet's own sonnets) to mark the occasion. Keats returned the compliment by placing a crown on Hunt's head, and each of them wrote a sonnet about the event. Afterwards Keats felt not only embarrassment but actual remorse. He had offended not a god but his sense of integrity. Even with a new book of verse his achievement was too slender to earn him laurels. That might come some day, but for the time being he had to put his artistic conscience to rest by composing an ode to the god of poetry. In this apology, entitled *Hymn to Apollo,* Keats reveals a more sober attitude toward his art. "Why was I not crush'd—such a pitiful germ?" he asks in a stridency of self-criticism that is absent from his earlier bravura.

That was 1817, when Keats was just beginning to lower his head from the clouds. The letters of 1818 show him with his feet on the ground. In the selections included under "The Poet and His Public," reverence for his art remains, but now Keats is absorbed in such practical matters as pleasing readers. The public virtually ignored the *Poems* of 1817. Though he could insist to Reynolds in April 1818, "I never wrote a single Line of Poetry with the least Shadow of public thought," Keats was actually worried about how *Endymion,* near publication, would be received. In October, after the reviewers had attacked *Endymion,* Keats could admit that he did care about their response, even if he looked on it as second in importance to his own. "My own domestic criticism has given me pain without comparison beyond what Blackwood or the . . . Quarterly could possibly inflict."

In 1818, then, the public became increasingly important in Keats's reckoning of his art. He realized that it is one thing to please the muse, his artistic conscience, or what Keats meant when he spoke of Apollo, and quite another thing to please the public. Here were the makings of a crisis in Keats's professional life. On what terms could he remain a poet? The artist in him longed to attain an ideal of excellence, while the man understandably sought public recognition and the subsistence that comes with it. Keats dealt with this dilemma characteristically. He saw that it was not an either/or situation and worked toward a larger goal that would embrace both ambitions. Before satisfying Apollo or the public, he would have to become a better craftsman with a master's work as evidence.

Vision and Revision: *Endymion* as a Test Case

Endymion was intended in the first instance as the work by which Keats would prove his poetic mastery. To do this he self-consciously undertook a formidable test of his abilities. "I must make 4000 Lines of one bare circumstance and fill them with Poetry," he wrote to his brother. That "circumstance" was the single episode from classical mythology in which Cynthia the moon goddess fell in love with Endymion the shepherd-boy. As if these conditions were not strenuous enough, he set himself an early deadline: the work, to begin in spring of 1817, was to be finished by fall. Either he would complete the project and demonstrate that he was a poet or admit defeat. "I put on no Laurels," he wrote to George, "till I shall have finished Endymion." Though his meaning was clear enough, he felt obliged to add, "I hope Apollo is not angered at my having made a Mockery at him at Hunt's."

As often when serious writing was in question, Keats decided on a change in surroundings. On April 14 he left the lodgings that he then shared with his brothers in Well Walk, Hampstead, and proceeded to the Isle of Wight. On April 18 he wrote to Reynolds from an inn near Carisbrooke Castle announcing that he would soon begin work—the first mention of the actual composition of *Endymion* in the letters. The atmosphere proved wrong, for he was suffering from loneliness. About a week later he traveled eastward along half the lower coast of England to Margate, joined his brother Tom there, and worked until mid-May, when he took a break to visit Canterbury. He must have finished the first book by early June, and on the 10th of the month he was back in Hampstead. He reported to Haydon in August that the second of the four books projected was then finished, but he was still behind schedule.

Hoping that another change of scene would stimulate production, at the beginning of September the poet took up an invitation from Bailey to stay at Magdalen Hall, Oxford. In the month that followed, Keats kept steadily at *Endymion* while Bailey read for his examinations. By the end of September, Book III was done, though by then Keats was heartily tired of the whole thing and scarcely pleased with his performance. One of his aims, however, was in process of fulfillment: he was proving to himself that he could write a sustained work, which if nothing else would provide "the fruit of Experience which I hope to gather in my next Poem."

Keats spent October back in Hampstead. The familiar surroundings seemed to break his momentum, for by month's end he was only three hundred lines into Book IV. His output for November promised to be even slimmer, and so at length he sought new surroundings: Burford Bridge in Surrey, not far to the south of London. Once again the change worked. On November 22 he wrote to Reynolds describing his climb up Box Hill, a local landmark, to watch the moon—a deliberate bid for inspiration, since the moon figured as a major preoccupation in Book IV. Within a week, on November 28, he could pronounce *Endymion* finished.

December meant a return to Well Walk and a start on the months-long process of copying (by hand, of course) and revision needed to put the poem in presentable form for publication. Though he was scarcely satisfied with it, Keats was determined that *Endymion* should reach the public as little marred by flaws as he could make it. And so he agonized over punctuation and minor deletions. He altered a line from Shakespeare's seventeenth sonnet, "The stretched metre of an antique song," as a motto to precede the poem. He coaxed a promise from Haydon to furnish a drawing for the frontispiece—a promise that was never fulfilled. What began as an exercise in mechanical drudgery became another experience in self-discovery.

Prolonged scrutiny forced Keats to criticize his work. If he saw where he failed, Keats also learned where he succeeded—the more important lesson by far. His keenest sense of achievement struck him as he was revising the lines beginning with 777 in Book I. The passage in question customarily takes its name from a phrase in the letters, the "Pleasure Thermometer"; essentially, it deals with the means—love chief among them—by which the spirit can break through the bonds of self to unite with another. His comment on the lines in a letter to John Taylor, his publisher, dated January 30, 1818, suggests that even months after their composition they came to the poet with all the freshness of discovery, the seed of future accomplishment. "My having written that Argument," he observed, "will perhaps be of the greatest Service to me of any thing I ever did. . . . It was a regular stepping of the Imagination towards a Truth." Another letter to Taylor, this one dated February 27, 1818, begins by correcting some misplaced commas in *Endymion*. From there Keats complains that the poem falls short of his aesthetic ideals, but his is a fruitful disappointment, for it precipitates a rare, incisive moment of theorizing about art. Keats proposes three "axioms" which take up major aspects of poetry. The first tries to account for poetry's special effect on its reader. He locates the power of poetry in a "fine excess," by which he means rich condensation. He rules out "Singularity"—here probably unusualness of thought—and in doing so comes to a restatement of Pope's definition of wit, "What oft was thought, but ne'er so well express'd." The second axiom addresses itself to form, which for Keats is dynamic, the inner principle of coherence and not a fixed formula. His comment on creativity, the third axiom, complements the first two. That fine excess, that organic unfolding, these are the flowerings of spontaneity; they cannot be forced.

One last preliminary, the hardest, remained before Keats was finished with the manuscript: this was the writing of a preface. As the time drew near when his work would bear the exposure of print, Keats began to lose courage. To ward off the expected blows of criticism, he wrote an abjectly self-effacing preface which, as Reynolds saw, was exactly the thing to invite an attack, not to deflect one. At Reynolds' urging (and he spoke for Taylor and Hessey, the publishers), Keats withdrew the original preface, wavered about including a preface at all, and at last produced a statement less apologetic than the first, but hardly self-assured.

Keats had reason to be worried about the reviews. The previous October (1817), *Blackwood's Edinburgh Magazine,* as part of an editorial policy of sensation, had launched an unscrupulous attack on Leigh Hunt as leader of what it called the "Cockney School of Poetry." At that time Keats was appalled. He wrote to Bailey on November 3, "I never read anything so virulent." Worse yet, additional installments were promised, and Keats found his own name capitalized with Hunt's in the motto above the article. "I have no doubt," he confided to Bailey, "that the second Number was intended for me." The expected attack appeared almost a year later on September 1, 1818, as a review of *Endymion*. It was merciless, putting Keats down not only for poetic lapses but also for his humble origins and his apothecary's training. That same month the *Quarterly*, more influential and therefore greater in its power to harm, followed suit. A few minor notices, one by Reynolds, appeared in Keats's defense, but as far as *Endymion* was concerned, the damage was done. Copies would remain unsold. The attacks affected Keats's reputation with the public for some time to come.

For all their vitriol, the reviews had a point. It would be false to make large artistic claims for *Endymion*, because the poem is downright uneven in quality. But to know a poet fully we must see where he is mended, and that is precisely the benefit of a slow-motion study of a long work in the making. The copious documentation from Keats's letters permits *Endymion* to become for the student of Keats what it was for the poet, an object lesson in creative growth.

Keats's year-and-a-half struggle with *Endymion*—its composition, revision, publication, and finally the reviews—was not wasted. On October 8, 1818, the month after the reviews were out, Keats sent his publisher Hessey what is certainly one of the mellowest letters he ever wrote. Any paraphrase would be an injustice, but the main point is clear: poets are made only through the ordeal of writing poems. To quote the letter, "The Genius of Poetry must work out its own salvation in a man: It cannot be matured by law & precept, but by sensation & watchfulness in itself—That which is creative must create itself." It was only months later, in the "vale of soul-making" letter of April 21, 1819, that Keats applied this principle more fervently to life. In that letter the poet was to say that every child is born with a spark of divinity (or what he called an intelligence), which becomes a soul through suffering in the world. This way of putting it makes Keats's view of the artist clearer. A man may—as one traditional view of the poet has it— be born with a divine gift; but that man will never be a poet until he develops his craftsmanship and refines his vision through the labor of artistic creation.

An Experiment with Form: The Sonnet

Endymion was the single longest poem that Keats wrote; his numerous sonnets were among the shortest. Charles Cowden Clarke, Keats's earliest mentor and friend, taught the poet while still an adolescent the standard forms of English verse. Spenser, Shakespeare, and Milton—all favorites of Keats—had firmly established the sonnet's place in the native poetic tradition, and now, after an eclipse during the late seventeenth and eighteenth centuries, the sonnet was regaining some of its previous popularity because of its use by such writers as Wordsworth, Coleridge, and Leigh Hunt. Sonnets mark several firsts in Keats's work. One of his first efforts at composition, *On Peace,* was a sonnet; so was the first verse he showed to Clarke, the poem on Leigh Hunt's release from prison. His first published work was the sonnet "*O Solitude! . . .*" And it is generally agreed that *On First Looking into Chapman's Homer,* a sonnet, is his first accomplished work. Keats quickly felt at home with the form. As a fledgling poet he could dash off a sonnet in fifteen minutes (as he did with *Written in Disgust of Vulgar Superstition*) , or he could write one to order on an assigned topic (as he did *On the Grasshopper and Cricket* in an impromptu competition with Hunt) .

While writing *Endymion,* Keats virtually abandoned the sonnet. Once the 4000-line narrative was complete, he returned to the 14-line lyric—but with a difference. He used the form much more sparingly. (Walter Jackson Bate, for one, has pointed out that whereas Keats had written at least 41 sonnets before January 1818, when *Endymion* was finished, he wrote only 25 after that date.) Also, Keats practically discarded the Petrarchan variety that he had employed exclusively before *Endymion* and substituted the Shakespearian form in its place. Of the 25 sonnets written after *Endymion,* only five adhere to the Petrarchan model; almost all of the rest are in the Shakespearian mold or a variation of it.

Keats had been reading Shakespeare's sonnets as he completed *Endymion* in November of 1817, and (as we have seen) he took the motto of that poem from one of them. Though Shakespeare's example as a sonneteer forced Keats to think better of the form, he was still dissatisfied with it. In April 1819 he turned that dissatisfaction to constructive result by a series of experiments. In the standard Shakespearian sonnet, the 14 lines are divided into three four-line groups or quatrains, rhyming *abab cdcd efef,* and a con-cluding couplet, rhyming *gg.* In his sonnet *To Sleep,* Keats tried moving the third quatrain to the end of the poem and inserting two lines, rhyming *bc,* in the space left between the second and third quatrains. The result was a rhyme scheme of *abab cdcd bc efef.* In the sonnet *On Fame* which begins "How fever'd is the man" he keeps the two standard Shakespearian quatrains at the beginning, but then moves the rhymed couplet from its normal position at lines 13 and 14 to lines 12 and 13, as if to insert it within the third quatrain. Instead of *efef gg,* then, the last six lines of the sonnet run *efe gg f.*

Keats recorded these sonnets on April 30, 1819, in a marathon letter to his brother and sister-in-law in America. In the same letter three days later he turned to questions of sonnet theory. He felt compelled to reject Shakespeare's model on the grounds that it was "too elegaic," meaning that like Gray's famous *Elegy Written in a Country Churchyard* it broke down mechanically into qua-trains. Whatever Keats's personal distaste for the Petrarchan or "legitimate" sonnet, as that variety was then called, it did resist this particular tendency to fall into fragments. Its basic structure is twofold, setting an octave, eight lines rhyming *abbaabba,* against a sestet, six lines which may rhyme in a variety of ways, but which ordinarily would include three different rhyme sounds such as *cdecde.* From Keats's point of view, however, the Petrarchan sonnet was also defective because of its "pouncing rhymes," an expression which apparently referred to the effect of the three consecutive couplets that occupy lines 2 through 7 of the octave. If the Petrar-chan sonnet avoids splitting into quatrains, it still breaks down into couplets for almost half its length. To show how structure of sound and meaning could otherwise be managed, Keats composed his sonnet on the sonnet, *"If by Dull Rhymes . . . ,"* included in the letter of May 3, 1819. This experimental piece succeeded in avoid-ing both the quatrains of the Shakespearian form and the couplets of the Petrarchan, but still offered no satisfactory pattern in their place.

Keats's experimentation and theorizing were yet to bear rich fruit, but not in the sonnet. The first evidence of substantial prog-ress appeared, as a matter of fact, just after the sonnets *To Sleep* and *On Fame* in the letter of April 30, 1819, in the last poem Keats wrote to that date, one on which he expended special care, and not a sonnet at all but an ode—the *Ode to Psyche*. Such scholars as H. W. Garrod and Walter Jackson Bate have shown that Keats was doing the kind of rearranging of quatrains and couplets in the *Ode to Psyche* that he had done in the two experimental sonnets copied in the same letter. In the original version (not included in this book) the first 14 lines of the ode could be considered a modified form of the Shakespearian sonnet. They begin with two standard quatrains, *ababcdcd,* then rearrange the next six lines to *effeef,* somewhat like the corresponding section of the sonnet *On Fame.*

In playing with lines of verse and pieces of stanzas, Keats was approaching the crucial realization that he need not confine himself to established metrical forms. He had to devise his own. So in the *Ode to Psyche* he overcame the limitations of the sonnet by stringing together several sonnetlike blocks of verse, creating a structure flexible enough to develop a significant theme. The real breakthrough occurred, not in the *Ode to Psyche,* but in Keats's invention of the stanza that served him as the basic metrical unit (subject to variation, particularly in *To Autumn*) for all of the other great odes, the works that support Keats's preeminence as a poet. (Besides the works just mentioned, these also include the *Ode on Melancholy,* the *Ode to a Nightingale,* and the *Ode on a Grecian Urn.*) The formula for the stanza was simple. It called for a quatrain from the Shakespearian sonnet rhyming *abab,* with a sestet from the Petrarchan rhyming *cdecde.* The stanza could be repeated as often as desired (there are three stanzas, for example, in the *Ode on Melancholy* and eight in the *Ode to a Nightingale*).

We want to call special attention to the ode form that Keats finally made from the sonnet because that form emblematizes the central meaning of his work. If we step back a sufficient distance, we can discern two impulses shaping his art. One is toward expansion, to say as much as possible about a subject. In *Endymion,* for instance, he resolved to "make 4000 Lines of one bare circumstance." The other impulse, which moves in the direction of contraction, surfaces in various ways. We catch it in the Keatsian delight with aphorism: "Beauty is truth, truth beauty," or "A thing of beauty is a joy for ever." As with language, so with form, especially the sonnet form; for Keats, as we know from the letters, it meant confinement.

Keats's theoretical "axioms" explore the nature of poetry in relation to a similar tension. His recognition that poetic power inheres in a "fine excess" derives as much from a feeling for distillation as from one for expansion. "Excess" implies quantity beyond the expected, whereas "fine"—insofar as it would refer to quantity —implies containment (it comes from the Latin word meaning boundary or limit). On the other hand, "excess" as it applies to quality denotes grossness; "fine" conveys the opposite. When in his second axiom Keats declares that "touches of Beauty should never be half way," he seems to call for surfeit. But when he completes the axiom by saying that the movement of a poem should be like the rise, progress, and setting of the sun, Keats invokes a principle by which every natural process has its appropriate limitations. Keats sees expansion and contraction, then, as necessarily interdependent.

The ode form that Keats made his own fulfills that interdependence he saw in poetry. The quatrain and sestet left over from the sonnet are units of contraction and serve to restrain. But against this metrical strictness Keats plays an open movement of the mind. The *Ode on a Grecian Urn* serves to illustrate. Here the speaker moves associatively, flinging out a series of questions and observations as he responds to each successive scene on the urn. In the ode's cumulative effect, the pressure of free mental activity exerts itself against prosodic closure. Thus are opposing forces in Keats's manner—*Endymion*'s diffuseness and the sonnet's narrowness— reconciled in the odal form. Keats discovered that in form, expansion and contraction need, and in fact nourish, each other. And to go a step further, does not this synthesis in form express the synthesis he achieved in his view of the world? His special theory of negative capability proposed the mind's indiscriminate going out to experience, an expansion to the point where the self risked annihilation. His later concept of identity works the other way: the self, by constantly defining its limits against the world, comes ultimately to its realization.

A Commercial Venture: *Otho the Great*

Keats's success with the odes of April and May of 1819 was personal as well as aesthetic. A measure of his new self-assurance could be found in his readiness to face the public again—in fact, to bid openly for its approval and financial reward. Keats's chronic embarrassment over money became acute during the summer of

1819 and pushed aside whatever misgivings may still have lingered from the reception of *Endymion*. Now more knowing in the ways of the literary world, he devised—with his friend Charles Brown as an accomplice—a strategy for commercial success. They would collaborate in writing a tragedy, *Otho the Great*, to be produced the following season in London. A play had the obvious advantage of circumventing Keats's literary enemies on the reviews by appealing directly to the public. If the venture prospered, Keats's reputation might be refurbished at the same time that his financial distress was relieved.

Keats took a hard look at what was making money, and then he wrote to order. For a while his hopes for success were well-founded. Even Brown (who had little literary talent) had scored a success five years earlier when his comic opera *Narensky* was produced at the Drury Lane Theater. The benefits of whatever experience may have accrued from that effort were now at Keats's disposal. Then too, Keats himself was no stranger to the theater. Besides being a frequent playgoer he had professional connections with that world. His friends—Hunt, Hazlitt, and Reynolds, who had once had a play produced—were all drama reviewers, Hazlitt one of the greatest in English stage history. Reynolds had enough faith in Keats's knowledge of the theater to ask the poet to write his column in *The Champion* while he was out of town. During that time, a matter of a few weeks during December 1817 and January 1818, Keats wrote three reviews. Together, then, he and Brown had a modest fund of observation and experience.

Bernice Slote has presented all the relevant stage history of that day in Part II of her book *Keats and the Dramatic Principle*, to which the following comments are indebted. Among the mainstays of the repertory, two kinds of plays then stood out: revivals of Shakespeare and what Miss Slote calls, by analogy with "Western" films, "Easterns"—action dramas in exotic Oriental settings with plenty of love and intrigue. The Gothic play, also popular, was a subclass of the "Eastern," following the same formula but set in the Middle Ages. To insure that their play would be a hit, Keats and Brown borrowed a little from each kind of play. From Shakespeare they took blank verse, stylistic mannerisms, and a flavor of tragedy; from the "Eastern," the melodramatic plot and a few flourishes of exoticism; from the Gothic play, the medieval setting. Since the taste of contemporary audiences was anything but fastidious, aesthetic objections to such a mixture were not to be found. We can take Keats at his word when—in a letter dated July 31, 1819—he toys with the idea of having an elephant appear onstage as part of Otho's menagerie.

Settling upon the kind of play to write was an easy matter compared with getting the play produced once it was written. A licensing law dating back to Fielding's time worked a particular hardship on playwrights, since it permitted only two theaters, Covent Garden and Drury Lane, to operate in London. To Keats and Brown there was no choice between the two. The company at Covent Garden played in a grand, formal style that looked quite old-fashioned since the emergence of a powerful new talent, Edmund Kean, at the Drury Lane. Kean was all energy and passion, and in the words of John Keats made "a revolution . . . in acting." Keats had already joined the partisans of this magnetic actor (Hazlitt was among them) when he devoted one of the three reviews that he wrote for *The Champion* entirely to extolling Kean. For Keats, then, Ludolph, the principal role in *Otho the Great,* had to be played by Kean, and that meant that the play had to be presented at Drury Lane.

Such were the plans, but they fell through. In the first place, word spread in late summer of 1819 that Kean would spend the approaching season on tour in America. The tour never materialized, but Robert William Elliston, the manager of Drury Lane, created other obstacles. He delayed his decision about producing the play, and when at last he agreed to do so, it was only for use in the next year's season, 1820–1821. Since Keats's financial needs were growing desperate, such a delay was intolerable. In the meantime, a new actor named George Macready was beginning to attract attention at Covent Garden, causing Keats to reconsider that company. He and Brown therefore withdrew their play from Drury Lane and sent it to the rival theater, where it was rejected, probably not even read. It was not to be performed—in London, or anywhere—until 1950.

In the light of Keats's aims, then, *Otho* was a failure. But as a measure of his growing ability to perform as a professional writer it must be rated a success. Brown has left a description of the manner in which Keats worked on this project. He would give Keats a skeletal outline of the plot and characters, one scene at a time. Without knowing what was to follow, Keats fleshed out

Brown's ideas in blank verse, until in the fifth act he declared his independence and after hearing Brown's proposals finished the play to suit his own taste. What is remarkable is the speed and efficiency with which Keats executed his part of the task. Keats set out for the Isle of Wight on June 27, 1819; even before Brown joined him there on July 22, he had finished one act. When they left for Winchester only three weeks later, four acts were complete. The fifth was dispatched scarcely more than a week after that. For most writers a five-act play would have been work enough for one summer, but for Keats it was merely a part-time endeavor. The principal work occupying him that season was *Lamia* (which he finished) and *The Fall of Hyperion* (which he did not).

The achievement of *Otho* lay in its demonstration that Keats commanded sufficient discipline and skill in his craft to produce in a short time a substantial composition that could meet the numerous, complex demands of the contemporary stage. It proved that, like a true professional, he could function effectively under pressure. As his active career as a poet effectively ended in September 1819, Keats was at last finding a way of reconciling the demands of both his muse and his public. He could that same fall compose the consummate ode *To Autumn* and state in a letter to Brown his intention to work as a journalist for whoever would pay him. Achievement had made a difference. Not yet twenty-three, Keats had already done enough to warrant his modestly phrased prophecy that he would be "among the English poets."

Among the English Poets

The models a man chooses make him what he is. What one poet thinks of another defines artistically who he is. A major theme of Bate's biography *John Keats* is that Keats achieved greatness precisely by keeping the great constantly in mind.

Any list of Keats's literary heroes begins with Shakespeare. However much his estimate of other writers may have fluctuated, Keats's admiration for this poet was unfaltering. He never tired of quoting from the poems and plays, which the letters show he knew well. Here was the master he would never outgrow. Of all the lasting good to come from this discipleship, the best came early, as lasting effects frequently do. Shakespeare served as catalyst for the doctrine of negative capability and that was Keats's declaration of independence. By it he claimed an artist's freedom from moral restraint and social consequences. It also freed Keats from the unexamined attachments that generated youthful effusions like his sonnet to Byron.

The moral neutrality essential to negative capability made way for further development. Inspired by Wordsworth, who would probably take second place to Shakespeare among his literary idols, Keats came to link the artist indissolubly with moral commitment. Wordsworth's peculiar strength for Keats was insight into suffering gained through experience, a quality that finally carried decisive weight in his estimate of other poets. The Italian poet Boiardo lived in the splendor of a castle, and therefore knew nothing of the darker, agonizing side of existence. "He was a noble Poet of Romance," Keats observed, "not a miserable and mighty Poet of the human Heart." By contrast, suffering engendered by public neglect seemed the hallmark of the English poet—Shakespeare included.

The wretchedness of their lives drew Keats to celebrate two poets in particular, Robert Burns and Thomas Chatterton, whom history has consigned to minor status. *Misery* was the word that Keats associated with Burns, whose life he saw as a struggle for emotional survival in a repressive society dominated by Scottish Calvinism. The life of Chatterton, the eighteenth-century poet to whose memory Keats dedicated *Endymion,* was even more tragic. After a precocious adolescence, Chatterton committed suicide at eighteen, becoming for a whole generation of Romantics the genius destroyed by public neglect. It is easy to see why Keats was drawn to him.

Milton struck Keats as a case almost exactly opposite to that of Burns and Chatterton. Here was a writer whose poetic attainments were so massive that he could not be denied a place among the first rank of poets, one whose artistry was so expert that it seemed under perfect control. Yet here also was a writer who, in Keats's misinformed view, had never passed through the refining fire of suffering. He seemed too conscious an artist to be a deeply feeling man. The foreign-sounding, Latinate style that Milton cultivated seemed the inevitable result of the life that he led. Keats would claim that Chatterton, who did suffer, wrote the purest English, and that the Scotsman Burns was actually Southern—that is, English—at heart, precisely because of his wretched life. To be truly in the English tradition, then, Keats demanded of a poet not only mastery of his craft but a depth of moral awareness as well.

We come, finally, to what Keats's view of others tells us about himself. At heart he is English. Though he admired figures from world literature like Homer and Dante, he felt at home with the poets of his land—but not of his time. His contemporaries had little to say to his imagination except for Wordsworth, about whom Keats anticipated the favorable judgment of history. His prescience in Wordsworth's case displayed Keats's affinity for excellence; and if greatness in another poet was his stimulus, greatness for himself was John Keats's goal.

1. THE POET AND REALITY

SKEPTICISM

The Critical Spirit of the Enlightenment

TO B. R. HAYDON
11 May 1817   Margate

I feel confident I should have been a rebel Angel had the opportunity been mine.

———•—•—•———

Keats wrote this letter after learning that the ordination of his friend Benjamin Bailey was delayed by the Bishop of Lincoln.

TO BENJAMIN BAILEY
3 November 1817   Hampstead

My dear Bailey,
Before I received your Letter I had heard of your disappointment—an unlook'd for piece of villainy. I am glad to

hear there was an hindrance to your speaking your Mind to the Bishop: for all may go straight yet—as to being ordained—but the disgust consequent cannot pass away in a hurry—it must be shocking to find in a sacred Profession such barefaced oppression and impertinence—The Stations and Grandeurs of the World have taken it into their heads that they cannot commit themselves towards and inferior in rank—but is not the impertinence from one above to one below more wretchedly mean than from the low to the high? There is something so nauseous in self-willed yawning impudence in the shape of conscience—it sinks the Bishop of Lincoln into a smashed frog putrifying: that a rebel against common decency should escape the Pillory! That a mitre should cover a Man guilty of the most coxcombical, tyranical and indolent impertinence! I repeat this word for the offence appears to me most especially *impertinent*—and a very serious return would be the Rod— Yet doth he sit in his Palace. Such is this World—and we live—you have surely in a continual struggle against the suffocation of accidents—we must bear (and my Spleen is mad at the thought thereof) the Proud Mans Contumely— O for a recourse somewhat human independant of the great Consolations of Religion and undepraved Sensations. of the Beautiful. the poetical in all things—O for a Remedy against such wrongs within the pale of the World! Should not those things be pure enjoymen{t} should they stand the chance of being contaminated by being called in as antagonists to Bishops? Would not earthly thing do? By Heavens my dear Bailey, I know you have a spice of what I mean— you can set me and have set it in all the rubs that may befal me you have I know a sort of Pride which would kick the Devil on the Jaw Bone and make him drunk with the kick—There is nothing so balmy to a soul imbittered as yours must be, as Pride—When we look at the Heavens we cannot be proud—but shall stocks and stones be impertinent and say it does not become us to kick them? At this Moment I take your hand let us walk up ⟨your⟩ yon Mountain of common sense now if our Pride be vainglorious such a support woud fail—yet you feel firm footing— now look beneath at that parcel of knaves and fools. Many a Mitre is moving among them. I cannot express how I despise the Man who would wrong or be impertinent to you—The thought that we are mortal makes us groan   I will speak of something else or my Spleen will get higher and higher—and I am not a bearer of the two egded Sword.

———————

TO GEORGE AND TOM KEATS
13 January 1818   Hampstead

My dear Brothers
I am certain I think of having a letter tomorrow morning for I expected one so much this morning, having been in town two days, at the end of which my expectations began to get up a little, I found two on the table, one from Bailey & one from Haydon, I am quite perplexed in a world of doubts & fancies—there is nothing stable in the world—uproar's your only musick, I do not mean to include Bailey in this & so I dismiss him from this, with all the oprobrium he deserves, that is in so many words, he is one of the noblest men alive at the present day.

———————

The following is from a key letter in which Keats deals at some length with the evolution of human consciousness both in its individual and collective forms. Keats has just pointed to Wordsworth as an explorer of new regions of awareness.

TO J. H. REYNOLDS
3 May 1818   Teignmouth

Here I must think Wordsworth is deeper than Milton— though I think it has depended more upon the general and gregarious advance of intellect, than individual greatness of Mind—From the Paradise Lost and the other Works of Milton, I hope it is not too presuming, even between ourselves to say, his Philosophy, human and divine, may be tolerably understood by one not much advanced in years, In his time englishmen were just emancipated from a great superstition—and Men had got hold of certain points and resting places in reasoning which were too newly born to be doubted, and too much ⟨oppressed⟩ by the Mass of

opposed

Europe not to be thought etherial and authentically divine —who could gainsay his ideas on virtue, vice, and Chastity in Comus, just at the time of the dismissal of Cod-pieces and a hundred other disgraces? who would not rest satisfied with his hintings at good and evil in the Paradise Lost, when just free from the inquisition and burrning in Smithfield? The Reformation produced such immediate and great⟨s⟩ benefits, that Protestantism was considered under the immediate eye of heaven, and its own remaining Dogmas and superstitions, then, as it were, regenerated, constituted those resting places and seeming sure points of Reasoning—from that I have mentioned, Milton, whatever he may have thought in the sequel, appears to have been content with these by his writings—He did not think into the human heart, as Wordsworth has done—Yet Milton as a Philosop⟨h⟩er, had sure as great powers as Wordsworth —What is then to be inferr'd? O many things—It proves there is really a grand march of intellect—, It proves that a mighty providence subdues the mightiest Minds to the service of the time being, whether it be in human Knowledge or Religion.

———•◆•———

TO GEORGE AND GEORGIANA KEATS
22 December 1818   Hampstead

People think of nothing but money-getting—now for me I am rather inclined to the liberal side of things—{but} I am reckoned lax in my christian principles.

———•◆•———

TO GEORGE AND GEORGIANA KEATS
14 February 1819   Hampstead

The only time I went out from Bedhampton was to see a Chapel consecrated. . . . The Consecration was— not amusing—there were numbers of carriages, and his house crammed with Clergy—they sanctified the Chapel—and it being a wet day consecrated the burial ground through the vestry window. I begin to hate Parsons—they did not make me love them that day—when I saw them in their proper colours—A Parson is a Lamb in a drawing room and a lion in a Vestry—The notions of Society will not permit a Parson to give way to his temper in any shape —so he festers in himself—his features get a peculiar diabolical self sufficient iron stupid exp[r]ession—He is continually acting—His mind is against every Man and every Mans mind is against him—He is an Hippocrite to the Believer and a Coward to the unbeliever—He must be either a Knave or an Ideot—And there is no Man so much to be pitied as an ideot parson—The soldier who is cheated into an esprit du corps—by a red coat, a Band and Colours for the purpose of nothing—is not half so pitiable as the Parson who is led by the nose by the Bench of Bishops—and is smothered in absurdities—a poor neces⟨s⟩sary subaltern of the Church—

The following passage is from the same letter. The Roman author, Pliny the Elder (23–79 A.D.), and the Frenchman, George Louis Leclerq Buffon (1707–1788), each wrote a work entitled *Natural History*. Both works include encyclopedic surveys of familiar as well as exotic animal species.

3 March 1819

Here is the parson at Hampstead quarreling with all the world, he is in the wrong by this same token; when the black Cloth was put up in the Church for the Queen's mourning, he asked the workmen to hang it the wrong side outwards, that it might be better when taken down, it being his perquisite—Parsons will always keep up their Character, but as it is said there are some animals, the Ancients knew, which we do not; let us hope our posterity will miss the black badger with tri-cornered hat; Who knows but some Revisor of Buffon or Pliny, may put an account of the parson in the Appendix; No one will then beleive it any more than we believe in the Phoenix. I think we may class the lawyer in the same natural history of Monsters; a green bag will hold as much as a lawn sleeve— The only difference is that the one is fustian, & the other flimsy.

Still from the same letter:

19 March 1819

I have no doubt that thousands of people never heard of have had hearts comp[l]etely disinterested: I can remember but two—Socrates and Jesus—their Histories evince it— What I heard a little time ago, Taylor observe with respect to Socrates, may be said of Jesus—That he was so great a⟨s⟩ man that though he transmitted no writing of his own to posterity, we have his Mind and his sayings and his greatness handed to us by others. It is to be lamented that the history of the latter was written and revised by Men interested in the pious frauds of Religion. Yet through all this I see his splendour.

———•—•—•———

This letter catches Keats in an uncharacteristic mood. He is helping his younger sister, not yet sixteen, prepare for her confirmation. The correspondent accounts for the tone, as the parson is a role to which Keats is obviously unaccustomed.

TO FANNY KEATS

31 March 1819   Hampstead

My dear Fanny,
I shall be going to town tomorrow and will call at the Nursery on the road for those roots and seeds you want, which I will send by the Walthamstow stage. The best way, I thought, for you to lean to answer those questions, is to read over the little book, which I sent from a Bookseller's in town, or you should have had a Letter with it—Tell me

whether it will do: if not I will put down the answers for you—I have not yet heard from George—Perhaps if I just give you the heads of the answers it may be better—though I think you will find them all in that little book—

Ans^r 1—It was instituted by John the Baptist when he baptised those people in the river Jordan who beleved through him in the coming of Christ—and more particularly when he baptised christ himself.

2 It corresponds to the Jewish Circumscision

3 The meaning is that we are confirmed members of Christ It is not administered till 14 years of age because before that age the mind not judged to be sufficiently mature and capaple. The act of confirmation imposes on the Christian self circumspection; as by that ceremony the Christian duties of God fathers and godmothers is annulled and put and end to—as you see in the catechisim—"they promise and vow three things in my name"—Confirmation absolves this obligation.

4 There are two Sacraments of our Church—Baptisim and the Lord's Supper. The Church of Rome has seven Sacraments. The church of Rome includes several ceremonies (I forget what they are) and the civil rite of marriage—I believe Confi[r]mation is a Sacrament with them —Extreme unction or the annointing the extremities of dying persons with holy water. The reason why we have but two Sacraments is—that it is proved from the Scriptures by the great protestant reformers—that only two are commanded by god—the rest adopted by the Church of Rome are human institutions.

5 You must here repeat your belief—and say the question is to hard for you.

6 Look in Isaia for *"A virgin shall conceive"* &c—Look in the Psalms for *"The Kings of the Earth set themselves and the Princes take counsel together"* and *"they parted my Garments among them &"* and *"My god, my god why has thou forsaken me &c"* In Jeremia *"Comfort ye, comfort ye &"* In Daniel The stone cut out of the mountain without hands that breaks the image in pieces is a type of the Kingdom of Christ—Look at the 2nd Chat. Isaiah—Chap 7-9—*'For unto us a Child is bo[r]n"* 11—Jeremiah Chap

xxxi Micah Chap 5—Zechariah Chap 6 and Chap 13 *verse 6*. Those I have marked will be sufficient—You will remember their completion in the ⟨test⟩ new testament—

7ᵗʰ The communion of saints is the fruition they enjoy in heaven among one another and in the Divinity of Christ—

8ᵗʰ It was instituted on the night of the feast of the Passover at the Last supper with the Twelve; the night Judas betrayed Christ—and you may see in the 26 Mathew—It corresponds to the "Feast of the Passover in the Jewish Ritual—

9 They expected Christ to be a temporal Prince and being disappointed, rejected him—

10—Look to the Catechisim—'What is your duty towards God?

11ᵗʰ The Prophecy to our first parents is this—Genesis 3 Chapter—verse [15] "And I will put enmity between thee and the woman and between thy seed and her seed; *it shall bruize thy head* and thou shall bruize his heel—Christ the Son of David by dying on the Cross triumphed over death and the grave from which he saved mankind; and in that way did he 'bruize the Serpent's head"—

Your affectionate Parson
John—

WRITTEN ON THE DAY THAT MR. LEIGH HUNT LEFT PRISON

What though, for showing truth to flatter'd state,
   Kind Hunt was shut in prison, yet has he,
   In his immortal spirit, been as free
As the sky-searching lark, and as elate.
Minion of grandeur! think you he did wait?
   Think you he naught but prison walls did see,
   Till, so unwilling, thou unturn'dst the key?
Ah, no! far happier, nobler was his fate!
In Spenser's halls he stray'd, and bowers fair,
   Culling enchanted flowers; and he flew   10
With daring Milton through the fields of air:

To regions of his own his genius true
Took happy flights. Who shall his fame impair
   When thou art dead, and all thy wretched crew?

February 2, 1815

TO KOSCIUSKO

Good Kosciusko, thy great name alone
   Is a full harvest whence to reap high feeling;
   It comes upon us like the glorious pealing
Of the wide spheres—an everlasting tone.
And now it tells me, that in worlds unknown,
   The names of heroes, burst from clouds concealing,
   And change to harmonies, for ever stealing
Through cloudless blue, and round each silver throne.
It tells me too, that on a happy day,
   When some good spirit walks upon the earth,   **10**
     Thy name with Alfred's, and the great of yore
  Gently commingling, gives tremendous birth
To a loud hymn, that sounds far, far away
     To where the great God lives for evermore.

December 1816

WRITTEN IN DISGUST OF VULGAR SUPERSTITION

The church bells toll a melancholy round,
   Calling the people to some other prayers,
   Some other gloominess, more dreadful cares,
More hearkening to the sermon's horrid sound.
Surely the mind of man is closely bound
   In some black spell; seeing that each one tears
   Himself from fireside joys, and Lydian airs,
And converse high of those with glory crown'd.
Still, still they toll, and I should feel a damp,—
   A chill as from a tomb, did I know   **10**
That they are dying like an outburnt lamp;
   That 'tis their sighing, wailing ere they go

Into oblivion;—that fresh flowers will grow,
And many glories of immortal stamp.

December 22, 1816

Nothing in This World Is Proveable

TO BENJAMIN BAILEY
22 November 1817   Burford Bridge

I am certain of nothing but of the holiness of the Heart's affections and the truth of Imagination. . . . I have never yet been able to perceive how any thing can be known for truth by consequitive reasoning—and yet it must be—Can it be that even the greatest Philosopher ever (when) arrived at his goal without putting aside numerous objections— . . . . for I assure you I sometimes feel not the influence of a Passion or Affection during a whole week—and so long this sometimes continues I begin to suspect myself and the genuiness of my feelings at other times—thinking them a few barren Tragedy-tears—

TO BENJAMIN BAILEY
13 March 1818   Teignmouth

You know my ideas about Religion—I do not think myself more in the right than other people and that nothing in this world is proveable. I wish I could enter into all your feelings on the subject merely for one short 10 Minutes and give you a Page or two to your liking. I am sometimes so very sceptical as to think Poetry itself a mere Jack a lanthern to amuse whoever may chance to be struck with its brilliance—As Tradesmen say every thing is worth what it will fetch, so probably every mental pursuit takes its reality and worth from the ardour of the pursuer—being in itself a nothing. . . . Now my dear fellow I must once for all tell you I have not one Idea of the truth of any of my speculations—I shall never be a Reasoner because I care not to be in the right, when retired from bickering and in a proper philosophical temper—

My thoughts have turned lately this way—The more we know the more inadequacy we discover in the world to satisfy us—this is an old observation; but I have made up my Mind never to take any thing for granted—but even to examine the truth of the commonest proverbs—

If you could really what is call'd enjoy yourself at a Party —if you can smile in peoples faces, and wish them to admire you *now,* you never have nor ever will love me—I see *life* in nothing but the cerrtainty of your Love—convince me of it my sweetest. If I am not somehow convinc'd I shall die of agony. If we love we must not live as other men and women do—I cannot brook the wolfsbane of fashion and foppery and tattle. You must be mine to die upon the rack if I want you.

READ ME A LESSON, MUSE, AND SPEAK IT LOUD

Read me a lesson, Muse, and speak it loud
   Upon the top of Nevis, blind in mist!
I look into the chasms, and a shroud
   Vapourous doth hide them,—just so much I wist
Mankind do know of hell; I look o'erhead,
   And there is sullen mist,—even so much
Mankind can tell of heaven; mist is spread
   Before the earth, beneath me,—even such,
Even so vague is man's sight of himself!
   Here are the craggy stones beneath my feet,—   10
Thus much I know that, a poor witless elf,
   I tread on them,—that all my eye doth meet
Is mist and crag, not only on this height,
But in the world of thought and mental might!

August 2, 1818

LAMIA

Part I

Upon a time, before the faery broods
Drove Nymph and Satyr from the prosperous woods,
Before king Oberon's bright diadem,
Sceptre, and mantle, clasp'd with dewy gem,
Frighted away the Dryads and the Fauns
From rushes green, and brakes, and cowslip'd lawns,
The ever-smitten Hermes empty left
His golden throne, bent warm on amorous theft:
From high Olympus had he stolen light,
On this side of Jove's clouds, to escape the sight   10
Of his great summoner, and made retreat
Into a forest on the shores of Crete.
For somewhere in that sacred island dwelt
A nymph, to whom all hoofed Satyrs knelt;
At whose white feet the languid Tritons poured
Pearls, while on land they wither'd and adored.
Fast by the springs where she to bathe was wont,
And in those meads where sometime she might haunt,
Were strewn rich gifts, unknown to any Muse,
Though Fancy's casket were unlock'd to choose.   20
Ah, what a world of love was at her feet!
So Hermes thought, and a celestial heat
Burnt from his winged heels to either ear,
That from a whiteness, as the lilly clear,
Blush'd into roses 'mid his golden hair,
Fallen in jealous curls about his shoulders bare.

From vale to vale, from wood to wood, he flew,
Breathing upon the flowers his passion new,
And wound with many a river to its head,
To find where this sweet nymph prepar'd her secret bed: 30
In vain; the sweet nymph might nowhere be found,
And so he rested, on the lonely ground,
Pensive, and full of painful jealousies
Of the Wood-Gods, and even the very trees.
There as he stood, he heard a mournful voice,

Such as once heard, in gentle heart, destroys
All pain but pity: thus the lone voice spake:
'When from this wreathed tomb shall I awake!
'When move in a sweet body fit for life,
'And love, and pleasure, and the ruddy strife   40
'Of hearts and lips! Ah, miserable me!'
The God, dove-footed, glided silently
Round bush and tree, soft-brushing, in his speed,
The taller grasses and full-flowering weed,
Until he found a palpitating snake,
Bright, and cirque-couchant in a dusky brake.

She was a gordian shape of dazzling hue,
Vermilion-spotted, golden, green, and blue;
Striped like a zebra, freckled like a pard,
Eyed like a peacock, and all crimson barr'd;   50
And full of silver moons, that, as she breathed,
Dissolv'd, or brighter shone, or interwreathed
Their lustres with the gloomier tapestries—
So rainbow-sided, touch'd with miseries,
She seem'd, at once, some penanced lady elf,
Some demon's mistress, or the demon's self.
Upon her crest she wore a wannish fire
Sprinkled with stars, like Ariadne's tiar:
Her head was serpent, but ah, bitter-sweet!
She had a woman's mouth with all its pearls complete: 60
And for her eyes: what could such eyes do there
But weep, and weep, that they were born so fair?
As Proserpine still weeps for her Sicilian air.
Her throat was serpent, but the words she spake
Came, as through bubbling honey, for Love's sake,
And thus; while Hermes on his pinions lay,
Like a stoop'd falcon ere he takes his prey.

'Fair Hermes, crown'd with feathers, fluttering light,
'I had a splendid dream of thee last night:
'I saw thee sitting, on a throne of gold,   70
'Among the Gods, upon Olympus old,
'The only sad one; for thou didst not hear
'The soft, lute-finger'd Muses chaunting clear,

'Nor even Apollo when he sang alone,
'Deaf to his throbbing throat's long, long melodious moan.
'I dreamt I saw thee, robed in purple flakes,
'Break amorous through the clouds, as morning breaks,
'And, swiftly as a bright Phœbean dart,
'Strike for the Cretan isle; and here thou art!
'Too gentle Hermes, hast thou found the maid?'   80
Whereat the star of Lethe not delay'd
His rosy eloquence, and thus inquired:
'Thou smooth-lipp'd serpent, surely high inspired!
'Thou beauteous wreath, with melancholy eyes,
'Possess whatever bliss thou canst devise,
'Telling me only where my nymph is fled,—
'Where she doth breathe!' 'Bright planet, thou hast said,'
Return'd the snake, 'but seal with oaths, fair God!'
'I swear,' said Hermes, 'by my serpent rod,
'And by thine eyes, and by thy starry crown!'   90
Light flew his earnest words, among the blossoms blown.
Then thus again the brilliance feminine:
'Too frail of heart! for this lost nymph of thine,
'Free as the air, invisibly, she strays
'About these thornless wilds; her pleasant days
'She tastes unseen; unseen her nimble feet
'Leave traces in the grass and flowers sweet;
'From weary tendrils, and bow'd branches green,
'She plucks the fruit unseen, she bathes unseen:
'And by my power is her beauty veil'd   100
'To keep it unaffronted, unassail'd
'By the love-glances of unlovely eyes,
'Of Satyrs, Fauns, and blear'd Silenus' sighs.
'Pale grew her immortality, for woe
'Of all these lovers, and she grieved so
'I took compassion on her, bade her steep
'Her hair in weïrd syrops, that would keep
'Her loveliness invisible, yet free
'To wander as she loves, in liberty.
'Thou shalt behold her, Hermes, thou alone,   110
'If thou wilt, as thou swearest, grant my boon!'
Then, once again, the charmed God began
An oath, and through the serpent's ears it ran

Warm, tremulous, devout, psalterian.
Ravish'd, she lifted her Circean head,
Blush'd a live damask, and swift-lisping said,
'I was a woman, let me have once more
'A woman's shape, and charming as before.
'I love a youth of Corinth—O the bliss!
'Give me my woman's form, and place me where he is.   120
'Stoop, Hermes, let me breathe upon thy brow,
'And thou shalt see thy sweet nymph even now.'
The God on half-shut feathers sank serene,
She breath'd upon his eyes, and swift was seen
Of both the guarded nymph near-smiling on the green.
It was no dream; or say a dream it was,
Real are the dreams of Gods, and smoothly pass
Their pleasures in a long immortal dream.
One warm, flush'd moment, hovering, it might seem
Dash'd by the wood-nymph's beauty, so he burn'd;   130
Then, lighting on the printless verdure, turn'd
To the swoon'd serpent, and with languid arm,
Delicate, put to proof the lythe Caducean charm.
So done, upon the nymph his eyes he bent
Full of adoring tears and blandishment,
And towards her stept: she, like a moon in wane,
Faded before him, cower'd, nor could restrain
Her fearful sobs, self-folding like a flower
That faints into itself at evening hour:
But the God fostering her chilled hand,   140
She felt the warmth, her eyelids open'd bland,
And, like new flowers at morning song of bees,
Bloom'd, and gave up her honey to the lees.
Into the green-recessed woods they flew;
Nor grew they pale, as mortal lovers do.

Left to herself, the serpent now began
To change; her elfin blood in madness ran,
Her mouth foam'd, and the grass, therewith besprent,
Wither'd at dew so sweet and virulent;
Her eyes in torture fix'd, and anguish drear,   150
Hot, glaz'd, and wide, with lid-lashes all sear,
Flash'd phosphor and sharp sparks, without one cooling tear.

The colours all inflam'd throughout her train,
She writh'd about, convuls'd with scarlet pain:
A deep volcanian yellow took the place
Of all her milder-mooned body's grace;
And, as the lava ravishes the mead,
Spoilt all her silver mail, and golden brede;
Made gloom of all her frecklings, streaks and bars,
Eclips'd her crescents, and lick'd up her stars: 160
So that, in moments few, she was undrest
Of all her sapphires, greens, and amethyst,
And rubious-argent: of all these bereft,
Nothing but pain and ugliness were left.
Still shone her crown; that vanish'd, also she
Melted and disappear'd as suddenly;
And in the air, her new voice luting soft,
Cried, 'Lycius! gentle Lycius!'—Borne aloft
With the bright mists about the mountains hoar
These words dissolv'd: Crete's forests heard no more.   170

   Whither fled Lamia, now a lady bright,
A full-born beauty new and exquisite?
She fled into that valley they pass o'er
Who go to Corinth from Cenchreas' shore;
And rested at the foot of those wild hills,
The rugged founts of the Peræan rills,
And of that other ridge whose barren back
Stretches, with all its mist and cloudy rack,
South-westward to Cleone. There she stood
About a young bird's flutter from a wood,   180
Fair, on a sloping green of mossy tread,
By a clear pool, wherein she passioned
To see herself escap'd from so sore ills,
While her robes flaunted with the daffodils.

   Ah, happy Lycius!—for she was a maid
More beautiful than ever twisted braid,
Or sigh'd, or blush'd, or on spring-flowered lea
Spread a green kirtle to the minstrelsy:
A virgin purest lipp'd, yet in the lore
Of love deep learned to the red heart's core: 190

Not one hour old, yet of sciential brain
To unperplex bliss from its neighbour pain;
Define their pettish limits, and estrange
Their points of contact, and swift counterchange;
Intrigue with the specious chaos, and dispart
Its most ambiguous atoms with sure art;
As though in Cupid's college she had spent
Sweet days a lovely graduate, still unshent,
And kept his rosy terms in idle languishment.

Why this fair creature chose so faerily   200
By the wayside to linger, we shall see;
But first 'tis fit to tell how she could muse
And dream, when in the serpent prison-house,
Of all she list, strange or magnificent:
How, ever, where she will'd, her spirit went;
Whether to faint Elysium, or where
Down through tress-lifting waves the Nereids fair
Wind into Thetis' bower by many a pearly stair;
Or where God Bacchus drains his cups divine,
Stretch'd out, at ease, beneath a glutinous pine;   210
Or where in Pluto's gardens palatine
Mulciber's columns gleam in far piazzian line.
And sometimes into cities she would send
Her dream, with feast and rioting to blend;
And once, while among mortals dreaming thus,
She saw the young Corinthian Lycius
Charioting foremost in the envious race,
Like a young Jove with calm uneager face,
And fell into a swooning love of him.
Now on the moth-time of that evening dim   220
He would return that way, as well she knew,
To Corinth from the shore; for freshly blew
The eastern soft wind, and his galley now
Grated the quaystones with her brazen prow
In port Cenchreas, from Egina isle
Fresh anchor'd; whither he had been awhile
To sacrifice to Jove, whose temple there
Waits with high marble doors for blood and incense rare.
Jove heard his vows, and better'd his desire;

For by some freakful chance he made retire   230
From his companions, and set forth to walk,
Perhaps grown wearied of their Corinth talk:
Over the solitary hills he fared,
Thoughtless at first, but ere eve's star appeared
His phantasy was lost, where reason fades,
In the calm'd twilight of Platonic shades.
Lamia beheld him coming, near, more near—
Close to her passing, in indifference drear,
His silent sandals swept the mossy green;
So neighbour'd to him, and yet so unseen   240
She stood: he pass'd, shut up in mysteries,
His mind wrapp'd like his mantle, while her eyes
Follow'd his steps, and her neck regal white
Turn'd—syllabling thus, 'Ah, Lycius bright,
'And will you leave me on the hills alone?
'Lycius, look back! and be some pity shown.'
He did; not with cold wonder fearingly,
But Orpheus-like at an Eurydice;
For so delicious were the words she sung,
It seem'd he had lov'd them a whole summer long: 250
And soon his eyes had drunk her beauty up,
Leaving no drop in the bewildering cup,
And still the cup was full,—while he, afraid
Lest she should vanish ere his lip had paid
Due adoration, thus began to adore;
Her soft look growing coy, she saw his chain so sure:
'Leave thee alone! Look back! Ah, Goddess, see
'Whether my eyes can ever turn from thee!
'For pity do not this sad heart belie—
'Even as thou vanishest so shall I die.   260
'Stay! though a Naiad of the rivers, stay!
'To thy far wishes will thy streams obey:
'Stay! though the greenest woods be thy domain,
'Alone they can drink up the morning rain:
'Though a descended Pleiad, will not one
'Of thine harmonious sisters keep in tune
'Thy spheres, and as thy silver proxy shine?
'So sweetly to these ravish'd ears of mine
'Came thy sweet greeting, that if thou shouldst fade

'Thy memory will waste me to a shade:— 270
'For pity do not melt!'—'If I should stay,'
Said Lamia, 'here, upon this floor of clay,
'And pain my steps upon these flowers too rough,
'What canst thou say or do of charm enough
'To dull the nice remembrance of my home?
'Thou canst not ask me with thee here to roam
'Over these hills and vales, where no joy is,—
'Empty of immortality and bliss!
'Thou art a scholar, Lycius, and must know
'That finer spirits cannot breathe below 280
'In human climes, and live: Alas! poor youth,
'What taste of purer air hast thou to soothe
'My essence? What serener palaces,
'Where I may all my many senses please,
'And by mysterious sleights a hundred thirsts appease?
'It cannot be—Adieu!' So said, she rose
Tiptoe with white arms spread. He, sick to lose
The amorous promise of her lone complain,
Swoon'd, murmuring of love, and pale with pain.
The cruel lady, without any show 290
Of sorrow for her tender favourite's woe,
But rather, if her eyes could brighter be,
With brighter eyes and slow amenity,
Put her new lips to his, and gave afresh
The life she had so tangled in her mesh:
And as he from one trance was wakening
Into another, she began to sing,
Happy in beauty, life, and love, and every thing,
A song of love, too sweet for earthly lyres,
While, like held breath, the stars drew in their panting
    fires. 300
And then she whisper'd in such trembling tone,
As those who, safe together met alone
For the first time through many anguish'd days,
Use other speech than looks; bidding him raise
His drooping head, and clear his soul of doubt,
For that she was a woman, and without
Any more subtle fluid in her veins
Than throbbing blood, and that the self-same pains

Inhabited her frail-strung heart as his.
And next she wonder'd how his eyes could miss 310
Her face so long in Corinth, where, she said,
She dwelt but half retir'd, and there had led
Days happy as the gold coin could invent
Without the aid of love; yet in content
Till she saw him, as once she pass'd him by,
Where 'gainst a column he lent thoughtfully
At Venus' temple porch, 'mid baskets heap'd
Of amorous herbs and flowers, newly reap'd
Late on that eve, as 'twas the night before
The Adonian feast; whereof she saw no more, 320
But wept alone those days, for why should she adore?
Lycius from death awoke into amaze,
To see her still, and singing so sweet lays;
Then from amaze into delight he fell
To hear her whisper woman's lore so well;
And every word she spake entic'd him on
To unperplex'd delight and pleasure known.
Let the mad poets say whate'er they please
Of the sweets of Faeries, Peris, Goddesses,
There is not such a treat among them all, 330
Haunters of cavern, lake, and waterfall,
As a real woman, lineal indeed
From Pyrrha's pebbles or old Adam's seed.
Thus gentle Lamia judg'd, and judg'd aright,
That Lycius could not love in half a fright,
So threw the goddess off, and won his heart
More pleasantly by playing woman's part,
With no more awe than what her beauty gave,
That, while it smote, still guaranteed to save.
Lycius to all made eloquent reply, 340
Marrying to every word a twinborn sigh;
And last, pointing to Corinth, ask'd her sweet,
If 'twas too far that night for her soft feet.
The way was short, for Lamia's eagerness
Made, by a spell, the triple league decrease
To a few paces; not at all surmised
By blinded Lycius, so in her comprized.
They pass'd the city gates, he knew not how,
So noiseless, and he never thought to know.

As men talk in a dream, so Corinth all,   350
Throughout her palaces imperial,
And all her populous streets and temples lewd,
Mutter'd, like tempest in the distance brew'd,
To the wide-spreaded night above her towers.
Men, women, rich and poor, in the cool hours,
Shuffled their sandals o'er the pavement white
Companion'd or alone; while many a light
Flared, here and there, from wealthy festivals,
And threw their moving shadows on the walls,
Or found them cluster'd in the corniced shade   360
Of some arch'd temple door, or dusky colonade.

   Muffling his face, of greeting friends in fear,
Her fingers he press'd hard, as one came near
With curl'd gray beard, sharp eyes, and smooth bald crown,
Slow-stepp'd, and robed in philosophic gown:
Lycius shrank closer, as they met and past,
Into his mantle, adding wings to haste,
While hurried Lamia trembled: 'Ah,' said he,
'Why do you shudder, love, so ruefully?
'Why does your tender palm dissolve in dew?'—   370
'I'm wearied,' said fair Lamia: 'tell me who
'Is that old man? I cannot bring to mind
'His features:—Lycius! wherefore did you blind
'Yourself from his quick eyes?' Lycius replied,
''Tis Apollonius sage, my trusty guide
'And good instructor; but to-night he seems
'The ghost of folly haunting my sweet dreams.'

   While yet he spake they had arrived before
A pillar'd porch, with lofty portal door,
Where hung a silver lamp, whose phosphor glow   380
Reflected in the slabbed steps below,
Mild as a star in water; for so new,
And so unsullied was the marble's hue,
So through the crystal polish, liquid fine,
Ran the dark veins, that none but feet divine
Could e'er have touch'd there. Sounds Æolian
Breath'd from the hinges, as the ample span
Of the wide doors disclos'd a place unknown

Some time to any, but those two alone,
And a few Persian mutes, who that same year   390
Were seen about the markets: none knew where
They could inhabit; the most curious
Were foil'd, who watch'd to trace them to their house:
And but the flitter-winged verse must tell,
For truth's sake, what woe afterwards befel,
'Twould humour many a heart to leave them thus,
Shut from the busy world of more incredulous.

Part II

Love in a hut, with water and a crust,
Is—Love, forgive us!—cinders, ashes, dust;
Love in a palace is perhaps at last
More grievous torment than a hermit's fast:—
That is a doubtful tale from faery land,
Hard for the non-elect to understand.
Had Lycius liv'd to hand his story down,
He might have given the moral a fresh frown,
Or clench'd it quite: but too short was their bliss
To breed distrust and hate, that make the soft voice hiss.   10
Beside, there, nightly, with terrific glare,
Love, jealous grown of so complete a pair,
Hover'd and buzz'd his wings, with fearful roar,
Above the lintel of their chamber door,
And down the passage cast a glow upon the floor.

For all this came a ruin: side by side
They were enthroned, in the even tide,
Upon a couch, near to a curtaining
Whose airy texture, from a golden string,
Floated into the room, and let appear   20
Unveil'd the summer heaven, blue and clear,
Betwixt two marble shafts:—there they reposed,
Where use had made it sweet, with eyelids closed,
Saving a tythe which love still open kept,
That they might see each other while they almost slept;
When from the slope side of a suburb hill,
Deafening the swallow's twitter, came a thrill

Of trumpets—Lycius started—the sounds fled,
But left a thought a-buzzing in his head.
For the first time, since first he harbour'd in   30
That purple-lined palace of sweet sin,
His spirit pass'd beyond its golden bourn
Into the noisy world almost forsworn.
The lady, ever watchful, penetrant,
Saw this with pain, so arguing a want
Of something more, more than her empery
Of joys; and she began to moan and sigh
Because he mused beyond her, knowing well
That but a moment's thought is passion's passing bell.
'Why do you sigh, fair creature?' whisper'd he: 40
'Why do you think?' return'd she tenderly:
'You have deserted me;—where am I now?
'Not in your heart while care weighs on your brow:
'No, no, you have dismiss'd me; and I go
'From your breast houseless: aye, it must be so.'
He answer'd, bending to her open eyes,
Where he was mirror'd small in paradise,
'My silver planet, both of eve and morn!
'Why will you plead yourself so sad forlorn,
'While I am striving how to fill my heart   50
'With deeper crimson, and a double smart?
'How to entangle, trammel up and snare
'Your soul in mine, and labyrinth you there
'Like the hid scent in an unbudded rose?
'Aye, a sweet kiss—you see your mighty woes.
'My thoughts! shall I unveil them? Listen then!
'What mortal hath a prize, that other men
'May be confounded and abash'd withal,
'But lets it sometimes pace abroad majestical,
'And triumph, as in thee I should rejoice   60
'Amid the hoarse alarm of Corinth's voice.
'Let my foes choke, and my friends shout afar,
'While through the thronged streets your bridal car
'Wheels round its dazzling spokes.'—The lady's cheek
Trembled; she nothing said, but, pale and meek,
Arose and knelt before him, wept a rain
Of sorrows at his words; at last with pain

Beseeching him, the while his hand she wrung,
To change his purpose. He thereat was stung,
Perverse, with stronger fancy to reclaim   70
Her wild and timid nature to his aim:
Beside, for all his love, in self despite,
Against his better self, he took delight
Luxurious in her sorrows, soft and new.
His passion, cruel grown, took on a hue
Fierce and sanguineous as 'twas possible
In one whose brow had no dark veins to swell.
Fine was the mitigated fury, like
Apollo's presence when in act to strike
The serpent—Ha, the serpent! certes, she   80
Was none. She burnt, she lov'd the tyranny,
And, all subdued, consented to the hour
When to the bridal he should lead his paramour.
Whispering in midnight silence, said the youth,
'Sure some sweet name thou hast, though, by my truth,
'I have not ask'd it, ever thinking thee
'Not mortal, but of heavenly progeny,
'As still I do. Hast any mortal name,
'Fit appellation for this dazzling frame?
'Or friends or kinsfolk on the citied earth,   90
'To share our marriage feast and nuptial mirth?'
'I have no friends,' said Lamia, 'no, not one;
'My presence in wide Corinth hardly known:
'My parents' bones are in their dusty urns
'Sepulchred, where no kindled incense burns,
'Seeing all their luckless race are dead, save me,
'And I neglect the holy rite for thee.
'Even as you list invite your many guests;
'But if, as now it seems, your vision rests
'With any pleasure on me, do not bid   100
'Old Apollonius—from him keep me hid.'
Lycius, perplex'd at words so blind and blank,
Made close inquiry; from whose touch she shrank,
Feigning a sleep; and he to the dull shade
Of deep sleep in a moment was betray'd.

It was the custom then to bring away
The bride from home at blushing shut of day,

Veil'd, in a chariot, heralded along
By strewn flowers, torches, and a marriage song,
With other pageants: but this fair unknown   110
Had not a friend. So being left alone,
 (Lycius was gone to summon all his kin)
And knowing surely she could never win
His foolish heart from its mad pompousness,
She set herself, high-thoughted, how to dress
The misery in fit magnificence.
She did so, but 'tis doubtful how and whence
Came, and who were her subtle servitors.
About the halls, and to and from the doors,
There was a noise of wings till in short space   120
The glowing banquet-room shone with wide-arched grace.
A haunting music, sole perhaps and lone
Supportress of the faery-roof, made moan
Throughout, as fearful the whole charm might fade.
Fresh carved cedar, mimicking a glade
Of palm and plantain, met from either side,
High in the midst, in honour of the bride:
Two palms and then two plantains, and so on,
From either side their stems branch'd one to one
All down the aisled place; and beneath all   130
There ran a stream of lamps straight on from wall to wall.
So canopied, lay an untasted feast
Teeming with odours. Lamia, regal drest,
Silently paced about, and as she went,
In pale contented sort of discontent,
Mission'd her viewless servants to enrich
The fretted splendour of each nook and niche.
Between the tree-stems, marbled plain at first,
Came jasper pannels; then anon, there burst
Forth creeping imagery of slighter trees,   140
And with the larger wove in small intricacies.
Approving all, she faded at self-will,
And shut the chamber up, close, hush'd and still,
Complete and ready for the revels rude,
When dreadful guests would come to spoil her solitude.

   The day appear'd, and all the gossip rout.
O senseless Lycius! Madman! wherefore flout

The silent-blessing fate, warm cloister'd hours,
And show to common eyes these secret bowers?
The herd approach'd; each guest, with busy brain,   150
Arriving at the portal, gaz'd amain,
And enter'd marveling: for they knew the street,
Remember'd it from childhood all complete
Without a gap, yet ne'er before had seen
That royal porch, that high-built fair demesne;
So in they hurried all, maz'd, curious and keen:
Save one, who look'd thereon with eye severe,
And with calm-planted steps walk'd in austere;
'Twas Apollonius: something too he laugh'd,
As though some knotty problem, that had daft   160
His patient thought, had now begun to thaw,
And solve and melt:—'twas just as he foresaw.

He met within the murmurous vestibule
His young disciple. "'Tis no common rule,
Lycius,' said he, 'for uninvited guest
'To force himself upon you, and infest
'With an unbidden presence the bright throng
'Of younger friends; yet must I do this wrong,
'And you forgive me.' Lycius blush'd, and led
The old man through the inner doors broad-spread;   170
With reconciling words and courteous mien
Turning into sweet milk the sophist's spleen.

Of wealthy lustre was the banquet-room,
Fill'd with pervading brilliance and perfume:
Before each lucid pannel fuming stood
A censer fed with myrrh and spiced wood,
Each by a sacred tripod held aloft,
Whose slender feet wide-swerv'd upon the soft
Wool-woofed carpets: fifty wreaths of smoke
From fifty censers their light voyage took   180
To the high roof, still mimick'd as they rose
Along the mirror'd walls by twin-clouds odorous.
Twelve sphered tables, by silk seats insphered,
High as the level of a man's breast rear'd
On libbard's paws, upheld the heavy gold

Of cups and goblets, and the store thrice told
Of Ceres' horn, and, in huge vessels, wine
Come from the gloomy tun with merry shine.
Thus loaded with a feast the tables stood,
Each shrining in the midst the image of a God.   190

When in an antichamber every guest
Had felt the cold full sponge to pleasure press'd,
By minist'ring slaves, upon his hands and feet,
And fragrant oils with ceremony meet
Pour'd on his hair, they all mov'd to the feast
In white robes, and themselves in order placed
Around the silken couches, wondering
Whence all this mighty cost and blaze of wealth could spring.

Soft went the music the soft air along,
While fluent Greek a vowel'd undersong   200
Kept up among the guests, discoursing low
At first, for scarcely was the wine at flow;
But when the happy vintage touch'd their brains,
Louder they talk, and louder come the strains
Of powerful instruments:—the gorgeous dyes,
The space, the splendour of the draperies,
The roof of awful richness, nectarous cheer,
Beautiful slaves, and Lamia's self, appear,
Now, when the wine has done its rosy deed,
And every soul from human trammels freed,   210
No more so strange; for merry wine, sweet wine,
Will make Elysian shades not too fair, too divine.
Soon was God Bacchus at meridian height;
Flush'd were their cheeks, and bright eyes double bright:
Garlands of every green, and every scent
From vales deflower'd, or forest-trees branch-rent,
In baskets of bright osier'd gold were brought
High as the handles heap'd, to suit the thought
Of every guest; that each, as he did please,
Might fancy-fit his brows, silk-pillow'd at his ease.   220

What wreath for Lamia? What for Lycius?
What for the sage, old Apollonius?

Upon her aching forehead be there hung
The leaves of willow and of adder's tongue;
And for the youth, quick, let us strip for him
The thyrsus, that his watching eyes may swim
Into forgetfulness; and, for the sage,
Let spear-grass and the spiteful thistle wage
War on his temples. Do not all charms fly
At the mere touch of cold philosophy? 230
There was an awful rainbow once in heaven:
We know her woof, her texture; she is given
In the dull catalogue of common things.
Philosophy will clip an Angel's wings,
Conquer all mysteries by rule and line,
Empty the haunted air, and gnomed mine—
Unweave a rainbow, as it erewhile made
The tender-person'd Lamia melt into a shade.

By her glad Lycius sitting, in chief place,
Scarce saw in all the room another face, 240
Till, checking his love trance, a cup he took
Full brimm'd, and opposite sent forth a look
'Cross the broad table, to beseech a glance
From his old teacher's wrinkled countenance,
And pledge him. The bald-head philosopher
Had fix'd his eye, without a twinkle or stir
Full on the alarmed beauty of the bride,
Brow-beating her fair form, and troubling her sweet pride.
Lycius then press'd her hand, with devout touch,
As pale it lay upon the rosy couch: 250
'Twas icy, and the cold ran through his veins;
Then sudden it grew hot, and all the pains
Of an unnatural heat shot to his heart.
'Lamia, what means this? Wherefore dost thou start?
'Know'st thou that man?' Poor Lamia answer'd not.
He gaz'd into her eyes, and not a jot
Own'd they the lovelorn piteous appeal:
More, more he gaz'd: his human senses reel:
Some hungry spell that loveliness absorbs;
There was no recognition in those orbs. 260
'Lamia!' he cried—and no soft-toned reply.

The many heard, and the loud revelry
Grew hush; the stately music no more breathes;
The myrtle sicken'd in a thousand wreaths.
By faint degrees, voice, lute, and pleasure ceased;
A deadly silence step by step increased,
Until it seem'd a horrid presence there,
And not a man but felt the terror in his hair.
'Lamia!' he shriek'd; and nothing but the shriek
With its sad echo did the silence break.   270
'Begone, foul dream!' he cried, gazing again
In the bride's face, where now no azure vein
Wander'd on fair-spaced temples; no soft bloom
Misted the cheek; no passion to illume
The deep-recessed vision:—all was blight;
Lamia, no longer fair, there sat a deadly white.
'Shut, shut those juggling eyes, thou ruthless man!
'Turn them aside, wretch! or the righteous ban
'Of all the Gods, whose dreadful images
'Here represent their shadowy presences,   280
'May pierce them on the sudden with the thorn
'Of painful blindness; leaving thee forlorn,
'In trembling dotage to the feeblest fright
'Of conscience, for their long offended might,
'For all thine impious proud-heart sophistries,
'Unlawful magic, and enticing lies.
'Corinthians! look upon that grey-beard wretch!
'Mark how, possess'd, his lashless eyelids stretch
'Around his demon eyes! Corinthians, see!
'My sweet bride withers at their potency.'   290
'Fool!' said the sophist, in an under-tone
Gruff with contempt; which a death-nighing moan
From Lycius answer'd, as heart-struck and lost,
He sank supine beside the aching ghost.
'Fool! Fool!' repeated he, while his eyes still
Relented not, nor mov'd; 'from every ill
'Of life have I preserv'd thee to this day,
'And shall I see thee made a serpent's prey?'
Then Lamia breath'd death breath; the sophist's eye,
Like a sharp spear, went through her utterly,   300
Keen, cruel, perceant, stinging: she, as well

As her weak hand could any meaning tell,
Motion'd him to be silent; vainly so,
He look'd and look'd again a level—No!
'A serpent!' echoed he; no sooner said,
Than with a frightful scream she vanished:
And Lycius' arms were empty of delight,
As were his limbs of life, from that same night.
On the high couch he lay!—his friends came round—
Supported him—no pulse, or breath they found,   310
And, in its marriage robe, the heavy body wound.

July–September 1819

EMPIRICISM

Immediate Experience, the Standard for Truth

The person whose genius is referred to in the following letter is Wordsworth.

TO J. H. REYNOLDS
3 May 1818   Teignmouth

In regard to his genius alone—we find what he says true as far as we have experienced and we can judge no further but by larger experience—for axioms in philosophy are not axioms until they are proved upon our pulses: We read fine——things but never feel them to thee full until we have gone the same steps as the Author.—I know this is not plain; you will know exactly my meaning when I say, that now I shall relish Hamlet more than I ever have done—Or, better—You are sensible no man can set down Venery as a bestial or joyless thing until he is sick of it and therefore all philosophizing on it would be mere wording. Until we are sick, we understand not;—in fine, as Byron says, "Knowledge is Sorrow"; and I go on to say that "Sorrow is Wisdom"—and further for aught we can know for certainty! "Wisdom is folly"—

The "unfortunate fellow" in the next letter is Robert Burns, whose house Keats visited on a walking tour through Scotland. *Riot* in the first sentence probably should read *rot*.

TO TOM KEATS
7 July 1818   Northern Ireland

Poor unfortunate fellow—his disposition was southern—how sad it is when a luxurious imagination is obliged in self defence to deaden its delicacy in vulgarity, and riot in thing[s] attainable that it may not have leisure to go mad after thing[s] which are not. No Man in such matters will be content with the experience of others—It is true that out of suffrance there is no greatness, no dignity; that in the most abstracted Pleasure there is no lasting happiness: yet who would not like to discover over again that Cleopatra was a Gipsey, Helen a Rogue and Ruth a deep one?

TO GEORGE AND GEORGIANA KEATS
31 December 1818   Hampstead

. . . and on my word I have thought so little that I have not one opinion upon any thing except in matters of taste —I never can feel certain of any truth but from a clear perception of its Beauty—and I find myself very young minded even in that perceptive power—which I hope will encrease—

TO GEORGE AND GEORGIANA KEATS
19 March 1819   Hampstead

May there not be superior beings amused with any graceful, though instinctive attitude my mind my fall into, as I am entertained with the alertness of a Stoat or the anxiety of a Deer? Though a quarrel in the streets is a thing to be hated, the energies displayed in it are fine; the commonest Man shows a grace in his quarrel—By a superior being our reasoning[s] may take the same tone—though erroneous they may be fine—This is the very thing in which consists poetry; and if so it is not so fine a thing as philosophy —For the same reason that an eagle is not so fine a thing as a truth—Give me this credit—Do you not think I strive —to know myself? Give me this credit—and you will not think that on my own accou[n]t I repeat Milton's lines

"How charming is divine Philosophy
Not harsh and crabbed as dull fools suppose
But musical as is Apollo's lute"—

No—no for myself—feeling grateful as I do to have got into a state of mind to relish them properly—Nothing ever becomes real till it is experienced—Even a Proverb is no proverb to you till your Life has illustrated it—

———

TO J. H. REYNOLDS
24 August 1819   Winchester

———My own being which I know to be becomes of more consequence to me than the crowds of Shadows in the Shape of Man and women that inhabit a kingdom. The Soul is a world of itself and has enough to do in its own home—Those whom I know already and who have grown as it were a part of myself I could not do without: but for the rest of Mankind they are as much a dream to me as Miltons Hierarchies.

WHY DID I LAUGH TO-NITE? NO VOICE WILL TELL

Why did I laugh to-night? No voice will tell:
    No God, no Demon of severe response,
Deigns to reply from Heaven or from Hell.
    Then to my human heart I turn at once.
Heart! Thou and I are here sad and alone;
    I say, why did I laugh! O mortal pain!
O Darkness! Darkness! ever must I moan,
    To question Heaven and Hell and Heart in vain.
Why did I laugh? I know this Being's lease,

My fancy to its utmost blisses spreads;   10
Yet would I on this very midnight cease,
    And the world's gaudy ensigns see in shreds;
Verse, Fame, and Beauty are intense indeed,
But Death intenser—Death is Life's high meed.

March 1819

ODE ON MELANCHOLY

I

No, no, go not to Lethe, neither twist
    Wolf's-bane, tight-rooted, for its poisonous wine;
Nor suffer thy pale forehead to be kiss'd
    By nightshade, ruby grape of Proserpine;
Make not your rosary of yew-berries,
    Nor let the beetle, nor the death-moth be
        Your mournful Psyche, nor the downy owl
A partner in your sorrow's mysteries;
    For shade to shade will come too drowsily,
        And drown the wakeful anguish of the soul.   10

II

But when the melancholy fit shall fall
    Sudden from heaven like a weeping cloud,
That fosters the droop-headed flowers all,
    And hides the green hill in an April shroud;
Then glut thy sorrow on a morning rose,
    Or on the rainbow of the salt sand-wave,
        Or on the wealth of globed peonies;
Or if thy mistress some rich anger shows,
    Emprison her soft hand, and let her rave,
        And feed deep, deep upon her peerless eyes.   20

III

She dwells with Beauty—Beauty that must die;
    And Joy, whose hand is ever at his lips
Bidding adieu; and aching Pleasure nigh,
    Turning to Poison while the bee-mouth sips:
Ay, in the very temple of delight

Veil'd Melancholy has her sovran shrine,
    Though seen of none save him whose strenuous tongue
Can burst Joy's grape against his palate fine;
His soul shall taste the sadness of her might,
    And be among her cloudy trophies hung.   30

May 1819

ODE ON INDOLENCE

'They toil not, neither do they spin.'

I

One morn before me were three figures seen,
  With bowed necks, and joined hands, side-faced;
And one behind the other stepp'd serene,
  In placid sandals, and in white robes graced;
They pass'd, like figures on a marble urn,
    When shifted round to see the other side;
      They came again; as when the urn once more
Is shifted round, the first seen shades return;
    And they were strange to me, as may betide
      With vases, to one deep in Phidian lore.   10

II

How is it, Shadows! that I knew ye not?
  How came ye muffled in so hush a mask?
Was it a silent deep-disguised plot
  To steal away, and leave without a task
My idle days? Ripe was the drowsy hour;
    The blissful cloud of summer-indolence
      Benumb'd my eyes; my pulse grew less and less;
Pain had no sting, and pleasure's wreath no flower:
    Oh, why did ye not melt, and leave my sense
      Unhaunted quite of all but—nothingness?   20

III

A third time came they by;—alas! wherefore?
  My sleep had been embroider'd with dim dreams;
My soul had been a lawn besprinkled o'er

With flowers, and stirring shades, and baffled beams.
The morn was clouded, but no shower fell,
  Tho' in her lids hung the sweet tears of May;
    The open casement press'd a new-leav'd vine,
  Let in the budding warmth and throstle's lay;
O Shadows! 'twas a time to bid farewell!
    Upon your skirts had fallen no tears of mine.   30

IV

A third time pass'd they by, and, passing, turn'd
  Each one the face a moment whiles to me;
Then faded, and to follow them I burn'd
  And ach'd for wings because I knew the three;
The first was a fair Maid, and Love her name;
  The second was Ambition, pale of cheek,
    And ever watchful with fatigued eye;
The last, whom I love more, the more of blame
  Is heap'd upon her, maiden most unmeek,—
    I knew to be my demon Poesy.   40

V

They faded, and, forsooth! I wanted wings:
  O folly! What is love! and where is it?
And for that poor Ambition! it springs
  From a man's little heart's short fever-fit;
For Poesy!—no,—she has not a joy,—
  At least for me,—so sweet as drowsy noons,
    And evenings steep'd in honied indolence;
O, for an age so shelter'd from annoy,
  That I may never know how change the moons,
    Or hear the voice of busy common-sense!   50

VI

So, ye Three Ghosts, adieu! Ye cannot raise
  My head cool-bedded in the flowery grass;
For I would not be dieted with praise,
  A pet-lamb in a sentimental farce!
Fade softly from my eyes, and be once more
  In masque-like figures on the dreamy urn;

Farewell! I yet have visions for the night,
And for the day faint visions there is store;
  Vanish, ye Phantoms! from my idle spright,
  Into the clouds, and never more return!   60

May 1819

Negative Capability

TO BENJAMIN BAILEY
22 November 1817   Burford Bridge

As soon as I had known Haydon three days I had got
enough of his character not to have been surp[r]ised at
such a Letter as he has hurt you with. Nor when I knew
it was it a principle with me to drop his acquaintance although with you it would have been an imperious feeling.
I wish you knew all that I think about Genius and the
Heart—and yet I think you are thoroughly acquainted
with my innermost breast in that respect or you could not
have known me even thus long and still hold me worthy
to be your dear friend. In passing however I must say of
one thing that has pressed upon me lately and encreased
my Humility and capability of submission and that is this
truth—Men of Genius are great as certain ethereal Chemi-
cals operating on the Mass of neutral intellect—by they
have not any individuality, any determined Character. I
would call the top and head of those who have a proper
self Men of Power—

. . . —you perhaps at one time thought there was such
a thing as Worldly Happiness to be arrived at, at certain
periods of time marked out—you have of necessity from
your disposition been thus led away—I scarcely remember
counting upon any Happiness—I look not for it if it be
not in the present hour—nothing startles me beyond the
Moment. The setting sun will always set me to rights—
or if a Sparrow come before my Window I take part in its
existence and pick about the Gravel.

Penetralium in the next letter seems a word Keats coined to signify the innermost region.

TO GEORGE AND TOM KEATS
27 (?) December 1817   Hampstead

I had not a dispute but a disquisition with Dilke, on various subjects; several things dovetailed in my mind, & at once it struck me, what quality went to form a Man of Achievement especially in Literature & which Shakespeare posessed so enormously—I mean *Negative Capability*, that is when man is capable of being in uncertainties, Mysteries, doubts, without any irritable reaching after fact & reason— Coleridge, for instance, would let go by a fine isolated verisimilitude caught from the Penetralium of mystery, from being incapable of remaining content with half knowledge. This pursued through Volumes would perhaps take us no further than this, that with a great poet the sense of Beauty overcomes every other consideration, or rather obliterates all consideration.

TO J. H. REYNOLDS
3 February 1818   Hampstead

It may be said that we ought to read our Contemporaries. that Wordsworth &c should have their due from us. but for the sake of a few fine imaginative or domestic passages, are we to be bullied into a certain Philosophy engendered in the whims of an Egotist—Every man has his speculations, but every man does not brood and peacock over them till he makes a false coinage and deceives himself— Many a man can travel to the very bourne of Heaven, and yet want confidence to put down his halfseeing. Sancho will invent a Journey heavenward as well as any body. We hate poetry that has a palpable design upon us—and if we do not agree, seems to put its hand in its breeches pocket. Poetry should be great & unobtrusive, a thing which enters into one's soul, and does not startle it or amaze it with itself but with its subject.

I have not read any Books—the Morning said I was right
—I had no Idea but of the Morning and the Thrush said I
was right—seeming to say—

'O thou whose face hath felt the Winter's wind;
  Whose eye has seen the Snow clouds hung in Mist
And the black-elm tops 'mong the freezing Stars
To thee the Spring will be a harvest-time—
O thou whose only book has been the light
Of supreme darkness which thou feddest on
Night after night, when Phœbus was away
To thee the Spring shall be a tripple morn—
O fret not after knowledge—I have none
And yet my song comes native with the warmth
O fret not after knowledge—I have none
And yet the Evening listens—He who saddens
At thought of Idleness cannot be idle,
And he's awake who thinks himself asleep.'

Now I am sensible all this is a mere sophistication, however it may neighbour to any truths, to excuse my own indolence—so I will not deceive myself that Man should be
equal with jove—but think himself very well off as a sort
of scullion-Mercury or even a humble Bee—It is not matter whether I am right or wrong either one way or another,
if there is sufficient to lift a little time from your Shoulders.

———•◆•———

                    —when we come to human Life
and the affections it is impossible how a parallel of breast
and head can be drawn— (you will forgive me for thus
                    treading
privately ⟨heading⟩ out my depth and take it for treading
                    tread
as schoolboys ⟨head⟩ the water⟨s⟩) —it is impossible to know

how far knowlege will console ⟨as⟩ for the death of a
friend and the ill "that flesh is heir to⟨o⟩—With respect to
the affections and Poetry you must know by a sympathy
my thoughts that way. . . .

The passages in the next letter are Keats's remembered ver-
sions from Milton's *Il Penseroso* (lines 97–98) and Shakespeare's
Troilus and Cressida (III, ii, 9–11).

TO GEORGE AND GEORGIANA KEATS
24 October 1818   Hampstead

The mighty abstract Idea I have of Beauty in all things
stifles the more divided and minute domestic happiness—
an amiable wife and sweet Children I contemplate as a
part of that Bea{u}ty. but I must have a thousand of those
beautiful particles to fill up my heart. I feel more and
more every day, as my imagination strengthens, that I do
not live in this world alone but in a thousand worlds—No
sooner am I alone than shapes of epic greatness are sta-
tioned around me, and serve my Spirit the office ⟨of⟩ which
is equivalent to a king's body guard—then 'Tragedy, with
scepter'd pall, comes sweeping by" According to my state
of mind I am with Achilles shouting in the Trenches or

                                         w
with Theocritus in the Vales of Sicily. Or I thro⟨ugh⟩ my
whole being into Triolus and repeating those lines, 'I
wander, like a lost soul upon the stygian Banks staying for
waftage," I melt into the air with a voluptuousness so delicate that I am content to be alone—

Iago (*Othello*) and Imogen (*Cymbeline*) among Shakespeare's
characters represent in the next letter the extremes of evil and
good. As Keats mentions, Saturn and Ops are characters from the
poem he was planning—*Hyperion.*

My dear Woodhouse,
Your Letter gave me a great satisfaction; more on account
of its friendliness, than any relish of that matter in it
which is accounted so acceptable in the 'genus irritabile'
The best answer I can give you is in a clerklike manner
to make some observations on two principle points, which
seem to point like indices into the midst of the whole pro
and con, about genius, and views and atchievements and
ambition and coetera. 1st As to the poetical Character itself, (I mean that sort of which, if I am any thing, I am a
Member; that sort distinguished from the wordsworthian
or egotistical sublime; which is a thing per se and stands
alone) it is not itself—it has no self—it is every thing and
nothing—It has no character—it enjoys light and shade;
it lives in gusto, be it foul or fair, high or low, rich or
poor, mean or elevated—It has as much delight in conceiving an Iago as an Imogen. What shocks the virtuous philos-
op[h]er, delights the camelion Poet. It does no harm from
its relish of the dark side of things any more than from its
taste for the bright one; because they both end in speculation. A Poet is the most unpoetical of any thing in existence; because he has no Identity—he is continually in for
—and filling some other Body—The Sun, the Moon, the
Sea and Men and Women who are creatures of impulse
are poetical and have about them an unchangeable attribute—the poet has none; no identity—he is certainly the
most unpoetical of all God's Creatures. If then he has no
self, and if I am a Poet, where is the Wonder that I
                              write
should say I would ⟨right⟩ no more? Might I not at that
very instant [have] been cogitating on the Characters of
saturn and Ops? It is a wretched thing to confess; but is a
very fact that not one word I ever utter can be taken for
granted as an opinion growing out of my identical nature
—how can it, when I have no nature? When I am in a
room with People if I ever am free from speculating on

creations of my own brain, then not myself goes home to myself: but the identity of every one in the room begins to to press upon me that, I am in a very little time anhilated— not only among Men; it would be the same in a Nursery of children: I know not whether I make myself wholly understood. . . .

In Keats's day the Methodists had a reputation for being zealots. When Keats calls Dilke in the following excerpt a "Godwin-Methodist," he means that his friend is a fanatic over the doctrines of William Godwin, author of *Political Justice*. Godwin's ideas, incidentally, were not Christian, certainly not Methodist.

TO GEORGE AND GEORGIANA KEATS
24 September 1819   Winchester

. . . yesterday Brown had four Letters from me all in a Lump—and the matter is clear'd up—Brown complained very much in his Letter to me of yesterday of the great alteration the Disposition of Dilke has undergone—He thinks of nothing but 'Political Justice' and his Boy—Now the first political duty a Man ought to have a Mind to is the happiness of his friends. I wrote Brown a comment on the subject, wherein I explained what I thought of Dilke's Character. Which resolved itself into this conclusion. That Dilke was a Man who cannot feel he has a personal identity unless he has made up his Mind about every thing. The only means of strengthening one's intellect is to make up ones mind about nothing—to let the mind be a thoroughfare for all thoughts. Not a select party. The genus is not scarce in population. All the stubborn arguers you meet with are of the same brood—They never begin upon a subject they have not preresolved on. They want to hammer their nail into you and if you turn the point, still they think you wrong. Dilke will never come at a truth as long as he lives; because he is always trying at it. He is a Godwin-methodist.

I may say that for 6 Months before I was taken ill I had
not passed a tranquil day—Either that gloom overspred
me or I was suffering under some passionate feeling, or if
I turn'd to versify that acerbated the poison of either sensation. The Beauties of Nature had lost their power over
me. How astonishingly (here I must premise that illness
as far as I can judge in so short a time has relieved my
Mind of a load of deceptive thoughts and images and
makes me perceive things in a truer light) —How astonishingly does the chance of leaving the world impress a sense
of its natural beauties on us. Like poor Falstaff, though I
do not babble, I think of green fields. I muse with the
greatest affection on every flower I have known from my
infancy—their shapes and coulours as are new to me as if
I had just created them with a superhuman fancy—It is
because they are connected with the most thoughtless
and happiest moments of our Lives—I have seen foreign
flowers in hothouses of the most beautiful nature, but I
do not care a straw for them. The simple flowers of our
sp[r]ing are what I want to see again.

TO FANNY BRAWNE
March (?) 1820

My Mind has been the most discontented and restless one
that ever was put into a body too small for it. I never felt
my Mind repose upon anything with complete and undis-
tracted enjoyment—upon no person but you.

I STOOD TIP-TOE UPON A LITTLE HILL

'Places of nestling green for Poets made.'
                    Story of Rimini

I stood tip-toe upon a little hill,
The air was cooling, and so very still,

That the sweet buds which with a modest pride
Pull droopingly, in slanting curve aside,
Their scantly leav'd, and finely tapering stems,
Had not yet lost those starry diadems
Caught from the early sobbing of the morn.
The clouds were pure and white as flocks new shorn,
And fresh from the clear brook; sweetly they slept
On the blue fields of heaven, and then there crept   10
A little noiseless noise among the leaves,
Born of the very sigh that silence heaves:
For not the faintest motion could be seen
Of all the shades that slanted o'er the green.
There was wide wand'ring for the greediest eye,
To peer about upon variety;
Far round the horizon's crystal air to skim,
And trace the dwindled edgings of its brim;
To picture out the quaint, and curious bending
Of a fresh woodland alley, never ending;   20
Or by the bowery clefts, and leafy shelves,
Guess where the jaunty streams refresh themselves.
I gazed awhile, and felt as light, and free
As though the fanning wings of Mercury
Had play'd upon my heels: I was light-hearted,
And many pleasures to my vision started;
So I straightway began to pluck a posey
Of luxuries bright, milky, soft and rosy.

A bush of May flowers with the bees about them;
Ah, sure no tasteful nook would be without them;   30
And let a lush laburnum oversweep them,
And let long grass grow round the roots to keep them
Moist, cool and green; and shade the violets,
That they may bind the moss in leafy nets.
A filbert hedge with wild briar overtwined,
And clumps of woodbine taking the soft wind
Upon their summer thrones; there too should be
The frequent chequer of a youngling tree,
That with a score of light green brethren shoots
From the quaint mossiness of aged roots: 40
Round which is heard a spring-head of clear waters

Babbling so wildly of its lovely daughters
The spreading blue-bells: it may haply mourn
That such fair clusters should be rudely torn
From their fresh beds, and scattered thoughtlessly
By infant hands, left on the path to die.

Open afresh your round of starry folds,
Ye ardent marigolds!
Dry up the moisture from your golden lids,
For great Apollo bids   50
That in these days your praises should be sung
On many harps, which he has lately strung;
And when again your dewiness he kisses,
Tell him, I have you in my world of blisses:
So haply when I rove in some far vale,
His mighty voice may come upon the gale.

Here are sweet peas, on tip-toe for a flight:
With wings of gentle flush o'er delicate white,
And taper fingers catching at all things,
To bind them all about with tiny rings.   60

Linger awhile upon some bending planks
That lean against a streamlet's rushy banks,
And watch intently Nature's gentle doings:
They will be found softer than ring-dove's cooings.
How silent comes the water round that bend;
Not the minutest whisper does it send
To the o'erhanging sallows: blades of grass
Slowly across the chequer'd shadows pass.
Why, you might read two sonnets, ere they reach
To where the hurrying freshnesses aye preach   70
A natural sermon o'er their pebbly beds;
Where swarms of minnows show their little heads,
Staying their wavy bodies 'gainst the streams,
To taste the luxury of sunny beams
Temper'd with coolness. How they ever wrestle
With their own sweet delight, and ever nestle
Their silver bellies on the pebbly sand.
If you but scantily hold out the hand,

That very instant not one will remain;
But turn your eye, and they are there again.   80
The ripples seem right glad to reach those cresses,
And cool themselves among the em'rald tresses;
The while they cool themselves, they freshness give,
And moisture, that the bowery green may live:
So keeping up an interchange of favours,
Like good men in the truth of their behaviours.
Sometimes goldfinches one by one will drop
From low hung branches; little space they stop;
But sip, and twitter, and their feathers sleek;
Then off at once, as in a wanton freak: 90
Or perhaps, to show their black, and golden wings,
Pausing upon their yellow flutterings.
Were I in such a place, I sure should pray
That naught less sweet, might call my thoughts away,
Than the soft rustle of a maiden's gown
Fanning away the dandelion's down;
Than the light music of her nimble toes
Patting against the sorrel as she goes.
How she would start, and blush, thus to be caught
Playing in all her innocence of thought.   100
O let me lead her gently o'er the brook,
Watch her half-smiling lips, and downward look;
O let me for one moment touch her wrist;
Let me one moment to her breathing list;
And as she leaves me may she often turn
Her fair eyes looking through her locks auburne.
What next? A tuft of evening primroses,
O'er which the mind may hover till it dozes;
O'er which it well might take a pleasant sleep,
But that 'tis ever startled by the leap   110
Of buds into ripe flowers; or by the flitting
Of diverse moths, that aye their rest are quitting;
Or by the moon lifting her silver rim
Above a cloud, and with a gradual swim
Coming into the blue with all her light.
O Maker of sweet poets, dear delight
Of this fair world, and all its gentle livers;
Spangler of clouds, halo of crystal rivers,

Mingler with leaves, and dew and tumbling streams,
Closer of lovely eyes to lovely dreams, 120
Lover of loneliness, and wandering,
Of upcast eye, and tender pondering!
Thee must I praise above all other glories
That smile us on to tell delightful stories.
For what has made the sage or poet write
But the fair paradise of Nature's light?
In the calm grandeur of a sober line,
We see the waving of the mountain pine;
And when a tale is beautifully staid,
We feel the safety of a hawthorn glade: 130
When it is moving on luxurious wings,
The soul is lost in pleasant smotherings:
Fair dewy roses brush against our faces,
And flowering laurels spring from diamond vases;
O'er head we see the jasmine and sweet briar,
And bloomy grapes laughing from green attire;
While at our feet, the voice of crystal bubbles
Charms us at once away from all our troubles:
So that we feel uplifted from the world,   '
Walking upon the white clouds wreath'd and curl'd. 140
So felt he, who first told, how Psyche went
On the smooth wind to realms of wonderment;
What Psyche felt, and Love, when their full lips
First touch'd; what amorous, and fondling nips
They gave each other's cheeks; with all their sighs,
And how they kist each other's tremulous eyes:
The silver lamp,—the ravishment,—the wonder—
The darkness,—loneliness,—the fearful thunder;
Their woes gone by, and both to heaven upflown,
To bow for gratitude before Jove's throne. 150
So did he feel, who pull'd the boughs aside,
That we might look into a forest wide,
To catch a glimpse of Fauns, and Dryades
Coming with softest rustle through the trees;
And garlands woven of flowers wild, and sweet,
Upheld on ivory wrists, or sporting feet:
Telling us how fair, trembling Syrinx fled
Arcadian Pan, with such a fearful dread.

Poor nymph,—poor Pan,—how he did weep to find,
Nought but a lovely sighing of the wind   160
Along the reedy stream; a half-heard strain,
Full of sweet desolation—balmy pain.

What first inspired a bard of old to sing
Narcissus pining o'er the untainted spring?
In some delicious ramble, he had found
A little space, with boughs all woven round;
And in the midst of all, a clearer pool
Then e'er reflected in its pleasant cool,
The blue sky here, and there, serenely peeping
Through tendril wreaths fantastically creeping.   170
And on the bank a lonely flower he spied,
A meek and forlorn flower, with naught of pride,
Drooping its beauty o'er the watery clearness,
To woo its own sad image into nearness:
Deaf to light Zephyrus it would not move;
But still would seem to droop, to pine, to love.
So while the poet stood in this sweet spot,
Some fainter gleamings o'er his fancy shot;
Nor was it long ere he had told the tale
Of young Narcissus, and sad Echo's bale.   180

Where had he been, from whose warm head out-flew
That sweetest of all songs, that ever new,
That aye refreshing, pure deliciousness,
Coming ever to bless
The wanderer by moonlight? to him bringing
Shapes from the invisible world, unearthly singing
From out the middle air, from flowery nests,
And from the pillowy silkiness that rests
Full in the speculation of the stars.
Ah! surely he had burst our mortal bars;   190
Into some wond'rous region he had gone,
To search for thee, divine Endymion!
He was a Poet, sure a lover too,
Who stood on Latmus' top, what time there blew
Soft breezes from the myrtle vale below;
And brought in faintness solemn, sweet, and slow

A hymn from Dian's temple; while upswelling,
The incense went to her own starry dwelling.
But though her face was clear as infant's eyes,
Though she stood smiling o'er the sacrifice,   200
The Poet wept at her so piteous fate,
Wept that such beauty should be desolate:
So in fine wrath some golden sounds he won,
And gave meek Cynthia her Endymion.

Queen of the wide air; thou most lovely queen
Of all the brightness that mine eyes have seen!
As thou exceedest all things in thy shine,
So every tale, does this sweet tale of thine.
O for three words of honey, that I might
Tell but one wonder of thy bridal night!   210

Where distant ships do seem to show their keels,
Phoebus awhile delay'd his mighty wheels,
And turn'd to smile upon thy bashful eyes,
Ere he his unseen pomp would solemnize.
The evening weather was so bright, and clear,
That men of health were of unusual cheer;
Stepping like Homer at the trumpet's call,
Or young Apollo on the pedestal:
And lovely women were as fair and warm,
As Venus looking sideways in alarm.   220
The breezes were ethereal, and pure,
And crept through half-closed lattices to cure
The languid sick; it cool'd their fever'd sleep,
And soothed them into slumbers full and deep.
Soon they awoke clear eyed: nor burnt with thirsting,
Nor with hot fingers, nor with temples bursting:
And springing up, they met the wond'ring sight
Of their dear friends, nigh foolish with delight;
Who feel their arms, and breasts, and kiss and stare,
And on their placid foreheads part the hair.   230
Young men, and maidens at each other gaz'd
With hands held back, and motionless, amaz'd
To see the brightness in each other's eyes;

And so they stood, fill'd with a sweet surprise,
Until their tongues were loos'd in poesy.
Therefore no lover did of anguish die:
But the soft numbers, in that moment spoken,
Made silken ties, that never may be broken.
Cynthia! I cannot tell the greater blisses,
That follow'd thine, and thy dear shepherd's kisses: 240
Was there a poet born?—but now no more,
My wand'ring spirit must no further soar.—

July–December 1816

AFTER DARK VAPOURS HAVE OPPRESS'D OUR PLAINS

After dark vapours have oppress'd our plains
   For a long dreary season, comes a day
   Born of the gentle South, and clears away
From the sick heavens all unseemly stains.
The anxious month, relieved of its pains,
   Takes as a long-lost right the feel of May;
   The eyelids with the passing coolness play
Like rose leaves with the drip of Summer rains.
The calmest thoughts come round us; as of leaves
   Budding—fruit ripening in stillness—Autumn suns   10
Smiling at eve upon the quiet sheaves—
Sweet Sappho's cheek—a smiling infant's breath—
   The gradual sand that through an hour-glass runs—
A woodland rivulet—a Poet's death.

January 31, 1817

ON LEIGH HUNT'S POEM "THE STORY OF RIMINI"

Who loves to peer up at the morning sun,
   With half-shut eyes and comfortable cheek,
   Let him, with this sweet tale, full often seek
For meadows where the little rivers run;
Who loves to linger with that brightest one

Of Heaven—Hesperus—let him lowly speak
These numbers to the night, and starlight meek,
Or moon, if that her hunting be begun.
He who knows these delights, and too is prone
    To moralize upon a smile or tear,   10
Will find at once a region of his own,
    A bower for his spirit, and will steer
To alleys where the fir-tree drops its cone,
    Where robins hop, and fallen leaves are sear.

March 1817

TO AUTUMN

I

Season of mists and mellow fruitfulness,
    Close bosom-friend of the maturing sun;
Conspiring with him how to load and bless
    With fruit the vines that round the thatch-eves run;
To bend with apples the moss'd cottage-trees,
    And fill all fruit with ripeness to the core;
        To swell the gourd, and plump the hazel shells
    With a sweet kernel; to set budding more,
And still more, later flowers for the bees,
Until they think warm days will never cease,   10
    For Summer has o'er-brimm'd their clammy cells.

II

Who hath not seen thee oft amid thy store?
    Sometimes whoever seeks abroad may find
Thee sitting careless on a granary floor,
    Thy hair soft-lifted by the winnowing wind;
Or on a half-reap'd furrow sound asleep,
    Drows'd with the fume of poppies, while thy hook
        Spares the next swath and all its twined flowers:
And sometimes like a gleaner thou dost keep
    Steady thy laden head across a brook;   20
    Or by a cyder-press, with patient look,
        Thou watchest the last oozings hours by hours.

III

Where are the songs of Spring? Ay, where are they?
　　Think not of them, thou hast thy music too,—
While barred clouds bloom the soft-dying day,
　　And touch the stubble-plains with rosy hue;
Then in a wailful choir the small gnats mourn
　　Among the river sallows, borne aloft
　　　　Or sinking as the light wind lives or dies;
And full-grown lambs loud bleat from hilly bourn;　　30
　　Hedge-crickets sing; and now with treble soft
　　The red-breast whistles from a garden-croft;
　　　　And gathering swallows twitter in the skies.

September 19, 1819

THE TRUTH OF THE IMAGINATION

TO BENJAMIN BAILEY
3 November 1817　　　Hampstead

O for a recourse somewhat human independant of the
great Consolations of Religion and undepraved Sensations.
of the Beautiful. the poetical in all things—

＿＿＿＿＿＿＿＿

The subject Keats mentions below is the nature of genius, the
discussion of which is included in the previous section (p. 68) on
"negative capability."

"My first Book and the little song I sent" refer respectively
to the first book of *Endymion* and the lyric "O Sorrow" which appears in the last book of *Endymion*.

In *Genesis* (ii: 21–22) God casts Adam into a deep sleep, re-
moves one of his ribs, and from it creates Eve. When Milton
retold the story in *Paradise Lost* (VIII, 452–490), he made a significant addition by having Adam dream of the mate created for
him. Milton's expansion served as a model for Keats in writing
his own parable of imaginative creation in *Endymion*. Like Adam,
Endymion dreams of his ideal beloved and ultimately wakes to
find her real.

But I am running my head into a Subject which I am certain I could not do justice to under five years s[t]udy and 3 vols octavo—and moreover long to be talking about the Imagination— . . . O I wish I was as certain of the end of all your troubles as that of your momentary start about the authenticity of the Imagination. I am certain of nothing but of the holiness of the Heart's affections and the truth of Imagination—What the imagination seizes as Beauty must be truth—whether it existed before or not—for I have the same Idea of all our Passions as of Love they are all in their sublime, creative of essential Beauty—In a Word, you may know my favorite Speculation by my first Book and the little song I sent in my last—which is a representation from the fancy of the probable mode of operating in these Matters—The Imagination may be compared to Adam's dream —he awoke and found it truth. I am the more zealous in this affair, because I have never yet been able to perceive how any thing can be known for truth by consequitive reasoning—and yet it must be—Can it be that even the greatest Philosopher ever ⟨when⟩ arrived at his goal without putting aside numerous objections—However it may be, O for a Life of Sensations rather than of Thoughts! It is 'a Vision in the form of Youth' a Shadow of reality to come —and this consideration has further conv[i]nced me for it has come as auxiliary to another favorite Speculation of mine, that we shall enjoy ourselves here after by having what we called happiness on Earth repeated in a finer tone and so repeated—And yet such a fate can only befall those who delight in sensation rather than hunger as you do after Truth—Adam's dream will do here and seems to be a conviction that Imagination and its empyreal reflection is the same as human Life and its spiritual repetition. But as I was saying—the simple imaginative Mind may have its rewards in the repeti[ti]on of its own silent Working coming continually on the spirit with a fine suddenness— to compare great things with small—have you never by being surprised with an old Melody—in a delicious place—

by a delicious voice, fe[l]t over again your very speculations and surmises at the time it first operated on your
soul—do you not remember forming to youself the
singer's face more beautiful that it was possible and yet
with the elevation of the Moment you did not think so—
even then you were mounted on the Wings of Imagination
so high—that the Prototype must be here after—that delicious face you will see—What a time! I am continually
running away from the subject—sure this cannot be exactly
the case with a complex Mind—one that is imaginative
and at the same time careful of its fruits—who would exist
partly on sensation partly on thought—to whom it is necessary that years should bring the philosophic Mind—
such an one I consider your's and therefore it is necessary
                                                       drink
to your eternal Happiness that you not only ⟨have⟩ this
old Wine of Heaven which I shall call the redigestion of
our most ethereal Musings on Earth; but also increase in
knowledge and know all things.

The subject Keats mentions in this letter is "fellowship with
essence" which is taken up in *Endymion*, I, 777–815. The five lines
of verse cited introduce that section.

TO JOHN TAYLOR
30 January 1818   Hampstead

My dear Taylor,
These Lines, as they now stand, about Happiness have
rung in my ears like a 'chime a mending'. see here,

                    Behold
Wherein Lies happiness Pæona? fold—

This appears to me the very contrary of blessed. I hope
this will appear to you more elegible.

Wherein lies Happiness? In that which becks
Our ready Minds to fellowship divine;
A fellowship with essence, till we shine

Full alchymized and free of space. Behold
The clear Religion of heaven—fold &c—

You must indulge me by putting this in for setting aside the badness of the other, such a preface is necessary to the Subject. The whole thing must I think have appeared to you, who are a consequitive Man, as a thing almost of mere words—but I assure you that when I wrote it, it was a regular stepping of the Imagination towards a Truth. My

Argument

having written that ⟨Passage⟩ will perhaps be of the greatest Service to me of any thing I ever did—It set before me at once the gradations of Happiness even like a kind of Pleasure Thermometer—and is my first Step towards the chief Attempt in the Drama—the playing of different Natures with Joy and Sorrow.

Do me this favor and believe Me, Your sincere friend

John Keats

———•·•·•———

TO BENJAMIN BAILEY
13 March 1818   Teignmouth

You know my ideas about Religion—I do not think myself more in the right than other people and that nothing in this world is proveable. I wish I could enter into all your feelings on the subject merely for one short 10 Minutes and give you a Page or two to your liking. I am sometimes so very sceptical as to think Poetry itself a mere Jack a lanthern to amuse whoever may chance to be struck with its brilliance—As Tradesmen say every thing is worth what it will fetch, so probably every mental pursuit takes its reality and worth from the ardour of the pursuer—being in itself a nothing—Ethereal things may at least be thus real, divided under three heads—Things real—things semireal—and no things—Things real—such as existences of Sun Moon & Stars and passages of Shakspeare—Things semireal such as Love, the Clouds &c which require a greeting of the Spirit to make them wholly exist—and Nothings which are made Great and dignified by an ardent pursuit—Which by the by stamps the burgundy mark on the bottles of our Minds, insomuch as they are able to *"con-*

sec[r]ate whate'er they look upon" I have written a Sonnet here of a somewhat collateral nature—so don't imagine it an a propos des bottes.

Four Seasons fill the Measure of the year;
   *Four Seasons are there in the mind of M**a**n.*
He hath his lusty spring when fancy clear
   Takes in all beauty with an easy span:
He hath his Summer, when luxuriously
   He chews the honied cud of fair spring thoughts,
Till, in his Soul dissolv'd they come to be
   Part of himself. He hath his Autumn ports
And Havens of repose, when his tired wings
   Are folded up, and he content to look
On Mists in idleness: to let fair things
   Pass by unheeded as a threshold brook.
    He hath his Winter too of pale Misfeature,
    Or else he would forget his mortal nature.

Aye this may be carried—but what am I talking of—it is an old maxim of mine and of course must be well known that evey point of thought is the centre of an intellectual world—the two uppermost thoughts in a Man's mind are the two poles of his World he revolves on them and every thing is southward or northward to him through their means—We take but three steps from feathers to iron.

———•—•—•———

TO JAMES RICE
24 March 1818   Teignmouth

What a happy thing it would be if we could settle our thoughts, make our minds up on any matter in five Minutes and remain content—that is to build a sort of mental Cottage of feelings quiet and pleasant—to have a sort of Philosophical Back Garden, and cheerful holiday-keeping front one—but Alas! this never can be: ⟨the⟩ for as the material Cottager knows there are such places as france and Italy and the Andes and the Burning Mountains—so the spiritual Cottager has knowledge of the terra semi incognita of things unearthly; and cannot for his Life, keep in the check rein—

———•—•—•———

TO B. R. HAYDON
8 April 1818   Teignmouth

I have ever been too sensible of the labyrinthian path to
eminence in Art (judging from Poetry) ever to think I
understood the emphasis of Painting. The innumerable
compositions and decompositions which take place between
the intellect and its thousand materials before it arrives at
that trembling delicate and snail-horn perception of
Beauty—I know not . . . .

TO TOM KEATS
27 June 1818   Lake District

What astonishes me more than any thing is the tone, the
coloring, the slate, the stone, the moss, the rock-weed; or,
if I may so say, the intellect, the countenance of such
places. The space, the magnitude of mountains and waterfalls are well imagined before one sees them; but this
countenance or intellectual tone must surpass every imagination and defy any remembrance. I shall learn poetry
here and shall henceforth write more than ever, for the abstract endeavor of being able to add a mite to that mass of
beauty which is harvested from these grand materials, by
the finest spirits, and put into etherial existence for the
relish of one's fellows. I cannot think with Hazlitt that
these scenes make man appear little. I never forgot my
stature so completely—I live in the eye; and my imagination, surpassed, is at rest—

In the next letter, Morris Birkbeck is a landowner with extensive holdings in Illinois. The poet's brother thought of buying land
from Birkbeck but finally settled in Kentucky.

TO GEORGE AND GEORGIANA KEATS
16 December 1818   Hampstead

How are you going on now? The going[s] on of the world
make me dizzy—there you are with Birkbeck—here I am

with brown—sometimes I fancy an immense separation, and sometimes, as at present, a direct communication of spirit with you. That will be one of the grandeurs of immortality—there will be no space and consequently the only commerce between spirits will be by their intelligence of each other—when they will completely understand each other—while we in this world merely comp[r]ehend each other in different degrees—the highe{r} the degree of good so higher is our Love and friendship—

TO CHARLES BROWN
23 September 1819   Winchester

Do not suffer me to disturb you unpleasantly: I do not mean that you should not suffer me to occupy your thoughts, but to occupy them pleasantly; for, I assure you, I am as far from being unhappy as possible. Imaginary grievances have always been ⟨my⟩ more my torment than real ones. You know this well. Real ones will never have any other effect upon me than to stimulate me to get out of or avoid them. This is easily accounted for. Our imaginary woes are conjured up by our passions, and are fostered by passionate feeling; our real ones come of themselves, and are opposed by an abstract exertion of mind. Real grievances are displacers of passion. The imaginary nail a man down for a sufferer, as on a cross; the real spur him up into an agent. I wish, at one view, you could see my heart towards you. 'Tis only from a high tone of feeling that I can put that word upon paper—out of poetry.

TO FANNY KEATS
23 August 1820   Hampstead

There are enough real distresses and evils in wait for every one to try the most vigorous health. Not that I would say yours are not real—but they are such as to tempt you to employ your imagination on them, rather than endeavour to dismiss them entirely. Do not diet your mind with grief, it destroys the constitution; but let your chief

care be of your health, and with that you will meet with
your share of Pleasure in the world—do not doubt it.

AS FROM THE DARKENING GLOOM A SILVER DOVE

As from the darkening gloom a silver dove
   Upsoars, and darts into the Eastern light,
   On pinions that naught moves but pure delight,
So fled thy soul into the realms above,
Regions of peace and everlasting love;
   Where happy spirits, crown'd with circlets bright
   Of starry beam, and gloriously bedight,
Taste the high joy none but the blest can prove.
There thou or joinest the immortal quire
   In melodies that even Heaven fair   **10**
Fill with superior bliss, or, at desire
   Of the omnipotent Father, cleavest the air
On holy message sent—What pleasures higher?
   Wherefore does any grief our joy impair?

December 1814

TO HOPE

When by my solitary hearth I sit,
   And hateful thoughts enwrap my soul in gloom;
When no fair dreams before my 'mind's eye' flit,
   And the bare heath of life presents no bloom;
     Sweet Hope, ethereal balm upon me shed,
     And wave thy silver pinions o'er my head.

Whene'er I wander, at the fall of night,
   Where woven boughs shut out the moon's bright ray,
Should sad Despondency my musings fright,
   And frown, to drive fair Cheerfulness away,   **10**
     Peep with the moon-beams through the leafy roof,
     And keep that fiend Despondence far aloof.

Should Disappointment, parent of Despair,
   Strive for her son to seize my careless heart;

When, like a cloud, he sits upon the air,
   Preparing on his spell-bound prey to dart:
      Chace him away, sweet Hope, with visage bright,
      And fright him as the morning frightens night!

Whene'er the fate of those I hold most dear
   Tells to my fearful breast a tale of sorrow,   20
O bright-eyed Hope, my morbid fancy cheer;
   Let me awhile thy sweetest comforts borrow:
      Thy heaven-born radiance around me shed,
      And wave thy silver pinions o'er my head!

Should e'er unhappy love my bosom pain,
   From cruel parents, or relentless fair;
O let me think it is not quite in vain
   To sigh out sonnets to the midnight air!
      Sweet Hope, ethereal balm upon me shed,
      And wave thy silver pinions o'er my head!   30

In the long vista of the years to roll,
   Let me not see our country's honour fade:
O let me see our land retain her soul,
   Her pride, her freedom; and not freedom's shade.
      From thy bright eyes unusual brightness shed—
      Beneath thy pinions canopy my head!

Let me not see the patriot's high bequest,
   Great liberty! how great in plain attire!
With the base purple of a court oppress'd,
   Bowing her head, and ready to expire: 40
      But let me see thee stoop from heaven on wings
      That fill the skies with silver glitterings!

And as, in sparkling majesty, a star
   Gilds the bright summit of some gloomy cloud;
Brightening the half veil'd face of heaven afar:
   So, when dark thoughts my boding spirit shroud,
      Sweet Hope, celestial influence round me shed,
      Waving thy silver pinions o'er my head.

February 1815

TO J. H. REYNOLDS, ESQ.

Dear Reynolds! as last night I lay in bed,
There came before my eyes that wonted thread
Of shapes, and shadows, and remembrances,
That every other minute vex and please:
Things all disjointed come from north and south,—
Two Witch's eyes above a Cherub's mouth,
Voltaire with casque and shield and habergeon,
And Alexander with his nightcap on;
Old Socrates a-tying his cravat,
And Hazlitt playing with Miss Edgeworth's cat;   10
And Junius Brutus, pretty well so so,
Making the best of's way towards Soho.

Few are there who escape these visitings,—
Perhaps one or two whose lives have patent wings,
And thro' whose curtains peeps no hellish nose,
No wild-boar tushes, and no Mermaid's toes;
But flowers bursting out with lusty pride,
And young Æolian harps personified;
Some Titian colours touch'd into real life,—
The sacrifice goes on; the pontiff knife   20
Gleams in the Sun, the milk-white heifer lows,
The pipes go shrilly, the libation flows:
A white sail shows above the green-head cliff,
Moves round the point, and throws her anchor stiff;
The mariners join hymn with those on land.

You know the Enchanted Castle,—it doth stand
Upon a rock, on the border of a Lake,
Nested in trees, which all do seem to shake
From some old magic-like Urganda's Sword.
O Phœbus! that I had thy sacred word   30
To show this Castle, in fair dreaming wise,
Unto my friend, while sick and ill he lies!

You know it well enough, where it doth seem
A mossy place, a Merlin's Hall, a dream;
You know the clear Lake, and the little Isles,

The mountains blue, and cold near neighbour rills,
All which elsewhere are but half animate;
There do they look alive to love and hate,
To smiles and frowns; they seem a lifted mound
Above some giant, pulsing underground.   40

Part of the Building was a chosen See,
Built by a banish'd Santon of Chaldee;
The other part, two thousand years from him,
Was built by Cuthbert de Saint Aldebrim;
Then there's a little wing, far from the Sun,
Built by a Lapland Witch turn'd maudlin Nun;
And many other juts of aged stone
Founded with many a mason-devil's groan.

The doors all look as if they op'd themselves,
The windows as if latch'd by Fays and Elves,   50
And from them comes a silver flash of light,
As from the westward of a Summer's night;
Or like a beauteous woman's large blue eyes
Gone mad thro' olden songs and poesies.

See! what is coming from the distance dim!
A golden Galley all in silken trim!
Three rows of oars are lightening, moment whiles,
Into the verd'rous bosoms of those isles;
Towards the shade, under the Castle wall,
It comes in silence,—now 'tis hidden all.   60
The Clarion sounds, and from a Postern-gate
An echo of sweet music doth create
A fear in the poor Herdsman, who doth bring
His beasts to trouble the enchanted spring,—
He tells of the sweet music, and the spot,
To all his friends, and they believe him not.

O that our dreamings all, of sleep or wake,
Would all their colours from the sunset take:
From something of material sublime,
Rather than shadow our own soul's day-time   70
In the dark void of night. For in the world

We jostle,—but my flag is not unfurl'd
On the Admiral-staff,—and so philosophize
I dare not yet! Oh, never will the prize,
High reason, and the lore of good and ill,
Be my award! Things cannot to the will
Be settled, but they tease us out of thought;
Or is it that imagination brought
Beyond its proper bound, yet still confin'd,
Lost in a sort of Purgatory blind,   80
Cannot refer to any standard law
Of either earth or heaven? It is a flaw
In happiness, to see beyond our bourn,—
It forces us in summer skies to mourn,
It spoils the singing of the Nightingale.

    Dear Reynolds! I have a mysterious tale,
And cannot speak it: the first page I read
Upon a Lampit rock of green sea-weed
Among the breakers; 'twas a quiet eve,
The rocks were silent, the wide sea did weave   90
An untumultuous fringe of silver foam
Along the flat brown sand; I was at home
And should have been most happy,—but I saw
Too far into the sea, where every maw
The greater on the less feeds evermore.—
But I saw too distinct into the core
Of an eternal fierce destruction,
And so from happiness I far was gone.
Still am I sick of it, and tho', to-day,
I've gather'd young spring-leaves, and flowers gay   100
Of periwinkle and wild strawberry,
Still do I that most fierce destruction see,—
The Shark at savage prey,—the Hawk at pounce,—
The gentle Robin, like a Pard or Ounce,
Ravening a worm,—Away, ye horrid moods!
Moods of one's mind! You know I hate them well.
You know I'd sooner be a clapping Bell
To some Kamtschatcan Missionary Church,
Than with these horrid moods be left i' the lurch.

March 25, 1818

TO HOMER

Standing aloof in giant ignorance,
   Of thee I hear and of the Cyclades,
As one who sits ashore and longs perchance
   To visit dolphin-coral in deep seas.
So thou wast blind;—but then the veil was rent,
   For Jove uncurtain'd Heaven to let thee live,
And Neptune made for thee a spumy tent,
   And Pan made sing for thee his forest-hive;
Aye on the shores of darkness there is light,
   And precipices show untrodden green,   **10**
There is a budding morrow in midnight,
   There is a triple sight in blindness keen;
Such seeing hadst thou, as it once befel
To Dian, Queen of Earth, and Heaven, and Hell.

April 1818

LINES WRITTEN IN THE HIGHLANDS AFTER A VISIT TO BURNS'S COUNTRY

There is a charm in footing slow across a silent plain,
Where patriot battle has been fought, where glory had the
    gain;
There is a pleasure on the heath where Druids old have been,
Where mantles grey have rustled by and swept the nettles
    green;
There is a joy in every spot made known by times of old,
New to the feet, although each tale a hundred times be told;
There is a deeper joy than all, more solemn in the heart,
More parching to the tongue than all, of more divine a smart,
When weary steps forget themselves upon a pleasant turf,
Upon hot sand, or flinty road, or sea-shore iron scurf,   **10**
Toward the castle or the cot, where long ago was born
One who was great through mortal days, and died of fame
    unshorn!
Light heather-bells may tremble then, but they are far away;
Wood-lark may sing from sandy fern,—the Sun may hear his
    lay;

Runnels may kiss the grass on shelves and shallows clear,
But their low voices are not heard, though come on travels
   drear;
Blood-red the Sun may set behind black mountain peaks;
Blue tides may sluice and drench their time in caves and
   weedy creeks;
Eagles may seem to sleep wing-wide upon the air;
Ring-doves may fly convuls'd across to some high-cedar'd
   lair;   20
But the forgotten eye is still fast lidded to the ground,
As Palmer's, that with weariness, mid-desert shrine hath
   found.
At such a time the soul's a child, in childhood is the brain;
Forgotten is the worldly heart—alone, it beats in vain.—
Aye, if a madman could have leave to pass a healthful day
To tell his forehead's swoon and faint when first began decay,
He might make tremble many a one whose spirit had gone
   forth
To find a Bard's low cradle-place about the silent North!
Scanty the hour and few the steps beyond the bourn of care,
Beyond the sweet and bitter world,—beyond it unaware!   30
Scanty the hour and few the steps, because a longer stay
Would bar return, and make a man forget his mortal way:
O horrible! to lose the sight of well remember'd face,
Of Brother's eyes, of Sister's brow—constant to every place;
Filling the air, as on we move, with portraiture intense;
More warm than those heroic tints that pain a painter's sense,
When shapes of old come striding by, and visages of old,
Locks shining black, hair scanty grey, and passions manifold.
No, no, that horror cannot be, for at the cable's length
Man feels the gentle anchor pull and gladdens in its
   strength:—   40
One hour, half-idiot, he stands by mossy waterfall,
But in the very next he reads his soul's memorial:—
He reads it on the mountain's height, where chance he may sit
   down
Upon rough marble diadem—that hill's eternal crown.
Yet be his anchor e'er so fast, room is there for a prayer
That man may never lose his mind on mountains black and
   bare;

That he may stray league after league some great birth-place
    to find
And keep his vision clear from speck, his inward sight unblind.

July 1818

FANCY

Ever let the fancy roam,
Pleasure never is at home:
At a touch sweet Pleasure melteth,
Like to bubbles when rain pelteth;
Then let winged Fancy wander
Through the thought still spread beyond her:
Open wide the mind's cage-door,
She'll dart forth, and cloudward soar.
O sweet Fancy! let her loose;
Summer's joys are spoilt by use,   10
And the enjoying of the Spring
Fades as does its blossoming;
Autumn's red-lipp'd fruitage too,
Blushing through the mist and dew,
Cloys with tasting: What do then?
Sit thee by the ingle, when
The sear faggot blazes bright,
Spirit of a winter's night;
When the soundless earth is muffled,
And the caked snow is shuffled   20
From the ploughboy's heavy shoon;
When the Night doth meet the Noon
In a dark conspiracy
To banish Even from her sky.
Sit thee there, and send abroad,
With a mind self-overaw'd,
Fancy, high-commission'd:—send her!
She has vassals to attend her:
She will bring, in spite of frost,
Beauties that the earth hath lost;   30
She will bring thee, all together,
All delights of summer weather;

All the buds and bells of May,
From dewy sward or thorny spray;
All the heaped Autumn's wealth,
With a still, mysterious stealth:
She will mix these pleasures up
Like three fit wines in a cup,
And thou shalt quaff it:—thou shalt hear
Distant harvest-carols clear;   40
Rustle of the reaped corn;
Sweet birds antheming the morn:
And, in the same moment—hark!
'Tis the early April lark,
Or the rooks, with busy caw,
Foraging for sticks and straw.
Thou shalt, at one glance, behold
The daisy and the marigold;
White-plum'd lillies, and the first
Hedge-grown primrose that hath burst;   50
Shaded hyacinth, alway
Sapphire queen of the mid-May;
And every leaf, and every flower
Pearled with the self-same shower.
Thou shalt see the field-mouse peep
Meagre from its celled sleep;
And the snake all winter-thin
Cast on sunny bank its skin;
Freckled nest-eggs thou shalt see
Hatching in the hawthorn-tree,   60
When the hen-bird's wing doth rest
Quiet on her mossy nest;
Then the hurry and alarm
When the bee-hive casts its swarm;
Acorns ripe down-pattering,
While the autumn breezes sing.

    Oh, sweet Fancy! let her loose;
Every thing is spoilt by use:
Where's the cheek that doth not fade,
Too much gaz'd at? Where's the maid   70

Whose lip mature is ever new?
Where's the eye, however blue,
Doth not weary? Where's the face
One would meet in every place?
Where's the voice, however soft,
One would hear so very oft?
At a touch sweet Pleasure melteth
Like to bubbles when rain pelteth.
Let, then, winged Fancy find
Thee a mistress to thy mind: 80
Dulcet-eyed as Ceres' daughter,
Ere the God of Torment taught her
How to frown and how to chide;
With a waist and with a side
White as Hebe's, when her zone
Slipt its golden clasp, and down
Fell her kirtle to her feet,
While she held the goblet sweet,
And Jove grew languid.—Break the mesh
Of the Fancy's silken leash;   90
Quickly break her prison-string
And such joys as these she'll bring.—
Let the winged Fancy roam,
Pleasure never is at home.

December 1818

THE EVE OF ST. AGNES

I

St. Agnes' Eve—Ah, bitter chill it was!
The owl, for all his feathers, was a-cold;
The hare limp'd trembling through the frozen grass,
And silent was the flock in woolly fold:
Numb were the Beadsman's fingers, while he told
His rosary, and while his frosted breath,
Like pious incense from a censer old,
Seem'd taking flight for heaven, without a death,
Past the sweet Virgin's picture, while his prayer he saith.

II

His prayer he saith, this patient, holy man;   10
Then takes his lamp, and riseth from his knees,
And back returneth, meagre, barefoot, wan,
Along the chapel aisle by slow degrees:
The sculptur'd dead, on each side, seem to freeze,
Emprison'd in black, purgatorial rails:
Knights, ladies, praying in dumb orat'ries,
He passeth by; and his weak spirit fails
To think how they may ache in icy hoods and mails.

III

Northward he turneth through a little door,
And scarce three steps, ere Music's golden tongue   20
Flatter'd to tears this aged man and poor;
But no—already had his deathbell rung:
The joys of all his life were said and sung:
His was harsh penance on St. Agnes' Eve:
Another way he went, and soon among
Rough ashes sat he for his soul's reprieve,
And all night kept awake, for sinners' sake to grieve.

IV

That ancient Beadsman heard the prelude soft;
And so it chanc'd, for many a door was wide,
From hurry to and fro. Soon, up aloft,   30
The silver, snarling trumpets 'gan to chide:
The level chambers, ready with their pride,
Were glowing to receive a thousand guests:
The carved angels, ever eager-eyed,
Star'd, where upon their heads the cornice rests,
With hair blown back, and wings put cross-wise on their
    breasts.

V

At length burst in the argent revelry,
With plume, tiara, and all rich array,
Numerous as shadows haunting faerily
The brain, new stuff'd, in youth, with triumphs gay   40
Of old romance. These let us wish away,

And turn, sole-thoughted, to one Lady there,
Whose heart had brooded, all that wintry day,
On love, and wing'd St. Agnes' saintly care,
As she had heard old dames full many times declare.

VI

They told her how, upon St. Agnes' Eve,
Young virgins might have visions of delight,
And soft adorings from their loves receive
Upon the honey'd middle of the night,
If ceremonies due they did aright;   50
As, supperless to bed they must retire,
And couch supine their beauties, lilly white;
Nor look behind, nor sideways, but require
Of Heaven with upward eyes for all that they desire.

VII

Full of this whim was thoughtful Madeline:
The music, yearning like a God in pain,
She scarcely heard: her maiden eyes divine,
Fix'd on the floor, saw many a sweeping train
Pass by—she heeded not at all: in vain
Came many a tiptoe, amorous cavalier,   60
And back retir'd; not cool'd by high disdain,
But she saw not: her heart was otherwhere:
She sigh'd for Agnes' dreams, the sweetest of the year.

VIII

She danc'd along with vague, regardless eyes,
Anxious her lips, her breathing quick and short:
The hallow'd hour was near at hand: she sighs
Amid the timbrels, and the throng'd resort
Of whisperers in anger, or in sport;
'Mid looks of love, defiance, hate, and scorn,
Hoodwink'd with faery fancy; all amort,   70
Save to St. Agnes and her lambs unshorn,
And all the bliss to be before to-morrow morn.

IX

So, purposing each moment to retire,
She linger'd still. Meantime, across the moors,

Had come young Porphyro, with heart on fire
For Madeline. Beside the portal doors,
Buttress'd from moonlight, stands he, and implores
All saints to give him sight of Madeline,
But for one moment in the tedious hours,
That he might gaze and worship all unseen;   80
Perchance speak, kneel, touch, kiss—in sooth such things have
    been.

X

He ventures in: let no buzz'd whisper tell:
All eyes be muffled, or a hundred swords
Will storm his heart, Love's fev'rous citadel:
For him, those chambers held barbarian hordes,
Hyena foemen, and hot-blooded lords,
Whose very dogs would execrations howl
Against his lineage: not one breast affords
Him any mercy, in that mansion foul,
Save one old beldame, weak in body and in soul.   90

XI

Ah, happy chance! the aged creature came,
Shuffling along with ivory-headed wand,
To where he stood, hid from the torch's flame,
Behind a broad hall-pillar, far beyond
The sound of merriment and chorus bland:
He startled her; but soon she knew his face,
And grasp'd his fingers in her palsied hand,
Saying, 'Mercy, Porphyro! hie thee from this place:
'They are all here to-night, the whole blood-thirsty race!

XII

'Get hence! get hence! there's dwarfish Hildebrand;   100
'He had a fever late, and in the fit
'He cursed thee and thine, both house and land:
'Then there's that old Lord Maurice, not a whit
'More tame for his gray hairs—Alas me! flit!
'Flit like a ghost away.'—'Ah, Gossip dear,
'We're safe enough; here in this arm-chair sit,

'And tell me how'—'Good Saints! not here, not here;
'Follow me, child, or else these stones will be thy bier.'

XIII

He follow'd through a lowly arched way,
Brushing the cobwebs with his lofty plume,   110
And as she mutter'd 'Well-a—well-a-day!'
He found him in a little moonlight room,
Pale, lattic'd, chill, and silent as a tomb.
'Now tell me where is Madeline,' said he,
'O tell me, Angela, by the holy loom
'Which none but secret sisterhood may see,
'When they St. Agnes' wool are weaving piously.'

XIV

'St. Agnes! Ah! it is St. Agnes' Eve—
'Yet men will murder upon holy days:
'Thou must hold water in a witch's sieve,   120
'And be liege-lord of all the Elves and Fays,
'To venture so: it fills me with amaze
'To see thee, Porphyro!—St. Agnes' Eve!
'God's help! my lady fair the conjuror plays
'This very night: good angels her deceive!
'But let me laugh awhile, I've mickle time to grieve.'

XV

Feebly she laugheth in the languid moon,
While Porphyro upon her face doth look,
Like puzzled urchin on an aged crone
Who keepeth clos'd a wond'rous riddle-book,   130
As spectacled she sits in chimney nook.
But soon his eyes grew brilliant, when she told
His lady's purpose; and he scarce could brook
Tears, at the thought of those enchantments cold,
And Madeline asleep in lap of legends old.

XVI

Sudden a thought came like a full-blown rose,
Flushing his brow, and in his pained heart

Made purple riot: then doth he propose
A stratagem, that makes the beldame start:
'A cruel man and impious thou art: 140
'Sweet lady, let her pray, and sleep, and dream
'Alone with her good angels, far apart
'From wicked men like thee. Go, go!—I deem
'Thou canst not surely be the same that thou didst seem.'

XVII

'I will not harm her, by all saints I swear,'
Quoth Porphyro: 'O may I ne'er find grace
'When my weak voice shall whisper its last prayer,
'If one of her soft ringlets I displace,
'Or look with ruffian passion in her face:
'Good Angela, believe me by these tears;   150
'Or I will, even in a moment's space,
'Awake, with horrid shout, my foemen's ears,
'And beard them, though they be more fang'd than wolves and
        bears.'

XVIII

'Ah! why wilt thou affright a feeble soul?
'A poor, weak, palsy-stricken, churchyard thing,
'Whose passing-bell may ere the midnight toll;
'Whose prayers for thee, each morn and evening,
'Were never miss'd.'—Thus plaining, doth she bring
A gentler speech from burning Porphyro;
So woful, and of such deep sorrowing,   160
That Angela gives promise she will do
Whatever he shall wish, betide her weal or woe.

XIX

Which was, to lead him, in close secrecy,
Even to Madeline's chamber, and there hide
Him in a closet, of such privacy
That he might see her beauty unespied,
And win perhaps that night a peerless bride,
While legion'd faeries pac'd the coverlet,
And pale enchantment held her sleepy-eyed.

Never on such a night have lovers met,
Since Merlin paid his Demon all the monstrous debt.

XX

'It shall be as thou wishest,' said the Dame:
'All cates and dainties shall be stored there
'Quickly on this feast-night: by the tambour frame
'Her own lute thou wilt see: no time to spare,
'For I am slow and feeble, and scarce dare
'On such a catering trust my dizzy head.
'Wait here, my child, with patience; kneel in prayer
'The while: Ah! thou must needs the lady wed,
'Or may I never leave my grave among the dead.' 180

XXI

So saying, she hobbled off with busy fear.
The lover's endless minutes slowly pass'd;
The dame return'd, and whisper'd in his ear
To follow her; with aged eyes aghast
From fright of dim espial. Safe at last,
Through many a dusky gallery, they gain
The maiden's chamber, silken, hush'd, and chaste;
Where Porphyro took covert, pleas'd amain.
His poor guide hurried back with agues in her brain.

XXII

Her falt'ring hand upon the balustrade, 190
Old Angela was feeling for the stair,
When Madeline, St. Agnes' charmed maid,
Rose, like a mission'd spirit, unaware:
With silver taper's light, and pious care,
She turn'd, and down the aged gossip led
To a safe level matting. Now prepare,
Young Porphyro, for gazing on that bed;
She comes, she comes again, like ring-dove fray'd and fled.

XXIII

Out went the taper as she hurried in;
Its little smoke, in pallid moonshine, died: 200
She clos'd the door, she panted, all akin

To spirits of the air, and visions wide:
No uttered syllable, or, woe betide!
But to her heart, her heart was voluble,
Paining with eloquence her balmy side;
As though a tongueless nightingale should swell
Her throat in vain, and die, heart-stifled, in her dell.

XXIV

A casement high and triple-arch'd there was,
All garlanded with carven imag'ries
Of fruits, and flowers, and bunches of knot-grass,   210
And diamonded with panes of quaint device,
Innumerable of stains and splendid dyes,
As are the tiger-moth's deep-damask'd wings;
And in the midst, 'mong thousand heraldries,
And twilight saints, and dim emblazonings,
A shielded scutcheon blush'd with blood of queens and kings.

XXV

Full on this casement shone the wintry moon,
And threw warm gules on Madeline's fair breast,
As down she knelt for heaven's grace and boon;
Rose-bloom fell on her hands, together prest,   220
And on her silver cross soft amethyst,
And on her hair a glory, like a saint:
She seem'd a splendid angel, newly drest,
Save wings, for heaven:—Porphyro grew faint:
She knelt, so pure a thing, so free from mortal taint.

XXVI

Anon his heart revives: her vespers done,
Of all its wreathed pearls her hair she frees;
Unclasps her warmed jewels one by one;
Loosens her fragrant boddice; by degrees
Her rich attire creeps rustling to her knees: 230
Half-hidden, like a mermaid in sea-weed,
Pensive awhile she dreams awake, and sees,
In fancy, fair St. Agnes in her bed,
But dares not look behind, or all the charm is fled.

XXVII

    Soon, trembling in her soft and chilly nest,
    In sort of wakeful swoon, perplex'd she lay,
    Until the poppied warmth of sleep oppress'd
    Her soothed limbs, and soul fatigued away;
    Flown, like a thought, until the morrow-day;
    Blissfully haven'd both from joy and pain;   240
    Clasp'd like a missal where swart Paynims pray;
    Blinded alike from sunshine and from rain,
As though a rose should shut, and be a bud again.

XXVIII

    Stol'n to this paradise, and so entranced,
    Porphyro gazed upon her empty dress,
    And listen'd to her breathing, if it chanced
    To wake into a slumberous tenderness;
    Which when he heard, that minute did he bless,
    And breath'd himself: then from the closet crept,
    Noiseless as fear in a wide wilderness,   250
    And over the hush'd carpet, silent, stept,
And 'tween the curtains peep'd, where, lo!—how fast she slept.

XXIX

    Then by the bed-side, where the faded moon
    Made a dim, silver twilight, soft he set
    A table, and, half anguish'd, threw thereon
    A cloth of woven crimson, gold, and jet:—
    O for some drowsy Morphean amulet!
    The boisterous, midnight, festive clarion,
    The kettle-drum, and far-heard clarinet,
    Affray his ears, though but in dying tone:—   260
The hall door shuts again, and all the noise is gone.

XXX

    And still she slept an azure-lidded sleep,
    In blanched linen, smooth, and lavender'd,
    While he from forth the closet brought a heap
    Of candied apple, quince, and plum, and gourd;
    With jellies soother than the creamy curd,
    And lucent syrops, tinct with cinnamon;

Manna and dates, in argosy transferr'd
From Fez; and spiced dainties, every one,
From silken Samarcand to cedar'd Lebanon.   270

XXXI

These delicates he heap'd with glowing hand
On golden dishes and in baskets bright
Of wreathed silver: sumptuous they stand
In the retired quiet of the night,
Filling the chilly room with perfume light.—
'And now, my love, my seraph fair, awake!
'Thou art my heaven, and I thine eremite:
'Open thine eyes, for meek St. Agnes' sake,
'Or I shall drowse beside thee, so my soul doth ache.'

XXXII

Thus whispering, his warm, unnerved arm   280
Sank in her pillow. Shaded was her dream
By the dusk curtains:—'twas a midnight charm
Impossible to melt as iced stream:
The lustrous salvers in the moonlight gleam;
Broad golden fringe upon the carpet lies:
It seem'd he never, never could redeem
From such a stedfast spell his lady's eyes;
So mus'd awhile, entoil'd in woofed phantasies.

XXXIII

Awakening up, he took her hollow lute,—
Tumultuous,—and, in chords that tenderest be,   290
He play'd an ancient ditty, long since mute,
In Provence call'd, 'La belle dame sans mercy:'
Close to her ear touching the melody;—
Wherewith disturb'd, she utter'd a soft moan:
He ceased—she panted quick—and suddenly
Her blue affrayed eyes wide open shone:
Upon his knees he sank, pale as smooth-sculptured stone.

XXXIV

Her eyes were open, but she still beheld,
Now wide awake, the vision of her sleep:

There was a painful change, that nigh expell'd   300
The blisses of her dream so pure and deep
At which fair Madeline began to weep,
And moan forth witless words with many a sigh;
While still her gaze on Porphyro would keep;
Who knelt, with joined hands and piteous eye,
Fearing to move or speak, she look'd so dreamingly.

XXXV

'Ah, Porphyro!' said she, 'but even now
'Thy voice was at sweet tremble in mine ear,
'Made tuneable with every sweetest vow;
'And those sad eyes were spiritual and clear: 310
'How chang'd thou art! how pallid, chill, and drear!
'Give me that voice again, my Porphyro,
'Those looks immortal, those complainings dear!
'Oh leave me not in this eternal woe,
'For if thou diest, my Love, I know not where to go.'

XXXVI

Beyond a mortal man impassion'd far
At these voluptuous accents, he arose,
Ethereal, flush'd, and like a throbbing star
Seen mid the sapphire heaven's deep repose;
Into her dream he melted, as the rose   320
Blendeth its odour with the violet,—
Solution sweet: meantime the frost-wind blows
Like Love's alarum pattering the sharp sleet
Against the window-panes; St. Agnes' moon hath set.

XXXVII

'Tis dark: quick pattereth the flaw-blown sleet:
'This is no dream, my bride, my Madeline!'
'Tis dark: the iced gusts still rave and beat:
'No dream, alas! alas! and woe is mine!
'Porphyro will leave me here to fade and pine.—
'Cruel! what traitor could thee hither bring?   330
'I curse not, for my heart is lost in thine,
'Though thou forsakest a deceived thing;—
'A dove forlorn and lost with sick unpruned wing.'

XXXVIII

'My Madeline! sweet dreamer! lovely bride!
'Say, may I be for aye thy vassal blest?
'Thy beauty's shield, heart-shap'd and vermeil dyed?
'Ah, silver shrine, here will I take my rest
'After so many hours of toil and quest,
'A famish'd pilgrim,—sav'd by miracle.
'Though I have found, I will not rob thy nest   340
'Saving of thy sweet self; if thou think'st well
'To trust, fair Madeline, to no rude infidel.

XXXIX

'Hark! 'tis an elfin-storm from faery land,
'Of haggard seeming, but a boon indeed:
'Arise—arise! the morning is at hand;—
'The bloated wassaillers will never heed:—
'Let us away, my love, with happy speed;
'There are no ears to hear, or eyes to see,—
'Drown'd all in Rhenish and the sleepy mead:
'Awake! arise! my love, and fearless be,   350
'For o'er the southern moors I have a home for thee.'

XL

She hurried at his words, beset with fears,
For there were sleeping dragons all around,
At glaring watch, perhaps, with ready spears—
Down the wide stairs a darkling way they found.—
In all the house was heard no human sound.
A chain-droop'd lamp was flickering by each door;
The arras, rich with horseman, hawk, and hound,
Flutter'd in the besieging wind's uproar;
And the long carpets rose along the gusty floor.   360

XLI

They glide, like phantoms, into the wide hall;
Like phantoms, to the iron porch, they glide;
Where lay the Porter, in uneasy sprawl,
With a huge empty flaggon by his side:
The wakeful bloodhound rose, and shook his hide,
But his sagacious eye an inmate owns:

By one, and one, the bolts full easy slide:—
The chains lie silent on the footworn stones;—
The key turns, and the door upon its hinges groans.

XLII

And they are gone: aye, ages long ago   370
These lovers fled away into the storm.
That night the Baron dreamt of many a woe,
And all his warrior-guests, with shade and form
Of witch, and demon, and large coffin-worm,
Were long be-nightmar'd. Angela the old
Died palsy-twitch'd, with meagre face deform;
The Beadsman, after thousand aves told,
For aye unsought for slept among his ashes cold.

January 1819

THE EVE OF SAINT MARK

Upon a Sabbath-day it fell;
Twice holy was the Sabbath-bell,
That call'd the folk to evening prayer;
The city streets were clean and fair
From wholesome drench of April rains;
And, on the western window panes,
The chilly sunset faintly told
Of unmatur'd green vallies cold,
Of the green thorny bloomless hedge,
Of rivers new with spring-tide sedge,   10
Of primroses by shelter'd rills,
And daisies on the aguish hills.
Twice holy was the Sabbath-bell:
The silent streets were crowded well
With staid and pious companies,
Warm from their fire-side orat'ries;
And moving, with demurest air,
To even-song, and vesper prayer.
Each arched porch, and entry low,
Was fill'd with patient folk and slow,   20

With whispers hush, and shuffling feet,
While play'd the organ loud and sweet.

The bells had ceas'd, the prayers begun,
And Bertha had not yet half done
A curious volume, patch'd and torn,
That all day long, from earliest morn,
Had taken captive her two eyes,
Among its golden broideries;
Perplex'd her with a thousand things,—
The stars of Heaven, and angels' wings,   30
Martyrs in a fiery blaze,
Azure saints in silver rays,
Moses' breastplate, and the seven
Candlesticks John saw in Heaven,
The winged Lion of Saint Mark,
And the Covenantal Ark,
With its many mysteries,
Cherubim and golden mice.

Bertha was a maiden fair,
Dwelling in the old Minster-square;   40
From her fire-side she could see,
Sidelong, its rich antiquity,
Far as the Bishop's garden-wall;
Where sycamores and elm-trees tall,
Full-leav'd, the forest had outstript,
By no sharp north-wind ever nipt,
So shelter'd by the mighty pile.
Bertha arose, and read awhile,
With forehead 'gainst the window-pane.
Again she try'd, and then again,   50
Until the dusk eve left her dark
Upon the legend of St. Mark.
From plaited lawn-frill, fine and thin,
She lifted up her soft warm chin,
With aching neck and swimming eyes,
And daz'd with saintly imageries.

All was gloom, and silent all,
Save now and then the still foot-fall

Of one returning homewards late,
Past the echoing minster-gate.

The clamorous daws, that all the day
Above tree-tops and towers play,
Pair by pair had gone to rest,
Each in its ancient belfry-nest,
Where asleep they fall betimes,
To music of the drowsy chimes.

All was silent, all was gloom,
Abroad and in the homely room:
Down she sat, poor cheated soul!
And struck a lamp from the dismal coal; 70
Lean'd forward, with bright drooping hair
And slant book, full against the glare.
Her shadow, in uneasy guise,
Hover'd about, a giant size,
On ceiling-beam and old oak chair,
The parrot's cage, and panel square;
And the warm angled winter screen,
On which were many monsters seen,
Call'd doves of Siam, Lima mice,
And legless birds of Paradise, 80
Macaw, and tender Avadavat,
And silken-furr'd Angora cat.
Untir'd she read, her shadow still
Glower'd about, as it would fill
The room with wildest forms and shades,
As though some ghostly queen of spades
Had come to mock behind her back,
And dance, and ruffle her garments black.
Untir'd she read the legend page,
Of holy Mark, from youth to age, 90
On land, on sea, in pagan chains,
Rejoicing for his many pains.
Sometimes the learned eremite,
With golden star, or dagger bright,
Referr'd to pious poesies
Written in smallest crow-quill size
Beneath the text; and thus the rhyme

Was parcell'd out from time to time: **98**
'Gif ye wol stonden hardie wight—   *98 a*
Amiddes of the blacke night—   *b*
Righte in the churche porch, pardie   *c*
Ye wol behold a companie   *d*
Appouchen thee full dolourouse   *e*
For sooth to sain from everich house   *f*
Be it in City or village   *g*
Wol come the Phantom and image   *h*
Of ilka gent and ilka carle   *i*
Whom coldè Deathè hath in parle   *j*
And wol some day that very year   *k*
Touchen with foulè venìme spear   *98 l*
And sadly do them all to die—   *m*
Hem all shalt thou see verilie—   *n*
And everichon shall by the[e] pass   *o*
All who must die that year Alas   *p*
——Als writith he of swevenis,
Men han beforne they wake in bliss,   **100**
Whanne that hir friendes thinke hem bound
In crimped shroude farre under grounde;
And how a litling child mote be
A saint er its nativitie,
Gif that the modre (God her blesse!)
Kepen in solitarinesse,
And kissen devoute the holy croce.
Of Goddes love, and Sathan's force,—
He writith; and thinges many mo: **110**
Of swiche thinges I may not show.
Bot I must tellen verilie
Somdel of Saintè Cicilie,
And chieflie what he auctorethe
Of Saintè Markis life and dethe:'

At length her constant eyelids come
Upon the fervent martyrdom;
Then lastly to his holy shrine,
Exalt amid the tapers' shine
At Venice,—

February 13–17, 1819

ODE TO FANNY

I

Physician Nature! let my spirit blood!
 O ease my heart of verse and let me rest;
Throw me upon thy Tripod, till the flood
 Of stifling numbers ebbs from my full breast.
A theme! a theme! great nature! give a theme;
  Let me begin my dream.
I come—I see thee, as thou standest there,
Beckon me not into the wintry air.

II

Ah! dearest love, sweet home of all my fears,
 And hopes, and joys, and panting miseries,—   10
To-night, if I may guess, thy beauty wears
  A smile of such delight,
  As brilliant and as bright,
 As when with ravished, aching, vassal eyes,
  Lost in soft amaze,
  I gaze, I gaze!

III

Who now, with greedy looks, eats up my feast?
 What stare outfaces now my silver moon!
Ah! keep that hand unravish'd at the least;
  Let, let, the amorous burn—   20
  But, pr'ythee, do not turn
 The current of your heart from me so soon.
  O! save, in charity,
  The quickest pulse for me.

IV

Save it for me, sweet love! though music breathe
 Voluptuous visions into the warm air;
Though swimming through the dance's dangerous wreath,
  Be like an April day,
  Smiling and cold and gay,
 A temperate lilly, temperate as fair;   30
  Then, Heaven! there will be
  A warmer June for me.

V

Why, this—you'll say, my Fanny! is not true:
  Put your soft hand upon your snowy side,
Where the heart beats: confess—'tis nothing new—
     Must not a woman be
     A feather on the sea,
  Sway'd to and fro by every wind and tide?
     Of as uncertain speed
     As blow-ball from the mead?   40

VI

I know it—and to know it is despair
  To one who loves you as I love, sweet Fanny!
Whose heart goes fluttering for you every where,
     Nor, when away you roam,
     Dare keep its wretched home,
  Love, love alone, has pains severe and many:
     Then, loveliest! keep me free
     From torturing jealousy.

VII

Ah! if you prize my subdued soul above
  The poor, the fading, brief, pride of an hour;   50
Let none profane my Holy See of love,
     Or with a rude hand break
     The sacramental cake:
  Let none else touch the just new-budded flower;
     If not—may my eyes close,
     Love! on their last repose.

February (?) 1819

LA BELLE DAME SANS MERCI

A Ballad

I

O, what can ail thee, knight-at-arms,
  Alone and palely loitering?
The sedge has wither'd from the lake,
  And no birds sing.

II

O, what can ail thee, knight-at-arms,
    So haggard and so woe-begone?
The squirrel's granary is full,
    And the harvest's done.

III

I see a lilly on thy brow,
    With anguish moist and fever dew;   10
And on thy cheeks a fading rose
    Fast withereth too.

IV

I met a lady in the meads,
    Full beautiful—a faery's child,
Her hair was long, her foot was light,
    And her eyes were wild.

V

I made a garland for her head,
    And bracelets too, and fragrant zone;
She look'd at me as she did love,
    And made sweet moan.   20

VI

I set her on my pacing steed,
    And nothing else saw all day long;
For sidelong would she bend, and sing
    A faery's song.

VII

She found me roots of relish sweet,
    And honey wild, and manna dew,
And sure in language strange she said—
    'I love thee true'.

VIII

She took me to her elfin grot,
    And there she wept and sigh'd full sore,   30
And there I shut her wild wild eyes
    With kisses four.

IX

And there she lulled me asleep
  And there I dream'd—Ah! woe betide!
The latest dream I ever dream'd
  On the cold hill side.

X

I saw pale kings and princes too,
  Pale warriors, death-pale were they all;
They cried—'La Belle Dame sans Merci
  Hath thee in thrall!'   40

XI

I saw their starved lips in the gloom,
  With horrid warning gaped wide,
And I awoke and found me here,
  On the cold hill's side.

XII

And this is why I sojourn here
  Alone and palely loitering,
Though the sedge has wither'd from the lake,
  And no birds sing.

April 21, 1819

ODE TO A NIGHTINGALE

I

My heart aches, and a drowsy numbness pains
  My sense, as though of hemlock I had drunk,
Or emptied some dull opiate to the drains
  One minute past, and Lethe-wards had sunk:
'Tis not through envy of thy happy lot,
  But being too happy in thine happiness,—
    That thou, light-winged Dryad of the trees,
      In some melodious plot
  Of beechen green, and shadows numberless,
    Singest of summer in full-throated ease.   10

II

O, for a draught of vintage! that hath been
  Cool'd a long age in the deep-delved earth,
Tasting of Flora and the country green,
  Dance, and Provençal song, and sunburnt mirth!
O for a beaker full of the warm South,
  Full of the true, the blushful Hippocrene,
    With beaded bubbles winking at the brim,
        And purple-stained mouth;
    That I might drink, and leave the world unseen,
      And with thee fade away into the forest dim: 20

III

Fade far away, dissolve, and quite forget
  What thou among the leaves hast never known,
The weariness, the fever, and the fret
  Here, where men sit and hear each other groan;
Where palsy shakes a few, sad, last gray hairs,
  Where youth grows pale, and spectre-thin, and dies;
    Where but to think is to be full of sorrow
        And leaden-eyed despairs,
    Where Beauty cannot keep her lustrous eyes,
      Or new Love pine at them beyond to-morrow.   30

IV

Away! away! for I will fly to thee,
  Not charioted by Bacchus and his pards,
But on the viewless wings of Poesy,
  Though the dull brain perplexes and retards:
Already with thee! tender is the night,
  And haply the Queen-Moon is on her throne,
    Cluster'd around by all her starry Fays;
        But here there is no light,
    Save what from heaven is with the breezes blown
      Through verdurous glooms and winding mossy ways.   40

V

I cannot see what flowers are at my feet,
  Nor what soft incense hangs upon the boughs,
But, in embalmed darkness, guess each sweet

Wherewith the seasonable month endows
The grass, the thicket, and the fruit-tree wild;
White hawthorn, and the pastoral eglantine;
Fast fading violets cover'd up in leaves;
And mid-May's eldest child,
The coming musk-rose, full of dewy wine,
The murmurous haunt of flies on summer eves.   50

VI

Darkling I listen; and, for many a time
I have been half in love with easeful Death,
Call'd him soft names in many a mused rhyme,
To take into the air my quiet breath;
Now more than ever seems it rich to die,
To cease upon the midnight with no pain,
While thou art pouring forth thy soul abroad
In such an ecstasy!
Still wouldst thou sing, and I have ears in vain—
To thy high requiem become a sod.   60

VII

Thou wast not born for death, immortal Bird!
No hungry generations tread thee down;
The voice I hear this passing night was heard
In ancient days by emperor and clown:
Perhaps the self-same song that found a path
Through the sad heart of Ruth, when, sick for home,
She stood in tears amid the alien corn;
The same that oft-times hath
Charm'd magic casements, opening on the foam
Of perilous seas, in faery lands forlorn.   70

VIII

Forlorn! the very word is like a bell
To toll me back from thee to my sole self!
Adieu! the fancy cannot cheat so well
As she is fam'd to do, deceiving elf.
Adieu! adieu! thy plaintive anthem fades
Past the near meadows, over the still stream,
Up the hill-side; and now 'tis buried deep
In the next valley-glades:

Was it a vision, or a waking dream?
    Fled is that music:—Do I wake or sleep?   **80**

May 1819

ODE ON A GRECIAN URN

I

Thou still unravish'd bride of quietness,
    Thou foster-child of silence and slow time,
Sylvan historian, who canst thus express
    A flowery tale more sweetly than our rhyme:
What leaf-fring'd legend haunts about thy shape
    Of deities or mortals, or of both,
        In Tempe or the dales of Arcady?
    What men or gods are these? What maidens loth?
What mad pursuit? What struggle to escape?
        What pipes and timbrels? What wild ecstasy?   **10**

II

Heard melodies are sweet, but those unheard
    Are sweeter; therefore, ye soft pipes, play on;
Not to the sensual ear, but, more endear'd,
    Pipe to the spirit ditties of no tone:
Fair youth, beneath the trees, thou canst not leave
    Thy song, nor ever can those trees be bare;
    Bold Lover, never, never canst thou kiss,
Though winning near the goal—yet, do not grieve;
    She cannot fade, though thou hast not thy bliss,
    For ever wilt thou love, and she be fair!   **20**

III

Ah, happy, happy boughs! that cannot shed
    Your leaves, nor ever bid the Spring adieu;
And, happy melodist, unwearied,
    For ever piping songs for ever new;
More happy love! more happy, happy love!
    For ever warm and still to be enjoy'd,
        For ever panting, and for ever young;
All breathing human passion far above,

That leaves a heart high-sorrowful and cloy'd,
    A burning forehead, and a parching tongue. 30

IV

Who are these coming to the sacrifice?
    To what green altar, O mysterious priest,
Lead'st thou that heifer lowing at the skies,
    And all her silken flanks with garlands drest?
What little town by river or sea shore,
    Or mountain-built with peaceful citadel,
      Is emptied of this folk, this pious morn?
And, little town, thy streets for evermore
    Will silent be; and not a soul to tell
      Why thou art desolate, can e'er return. 40

V

O Attic shape! Fair attitude! with brede
    Of marble men and maidens overwrought,
With forest branches and the trodden weed;
    Thou, silent form, dost tease us out of thought
As doth eternity: Cold Pastoral!
    When old age shall this generation waste,
      Thou shalt remain, in midst of other woe
Than ours, a friend to man, to whom thou say'st,
    'Beauty is truth, truth beauty,'—that is all
      Ye know on earth, and all ye need to know. 50

May 1819

THE MORAL DIMENSION

The Need to Know

The reference to "Solomon's directions" that appears in the following letter is to the *Book of Proverbs*, iv, 5.

TO JOHN TAYLOR
24 April 1818   Teignmouth

I was purposing to travel over the north this Summer—
there is but one thing to prevent me—I know nothing I

have read nothing and I mean to follow Solomon's directions of 'get Wisdom—get understanding'—I find cavalier days are gone by. I find that I can have no enjoyment in the World but continual drinking of Knowledge—I find there is no worthy pursuit but the idea of doing some good for the world—some do it with their society—some with their wit—some with their benevolence—some with a sort of power of conferring pleasure and good humour on all they meet and in a thousand ways all equally dutiful to the command of Great Nature—there is but one way for me—the road lies though application study and thought. I will pursue it and to that end purpose retiring for some years. I have been hovering for some time between an exquisite sense of the luxurious and a love for Philosophy—were I calculated for the former I should be glad—but as I am not I shall turn all my soul to the latter.

TO J. H. REYNOLDS
27 April 1818   Teignmouth

I shall perhaps remain here some Months.—I have written to George for some Books—shall learn Greek, and very likely Italian—and in other ways prepare myself to ask Hazlitt in about a years time the best metaphysical road
to be
I can take.—For although I take poetry (of the) Chief, there is something else wanting to one who passes his life among Books and thoughts on Books—I long to feast upon old Homer as we have upon Shakespeare. and as I have lately upon Milton.—if you understood Greek, and would read me passages, now and then, explaining their meaning, 't would be, from its mistiness, perhaps a greater luxury than reading the thing one's self.

Authorities have not agreed on the meaning of the phrase "Pip-civilian" in the following letter. *Civilian* can mean lawyer; *pip* can mean a small seed and in any case the word suggests something diminutive. Context and common sense suggest that "Pip-civilian" means a novice or amateur lawyer. This meaning works because Reynolds and Rice were lawyers. The phrase "The Burden of the Mystery" comes from Wordsworth's *Tintern Abbey*, line 38.

———•◦•———

TO J. H. REYNOLDS
3 May 1818   Teignmouth

Were I to study physic or rather Medicine again,—I feel it would not make the least difference in my Poetry; when
                                            is
the Mind is in its infancy a Bias ⟨in⟩ in reality a Bias, but when we have acquired more strength, a Bias becomes no Bias. Every department of knowledge we see excellent and calculated towards a great whole. I am so convinced of this, that I am glad at not having given away my medical Books, which I shall again look over to keep alive the little I know thitherwards; and moreover intend through you and Rice to become a sort of Pip-civilian. An extensive knowledge is needful to thinking people—it takes away the heat and fever; and helps, by widening speculation, to ease the Burden of the Mystery: a thing I begin to understand a little, and which weighed upon you in the most gloomy and true sentence in your Letter. The difference of high Sensations with and without knowledge appears to me this—in the latter case we are falling continually ten thousand fathoms deep and being blown up
                                                bare
again without wings and with all [the] horror of a ⟨Case⟩ shoulderd Creature—in the former case, our shoulders are
                                    air
fledge⟨d⟩, and we go thro' the same ⟨Fir⟩ and space without fear. This is running one's rigs on the score of abstracted benefit—when we come to human Life and the affections it is impossible how a parallel of breast and head can be
                                            treading
drawn— (you will forgive me for thus privately ⟨heading⟩
                                            tread
out my depth and take it for treading as schoolboys ⟨head⟩

the water⟨s⟩) —it is impossible to know how far knowledge

us

will console ⟨as⟩ for the death of a friend and the ill "that flesh is heir to". . . .

———•—•—•———

The following passage will make sense if *and* is substituted for the second *to*.

TO BENJAMIN BAILEY
18 July 1818   Inverary, Scotland

I think I have as far as a Man can do who has Books to read to subjects to think upon—for that reason I have been no where else except to Wentworth place so nigh at hand— . . . I should not have consented to myself these four Months tramping in the highlands but that I thought it would give me more experience, rub off more Prejudice, use [me] to more hardship, identify finer scenes load me with grander Mountains, and strengthen more my reach in Poetry, than would stopping at home among Books even though I should reach Homer—

———•—•—•———

TO RICHARD WOODHOUSE
18 December 1818   Hampstead

I have a new leaf to turn over—I must work—I must read —I must write—I am unable to affrod time for new acquaintances—I am scarcely able to do my duty to those I have—

———•—•—•———

TO GEORGE AND GEORGIANA KEATS
21 September 1819   Winchester

Some think I have lost that poetic ardour and fire 't is said I once had—the fact is perhaps I have: but instead of that I hope I shall substitute a more thoughtful and quiet power. I am more frequently, now, contented to read and think—but now & then, haunted with ambitious

thoughts. Qui[e]ter in my pulse, improved in my diges-
tion; exerting myself against vexing speculations—scarcely
content to write the best verses for the fever they leave
behind. I want to compose without this fever. I hope I
one day shall.

———•◦•◦•———

TO B. R. HAYDON
3 October 1819   Winchester

Though at this present "I have great dispositions to *write*"
I feel every day more and more content to read. Books
are becoming more interesting and valuable to me—I may
say I could not live without them. If in the course of a
fortnight you can procure me a ticket to the british
musœum I will make a better use of it than I did in the
first instance.

———•◦•◦•———

TO FANNY BRAWNE
February (?) 1820

I must make myself as good a Philosopher as possible.
Now I have had opportunities of passing nights anxious
and awake I have found other thoughts intrude upon me.
"If I should die," said I to myself, "I have left no immortal work behind me—nothing to make my friends proud
of my memory—but I have lov'd the principle of beauty
in all things, and if I had had time I would have made
myself remember'd."

HYPERION

A Fragment

Book I

Deep in the shady sadness of a vale
Far sunken from the healthy breath of morn,
Far from the fiery noon, and eve's one star,
Sat gray-hair'd Saturn, quiet as a stone,

Still as the silence round about his lair;
Forest on forest hung about his head
Like cloud on cloud. No stir of air was there,
Not so much life as on a summer's day
Robs not one light seed from the feather'd grass,
But where the dead leaf fell, there did it rest.   10
A stream went voiceless by, still deadened more
By reason of his fallen divinity
Spreading a shade: the Naiad 'mid her reeds
Press'd her cold finger closer to her lips.

Along the margin-sand large foot-marks went,
No further than to where his feet had stray'd,
And slept there since. Upon the sodden ground
His old right hand lay nerveless, listless, dead,
Unsceptred; and his realmless eyes were closed;
While his bow'd head seem'd list'ning to the Earth,   20
His ancient mother, for some comfort yet.

It seem'd no force could wake him from his place;
But there came one, who with a kindred hand
Touch'd his wide shoulders, after bending low
With reverence, though to one who knew it not.
She was a Goddess of the infant world;
By her in stature the tall Amazon
Had stood a pigmy's height: she would have ta'en
Achilles by the hair and bent his neck;
Or with a finger stay'd Ixion's wheel.   30
Her face was large as that of Memphian sphinx,
Pedestal'd haply in a palace court,
When sages look'd to Egypt for their lore.
But oh! how unlike marble was that face:
How beautiful, if sorrow had not made
Sorrow more beautiful than Beauty's self.
There was a listening fear in her regard,
As if calamity had but begun;
As if the vanward clouds of evil days
Had spent their malice, and the sullen rear   40
Was with its stored thunder labouring up.
One hand she press'd upon that aching spot

Where beats the human heart, as if just there,
Though an immortal, she felt cruel pain:
The other upon Saturn's bended neck
She laid, and to the level of his ear
Leaning with parted lips, some words she spake
In solemn tenour and deep organ tone:
Some mourning words, which in our feeble tongue
Would come in these like accents; O how frail   50
To that large utterance of the early Gods!
'Saturn, look up!—though wherefore, poor old King?
'I have no comfort for thee, no not one:
'I cannot say, "O wherefore sleepest thou?"
'For heaven is parted from thee, and the earth
'Knows thee not, thus afflicted, for a God;
'And ocean too, with all its solemn noise,
'Has from thy sceptre pass'd; and all the air
'Is emptied of thine hoary majesty.
'Thy thunder, conscious of the new command,   60
'Rumbles reluctant o'er our fallen house;
'And thy sharp lightning in unpractis'd hands
'Scorches and burns our once serene domain.
'O aching time! O moments big as years!
'All as ye pass swell out the monstrous truth,
'And press it so upon our weary griefs
'That unbelief has not a space to breathe.
'Saturn, sleep on:—O thoughtless, why did I
'Thus violate thy slumbrous solitude?
'Why should I ope thy melancholy eyes?   70
'Saturn, sleep on! while at thy feet I weep.'

    As when, upon a tranced summer-night,
Those green-rob'd senators of mighty woods,
Tall oaks, branch-charmed by the earnest stars,
Dream, and so dream all night without a stir,
Save from one gradual solitary gust
Which comes upon the silence, and dies off,
As if the ebbing air had but one wave;
So came these words and went; the while in tears
She touch'd her fair large forehead to the ground,   80

Just where her falling hair might be outspread
A soft and silken mat for Saturn's feet.
One moon, with alteration slow, had shed
Her silver seasons four upon the night,
And still these two were postured motionless,
Like natural sculpture in cathedral cavern;
The frozen God still couchant on the earth,
And the sad Goddess weeping at his feet:
Until at length old Saturn lifted up
His faded eyes, and saw his kingdom gone,   90
And all the gloom and sorrow of the place,
And that fair kneeling Goddess; and then spake,
As with a palsied tongue, and while his beard
Shook horrid with such aspen-malady:
'O tender spouse of gold Hyperion,
'Thea, I feel thee ere I see thy face;
'Look up, and let me see our doom in it;
'Look up, and tell me if this feeble shape
'Is Saturn's; tell me, if thou hear'st the voice
'Of Saturn; tell me, if this wrinkling brow,   100
'Naked and bare of its great diadem,
'Peers like the front of Saturn. Who had power
'To make me desolate? whence came the strength?
'How was it nurtur'd to such bursting forth,
'While Fate seem'd strangled in my nervous grasp?
'But it is so; and I am smother'd up,
'And buried from all godlike exercise
'Of influence benign on planets pale,
'Of admonitions to the winds and seas,
'Of peaceful sway above man's harvesting,   110
'And all those acts which Deity supreme
'Doth ease its heart of love in.—I am gone
'Away from my own bosom: I have left
'My strong identity, my real self,
'Somewhere between the throne, and where I sit
'Here on this spot of earth. Search, Thea, search!
'Open thine eyes eterne, and sphere them round
'Upon all space: space starr'd, and lorn of light;
'Space region'd with life-air; and barren void;

'Spaces of fire, and all the yawn of hell.—   120
'Search, Thea, search! and tell me, if thou seest
'A certain shape or shadow, making way
'With wings or chariot fierce to repossess
'A heaven he lost erewhile: it must—it must
'Be of ripe progress—Saturn must be King.
'Yes, there must be a golden victory;
'There must be Gods thrown down, and trumpets blown
'Of triumph calm, and hymns of festival
'Upon the gold clouds metropolitan,
'Voices of soft proclaim, and silver stir   130
'Of strings in hollow shells; and there shall be
'Beautiful things made new, for the surprise
'Of the sky-children; I will give command:
'Thea! Thea! Thea! where is Saturn?'

    This passion lifted him upon his feet,
And made his hands to struggle in the air,
His Druid locks to shake and ooze with sweat,
His eyes to fever out, his voice to cease.
He stood, and heard not Thea's sobbing deep;
A little time, and then again he snatch'd   140
Utterance thus.—'But cannot I create?
'Cannot I form? Cannot I fashion forth
'Another world, another universe,
'To overbear and crumble this to naught?
'Where is another chaos? Where?'—That word
Found way unto Olympus, and make quake
The rebel three.—Thea was startled up,
And in her bearing was a sort of hope,
As thus she quick-voic'd spake, yet full of awe.
'This cheers our fallen house: come to our friends,   150
'O Saturn! come away, and give them heart;
'I know the covert, for thence came I hither.'
Thus brief; then with beseeching eyes she went
With backward footing through the shade a space:
He follow'd, and she turn'd to lead the way
Through aged boughs, that yielded like the mist
Which eagles cleave upmounting from their nest.

Meanwhile in other realms big tears were shed,
More sorrow like to this, and such like woe,
Too huge for mortal tongue or pen of scribe: 160
The Titans fierce, self-hid, or prison-bound,
Groan'd for the old allegiance once more,
And listen'd in sharp pain for Saturn's voice.
But one of the whole mammoth-brood still kept
His sov'reignty, and rule, and majesty;—
Blazing Hyperion on his orbed fire
Still sat, still snuff'd the incense, teeming up
From man to the sun's God; yet unsecure:
For as among us mortals omens drear
Fright and perplex, so also shuddered he—   170
Not at dog's howl, or gloom-bird's hated screech,
Or the familiar visiting of one
Upon the first toll of his passing-bell,
Or prophesyings of the midnight lamp;
But horrors, portion'd to a giant nerve,
Oft made Hyperion ache. His palace bright
Bastion'd with pyramids of glowing gold,
And touch'd with shade of bronzed obelisks,
Glar'd a blood-red through all its thousand courts,
Arches, and domes, and fiery galleries;   180
And all its curtains of Aurorian clouds
Flush'd angerly: while sometimes eagle's wings,
Unseen before by Gods or wondering men,
Darken'd the place; and neighing steeds were heard,
Not heard before by Gods or wondering men.
Also, when he would taste the spicy wreaths
Of incense, breath'd aloft from sacred hills,
Instead of sweets, his ample palate took
Savour of poisonous brass and metal sick:
And so, when harbour'd in the sleepy west,   190
After the full completion of fair day,—
For rest divine upon exalted couch
And slumber in the arms of melody,
He pac'd away the pleasant hours of ease
With stride colossal, on from hall to hall;
While far within each aisle and deep recess,

His winged minions in close clusters stood,
Amaz'd and full of fear; like anxious men
Who on wide plains gather in panting troops,
When earthquakes jar their battlements and towers.   200
Even now, while Saturn, rous'd from icy trance,
Went step for step with Thea through the woods,
Hyperion, leaving twilight in the rear,
Came slope upon the threshold of the west;
Then, as was wont, his palace-door flew ope
In smoothest silence, save what solemn tubes,
Blown by the serious Zephyrs, gave of sweet
And wandering sounds, slow-breathed melodies;
And like a rose in vermeil tint and shape,
In fragrance soft, and coolness to the eye,   210
That inlet to severe magnificence
Stood full blown, for the God to enter in.

   He enter'd, but he enter'd full of wrath;
His flaming robes stream'd out beyond his heels,
And gave a roar, as if of earthly fire,
That scar'd away the meek ethereal Hours
And made their dove-wings tremble. On he flared,
From stately nave to nave, from vault to vault,
Through bowers of fragrant and enwreathed light,
And diamond-paved lustrous long arcades,   220
Until he reach'd the great main cupola;
There standing fierce beneath, he stamped his foot,
And from the basement deep to the high towers
Jarr'd his own golden region; and before
The quavering thunder thereupon had ceas'd,
His voice leapt out, despite of godlike curb,
To this result: 'O dreams of day and night!
'O monstrous forms! O effigies of pain!
'O spectres busy in a cold, cold gloom!
'O lank-ear'd Phantoms of black-weeded pools!   230
'Why do I know ye? why have I seen ye? why
'Is my eternal essence thus distraught
'To see and to behold these horrors new?
'Saturn is fallen, am I too to fall?
'Am I to leave this haven of my rest,

'This cradle of my glory, this soft clime,
'This calm luxuriance of blissful light,
'These crystalline pavilions, and pure fanes,
'Of all my lucent empire? It is left
'Deserted, void, nor any haunt of mine.   240
'The blaze, the splendor, and the symmetry,
'I cannot see—but darkness, death and darkness.
'Even here, into my centre of repose,
'The shady visions come to domineer,
'Insult, and blind, and stifle up my pomp.—
'Fall!—No, by Tellus and her briny robes!
'Over the fiery frontier of my realms
'I will advance a terrible right arm
'Shall scare that infant thunderer, rebel Jove,
'And bid old Saturn take his throne again.'—   250
He spake, and ceas'd, the while a heavier threat
Held struggle with his throat but came not forth;
For as in theatres of crowded men
Hubbub increases more they call out 'Hush!'
So at Hyperion's words the Phantoms pale
Bestirr'd themselves, thrice horrible and cold;
And from the mirror'd level where he stood
A mist arose, as from a scummy marsh.
At this, through all his bulk an agony
Crept gradual, from the feet unto the crown,   260
Like a lithe serpent vast and muscular
Making slow way, with head and neck convuls'd
From over-strained might. Releas'd, he fled
To the eastern gates, and full six dewy hours
Before the dawn in season due should blush,
He breath'd fierce breath against the sleepy portals,
Clear'd them of heavy vapours, burst them wide
Suddenly on the ocean's chilly streams.
The planet orb of fire, whereon he rode
Each day from east to west the heavens through,   270
Spun round in sable curtaining of clouds;
Not therefore veiled quite, blindfold, and hid,
But ever and anon the glancing spheres,
Circles, and arcs, and broad-belting colure,
Glow'd through, and wrought upon the muffling dark

Sweet-shaped lightnings from the nadir deep
Up to the zenith,—hieroglyphics old
Which sages and keen-eyed astrologers
Then living on the earth, with labouring thought
Won from the gaze of many centuries: 280
Now lost, save what we find on remnants huge
Of stone, or marble swart; their import gone,
Their wisdom long since fled.—Two wings this orb
Possess'd for glory, two fair argent wings,
Ever exalted at the God's approach:
And now, from forth the gloom their plumes immense
Rose, one by one, till all outspreaded were;
While still the dazzling globe maintain'd eclipse,
Awaiting for Hyperion's command.
Fain would he have commanded, fain took throne   290
And bid the day begin, if but for change.
He might not:—No, though a primeval God:
The sacred seasons might not be disturb'd.
Therefore the operations of the dawn
Stay'd in their birth, even as here 'tis told.
Those silver wings expanded sisterly,
Eager to sail their orb; the porches wide
Open'd upon the dusk demesnes of night;
And the bright Titan, phrenzied with new woes,
Unus'd to bend, by hard compulsion bent   300
His spirit to the sorrow of the time;
And all along a dismal rack of clouds,
Upon the boundaries of day and night,
He stretch'd himself in grief and radiance faint.
There as he lay, the Heaven with its stars
Look'd down on him with pity, and the voice
Of Cœlus, from the universal space,
Thus whisper'd low and solemn in his ear.
'O brightest of my children dear, earth-born
'And sky-engendered, Son of Mysteries   310
'All unrevealed even to the powers
'Which met at thy creating; at whose joys
'And palpitations sweet, and pleasures soft,
'I, Cœlus, wonder, how they came and whence;
'And at the fruits thereof what shapes they be,

'Distinct, and visible; symbols divine,
'Manifestations of that beauteous life
'Diffus'd unseen throughout eternal space:
'Of these new-form'd art thou, oh brightest child!
'Of these, thy brethren and the Goddesses!   320
'There is sad feud among ye, and rebellion
'Of son against his sire. I saw him fall,
'I saw my first-born tumbled from his throne!
'To me his arms were spread, to me his voice
'Found way from forth the thunders round his head!
'Pale wox I, and in vapours hid my face.
'Art thou, too, near such doom? vague fear there is:
'For I have seen my sons most unlike Gods.
'Divine ye were created, and divine
'In sad demeanour, solemn, undisturb'd,   330
'Unruffled, like high Gods, ye liv'd and ruled:
'Now I behold in you fear, hope, and wrath;
'Actions of rage and passion; even as
'I see them, on the mortal world beneath,
'In men who die.—This is the grief, O Son!
'Sad sign of ruin, sudden dismay, and fall!
'Yet do thou strive; as thou art capable,
'As thou canst move about, an evident God;
'And canst oppose to each malignant hour
'Ethereal presence:—I am but a voice;   340
'My life is but the life of winds and tides,
'No more than winds and tides can I avail:—
'But thou canst.—Be thou therefore in the van
'Of circumstance; yea, seize the arrow's barb
'Before the tense string murmur.—To the earth!
'For there thou wilt find Saturn, and his woes.
'Meantime I will keep watch on thy bright sun,
'And of thy seasons be a careful nurse.'—
Ere half this region-whisper had come down,
Hyperion arose, and on the stars   350
Lifted his curved lids, and kept them wide
Until it ceas'd; and still he kept them wide:
And still they were the same bright, patient stars.
Then with a slow incline of his broad breast,
Like to a diver in the pearly seas,

Forward he stoop'd over the airy shore,
And plung'd all noiseless into the deep night.

Book II

Just at the self-same beat of Time's wide wings
Hyperion slid into the rustled air,
And Saturn gain'd with Thea that sad place
Where Cybele and the bruised Titans mourn'd.
It was a den where no insulting light
Could glimmer on their tears; where their own groans
They felt, but heard not, for the solid roar
Of thunderous waterfalls and torrents hoarse,
Pouring a constant bulk, uncertain where.
Crag jutting forth to crag, and rocks that seem'd   10
Ever as if just rising from a sleep,
Forehead to forehead held their monstrous horns;
And thus in thousand hugest phantasies
Made a fit roofing to this nest of woe.
Instead of thrones, hard flint they sat upon,
Couches of rugged stone, and slaty ridge
Stubborn'd with iron. All were not assembled:
Some chain'd in torture, and some wandering.
Cœus, and Gyges, and Briareüs,
Typhon, and Dolor, and Porphyrion,   20
With many more, the brawniest in assault,
Were pent in regions of laborious breath;
Dungeon'd in opaque element, to keep
Their clenched teeth still clench'd, and all their limbs
Lock'd up like veins of metal, crampt and screw'd;
Without a motion, save of their big hearts
Heaving in pain, and horribly convuls'd
With sanguine feverous boiling gurge of pulse.
Mnemosyne was straying in the world;
Far from her moon had Phoebe wandered;   30
And many else were free to roam abroad,
But for the main, here found they covert drear.
Scarce images of life, one here, one there,
Lay vast and edgeways; like a dismal cirque
Of Druid stones, upon a forlorn moor,

When the chill rain begins at shut of eve,
In dull November, and their chancel vault,
The Heaven itself, is blinded throughout night.
Each one kept shroud, nor to his neighbour gave
Or word, or look, or action of despair. 40
Creüs was one; his ponderous iron mace
Lay by him, and a shatter'd rib of rock
Told of his rage, ere he thus sank and pined.
Iäpetus another; in his grasp,
A serpent's plashy neck; its barbed tongue
Squeez'd from the gorge, and all its uncurl'd length
Dead; and because the creature could not spit
Its poison in the eyes of conquering Jove.
Next Cottus: prone he lay, chin uppermost,
As though in pain; for still upon the flint 50
He ground severe his skull, with open mouth
And eyes at horrid working. Nearest him
Asia, born of most enormous Caf,
Who cost her mother Tellus keener pangs,
Though feminine, than any of her sons:
More thought than woe was in her dusky face,
For she was prophesying of her glory;
And in her wide imagination stood
Palm-shaded temples, and high rival fanes,
By Oxus or in Ganges' sacred isles. 60
Even as Hope upon her anchor leans,
So leant she, not so fair, upon a tusk
Shed from the broadest of her elephants.
Above her, on a crag's uneasy shelve,
Upon his elbow rais'd, all prostrate else,
Shadow'd Enceladus; once tame and mild
As grazing ox unworried in the meads;
Now tiger-passion'd, lion-thoughted, wroth,
He meditated, plotted, and even now
Was hurling mountains in that second war, 70
Not long delay'd, that scar'd the younger Gods
To hide themselves in forms of beast and bird.
Not far hence Atlas; and beside him prone
Phorcus, the sire of Gorgons. Neighbour'd close
Oceanus, and Tethys, in whose lap

Sobb'd Clymene among her tangled hair.
In midst of all lay Themis, at the feet
Of Ops the queen all clouded round from sight;
No shape distinguishable, more than when
Thick night confounds the pine-tops with the clouds: 80
And many else whose names may not be told.
For when the Muse's wings are air-ward spread,
Who shall delay her flight? And she must chaunt
Of Saturn, and his guide, who now had climb'd
With damp and slippery footing from a depth
More horrid still. Above a sombre cliff
Their heads appear'd, and up their stature grew
Till on the level height their steps found ease:
Then Thea spread abroad her trembling arms
Upon the precincts of this nest of pain,   90
And sidelong fix'd her eye on Saturn's face:
There saw she direst strife; the supreme God
At war with all the frailty of grief,
Of rage, of fear, anxiety, revenge,
Remorse, spleen, hope, but most of all despair.
Against these plagues he strove in vain; for Fate
Had pour'd a mortal oil upon his head,
A disanointing poison: so that Thea,
Affrighted, kept her still, and let him pass
First onwards in, among the fallen tribe.   100

As with us mortal men, the laden heart
Is persecuted more, and fever'd more,
When it is nighing to the mournful house
Where other hearts are sick of the same bruise;
So Saturn, as he walk'd into the midst,
Felt faint, and would have sunk among the rest,
But that he met Enceladus's eye,
Whose mightiness, and awe of him, at once
Came like an inspiration; and he shouted,
'Titans, behold your God!' at which some groan'd;   110
Some started on their feet; some also shouted;
Some wept, some wail'd, all bow'd with reverence;
And Ops, uplifting her black folded veil,
Show'd her pale cheeks, and all her forehead wan,

Her eye-brows thin and jet, and hollow eyes.
There is a roaring in the bleak-grown pines
When Winter lifts his voice; there is a noise
Among immortals when a God gives sign,
With hushing finger, how he means to load
His tongue with the full weight of utterless thought,   120
With thunder, and with music, and with pomp:
Such noise is like the roar of bleak-grown pines:
Which, when it ceases in this mountain'd world,
No other sound succeeds; but ceasing here,
Among these fallen, Saturn's voice therefrom
Grew up like organ, that begins anew
Its strain, when other harmonies, stopt short,
Leave the dinn'd air vibrating silverly.
Thus grew it up—'Not in my own sad breast,
'Which is its own great judge and searcher out,   130
'Can I find reason why ye should be thus:
'Not in the legends of the first of days,
'Studied from that old spirit-leaved book
'Which starry Uranus with finger bright
'Sav'd from the shores of darkness, when the waves
'Low-ebb'd still hid it up in shallow gloom;—
'And the which book ye know I ever kept
'For my firm-based footstool:—Ah, infirm!
'Not there, nor in sign, symbol, or portent
'Of element, earth, water, air, and fire,—   140
'At war, at peace, or inter-quarreling
'One against one, or two, or three, or all
'Each several one against the other three,
'As fire with air loud warring when rain-floods
'Drown both, and press them both against earth's face,
'Where, finding sulphur, a quadruple wrath
'Unhinges the poor world;—not in that strife,
'Wherefrom I take strange lore, and read it deep,
'Can I find reason why ye should be thus:
'No, no-where can unriddle, though I search,   150
'And pore on Nature's universal scroll
'Even to swooning, why ye, Divinities,
'The first-born of all shap'd and palpable Gods,
'Should cower beneath what, in comparison,

'Is untremendous might. Yet ye are here,
'O'erwhelm'd, and spurn'd, and batter'd, ye are here!
'O Titans, shall I say, "Arise!"—Ye groan:
'Shall I say "Crouch!"—Ye groan. What can I then?
'O Heaven wide! O unseen parent dear!
'What can I? Tell me, all ye brethren Gods,   160
'How we can war, how engine our great wrath!
'O speak your counsel now, for Saturn's ear
'Is all a-hunger'd. Thou, Oceanus,
'Ponderest high and deep; and in thy face
'I see, astonied, that severe content
'Which comes of thought and musing: give us help!'

   So ended Saturn; and the God of the Sea,
Sophist and sage, from no Athenian grove,
But cogitation in his watery shades,
Arose, with locks not oozy, and began,   170
In murmurs, which his first-endeavouring tongue
Caught infant-like from the far-foamed sands.
'O ye, whom wrath consumes! who, passion-stung,
'Writhe at defeat, and nurse your agonies!
'Shut up your senses, stifle up your ears,
'My voice is not a bellows unto ire.
'Yet listen, ye who will, whilst I bring proof
'How ye, perforce, must be content to stoop:
'And in the proof much comfort will I give,
'If ye will take that comfort in its truth.   180
'We fall by course of Nature's law, not force
'Of thunder, or of Jove. Great Saturn, thou
'Hast sifted well the atom-universe;
'But for this reason, that thou art the King,
'And only blind from sheer supremacy,
'One avenue was shaded from thine eyes,
'Through which I wandered to eternal truth.
'And first, as thou wast not the first of powers,
'So art thou not the last; it cannot be:
'Thou art not the beginning nor the end.   190
'From chaos and parental darkness came
'Light, the first fruits of that intestine broil,
'That sullen ferment, which for wondrous ends

'Was ripening in itself. The ripe hour came,
'And with it light, and light, engendering
'Upon its own producer, forthwith touch'd
'The whole enormous matter into life.
'Upon that very hour, our parentage,
'The Heavens, and the Earth, were manifest:
'Then thou first born, and we the giant race,   200
'Found ourselves ruling new and beauteous realms.
'Now comes the pain of truth, to whom 'tis pain;
'O folly! for to bear all naked truths,
'And to envisage circumstance, all calm,
'That is the top of sovereignty. Mark well!
'As Heaven and Earth are fairer, fairer far
'Than Chaos and blank Darkness, though once chiefs;
'And as we show beyond that Heaven and Earth
'In form and shape compact and beautiful,
'In will, in action free, companionship,   210
'And thousand other signs of purer life;
'So on our heels a fresh perfection treads,
'A power more strong in beauty, born of us
'And fated to excel us, as we pass
'In glory that old Darkness: nor are we
'Thereby more conquer'd, than by us the rule
'Of shapeless Chaos. Say, doth the dull soil
'Quarrel with the proud forests it hath fed,
'And feedeth still, more comely than itself?
'Can it deny the chiefdom of green groves?   220
'Or shall the tree be envious of the dove
'Because it cooeth, and hath snowy wings
'To wander wherewithal and find its joys?
'We are such forest-trees, and our fair boughs
'Have bred forth, not pale solitary doves,
'But eagles golden-feather'd, who do tower
'Above us in their beauty, and must reign
'In right thereof; for 'tis the eternal law
'That first in beauty should be first in might:
'Yea, by that law, another race may drive   230
'Our conquerors to mourn as we do now.
'Have ye beheld the young God of the Seas,
'My dispossessor? Have ye seen his face?

'Have ye beheld his chariot, foam'd along
'By noble winged creatures he hath made?
'I saw him on the calmed waters scud,
'With such a glow of beauty in his eyes,
'That it enforc'd me to bid sad farewell
'To all my empire: farewell sad I took,
'And hither came, to see how dolorous fate   240
'Had wrought upon ye; and how I might best
'Give consolation in this woe extreme.
'Receive the truth, and let it be your balm.'

   Whether through poz'd conviction, or disdain,
They guarded silence, when Oceanus
Left murmuring, what deepest thought can tell?
But so it was, none answer'd for a space,
Save one whom none regarded, Clymene;
And yet she answer'd not, only complain'd,
With hectic lips, and eyes up-looking mild,   250
Thus wording timidly among the fierce:
'O Father, I am here the simplest voice,
'And all my knowledge is that joy is gone,
'And this thing woe crept in among our hearts,
'There to remain for ever, as I fear:
'I would not bode of evil, if I thought
'So weak a creature could turn off the help
'Which by just right should come of mighty Gods;
'Yet let me tell my sorrow, let me tell
'Of what I heard, and how it made me weep,   260
'And know that we had parted from all hope.
'I stood upon a shore, a pleasant shore,
'Where a sweet clime was breathed from a land
'Of fragrance, quietness, and trees, and flowers
'Full of calm joy it was, as I of grief;
'Too full of joy and soft delicious warmth;
'So that I felt a movement in my heart
'To chide, and to reproach that solitude
'With songs of misery, music of our woes;
'And sat me down, and took a mouthed shell   270
'And murmur'd into it, and made melody—
'O melody no more! for while I sang,

'And with poor skill let pass into the breeze
'The dull shell's echo, from a bowery strand
'Just opposite, an island of the sea,
'There came enchantment with the shifting wind,
'That did both drown and keep alive my ears.
'I threw my shell away upon the sand,
'And a wave fill'd it, as my sense was fill'd
'With that new blissful golden melody.   280
'A living death was in each gush of sounds,
'Each family of rapturous hurried notes,
'That fell, one after one, yet all at once,
'Like pearl beads dropping sudden from their string:
'And then another, then another strain,
'Each like a dove leaving its olive perch,
'With music wing'd instead of silent plumes,
'To hover round my head, and make me sick
'Of joy and grief at once. Grief overcame,
'And I was stopping up my frantic ears,   290
'When, past all hindrance of my trembling hands,
'A voice came sweeter, sweeter than all tune,
'And still it cried, "Apollo! young Apollo!
' "The morning-bright Apollo! young Apollo!"
'I fled, it follow'd me, and cried "Apollo!"
'O Father, and O Brethren, had ye felt
'Those pains of mine; O Saturn, hadst thou felt,
'Ye would not call this too indulged tongue
'Presumptuous, in thus venturing to be heard.'

So far her voice flow'd on, like timorous brook   300
That, lingering along a pebbled coast,
Doth fear to meet the sea: but sea it met,
And shudder'd; for the overwhelming voice
Of huge Enceladus swallow'd it in wrath:
The ponderous syllables, like sullen waves
In the half-glutted hollows of reef-rocks,
Came booming thus, while still upon his arm
He lean'd; not rising, from supreme contempt.
'Or shall we listen to the over-wise,
'Or to the over-foolish, Giant-Gods?   310
'Not thunderbolt on thunderbolt, till all

'That rebel Jove's whole armoury were spent,
'Not world on world upon these shoulders piled,
'Could agonize me more than baby-words
'In midst of this dethronement horrible.
'Speak! roar! shout! yell! ye sleepy Titans all.
'Do ye forget the blows, the buffets vile?
'Are ye not smitten by a youngling arm?
'Dost thou forget, sham Monarch of the Waves,
'Thy scalding in the seas? What, have I rous'd   320
'Your spleens with so few simple words as these?
'O joy! for now I see ye are not lost:
'O joy! for now I see a thousand eyes
'Wide-glaring for revenge!'—As this he said,
He lifted up his stature vast, and stood,
Still without intermission speaking thus:
'Now ye are flames, I'll tell you how to burn,
'And purge the ether of our enemies;
'How to feed fierce the crooked stings of fire,
'And singe away the swollen clouds of Jove,   330
'Stifling that puny essence in its tent.
'O let him feel the evil he hath done;
'For though I scorn Oceanus's lore,
'Much pain have I for more than loss of realms:
'The days of peace and slumberous calm are fled;
'Those days, all innocent of scathing war,
'When all the fair Existences of heaven
'Came open-eyed to guess what we would speak:—
'That was before our brows were taught to frown,
'Before our lips knew else but solemn sounds;   340
'That was before we knew the winged thing,
'Victory, might be lost, or might be won.
'And be ye mindful that Hyperion,
'Our brightest brother, still is undisgraced—
'Hyperion, lo! his radiance is here!'

    All eyes were on Enceladus's face,
And they beheld, while still Hyperion's name
Flew from his lips up to the vaulted rocks,
A pallid gleam across his features stern:

Not savage, for he saw full many a God   350
Wroth as himself. He look'd upon them all,
And in each face he saw a gleam of light,
But splendider in Saturn's, whose hoar locks
Shone like the bubbling foam about a keel
When the prow sweeps into a midnight cove.
In pale and silver silence they remain'd,
Till suddenly a splendour, like the morn,
Pervaded all the beetling gloomy steeps,
All the sad spaces of oblivion,
And every gulf, and every chasm old,   360
And every height, and every sullen depth,
Voiceless, or hoarse with loud tormented streams:
And all the everlasting cataracts,
And all the headlong torrents far and near,
Mantled before in darkness and huge shade,
Now saw the light and made it terrible.
It was Hyperion:—a granite peak
His bright feet touch'd, and there he stay'd to view
The misery his brilliance had betray'd
To the most hateful seeing of itself.   370
Golden his hair of short Numidian curl,
Regal his shape majestic, a vast shade
In midst of his own brightness, like the bulk
Of Memnon's image at the set of sun
To one who travels from the dusking East:
Sighs, too, as mournful as that Memnon's harp
He utter'd, while his hands contemplative
He press'd together, and in silence stood.
Despondence seiz'd again the fallen Gods
At sight of the dejected King of Day,   380
And many hid their faces from the light:
But fierce Enceladus sent forth his eyes
Among the brotherhood; and, at their glare,
Uprose Iäpetus, and Creüs too,
And Phorcus, sea-born, and together strode
To where he towered on his eminence.
There those four shouted forth old Saturn's name;
Hyperion from the peak loud answered, 'Saturn!'

Saturn sat near the Mother of the Gods,
In whose face was no joy, though all the Gods   390
Gave from their hollow throats the name of 'Saturn!'

Book III

Thus in alternate uproar and sad peace,
Amazed were those Titans utterly.
O leave them, Muse! O leave them to their woes;
For thou art weak to sing such tumults dire:
A solitary sorrow best befits
Thy lips, and antheming a lonely grief.
Leave them, O Muse! for thou anon wilt find
Many a fallen old Divinity
Wandering in vain about bewildered shores.
Meantime touch piously the Delphic harp,   10
And not a wind of heaven but will breathe
In aid soft warble from the Dorian flute;
For lo! 'tis for the Father of all verse.
Flush every thing that hath a vermeil hue,
Let the rose glow intense and warm the air,
And let the clouds of even and of morn
Float in voluptuous fleeces o'er the hills;
Let the red wine within the goblet boil,
Cold as a bubbling well; let faint-lipp'd shells,
On sands, or in great deeps, vermilion turn   20
Through all their labyrinths; and let the maid
Blush keenly, as with some warm kiss surpris'd.
Chief isle of the embowered Cyclades,
Rejoice, O Delos, with thine olives green,
And poplars, and lawn-shading palms, and beech,
In which the Zephyr breathes the loudest song,
And hazels thick, dark-stemm'd beneath the shade:
Apollo is once more the golden theme!
Where was he, when the Giant of the Sun
Stood bright, amid the sorrow of his peers?   30
Together had he left his mother fair
And his twin-sister sleeping in their bower,
And in the morning twilight wandered forth
Beside the osiers of a rivulet,

Full ankle-deep in lillies of the vale.
The nightingale had ceas'd, and a few stars
Were lingering in the heavens, while the thrush
Began calm-throated. Throughout all the isle
There was no covert, no retired cave
Unhaunted by the murmurous noise of waves,   40
Though scarcely heard in many a green recess.
He listen'd, and he wept, and his bright tears
Went trickling down the golden bow he held.
Thus with half-shut suffused eyes he stood,
While from beneath some cumbrous boughs hard by
With solemn step an awful Goddess came,
And there was purport in her looks for him,
Which he with eager guess began to read
Perplex'd, the while melodiously he said:
'How cam'st thou over the unfooted sea?   50
'Or hath that antique mien and robed form
'Mov'd in these vales invisible till now?
'Sure I have heard those vestments sweeping o'er
'The fallen leaves, when I have sat alone
'In cool mild-forest. Surely I have traced
'The rustle of those ample skirts about
'These grassy solitudes, and seen the flowers
'Lift up their heads, as still the whisper pass'd.
'Goddess! I have beheld those eyes before,
'And their eternal calm, and all that face,   60
'Or I have dream'd.'—'Yes,' said the supreme shape,
'Thou hast dream'd of me; and awaking up
'Didst find a lyre all golden by thy side,
'Whose strings touch'd by thy fingers, all the vast
'Unwearied ear of the whole universe
'Listen'd in pain and pleasure at the birth
'Of such new tuneful wonder. Is't not strange
'That thou shouldst weep, so gifted? Tell me, youth,
'What sorrow thou canst feel; for I am sad
'When thou dost shed a tear: explain thy griefs   70
'To one who in this lonely isle hath been
'The watcher of thy sleep and hours of life,
'From the young day when first thy infant hand
'Pluck'd witless the weak flowers, till thine arm

'Could bend that bow heroic to all times.
'Show thy heart's secret to an ancient Power
'Who hath forsaken old and sacred thrones
'For prophecies of thee, and for the sake
'Of loveliness new born.'—Apollo then,
With sudden scrutiny and gloomless eyes,   80
Thus answer'd, while his white melodious throat
Throbb'd with the syllables.—'Mnemosyne!
'Thy name is on my tongue, I know not how;
'Why should I tell thee what thou so well seest?
'Why should I strive to show what from thy lips
'Would come no mystery? For me, dark, dark,
'And painful vile oblivion seals my eyes:
'I strive to search wherefore I am so sad,
'Until a melancholy numbs my limbs;
'And then upon the grass I sit, and moan,   90
'Like one who once had wings.—O why should I
'Feel curs'd and thwarted, when the liegeless air
'Yields to my step aspirant? why should I
'Spurn the green turf as hateful to my feet?
'Goddess benign, point forth some unknown thing:
'Are there not other regions than this isle?
'What are the stars? There is the sun, the sun!
'And the most patient brilliance of the moon!
'And stars by thousands! Point me out the way
'To any one particular beauteous star,   100
'And I will flit into it with my lyre
'And make its silvery splendour pant with bliss.
'I have heard the cloudy thunder: Where is power?
'Whose hand, whose essence, what divinity
'Makes this alarum in the elements,
'While I here idle listen on the shores
'In fearless yet in aching ignorance?
'O tell me, lonely Goddess, by thy harp,
'That waileth every morn and eventide,
'Tell me why thus I rave, about these groves!   110
'Mute thou remainest—mute! yet I can read
'A wondrous lesson in thy silent face:
'Knowledge enormous makes a God of me.
'Names, deeds, grey legends, dire events, rebellions,

'Majesties, sovran voices, agonies,
'Creations and destroyings, all at once
'Pour into the wide hollows of my brain,
'And deify me, as if some blithe wine
'Or bright elixir peerless I had drunk,
'And so become immortal.'—Thus the God,   120
While his enkindled eyes, with level glance
Beneath his white soft temples, stedfast kept
Trembling with light upon Mnemosyne.
Soon wild commotions shook him, and made flush
All the immortal fairness of his limbs;
Most like the struggle at the gate of death;
Or liker still to one who should take leave
Of pale immortal death, and with a pang
As hot as death's is chill, with fierce convulse
Die into life: so young Apollo anguish'd: 130
His very hair, his golden tresses famed
Kept undulation round his eager neck.
During the pain Mnemosyne upheld
Her arms as one who prophesied.—At length
Apollo shriek'd:—and lo! from all his limbs
Celestial   *   *   *   *   *   *
*   *   *   *   *   *   *   *

*September 1818
to early spring 1819.*

A Tragic Sense

TO J. H. REYNOLDS
3 May 1818   Teignmouth

My Branchings out therefrom have been numerous: one of
them is the consideration of Wordsworth's genius and as
a help, in the manner of gold being the meridian Line of
worldly wealth,—how he differs from Milton.—And here I
have nothing but surmises, from an uncertainty whether
Miltons apparently less anxiety for Humanity proceeds
from his seeing further or no than Wordsworth: And
whether Wordsworth has in truth epic passion(s), and

martyrs himself to the human heart, the main region of
his song—

—————•—•—•—————

—were it in my choice I would reject a petrarchal corona-
tion—on accou[n]t of my dying day, and because women
have Cancers. I should not by rights speak in this tone to
you—for it is an incendiary spirit that would do so. Yet I
am not old enough or magnanimous enough to anihilate
self—and it would perhaps be paying you an ill compliment. I was in hopes some little time back to be able to
releive your dullness by my spirits—to point out things in
the world worth your enjoyment—and now I am never
alone without rejoicing that there is such a thing as death
—without placing my ultimate in the glory of dying for a
great human purpose Perphaps if my affairs were in a
different state I should not have written the above—you
shall judge—I have two Brothers one is driven by the
'burden of Society' to America the other, with an exquisite
love of Life, is in a lingering state—My Love for my
Brothers from the early loss of our parents and even for
earlier Misfortunes has grown into a affection 'passing
the Love of Women'—I have been ill temper'd with them,
I have vex'd them—but the thought of them has always
stifled the impression that any woman might otherwise
have made upon me—I have a Sister too and may not follow them, either to America or to the Grave—Life must
be undergone, and I certainly derive a consolation from
the thought of writing one or two more Poems before it
ceases—

—————•—•—•—————

I wish I could say Tom was any better. His identity
presses upon me so all day that I am obliged to go out—
and although I intended to have given some time to study

alone I am obliged to write, and plunge into abstract images to ease myself of his countenance his voice and feebleness—so that I live now in a continual fever—it must be poisonous to life although I feel well. Imagine 'the hateful siege of contraries'—if I think of fame of poetry it seems a crime to me, and yet I must do so or suffer—I am sorry to give you pain—I am almost resolv'd to burn this—but I really have not self possession and magninimity enough to manage the thing othe[r]wise— after all it may be a nervousness proceeding from the Mercury—

———•——•——•———

TO RICHARD WOODHOUSE
27 October 1818   Hampstead

In the second place I will speak of my views, and of the life I purpose to myself—I am ambitious of doing the world some good: if I should be spared that may be the work of maturer years—in the interval I will assay to reach to as high a summit in Poetry as the nerve bestowed upon me will suffer. The faint conceptions I have of Poems to come brings the blood frequently into my forehead—All I hope is that I may not lose all interest in human affairs—that the solitary indifference I feel for applause even from the finest Spirits, will not blunt any acuteness of vision I may have. I do not think it will—I feel assured I should write from the mere yearning and fondness I have for the Beautiful even if my night's labours should be burnt every morning and no eye ever shine upon them. But even now I am perhaps not speaking from myself; but from some character in whose soul I now live. I am sure however that this next sentence is from myself. I feel your anxiety, good opinion and friendliness in the highest degree. . . .

———•——•——•———

The first choice referred to in the next letter is a job as surgeon on a ship to India. The *Indiaman* mentioned in the 9 June letter to Sarah Jeffrey (below) is that ship.

31 May 1819   Hampstead

I have the choice as it were of two Poisons (yet I ought
not to call this a Poison) the one is voyaging to and from
India for a few years; the other is leading a fevrous life
alone with Poetry—This latter will suit me best—for I
cannot resolve to give up my Studies.

The Renaissance Italians treated the Raphaels mentioned in
the next letter with generous patronage. Boyardo, an extreme
example of a pampered writer, is Matteo Maria Boiardo (fifteenth-
century poet).

TO SARAH JEFFREY
9 June 1819   Hampstead

Your advice about the Indiaman is a very wise advice, because it just suits me, though you are a little in the wrong
concerning its destroying the energies of Mind: on the
contrary it would be the finest thing in the world to
strengthen them—To be thrown among people who care
not for you, with whom you have no sympathies forces the
Mind upon its own resourses, and leaves it free to make its
speculations of the differences of human character and to
class them with the calmness of a Botanist. An Indiaman
is a little world. One of the great reasons that the english
have produced the finest writers in the world; is, that the
English world has ill-treated them during their lives and
foster'd them after their deaths. They have in general
been trampled aside into the bye paths of life and seen
the festerings of Society. They have not been treated like
the Raphaels of Italy. And where is the Englishman and
Poet who has given a magnificent Entertainment at the
christening of one of his Hero's Horses as Boyardo did?
He had a Castle in the Appenine. He was a noble Poet of
Romance; not a miserable and mighty Poet of the human
Heart. The middle age of Shakspeare was all couded over;
his days were not more happy than Hamlet's who is per-

haps more like Shakspeare himself in his common every day Life than any other of his Characters—Ben Johnson was a common Soldier and in the Low countries, in the face of two armies, fought a single combat with a french Trooper and slew him—For all this I will not go on board an Indiaman, nor for examples sake run my head into dark alleys: I dare say my discipline is to come, and plenty of it too. I have been very idle lately, very averse to writing; both from the overpowering idea of our dead poets and from abatement of my love of fame. I hope I am a little more of a Philosopher than I was, consequently a little less of a versifying Pet-lamb.

------•-•-•-•------

TO BENJAMIN BAILEY
14 August 1819   Winchester

I am convinced more and more every day that (excepting the human friend Philosopher) a fine writer is the most genuine Being in the World—

------•-•-•-•------

TO J. H. REYNOLDS
24 August 1819   Winchester

I am convinced more and more day by day that fine writing is next to fine doing the top thing in the world; the Paradise Lost becomes a greater wonder—

TO GEORGE FELTON MATHEW

Sweet are the pleasures that to verse belong,
And doubly sweet a brotherhood in song;
Nor can remembrance, Mathew! bring to view
A fate more pleasing, a delight more true
Than that in which the brother Poets joy'd,
Who with combined powers, their wit employ'd
To raise a trophy to the drama's muses.
The thought of this great partnership diffuses
Over the genius-loving heart, a feeling
Of all that's high, and great, and good, and healing.   10

Too partial friend! fain would I follow thee
Past each horizon of fine poesy;
Fain would I echo back each pleasant note
As o'er Sicilian seas, clear anthems float
'Mong the light skimming gondolas far parted,
Just when the sun his farewell beam has darted:
But 'tis impossible; far different cares
Beckon me sternly from soft 'Lydian airs,'
And hold my faculties so long in thrall,
That I am oft in doubt whether at all   20
I shall again see Phœbus in the morning:
Or flush'd Aurora in the roseate dawning!
Or a white Naiad in a rippling stream;
Or a rapt seraph in a moonlight beam;
Or again witness what with thee I've seen,
The dew by fairy feet swept from the green,
After a night of some quaint jubilee
Which every elf and fay had come to see:
When bright processions took their airy march
Beneath the curved moon's triumphal arch.   30
But might I now each passing moment give
To the coy muse, with me she would not live
In this dark city, nor would condescend
'Mid contradictions her delights to lend.
Should e'er the fine-eyed maid to me be kind,
Ah! surely it must be whene'er I find
Some flowery spot, sequester'd, wild, romantic,
That often must have seen a poet frantic;
Where oaks, that erst the Druid knew, are growing,
And flowers, the glory of one day, are blowing;   40
Where the dark-leav'd laburnum's drooping clusters
Reflect athwart the stream their yellow lustres,
And intertwined the cassia's arms unite,
With its own drooping buds, but very white.
Where on one side are covert branches hung,
'Mong which the nightingales have always sung
In leafy quiet: where to pry, aloof,
Atween the pillars of the sylvan roof,
Would be to find where violet beds were nestling,
And where the bee with cowslip bells was wrestling.   50

There must be too a ruin dark, and gloomy,
To say 'joy not too much in all that's bloomy.'

Yet this is vain—O Mathew lend thy aid
To find a place where I may greet the maid—
Where we may soft humanity put on,
And sit, and rhyme and think on Chatterton;
And that warm-hearted Shakspeare sent to meet him
Four laurell'd spirits, heaven-ward to intreat him.
With reverence would we speak of all the sages
Who have left streaks of light athwart their ages: 60
And thou shouldst moralize on Milton's blindness,
And mourn the fearful dearth of human kindness
To those who strove with the bright golden wing
Of genius, to flap away each sting
Thrown by the pitiless world. We next could tell
Of those who in the cause of freedom fell;
Of our own Alfred, of Helvetian Tell;
Of him whose name to ev'ry heart's a solace,
High-minded and unbending William Wallace.
While to the rugged north our musing turns   70
We well might drop a tear for him, and Burns.
Felton! without incitements such as these,
How vain for me the niggard Muse to tease:
For thee, she will thy every dwelling grace,
And make 'a sun-shine in a shady place:'
For thou wast once a flowret blooming wild,
Close to the source, bright, pure, and undefil'd,
Whence gush the streams of song: in happy hour
Came chaste Diana from her shady bower,
Just as the sun was from the east uprising;   80
And, as for him some gift she was devising,
Beheld thee, pluck'd thee, cast thee in the stream
To meet her glorious brother's greeting beam.
I marvel much that thou hast never told
How, from a flower, into a fish of gold
Apollo chang'd thee; how thou next didst seem
A black-eyed swan upon the widening stream;
And when thou first didst in that mirror trace
The placid features of a human face:

That thou hast never told thy travels strange, 90
And all the wonders of the mazy range
O'er pebbly crystal, and o'er golden sands;
Kissing thy daily food from Naiad's pearly hands.

November 1815

ON SEEING THE ELGIN MARBLES

My spirit is too weak—mortality
   Weighs heavily on me like unwilling sleep,
   And each imagin'd pinnacle and steep
Of godlike hardship, tells me I must die
Like a sick Eagle looking at the sky.
   Yet 'tis a gentle luxury to weep
   That I have not the cloudy winds to keep,
Fresh for the opening of the morning's eye.
Such dim-conceived glories of the brain
   Bring round the heart an undescribable feud; 10
So do these wonders a most dizzy pain,
   That mingles Grecian grandeur with the rude
Wasting of old Time—with a billowy main—
   A sun—a shadow of a magnitude.

March 1817

ON SITTING DOWN TO READ KING LEAR ONCE AGAIN

O golden tongued Romance, with serene lute!
   Fair plumed Syren, Queen of far-away!
   Leave melodizing on this wintry day,
Shut up thine olden pages, and be mute:
Adieu! for, once again, the fierce dispute
   Betwixt damnation and impassion'd clay
   Must I burn through; once more humbly assay
The bitter-sweet of this Shakespearian fruit:
Chief Poet! and ye clouds of Albion,
   Begetters of our deep eternal theme! 10

When through the old oak Forest I am gone,
     Let me not wander in a barren dream,
But, when I am consumed in the fire,
Give me new Phœnix wings to fly at my desire.

January 22, 1818

ISABELLA;
or,
THE POT OF BASIL

A Story from Boccaccio

I

Fair Isabel, poor simple Isabel!
     Lorenzo, a young palmer in Love's eye!
They could not in the self-same mansion dwell
     Without some stir of heart, some malady;
They could not sit at meals but feel how well
     It soothed each to be the other by;
They could not, sure, beneath the same roof sleep
But to each other dream, and nightly weep.

II

With every morn their love grew tenderer,
     With every eve deeper and tenderer still;   10
He might not in house, field, or garden stir,
     But her full shape would all his seeing fill;
And his continual voice was pleasanter
     To her, than noise of trees or hidden rill;
Her lute-string gave an echo of his name,
She spoilt her half-done broidery with the same.

III

He knew whose gentle hand was at the latch
     Before the door had given her to his eyes;
And from her chamber-window he would catch
     Her beauty farther than the falcon spies;   20
And constant as her vespers would he watch,

Because her face was turn'd to the same skies;
And with sick longing all the night outwear,
To hear her morning-step upon the stair.

IV

A whole long month of May in this sad plight
    Made their cheeks paler by the break of June:
'To-morrow will I bow to my delight,
    'To-morrow will I ask my lady's boon.'—
'O may I never see another night,
    'Lorenzo, if thy lips breathe not love's tune.'—   30
So spake they to their pillows; but, alas,
Honeyless days and days did he let pass;

V

Until sweet Isabella's untouch'd cheek
    Fell sick within the rose's just domain,
Fell thin as a young mother's, who doth seek
    By every lull to cool her infant's pain:
'How ill she is,' said he, 'I may not speak,
    'And yet I will, and tell my love all plain:
'If looks speak love-laws, I will drink her tears,
'And at the least 'twill startle off her cares.'   40

VI

So said he one fair morning, and all day
    His heart beat awfully against his side;
And to his heart he inwardly did pray
    For power to speak; but still the ruddy tide
Stifled his voice, and puls'd resolve away—
    Fever'd his high conceit of such a bride,
Yet brought him to the meekness of a child:
Alas! when passion is both meek and wild!

VII

So once more he had wak'd and anguished
    A dreary night of love and misery,   50
If Isabel's quick eye had not been wed
    To every symbol on his forehead high;
She saw it waxing very pale and dead,

And straight all flush'd; so, lisped tenderly,
'Lorenzo!'—here she ceas'd her timid quest,
But in her tone and look he read the rest.

VIII
'O Isabella, I can half perceive
    'That I may speak my grief into thine ear;
'If thou didst ever anything believe,
    'Believe how I love thee, believe how near   60
'My soul is to its doom: I would not grieve
    'Thy hand by unwelcome pressing, would not fear
'Thine eyes by gazing; but I cannot live
'Another night, and not my passion shrive.

IX
'Love! thou art leading me from wintry cold,
    'Lady! thou leadest me to summer clime,
'And I must taste the blossoms that unfold
    'In its ripe warmth this gracious morning time.'
So said, his erewhile timid lips grew bold,
    And poesied with hers in dewy rhyme: 70
Great bliss was with them, and great happiness
Grew, like a lusty flower in June's caress.

X
Parting they seem'd to tread upon the air,
    Twin roses by the zephyr blown apart
Only to meet again more close, and share
    The inward fragrance of each other's heart.
She, to her chamber gone, a ditty fair
    Sang, of delicious love and honey'd dart;
He with light steps went up a western hill,
And bade the sun farewell, and joy'd his fill.   80

XI
All close they met again, before the dusk
    Had taken from the stars its pleasant veil,
All close they met, all eves, before the dusk
    Had taken from the stars its pleasant veil,
Close in a bower of hyacinth and musk,

Unknown of any, free from whispering tale.
Ah! better had it been for ever so,
Than idle ears should pleasure in their woe.

XII

Were they unhappy then?—It cannot be—
    Too many tears for lovers have been shed,   90
Too many sighs give we to them in fee,
    Too much of pity after they are dead,
Too many doleful stories do we see,
    Whose matter in bright gold were best be read;
Except in such a page where Theseus' spouse
Over the pathless waves towards him bows.

XIII

But, for the general award of love,
    The little sweet doth kill much bitterness;
Though Dido silent is in under-grove,
    And Isabella's was a great distress,   100
Though young Lorenzo in warm Indian clove
    Was not embalm'd, this truth is not the less—
Even bees, the little almsmen of spring-bowers,
Know there is richest juice in poison-flowers.

XIV

With her two brothers this fair lady dwelt,
    Enriched from ancestral merchandize,
And for them many a weary hand did swelt
    In torched mines and noisy factories,
And many once proud-quiver'd loins did melt
    In blood from stinging whip;—with hollow eyes   110
Many all day in dazzling river stood,
To take the rich-ored driftings of the flood.

XV

For them the Ceylon diver held his breath,
    And went all naked to the hungry shark;
For them his ears gush'd blood; for them in death
    The seal on the cold ice with piteous bark
Lay full of darts; for them alone did seethe

A thousand men in troubles wide and dark:
Half-ignorant, they turn'd an easy wheel,
That set sharp racks at work, to pinch and peel.   120

XVI

Why were they proud? Because their marble founts
    Gush'd with more pride than do a wretch's tears?—
Why were they proud? Because fair orange-mounts
    Were of more soft ascent than lazar stairs?—
Why were they proud? Because red-lin'd accounts
    Were richer than the songs of Grecian years?—
Why were they proud? again we ask aloud,
Why in the name of Glory were they proud?

XVII

Yet were these Florentines as self-retired
    In hungry pride and gainful cowardice,   130
As two close Hebrews in that land inspired,
    Paled in and vineyarded from beggar-spies;
The hawks of ship-mast forests—the untired
    And pannier'd mules for ducats and old lies—
Quick cat's-paws on the generous stray-away,—
Great wits in Spanish, Tuscan, and Malay.

XVIII

How was it these same ledger-men could spy
    Fair Isabella in her downy nest?
How could they find out in Lorenzo's eye
    A straying from his toil? Hot Egypt's pest   140
Into their vision covetous and sly!
    How could these money-bags see east and west?—
Yet so they did—and every dealer fair
Must see behind, as doth the hunted hare.

XIX

O eloquent and famed Boccaccio!
    Of thee we now should ask forgiving boon,
And of thy spicy myrtles as they blow,
    And of thy roses amorous of the moon,
And of thy lillies, that do paler grow

Now they can no more hear thy ghittern's tune,   150
For venturing syllables that ill beseem
The quiet glooms of such a piteous theme.

XX

Grant thou a pardon here, and then the tale
   Shall move on soberly, as it is meet;
There is no other crime, no mad assail
   To make old prose in modern rhyme more sweet:
But it is done—succeed the verse or fail—
   To honour thee, and thy gone spirit greet;
To stead thee as a verse in English tongue,
An echo of thee in the north-wind sung.   160

XXI

These brethren having found by many signs
   What love Lorenzo for their sister had,
And how she lov'd him too, each unconfines
   His bitter thoughts to other, well nigh mad
That he, the servant of their trade designs,
   Should in their sister's love be blithe and glad,
When 'twas their plan to coax her by degrees
To some high noble and his olive-trees.

XXII

And many a jealous conference had they,
   And many times they bit their lips alone,   170
Before they fix'd upon a surest way
   To make the youngster for his crime atone;
And at the last, these men of cruel clay
   Cut Mercy with a sharp knife to the bone;
For they resolved in some forest dim
To kill Lorenzo, and there bury him.

XXIII

So on a pleasant morning, as he leant
   Into the sun-rise, o'er the balustrade
Of the garden-terrace, towards him they bent
   Their footing through the dews; and to him said,   180
'You seem there in the quiet of content,

'Lorenzo, and we are most loth to invade
'Calm speculation; but if you are wise,
    'Bestride your steed while cold is in the skies.

XXIV

'To-day we purpose, aye, this hour we mount
    'To spur three leagues towards the Apennine;
'Come down, we pray thee, ere the hot sun count
    'His dewy rosary on the eglantine.'
Lorenzo, courteously as he was wont,
    Bow'd a fair greeting to these serpents' whine;   190
And went in haste, to get in readiness,
With belt, and spur, and bracing huntsman's dress.

XXV

And as he to the court-yard pass'd along,
    Each third step did he pause, and listen'd oft
If he could hear his lady's matin-song,
    Or the light whisper of her footstep soft;
And as he thus over his passion hung,
    He heard a laugh full musical aloft;
When, looking up, he saw her features bright
Smile through an in-door lattice, all delight.   200

XXVI

'Love, Isabel!' said he, 'I was in pain
    'Lest I should miss to bid thee a good morrow:
'Ah! what if I should lose thee, when so fain
    'I am to stifle all the heavy sorrow
'Of a poor three hours' absence? but we'll gain
    'Out of the amorous dark what day doth borrow.
'Good bye! I'll soon be back.'—'Good bye!' said she:—
And as he went she chanted merrily.

XXVII

So the two brothers and their murder'd man
    Rode past fair Florence, to where Arno's stream   210
Gurgles through straiten'd banks, and still doth fan
    Itself with dancing bulrush, and the bream
Keeps head against the freshets. Sick and wan

The brothers' faces in the ford did seem,
Lorenzo's flush with love.—They pass'd the water
Into a forest quiet for the slaughter.

XXVIII

There was Lorenzo slain and buried in,
   There in that forest did his great love cease;
Ah! when a soul doth thus its freedom win,
   It aches in loneliness—is ill at peace   220
As the break-covert blood-hounds of such sin:
   They dipp'd their swords in the water, and did tease
Their horses homeward, with convulsed spur,
Each richer by his being a murderer.

XXIX

They told their sister how, with sudden speed,
   Lorenzo had ta'en ship for foreign lands,
Because of some great urgency and need
   In their affairs, requiring trusty hands.
Poor Girl! put on thy stifling widow's weed,
   And 'scape at once from Hope's accursed bands;   230
To-day thou wilt not see him, nor to-morrow,
And the next day will be a day of sorrow.

XXX

She weeps alone for pleasures not to be;
   Sorely she wept until the night came on,
And then, instead of love, O misery!
   She brooded o'er the luxury alone:
His image in the dusk she seem'd to see,
   And to the silence made a gentle moan,
Spreading her perfect arms upon the air,
And on her couch low murmuring 'Where? O where?'   240

XXXI

But Selfishness, Love's cousin, held not long
   Its fiery vigil in her single breast;
She fretted for the golden hour, and hung
   Upon the time with feverish unrest—
Not long—for soon into her heart a throng

Of higher occupants, a richer zest,
Came tragic; passion not to be subdued,
And sorrow for her love in travels rude.

XXXII

In the mid days of autumn, on their eves
    The breath of Winter comes from far away,   250
And the sick west continually bereaves
    Of some gold tinge, and plays a roundelay
Of death among the bushes and the leaves,
    To make all bare before he dares to stray
From his north cavern. So sweet Isabel
By gradual decay from beauty fell,

XXXIII

Because Lorenzo came not. Oftentimes
    She ask'd her brothers, with an eye all pale,
Striving to be itself, what dungeon climes
    Could keep him off so long? They spake a tale   260
Time after time, to quiet her. Their crimes
    Came on them, like a smoke from Hinnom's vale;
And every night in dreams they groan'd aloud,
To see their sister in her snowy shroud.

XXXIV

And she had died in drowsy ignorance,
    But for a thing more deadly dark than all;
It came like a fierce potion, drunk by chance,
    Which saves a sick man from the feather'd pall
For some few gasping moments; like a lance,
    Waking an Indian from his cloudy hall   270
With cruel pierce, and bringing him again
Sense of the gnawing fire at heart and brain.

XXXV

It was a vision.—In the drowsy gloom,
    The dull of midnight, at her couch's foot
Lorenzo stood, and wept: the forest tomb
    Had marr'd his glossy hair which once could shoot
Lustre into the sun, and put cold doom

Upon his lips, and taken the soft lute
From his lorn voice, and past his loamed ears
Had made a miry channel for his tears.   280

XXXVI

Strange sound it was, when the pale shadow spake;
    For there was striving, in its piteous tongue,
To speak as when on earth it was awake,
    And Isabella on its music hung:
Languor there was in it, and tremulous shake,
    As in a palsied Druid's harp unstrung;
And through it moan'd a ghostly under-song,
Like hoarse night-gusts sepulchral briars among.

XXXVII

Its eyes, though wild, were still all dewy bright
    With love, and kept all phantom fear aloof   290
From the poor girl by magic of their light,
    The while it did unthread the horrid woof
Of the late darken'd time,—the murderous spite
    Of pride and avarice,—the dark pine roof
In the forest,—and the sodden turfed dell,
Where, without any word, from stabs he fell.

XXXVIII

Saying moreover, 'Isabel, my sweet!
    'Red whortle-berries droop above my head,
'And a large flint-stone weighs upon my feet;
    'Around me beeches and high chestnuts shed   300
'Their leaves and prickly nuts; a sheep-fold bleat
    'Comes from beyond the river to my bed:
'Go, shed one tear upon my heather-bloom,
'And it shall comfort me within the tomb.

XXXIX

'I am a shadow now, alas! alas!
    'Upon the skirts of human-nature dwelling
'Alone: I chant alone the holy mass,
    'While little sounds of life are round me knelling,
'And glossy bees at noon do fieldward pass,

'And many a chapel bell the hour is telling,   310
'Paining me through: those sounds grow strange to me,
'And thou art distant in Humanity.

XL

'I know what was, I feel full well what is,
    'And I should rage, if spirits could go mad;
'Though I forget the taste of earthly bliss,
    'That paleness warms my grave, as though I had
'A Seraph chosen from the bright abyss
    'To be my spouse: thy paleness makes me glad;
'Thy beauty grows upon me, and I feel
'A greater love through all my essence steal.'   320

XLI

The Spirit mourn'd 'Adieu!'—dissolv'd and left
    The atom darkness in a slow turmoil;
As when of healthful midnight sleep bereft,
    Thinking on rugged hours and fruitless toil,
We put our eyes into a pillowy cleft,
    And see the spangly gloom froth up and boil:
It made sad Isabella's eyelids ache,
And in the dawn she started up awake;

XLII

'Ha! ha!' said she, 'I knew not this hard life,
    'I thought the worst was simple misery;   330
'I thought some Fate with pleasure or with strife
    'Portion'd us—happy days, or else to die;
'But there is crime—a brother's bloody knife!
    'Sweet Spirit, thou hast school'd my infancy:
'I'll visit thee for this, and kiss thine eyes,
'And greet thee morn and even in the skies.'

XLIII

When the full morning came, she had devised
    How she might secret to the forest hie;
How she might find the clay, so dearly prized,
    And sing to it one latest lullaby;   340
How her short absence might be unsurmised,

While she the inmost of the dream would try.
Resolv'd, she took with her an aged nurse,
And went into that dismal forest-hearse.

XLIV

See, as they creep along the river side,
   How she doth whisper to that aged Dame,
And, after looking round the champaign wide,
   Shows her a knife.—'What feverous hectic flame
'Burns in thee, child?—What good can thee betide,
   'That thou should'st smile again?'—The evening came,   350
And they had found Lorenzo's earthy bed;
The flint was there, the berries at his head.

XLV

Who hath not loiter'd in a green church-yard,
   And let his spirit, like a demon-mole,
Work through the clayey soil and gravel hard,
   To see scull, coffin'd bones, and funeral stole;
Pitying each form that hungry Death hath marr'd
   And filling it once more with human soul?
Ah! this is holiday to what was felt
When Isabella by Lorenzo knelt.   360

XLVI

She gaz'd into the fresh-thrown mould, as though
   One glance did fully all its secrets tell;
Clearly she saw, as other eyes would know
   Pale limbs at bottom of a crystal well;
Upon the murderous spot she seem'd to grow,
   Like to a native lilly of the dell:
Then with her knife, all sudden, she began
To dig more fervently than misers can.

XLVII

Soon she turn'd up a soiled glove, whereon
   Her silk had play'd in purple phantasies,   370
She kiss'd it with a lip more chill than stone,
   And put it in her bosom, where it dries
And freezes utterly unto the bone

Those dainties made to still an infant's cries:
Then 'gan she work again; nor stay'd her care,
But to throw back at times her veiling hair.

XLVIII

That old nurse stood beside her wondering,
  Until her heart felt pity to the core
At sight of such a dismal labouring,
  And so she kneeled, with her locks all hoar,   380
And put her lean hands to the horrid thing:
  Three hours they labour'd at this travail sore;
At last they felt the kernel of the grave,
And Isabella did not stamp and rave.

XLIX

Ah! wherefore all this wormy circumstance?
  Why linger at the yawning tomb so long?
O for the gentleness of old Romance,
  The simple plaining of a minstrel's song!
Fair reader, at the old tale take a glance,
  For here, in truth, it doth not well belong   390
To speak:—O turn thee to the very tale,
And taste the music of that vision pale.

L

With duller steel than the Perséan sword
  They cut away no formless monster's head,
But one, whose gentleness did well accord
  With death, as life. The ancient harps have said,
Love never dies, but lives, immortal Lord:
  If Love impersonate was ever dead,
Pale Isabella kiss'd it, and low moan'd.
'Twas love; cold,—dead indeed, but not dethroned.   400

LI

In anxious secrecy they took it home,
  And then the prize was all for Isabel:
She calm'd its wild hair with a golden comb,
  And all around each eye's sepulchral cell
Pointed each fringed lash; the smeared loam

With tears, as chilly as a dripping well,
She drench'd away:—and still she comb'd, and kept
Sighing all day—and still she kiss'd, and wept.

LII

Then in a silken scarf,—sweet with the dews
   Of precious flowers pluck'd in Araby,   410
And divine liquids come with odorous ooze
   Through the cold serpent-pipe refreshfully,—
She wrapp'd it up; and for its tomb did choose
   A garden-pot, wherein she laid it by,
And cover'd it with mould, and o'er it set
Sweet Basil, which her tears kept ever wet.

LIII

And she forgot the stars, the moon, and sun,
   And she forgot the blue above the trees,
And she forgot the dells where waters run,
   And she forgot the chilly autumn breeze;   420
She had no knowledge when the day was done,
   And the new morn she saw not: but in peace
Hung over her sweet Basil evermore,
And moisten'd it with tears unto the core.

LIV

And so she ever fed it with thin tears,
   Whence thick, and green, and beautiful it grew,
So that it smelt more balmy than its peers
   Of Basil-tufts in Florence; for it drew
Nurture besides, and life, from human fears,
   From the fast mouldering head there shut from view: 430
So that the jewel, safely casketed,
Came forth, and in perfumed leafits spread.

LV

O Melancholy, linger here awhile!
   O Music, Music, breathe despondingly!
O Echo, Echo, from some sombre isle,
   Unknown, Lethean, sigh to us—O sigh!
Spirits in grief, lift up your heads, and smile;

Lift up your heads, sweet Spirits, heavily,
And make a pale light in your cypress glooms,
Tinting with silver wan your marble tombs. 440

LVI
Moan hither, all ye syllables of woe,
   From the deep throat of sad Melpomene!
Through bronzed lyre in tragic order go,
   And touch the strings into a mystery;
Sound mournfully upon the winds and low;
   For simple Isabel is soon to be
Among the dead: She withers, like a palm
Cut by an Indian for its juicy balm.

LVII
O leave the palm to wither by itself;
   Let not quick Winter chill its dying hour!— 450
It may not be—those Baälites of pelf,
   Her brethren, noted the continual shower
From her dead eyes; and many a curious elf,
   Among her kindred, wonder'd that such dower
Of youth and beauty should be thrown aside
By one mark'd out to be a Noble's bride.

LVIII
And, furthermore, her brethren wonder'd much
   Why she sat drooping by the Basil green,
And why it flourish'd, as by magic touch;
   Greatly they wonder'd what the thing might mean: 460
They could not surely give belief, that such
   A very nothing would have power to wean
Her from her own fair youth, and pleasures gay,
And even remembrance of her love's delay.

LIX
Therefore they watch'd a time when they might sift
   This hidden whim; and long they watch'd in vain;
For seldom did she go to chapel-shrift,
   And seldom felt she any hunger-pain;

And when she left, she hurried back, as swift
   As bird on wing to breast its eggs again;   470
And, patient as a hen-bird, sat her there
Beside her Basil, weeping through her hair.

LX

Yet they contriv'd to steal the Basil-pot,
   And to examine it in secret place;
The thing was vile with green and livid spot,
   And yet they knew it was Lorenzo's face:
The guerdon of their murder they had got,
   And so left Florence in a moment's space,
Never to turn again.—Away they went,
With blood upon their heads, to banishment.   480

LXI

O Melancholy, turn thine eyes away!
   O Music, Music, breathe despondingly!
O Echo, Echo, on some other day,
   From isles Lethean, sigh to us—O sigh!
Spirits of grief, sing not your 'Well-a-way!'
   For Isabel, sweet Isabel, will die;
Will die a death too lone and incomplete,
Now they have ta'en away her Basil sweet.

LXII

Piteous she look'd on dead and senseless things,
   Asking for her lost Basil amorously;   490
And with melodious chuckle in the strings
   Of her lorn voice, she oftentimes would cry
After the Pilgrim in his wanderings,
   To ask him where her Basil was; and why
'Twas hid from her: 'For cruel 'tis,' said she,
'To steal my Basil-pot away from me.'

LXIII

And so she pined, and so she died forlorn,
   Imploring for her Basil to the last.
No heart was there in Florence but did mourn
   In pity of her love, so overcast.   500

And a sad ditty of this story born
　　From mouth to mouth through all the country pass'd:
Still is the burthen sung—'O cruelty,
'To steal my Basil-pot away from me.'

April 1818

ON VISITING THE TOMB OF BURNS

The town, the churchyard, and the setting sun,
　　The clouds, the trees, the rounded hills all seem,
　　Though beautiful, cold—strange—as in a dream,
I dreamed long ago, now new begun.
The short-liv'd, paly Summer is but won
　　From Winter's ague, for one hour's gleam;
　　Though sapphire-warm, their stars do never beam:
All is cold Beauty; pain is never done:
For who has mind to relish, Minos-wise,
　　The Real of Beauty, free from that dead hue 　　　　　　10
　　　　Sickly imagination and sick pride
　　Cast wan upon it! Burns! with honour due
　　　　I oft have honour'd thee. Great shadow, hide
Thy face; I sin against thy native skies.

July 1818

THE FALL OF HYPERION

A Dream

Canto I

Fanatics have their dreams, wherewith they weave
A paradise for a sect; the savage too
From forth the loftiest fashion of his sleep
Guesses at Heaven; pity these have not
Trac'd upon vellum or wild Indian leaf
The shadows of melodious utterance.
But bare of laurel they live, dream, and die;
For Poesy alone can tell her dreams,

With the fine spell of words alone can save
Imagination from the sable charm
And dumb enchantment. Who alive can say,
'Thou art no Poet—may'st not tell thy dreams?'
Since every man whose soul is not a clod
Hath visions, and would speak, if he had loved,
And been well nurtured in his mother tongue.
Whether the dream now purpos'd to rehearse
Be poet's or fanatic's will be known
When this warm scribe my hand is in the grave.

    Methought I stood where trees of every clime,
Palm, myrtle, oak, and sycamore, and beech,
With plantain, and spice-blossoms, made a screen;
In neighbourhood of fountains (by the noise
Soft-showering in my ears), and, (by the touch
Of scent,) not far from roses. Turning round
I saw an arbour with a drooping roof
Of trellis vines, and bells, and larger blooms,
Like floral censers, swinging light in air;
Before its wreathed doorway, on a mound
Of moss, was spread a feast of summer fruits,
Which, nearer seen, seem'd refuse of a meal
By angel tasted or our Mother Eve;
For empty shells were scattered on the grass,
And grape-stalks but half bare, and remnants more,
Sweet-smelling, whose pure kinds I could not know.
Still was more plenty than the fabled horn
Thrice emptied could pour forth, at banqueting
For Proserpine return'd to her own fields,
Where the white heifers low. And appetite
More yearning than on Earth I ever felt
Growing within, I ate deliciously;
And, after not long, thirsted, for thereby
Stood a cool vessel of transparent juice
Sipp'd by the wander'd bee, the which I took,
And, pledging all the mortals of the world,
And all the dead whose names are in our lips,
Drank. That full draught is parent of my theme.
No Asian poppy nor elixir fine

Of the soon-fading jealous Caliphat;
No poison gender'd in close monkish cell,
To thin the scarlet conclave of old men,   50
Could so have rapt unwilling life away.
Among the fragrant husks and berries crush'd,
Upon the grass I struggled hard against
The domineering potion; but in vain:
The cloudy swoon came on, and down I sank,
Like a Silenus on an antique vase.
How long I slumber'd 'tis a chance to guess.
When sense of life return'd, I started up
As if with wings; but the fair trees were gone,
The mossy mound and arbour were no more: 60
I look'd around upon the carved sides
Of an old sanctuary with roof august,
Builded so high, it seem'd that filmed clouds
Might spread beneath, as o'er the stars of heaven;
So old the place was, I remember'd none
The like upon the Earth: what I had seen
Of grey cathedrals, buttress'd walls, rent towers,
The superannuations of sunk realms,
Or Nature's rocks toil'd hard in waves and winds,
Seem'd but the faulture of decrepit things   70
To that eternal domed Monument.—
Upon the marble at my feet there lay
Store of strange vessels and large draperies,
Which needs had been of dyed asbestos wove,
Or in that place the moth could not corrupt,
So white the linen, so, in some, distinct
Ran imageries from a sombre loom.
All in a mingled heap confus'd there lay
Robes, golden tongs, censer and chafing-dish,
Girdles, and chains, and holy jewelries.   80

    Turning from these with awe, once more I rais'd
My eyes to fathom the space every way;
The embossed roof, the silent massy range
Of columns north and south, ending in mist
Of nothing, then to eastward, where black gates
Were shut against the sunrise evermore.—

Then to the west I look'd, and saw far off
An image, huge of feature as a cloud,
At level of whose feet an altar slept,
To be approach'd on either side by steps,   90
And marble balustrade, and patient travail
To count with toil the innumerable degrees.
Towards the altar sober-paced I went,
Repressing haste, as too unholy there;
And, coming nearer, saw beside the shrine
One minist'ring; and there arose a flame.—
When in mid-May the sickening East wind
Shifts sudden to the south, the small warm rain
Melts out the frozen incense from all flowers,
And fills the air with so much pleasant health   100
That even the dying man forgets his shroud;—
Even so that lofty sacrificial fire,
Sending forth Maian incense, spread around
Forgetfulness of everything but bliss,
And clouded all the altar with soft smoke;
From whose white fragrant curtains thus I heard
Language pronounc'd: 'If thou canst not ascend
'These steps, die on that marble where thou art.
'Thy flesh, near cousin to the common dust,
'Will parch for lack of nutriment—thy bones   110
'Will wither in few years, and vanish so
'That not the quickest eye could find a grain
'Of what thou now art on that pavement cold.
'The sands of thy short life are spent this hour,
'And no hand in the universe can turn
'Thy hourglass, if these gummed leaves be burnt
'Ere thou canst mount up these immortal steps.'
I heard, I look'd: two senses both at once,
So fine, so subtle, felt the tyranny
Of that fierce threat and the hard task proposed.   120
Prodigious seem'd the toil; the leaves were yet
Burning—when suddenly a palsied chill
Struck from the paved level up my limbs,
And was ascending quick to put cold grasp
Upon those streams that pulse beside the throat:
I shriek'd, and the sharp anguish of my shriek

Stung my own ears—I strove hard to escape
The numbness; strove to gain the lowest step.
Slow, heavy, deadly was my pace: the cold
Grew stifling, suffocating, at the heart;   130
And when I clasp'd my hands I felt them not.
One minute before death, my iced foot touch'd
The lowest stair; and as it touch'd, life seem'd
To pour in at the toes: I mounted up,
As once fair angels on a ladder flew
From the green turf to Heaven—'Holy Power,'
Cried I, approaching near the horned shrine,
'What am I that should so be saved from death?
'What am I that another death come not
'To choke my utterance sacrilegious, here?'   140
Then said the veiled shadow—'Thou hast felt
'What 'tis to die and live again before
'Thy fated hour, that thou hadst power to do so
'Is thy own safety; thou hast dated on
'Thy doom.'—'High Prophetess,' said I, 'purge off,
'Benign, if so it please thee, my mind's film.'—
'None can usurp this height,' return'd that shade,
'But those to whom the miseries of the world
'Are misery, and will not let them rest.
'All else who find a haven in the world,   150
'Where they may thoughtless sleep away their days,
'If by a chance into this fane they come,
'Rot on the pavement where thou rottedst half.'—
'Are there not thousands in the world,' said I,
Encourag'd by the sooth voice of the shade,
'Who love their fellows even to the death,
'Who feel the giant agony of the world,
'And more, like slaves to poor humanity,
'Labour for mortal good? I sure should see
'Other men here; but I am here alone.'   160
'Those whom thou spak'st of are no vision'ries,'
Rejoin'd that voice—'They are no dreamers weak,
'They seek no wonder but the human face;
'No music but a happy-noted voice—
'They come not here, they have no thought to come—
'And thou art here, for thou art less than they—

'What benefit canst thou, or all thy tribe,
'To the great world? Thou art a dreaming thing,
'A fever of thyself—think of the Earth;
'What bliss even in hope is there for thee?   170
'What haven? every creature hath its home;
'Every sole man hath days of joy and pain,
'Whether his labours be sublime or low—
'The pain alone; the joy alone; distinct:
'Only the dreamer venoms all his days,
'Bearing more woe than all his sins deserve.
'Therefore, that happiness be somewhat shar'd,
'Such things as thou art are admitted oft
'Into like gardens thou didst pass erewhile,
'And suffer'd in these temples: for that cause   180
'Thou standest safe beneath this statue's knees.'
'That I am favour'd for unworthiness,
'By such propitious parley medicin'd
'In sickness not ignoble, I rejoice,
'Aye, and could weep for love of such award.'
So answer'd I, continuing, 'If it please,
'Majestic shadow, tell me: sure not all
'Those melodies sung into the World's ear
'Are useless: sure a poet is a sage;
'A humanist, physician to all men.   190
'That I am none I feel, as vultures feel
'They are no birds when eagles are abroad.
'What am I then: Thou spakest of my tribe:
'What tribe?' The tall shade veil'd in drooping white
Then spake, so much more earnest, that the breath
Moved the thin linen folds that drooping hung
About a golden censer from the hand
Pendent—'Art thou not of the dreamer tribe?
'The poet and the dreamer are distinct,
'Diverse, sheer opposite, antipodes.   200
'The one pours out a balm upon the World,
'The other vexes it.' Then shouted I
Spite of myself, and with a Pythia's spleen,
'Apollo! faded! O far flown Apollo!
'Where is thy misty pestilence to creep
'Into the dwellings, through the door crannies

'Of all mock lyrists, large self worshipers
'And careless Hectorers in proud bad verse.
'Though I breathe death with them it will be life
'To see them sprawl before me into graves.   210
'Majestic shadow, tell me where I am,
'Whose altar this; for whom this incense curls;
'What image this whose face I cannot see,
'For the broad marble knees; and who thou art,
'Of accent feminine so courteous?'

     Then the tall shade, in drooping linens veil'd,
Spoke out, so much more earnest, that her breath
Stirr'd the thin folds of gauze that drooping hung
About a golden censer from her hand
Pendent; and by her voice I knew she shed   220
Long-treasured tears. 'This temple, sad and lone,
'Is all spar'd from the thunder of a war
'Foughten long since by giant hierarchy
'Against rebellion: this old image here,
'Whose carved features wrinkled as he fell,
'Is Saturn's; I Moneta, left supreme
'Sole Priestess of this desolation,'—
I had no words to answer, for my tongue,
Useless, could find about its roofed home
No syllable of a fit majesty   230
To make rejoinder to Moneta's mourn.
There was a silence, while the altar's blaze
Was fainting for sweet food: I look'd thereon,
And on the paved floor, where nigh were piled
Faggots of cinnamon, and many heaps
Of other crisped spice-wood—then again
I look'd upon the altar, and its horns
Whiten'd with ashes, and its lang'rous flame,
And then upon the offerings again;
And so by turns—till sad Moneta cried,   240
'The sacrifice is done, but not the less
'Will I be kind to thee for thy good will.
'My power, which to me is still a curse,
'Shall be to thee a wonder; for the scenes
'Still swooning vivid through my globed brain,

'With an electral changing misery,
'Thou shalt with those dull mortal eyes behold,
'Free from all pain, if wonder pain thee not.'
As near as an immortal's sphered words
Could to a mother's soften, were these last: 250
And yet I had a terror of her robes,
And chiefly of the veils, that from her brow
Hung pale, and curtain'd her in mysteries,
That made my heart too small to hold its blood.
This saw that Goddess, and with sacred hand
Parted the veils. Then saw I a wan face,
Not pin'd by human sorrows, but bright-blanch'd
By an immortal sickness which kills not;
It works a constant change, which happy death
Can put no end to; deathwards progressing   260
To no death was that visage; it had past
The lilly and the snow; and beyond these
I must not think now, though I saw that face—
But for her eyes I should have fled away.
They held me back, with a benignant light,
Soft mitigated by divinest lids
Half-closed, and visionless entire they seem'd
Of all external things;—they saw me not,
But in blank splendor, beam'd like the mild moon,
Who comforts those she sees not, who knows not   270
What eyes are upward cast. As I had found
A grain of gold upon a mountain side,
And twing'd with avarice strain'd out my eyes
To search its sullen entrails rich with ore,
So at the view of sad Moneta's brow,
I ach'd to see what things the hollow brain
Behind enwombed: what high tragedy
In the dark secret chambers of her skull
Was acting, that could give so dread a stress
To her cold lips, and fill with such a light   280
Her planetary eyes; and touch her voice
With such a sorrow—'Shade of Memory!'—
Cried I, with act adorant at her feet,
'By all the gloom hung round thy fallen house,
'By this last temple, by the golden age,

'By great Apollo, thy dear Foster Child,
'And by thyself, forlorn divinity,
'The pale Omega of a withered race,
'Let me behold, according as thou saidst,
'What in thy brain so ferments to and fro!'   290
No sooner had this conjuration pass'd
My devout lips, than side by side we stood
 (Like a stunt bramble by a solemn pine)
Deep in the shady sadness of a vale,
Far sunken from the healthy breath of morn,
Far from the fiery noon and eve's one star.
Onward I look'd beneath the gloomy boughs,
And saw, what first I thought an image huge,
Like to the image pedestal'd so high
In Saturn's temple. Then Moneta's voice   300
Came brief upon mine ear—'So Saturn sat
'When he had lost his Realms—' whereon there grew
A power within me of enormous ken
To see as a god sees, and take the depth
Of things as nimbly as the outward eye
Can size and shape pervade. The lofty theme
At those few words hung vast before my mind,
With half-unravel'd web. I set myself
Upon an eagle's watch, that I might see,
And seeing ne'er forget. No stir of life   310
Was in this shrouded vale, not so much air
As in the zoning of a summer's day
Robs not one light seed from the feather'd grass,
But where the dead leaf fell there did it rest:
A stream went voiceless by, still deaden'd more
By reason of the fallen divinity
Spreading more shade; the Naiad 'mid her reeds
Prest her cold finger closer to her lips.

    Along the margin-sand large footmarks went
No farther than to where old Saturn's feet   320
Had rested, and there slept, how long a sleep!
Degraded, cold, upon the sodden ground
His old right hand lay nerveless, listless, dead,

Unsceptred; and his realmless eyes were clos'd,
While his bow'd head seem'd listening to the Earth,
His ancient mother, for some comfort yet.

It seem'd no force could wake him from his place;
But there came one who, with a kindred hand
Touch'd his wide shoulders after bending low
With reverence, though to one who knew it not.   330
Then came the griev'd voice of Mnemosyne,
And griev'd I hearken'd. 'That divinity
'Whom thou saw'st step from yon forlornest wood,
'And with slow pace approach our fallen King,
'Is Thea, softest-natur'd of our Brood.'
I mark'd the Goddess in fair statuary
Surpassing wan Moneta by the head,
And in her sorrow nearer woman's tears.
There was a listening fear in her regard,
As if calamity had but begun;   340
As if the vanward clouds of evil days
Had spent their malice, and the sullen rear
Was with its stored thunder labouring up.
One hand she press'd upon that aching spot
Where beats the human heart, as if just there,
Though an immortal, she felt cruel pain;
The other upon Saturn's bended neck
She laid, and to the level of his hollow ear
Leaning with parted lips, some words she spake
In solemn tenor and deep organ tune;   350
Some mourning words, which in our feeble tongue
Would come in this-like accenting; how frail
To that large utterance of the early Gods!

'Saturn! look up—and for what, poor lost King?
'I have no comfort for thee; no not one;
'I cannot cry, wherefore thus sleepest thou?
'For Heaven is parted from thee, and the Earth
'Knows thee not, so afflicted, for a God;
'And Ocean too, with all its solemn noise,
'Has from thy sceptre pass'd, and all the air   360
'Is emptied of thine hoary majesty:

'Thy thunder, captious at the new command,
'Rumbles reluctant o'er our fallen house;
'And thy sharp lightning, in unpracticed hands,
'Scorches and burns our once serene domain.
'With such remorseless speed still come new woes,
'That unbelief has not a space to breathe.
'Saturn! sleep on:—Me thoughtless, why should I
'Thus violate thy slumbrous solitude?
'Why should I ope thy melancholy eyes?   370
'Saturn, sleep on, while at thy feet I weep.'

   As when upon a tranced summer-night
Forests, branch-charmed by the earnest stars,
Dream, and so dream all night without a noise,
Save from one gradual solitary gust,
Swelling upon the silence; dying off;
As if the ebbing air had but one wave;
So came these words, and went; the while in tears
She prest her fair large forehead to the earth,
Just where her fallen hair might spread in curls,   380
A soft and silken mat for Saturn's feet.
Long, long those two were postured motionless,
Like sculpture builded-up upon the grave
Of their own power. A long awful time
I look'd upon them: still they were the same;
The frozen God still bending to the earth,
And the sad Goddess weeping at his feet,
Moneta silent. Without stay or prop,
But my own weak mortality, I bore
The load of this eternal quietude,   390
The unchanging gloom, and the three fixed shapes
Ponderous upon my senses, a whole moon.
For by my burning brain I measured sure
Her silver seasons shedded on the night,
And ever day by day methought I grew
More gaunt and ghostly.—Oftentimes I pray'd
Intense, that Death would take me from the Vale
And all its burthens—gasping with despair
Of change, hour after hour I curs'd myself;
Until old Saturn rais'd his faded eyes,   400

And look'd around and saw his kingdom gone,
And all the gloom and sorrow of the place,
And that fair kneeling Goddess at his feet.
As the moist scent of flowers, and grass, and leaves,
Fills forest dells with a pervading air,
Known to the woodland nostril, so the words
Of Saturn fill'd the mossy glooms around,
Even to the hollows of time-eaten oaks,
And to the windings of the foxes' hole,
With sad low tones, while thus he spake, and sent   410
Strange musings to the solitary Pan.
'Moan, brethren, moan; for we are swallow'd up
'And buried from all Godlike exercise
'Of influence benign on planets pale,
'And peaceful sway above man's harvesting,
'And all those acts which Deity supreme
'Doth ease its heart of love in. Moan and wail,
'Moan, brethren, moan; for lo, the rebel spheres
'Spin round, the stars their ancient courses keep,
'Clouds still with shadowy moisture haunt the earth,   420
'Still suck their fill of light from sun and moon;
'Still buds the tree, and still the sea-shores murmur;
'There is no death in all the Universe,
'No smell of death—there shall be death—Moan, moan,
'Moan, Cybele, moan; for thy pernicious Babes
'Have changed a god into a shaking Palsy.
'Moan, brethren, moan, for I have no strength left,
'Weak as the reed—weak—feeble as my voice—
'O, O, the pain, the pain of feebleness.
'Moan, moan, for still I thaw—or give me help;   430
'Throw down those imps, and give me victory.
'Let me hear other groans, and trumpets blown
'Of triumph calm, and hymns of festival,
'From the gold peaks of Heaven's high-piled clouds;
'Voices of soft proclaim, and silver stir
'Of strings in hollow shells; and let there be
'Beautiful things made new for the surprise
'Of the sky-children.' So he feebly ceas'd,
With such a poor and sickly sounding pause,
Methought I heard some old man of the earth   440

Bewailing earthly loss; nor could my eyes
And ears act with that pleasant unison of sense
Which marries sweet sound with the grace of form,
And dolorous accent from a tragic harp
With large-limb'd visions.—More I scrutinized:
Still fix'd he sat beneath the sable trees,
Whose arms spread straggling in wild serpent forms,
With leaves all hush'd; his awful presence there
  (Now all was silent) gave a deadly lie
To what I erewhile heard—only his lips   450
Trembled amid the white curls of his beard.
They told the truth, though, round, the snowy locks
Hung nobly, as upon the face of heaven
A mid-day fleece of clouds. Thea arose,
And stretched her white arm through the hollow dark,
Pointing some whither: whereat he too rose
Like a vast giant, seen by men at sea
To grow pale from the waves at dull midnight.
They melted from my sight into the woods;
Ere I could turn, Moneta cried, 'These twain   460
'Are speeding to the families of grief,
'Where roof'd in by black rocks they waste, in pain
'And darkness, for no hope.'—And she spake on,
As ye may read who can unwearied pass
Onward from the Antichamber of this dream,
Where even at the open doors awhile
I must delay, and glean my memory
Of her high phrase:—perhaps no further dare.

End of Canto I

Canto II

'Mortal, that thou may'st understand aright,
'I humanize my sayings to thine ear,
'Making comparisons of earthly things;
'Or thou might'st better listen to the wind,
'Whose language is to thee a barren noise,
'Though it blows legend-laden thro' the trees.—
'In melancholy realms big tears are shed,

'More sorrow like to this, and such like woe,
'Too huge for mortal tongue, or pen of scribe.
'The Titans fierce, self hid or prison bound,   10
'Groan for the old allegiance once more,
'Listening in their doom for Saturn's voice.
'But one of our whole eagle-brood still keeps
'His sov'reignty, and rule, and majesty;
'Blazing Hyperion on his orbed fire
'Still sits, still snuffs the incense teeming up
'From Man to the Sun's God: yet unsecure.
'For as upon the earth dire prodigies
'Fright and perplex, so also shudders he:
'Nor at dog's howl or gloom-bird's Even screech,   20
'Or the familiar visitings of one
'Upon the first toll of his passing bell:
'But horrors, portioned to a giant nerve,
'Make great Hyperion ache. His palace bright,
'Bastion'd with pyramids of glowing gold,
'And touch'd with shade of bronzed obelisks,
'Glares a blood-red thro' all the thousand courts,
'Arches, and domes, and fiery galleries:
'And all its curtains of Aurorian clouds
'Flush angerly; when he would taste the wreaths   30
'Of incense breathed aloft from sacred hills,
'Instead of sweets, his ample palate takes
'Savour of poisonous brass and metals sick.
'Wherefore when harbour'd in the sleepy West,
'After the full completion of fair day,
'For rest divine upon exalted couch
'And slumber in the arms of melody,
'He paces through the pleasant hours of ease
'With strides colossal, on from hall to hall;
'While far within each aisle and deep recess   40
'His winged minions in close clusters stand
'Amaz'd, and full of fear; like anxious men,
'Who on a wide plain gather in sad troops,
'When earthquakes jar their battlements and towers.
'Even now, while Saturn, roused from icy trance,
'Goes, step for step, with Thea from yon woods,
'Hyperion, leaving twilight in the rear,

'Is sloping to the threshold of the West.—
'Thither we tend.'—Now in clear light I stood,
Reliev'd from the dusk vale. Mnemosyne   50
Was sitting on a square-edg'd polish'd stone,
That in its lucid depth reflected pure
Her priestess-garments.—My quick eyes ran on
From stately nave to nave, from vault to vault,
Through bow'rs of fragrant and enwreathed light
And diamond-paved lustrous long arcades.
Anon rush'd by the bright Hyperion;
His flaming robes stream'd out beyond his heels,
And gave a roar, as if of earthly fire,
That scared away the meek ethereal hours,   60
And made their dove-wings tremble. On he flared.

July–September 1819

IDENTITY

TO J. H. REYNOLDS
19 February 1818   Hampstead

Now it appears to me that almost any Man may like the
Spider spin from his own inwards his own airy Citadel—
the points of leaves and twigs on which the Spider begins
her work are few and she fills the Air with a beautiful cir-
cuiting: man should be content with as few points to tip
with the fine Webb of his Soul and weave a tapestry empyrean—full of Symbols for his spiritual eye, of softness
for his spiritual touch, of space for his wandering of distinctness for his Luxury—But the Minds of Mortals are so
different and bent on such diverse Journeys that it may at
first appear impossible for any common taste and fellowship to exist ⟨bettween⟩ between two or three under these
suppositions—It is however quite the contrary—Minds
would leave each other in contrary directions, traverse
each other in Numberless points, and all last greet each
other at the Journeys end—A old Man and a child would
talk together and the old Man be led on his Path, and the
child left thinking—Man should not dispute or assert but

whisper results to his neighbour, and thus by every germ of Spirit sucking the Sap from mould ethereal every human might become great. . . .

Keats addresses his sister-in-law Georgiana as *Sister*. The Fanny is his blood sister, not his beloved Fanny Brawne.

TO GEORGE AND GEORGIANA KEATS
14 October 1818   Hampstead

—If you were here my dear Sister I could not pronounce the words which I can write to you from a distance: I have a tenderness for you, and an admiration which I feel to be as great and more chaste than I can have for any woman in the world. You will mention Fanny—her character is not formed; her identity does not press upon me as yours does. I hope from the bottom of my heart that I may one day feel as much for her as I do for you—I know not how it is, but I have never made any acquaintance of my own—nearly all through your medium my dear Brother —through you I know not only a Sister but a glorious human being—

TO RICHARD WOODHOUSE
27 October 1818   Hampstead

It is a wretched thing to confess; but is a very fact that not one word I ever utter can be taken for granted as an opinion growing out of my identical nature—how can it, when I have no nature? When I am in a room with People if I ever am free from speculating on creations of my own brain, then not myself goes home to myself: but the identity of every one in the room begins to to press upon me that, I am in a very little time anhilated—not only among Men; it would be the same in a Nursery of children: I know not whether I make myself wholly understood. . . .

16 December 1818   Hampstead

—Suppose Brown or Haslam or any one whom I understand in the n{e}ther degree to what I do you, were in America, they would be so much the farth{er} from me in proportion as their identity was less impressed upon me. Now the reason why I do not feel at the present moment so far from you is that I rememb{er} your Ways and Manners and actions; I known you manner of thinking, you manner of feeling: I know what shape your joy or your sorrow w{ou}ld take, I know the manner of you walking, standing, sauntering, sitting down, laugh{ing,} punning, and evey action so truly that you seem near to me. You will rem{em}ber me in the same manner—

TO GEORGE AND GEORGIANA KEATS
17 March 1819   Hampstead

—An indolent day—fill'd with speculations even of an unpleasant colour—is bearable and even pleasant alone— when one's thoughts cannot find out any th[i]ng better in the world; and experience has told us that locomotion is no change: but to have nothing to do, and to be surrounded with unpleasant human identities; who press upon one just enough to prevent one getting into a lazy position; and not enough to interest or rouse one; is a capital punishment of a capital crime: for is not giving up, through goodnature, one's time to people who have no light and shade a capital crime?

The designation of this world as "a vale of tears" comes from the medieval hymn *Salve Regina*. By borrowing this phrase to describe his humanistic view of man's destiny in the following letter, Keats challenged the Christian position; at the same time his use of such language claims religious significance for his own statement. Salvation, for Keats, consists in psychic formation.

Vishnu is one of the two principal gods of Hinduism. Like Christ, Vishnu came to earth to save mankind. Oromanes seems to be a name from the popular literature of Keats's day and has no importance in world religion.

—The common cognomen of this world among the mis-guided and superstitious is a 'vale of tears' from which we are to be redeemed by a certain arbitrary interposition of God and taken to Heaven—What a little circumscribe[d] straightened notion! Call the world if you Please '"The vale of Soul-making" Then you will find out the use of the world (I am speaking now in the highest terms for hu-man nature admitting it to be immortal which I will here take for granted for the purpose of showing a thought which has struck me concerning it) I say *Soul making*' Soul as distinguished from an Intelligence—There may be intelligences or sparks of the divinity in millions—but they are not Souls ⟨the⟩ till they acquire identities, till each one is personally itself. I[n]telligences are atoms of perception—they know and they see and they are pure, in short they are God—how then are Souls to be made? How then are these sparks which are God to have identity given them—so as ever to possess a bliss peculiar to each ones individual existence? How, but by the medium of a world like this? This point I sincerely wish to consider because I think it a grander system of salvation than the chryst⟨e⟩ain religion—or rather it is a system of Spirit-creation—This is effected by three grand materials acting the one upon the other for a series of years—These three Materials are the *Intelligence*—the *human heart* (as dis-tinguished from intelligence or Mind) and the *World* or *Elemental space* suited for the proper action of *Mind and Heart* on each other for the purpose of forming the *Soul* or *Intelligence destined to possess the sense of Identity*. I can scarcely express what I but dimly perceive—and yet I think I perceive it—that you may judge the more clearly I will put it in the most homely form possible—I will call the *world* a School instituted for the purpose of teaching little children to read—I will call the *human heart* the *horn Book* used in that School—and I will call the *Child able to read, the Soul* made from that *school* and its *hornbook*. Do you not see how necessary a World of Pains and troubles is to school an Intelligence and make it a soul? A Place where the heart must feel and suffer in a thousand diverse ways! Not merely is the Heart a Hornbook, It is the Minds Bible, it is the Minds experience, it is the teat from which the Mind or intelligence sucks its identity—As various as the Lives of Men are—so various become their souls, and thus does God make individual beings, Souls, Identical Souls of the sparks of his own essence—This appears to me a faint sketch of a system of Salvation which does not affront our reason and humanity—I am convinced that many difficulties which christians labour under would vanish before it—There is one wh[i]ch even now Strikes me—the Salvation of Children—In them the Spark or intelligence returns to God without any identity—it having had no time to learn of, and be altered by, the heart—or seat of the human Passions—It is pretty generally suspected that the chr[i]stian scheme has been coppied from the ancient persian and greek Philosophers. Why may they not have made this simple thing even more simple for common apprehension by introducing Mediators and Personages in the same manner as in the hethen mythology abstractions are personified—Seriously I think it probable that this System of Soul-making—may have been the Parent of all the more palpable and personal Schemes of Redemption, among the Zoroastrians the Christians and the Hindoos. For as one part of the human species must have their carved Jupiter; so another part must have the palpable and named Mediatior and saviour, their Christ their Oromanes and their Vishnu—If what I have said should not be plain enough, as I fear it may not be, I will but you in the place where I began in this series of thoughts—I mean, I began by seeing how man was formed by circumstances —and what are circumstances?—but touchstones of his heart—? and what are touch stones?—but proovings of his hearrt?—and what are proovings of his heart but fortifiers or alterers of his nature? and what is his altered nature but his soul?—and what was his soul before it came into the world and had These provings and alterations and per-fectionings?—An intelligence(s)—without Identity—and how is this Identity to be made? Through the medium of the Heart? And how is the heart to become this Medium but in a world of Circumstances?—There now I think what with Poetry and Theology you may thank your Stars that my pen is not very long winded—

Thomas Hammond, mentioned in the next letter, was the surgeon to whom Keats was apprenticed, beginning in 1811.

TO GEORGE AND GEORGIANA KEATS
21 September 1819   Winchester

—You see I keep adding a sheet daily till I send the packet off—which I shall not do for a few days as I am inclined to write a good deal: for there can be nothing so remembrancing and enchaining as a good long letter be it composed of what it may—From the time you left me, our friends say I have altered completely—am not the same person—perhaps in this letter I am for in a letter one takes up one's existence from the time we last met—I dare say you have altered also—every man does—Our bodies every seven years are completely fresh-materiald—seven years ago it was not this hand that clench'd itself against Hammond—We are like the relict garments of a Saint: the same and not the same: for the careful Monks patch it and patch it: till there's not a thread of the original garment left, and still they show it for St Anthony's shirt. This is the reason why men who had been bosom friends, on being separated for any number of years, afterwards meet coldly, neither of them know-ing why—The fact is they are both altered—Men who live together have a silent ⟨p⟩ moulding and influencing power over each other—They interassimulate. 'T is an uneasy thought that in seven years the same hands cannot greet

each other again. All this may be obviated by a willful
and dramatic exercise of our Minds towards each other.

ODE TO PSYCHE

O Goddess! hear these tuneless numbers, wrung
   By sweet enforcement and remembrance dear,
And pardon that thy secrets should be sung
   Even into thine own soft-conched ear:
Surely I dreamt to-day, or did I see
   The winged Psyche with awaken'd eyes?
I wander'd in a forest thoughtlessly,
   And, on the sudden, fainting with surprise,
Saw two fair creatures, couched side by side
   In deepest grass, beneath the whisp'ring roof   10
   Of leaves and trembled blossoms, where there ran
      A brooklet, scarce espied.

'Mid hush'd, cool-rooted flowers, fragrant-eyed,
   Blue, silver-white, and budded Tyrian,
They lay calm-breathing on the bedded grass;
   Their arms embraced, and their pinions too;
   Their lips touch'd not, but had not bade adieu,
As if disjoined by soft-handed slumber,
And ready still past kisses to outnumber
   At tender eye-dawn of aurorean love: 20
      The winged boy I knew;
   But who wast thou, O happy, happy dove?
      His Psyche true!

O latest born and loveliest vision far
   Of all Olympus' faded hierarchy!
Fairer than Phœbe's sapphire-region'd star,
   Or Vesper, amorous glow-worm of the sky;
Fairer than these, though temple thou hast none,
      Nor altar heap'd with flowers;
Nor virgin-choir to make delicious moan   30
      Upon the midnight hours;
No voice, no lute, no pipe, no incense sweet
   From chain-swung censer teeming;

No shrine, no grove, no oracle, no heat
    Of pale-mouth'd prophet dreaming.

O brightest! though too late for antique vows,
    Too, too late for the fond believing lyre,
When holy were the haunted forest boughs,
    Holy the air, the water, and the fire;
Yet even in these days so far retir'd   40
    From happy pieties, thy lucent fans,
    Fluttering among the faint Olympians,
I see, and sing, by my own eyes inspir'd.
So let me be thy choir, and make a moan
        Upon the midnight hours;
Thy voice, thy lute, thy pipe, thy incense sweet
    From swinged censer teeming;
Thy shrine, thy grove, thy oracle, thy heat
    Of pale-mouth'd prophet dreaming.

Yes, I will be thy priest, and build a fane   50
    In some untrodden region of my mind,
Where branched thoughts, new grown with pleasant pain,
    Instead of pines shall murmur in the wind:
Far, far around shall those dark-cluster'd trees
    Fledge the wild-ridged mountains steep by steep;
And there by zephyrs, streams, and birds, and bees,
    The moss-lain Dryads shall be lull'd to sleep;
And in the midst of this wide quietness
A rosy sanctuary will I dress
With the wreath'd trellis of a working brain,   60
    With buds, and bells, and stars without a name,
With all the gardener Fancy e'er could feign,
    Who breeding flowers, will never breed the same:
And there shall be for thee all soft delight
    That shadowy thought can win,
A bright torch, and a casement ope at night,
    To let the warm Love in!

April 1819

2. THE POET AT HIS CRAFT

CALLING OR CAREER

The Poet and His Muse

TO J. H. REYNOLDS
18 April 1817   Carisbrooke, Isle of Wight

I find that I cannot exist without poetry—without eternal poetry—half the day will not do—the whole of it—I began with a little, but habit has made me a Leviathan—I had become all in a Tremble from not having written any thing of late—the Sonnet over leaf did me some good. I slept the better last night for it—this Morning, however, I am nearly as bad again—Just now I opened Spencer, and the first Lines I saw were these.—

> *"The noble Heart that harbors vertuous thought,*
> *And is with Child of glorious great intent,*
> *Can never rest, until it forth have brought*
> *Th' eternal Brood of Glory excellent—"*

Phaeton is a son of Hyperion who gives his name to the carriage, referred to in the next letter, that moves the sun. He is the mythological counterpart of the teen-age driver who wrecks his father's car.

10 May 1817   Margate

—I went to the Isle of Wight—thought so much about Poetry so long together that I could not get to sleep at night— . . . —I have asked myself so often why I should be a Poet more than other Men,—seeing how great a thing it is,—how great things are to be gained by it—What a thing to be in the Mouth of Fame—that at last the Idea has grown so monstrously beyond my seeming Power of attainment that the other day I nearly consented with myself to drop into a Phæton—yet 't is a disgrace to fail even in a huge attempt, and at this moment I drive the thought from me.

———————•◆•———————

TO B. R. HAYDON
10 May 1817   Margate

I read and write about eight hours a day. There is an old saying well begun is half done"—'t is a bad one. I would use instead—Not begun at all 'till half done" so according to that I have not begun my Poem and consequently (a priori) can say nothing about it. Thank God! I do begin arduously where I leave off, notwithstanding occasional depressions: and I hope for the support of a High Power while I clime this little eminence and especially in my Years of more momentous Labor. I remember your saying that you had notions of a good Genius presiding over you —I have of late had the same thought. for things which [I] do half at Random are afterwards confirmed by my judgment in a dozen features of Propriety—Is it too daring to Fancy Shakspeare this Presider? When in the Isle of W⟨h⟩ight I met with a Shakspeare in the Passage of the House at which I lodged—it comes nearer to my idea of him than any I have seen—I was but there a Week yet the old Woman made me take it with me though I went off in a hurry—Do you not think this is ominous of good? I am glad you say every Man of great Views is at times tormented as I am— . . .

From the same letter, 11 May 1817:

I wrote to Hunt yesterday—scar[c]ely know what I said in it—I could not talk about Poetry in the way I should have liked for I was not in humor with either his or mine. His self delusions are very lamentable they have inticed him into a Situation which I should be less eager after than that of a galley Slave—what you observe thereon is very true must be in time. Perhaps it is a self delusion to say so—but I think I could not be deceived in the Manner that Hunt is—may I die tomorrow if I am to be. There is no greater Sin after the 7 deadly than to flatter oneself into an idea of being a great Poet—or one of those beings who are privileged to wear out their Lives in the pursuit of Honor—how comfortable a feel it is that such a Crime must bring its heavy Penalty? That if one be a Selfdeluder accounts will be balanced?

———•—•—•———

TO J. A. HESSEY
8 October 1818   Hampstead

—I will write independantly.—I have written independently *without Judgment*—I may write independently *&* *with judgment* hereafter.—The Genius of Poetry must work out its own salvation in a man: It cannot be matured by law & precept, but by sensation & watchfulness in itself—That which is creative must create itself—In Endymion, I leaped headlong into the Sea, and thereby have become better acquainted with the Soundings, the quicksands, & the rocks, than if I had ⟨stayed⟩ stayed upon the green shore, and piped a silly pipe, and took tea & comfortable advice.—I was never afraid of failure; for I would sooner fail than not be among the greatest—

18 December 1818   Hampstead

—I am passing a Quiet day—which I have not done a long while—and if I do continue so—I feel I must again begin with my poetry—for if I am not in action mind or Body I am in pain—and from that I suffer greatly by going into parties where from the rules of society and a natural pride I am obliged to smother my Spirit and look like an Idiot—because I feel my impulses given way to would too much amaze them—I live under an everlasting restraint—Never relieved except when I am composing—so I will write away.

TO B. R. HAYDON
8 March 1819   Hampstead

A friend of mine observed the other day that if Lord Bacon were to make any remark in a party of the present day, the conversation would stop on the sudden. I am convinced of this, and from this I have come to the resolution never to write for the sake of writing, or making a poem, but from running over with any little knowledge and experience which many years of reflection may perhaps give me—otherwise I will be dumb. What Imagination I have I shall enjoy, and greatly, for I have experienced the satisfaction of having great conceptions without the toil of sonnetteering. I will not spoil my love of gloom by writing an ode to darkness; and with respect to my livelihood I will not write for it, for I will not mix with that most vulgar of all crowds the literary. [Such things I ratify by looking upon myself, and trying myself at lifting mental weights, as it were.] I am three and twenty with little knowlege and middling intellect. It is true that in the height of enthusiasm I have been cheated into some fine passages, but that is nothing.

ODE TO APOLLO

In thy western halls of gold
   When thou sittest in thy state,
Bards, that erst sublimely told
   Heroic deeds, and sang of fate,
With fervour seize their adamantine lyres,
Whose chords are solid rays, and twinkle radiant fires.

Here Homer with his nervous arms
   Strikes the twanging harp of war,
And even the western splendour warms,
   While the trumpets sound afar: 10
But, what creates the most intense surprise,
His soul looks out through renovated eyes.

Then, through thy Temple wide, melodious swells
   The sweet majestic tone of Maro's lyre:
The soul delighted on each accent dwells,—
   Enraptur'd dwells,—not daring to respire,
The while he tells of grief around a funeral pyre.

'Tis awful silence then again;
   Expectant stand the spheres;
   Breathless the laurell'd peers,   20
Nor move, till ends the lofty strain,
Nor move till Milton's tuneful thunders cease,
And leave once more the ravish'd heavens in peace.

Thou biddest Shakspeare wave his hand,
   And quickly forward spring
The Passions—a terrific band—
   And each vibrates the string
That with its tyrant temper best accords,
While from their Master's lips pour forth the inspiring words.

A silver trumpet Spenser blows,   30
   And, as its martial notes to silence flee,
From a virgin chorus flows
   A hymn in praise of spotless Chastity.

'Tis still! Wild warblings from the Æolian lyre
Enchantment softly breathe, and tremblingly expire.

Next thy Tasso's ardent numbers
   Float along the pleased air,
Calling youth from idle slumbers,
   Rousing them from Pleasure's lair:—
Then o'er the strings his fingers gently move,   40
And melt the soul to pity and to love.

But when *Thou* joinest with the Nine,
And all the powers of song combine,
   We listen here on earth:
The dying tones that fill the air,
And charm the ear of evening fair,
From thee, great God of Bards, receive their heavenly birth.

February 1815

TO CHARLES COWDEN CLARKE

Oft have you seen a swan superbly frowning,
And with proud breast his own white shadow crowning;
He slants his neck beneath the waters bright
So silently, it seems a beam of light
Come from the galaxy: anon he sports,—
With outspread wings the Naiad Zephyr courts,
Or ruffles all the surface of the lake
In striving from its crystal face to take
Some diamond water drops, and them to treasure
In milky nest, and sip them off at leisure.   10
But not a moment can he there insure them,
Nor to such downy rest can he allure them;
For down they rush as though they would be free,
And drop like hours into eternity.
Just like that bird am I in loss of time,
Whene'er I venture on the stream of rhyme;
With shatter'd boat, oar snapt, and canvass rent
I slowly sail, scarce knowing my intent;

Still scooping up the water with my fingers,
In which a trembling diamond never lingers. 20
By this, friend Charles, you may full plainly see
Why I have never penn'd a line to thee:
Because my thoughts were never free, and clear,
And little fit to please a classic ear;
Because my wine was of too poor a savour
For one whose palate gladdens in the flavour
Of sparkling Helicon:—small good it were
To take him to a desert rude, and bare,
Who had on Baiae's shore reclin'd at ease,
While Tasso's page was floating in a breeze. 30
That gave soft music from Armida's bowers,
Mingled with fragrance from her rarest flowers:
Small good to one who had by Mulla's stream
Fondled the maidens with the breasts of cream;
Who had beheld Belphœbe in a brook,
And lovely Una in a leafy nook,
And Archimago leaning o'er his book:
Who had of all that's sweet tasted, and seen,
From silv'ry ripple, up to beauty's queen;
From the sequester'd haunts of gay Titania, 40
To the blue dwelling of divine Urania:
One, who, of late, had ta'en sweet forest walks
With him who elegantly chats, and talks—
The wrong'd Libertas,—who has told you stories
Of laurel chaplets, and Apollo's glories;
Of troops chivalrous prancing through a city,
And tearful ladies made for love, and pity:
With many else which I have never known.
Thus have I thought; and days on days have flown
Slowly, or rapidly—unwilling still 50
For you to try my dull, unlearned quill.
Nor should I now, but that I've known you long;
That you first taught me all the sweets of song:
The grand, the sweet, the terse, the free, the fine;
What swell'd with pathos, and what right divine:
Spenserian vowels that elope with ease,
And float along like birds o'er summer seas;
Miltonian storms, and more, Miltonian tenderness;

Michael in arms, and more, meek Eve's fair slenderness,
Who read for me the sonnet swelling loudly   60
Up to its climax and then dying proudly?
Who found for me the grandeur of the ode,
Growing, like Atlas, stronger from its load?
Who let me taste that more than cordial dram,
The sharp, the rapier-pointed epigram?
Show'd me that epic was of all the king,
Round, vast, and spanning all like Saturn's ring?
You too upheld the veil from Clio's beauty,
And pointed out the patriot's stern duty;
The might of Alfred, and the shaft of Tell;   70
The hand of Brutus, that so grandly fell
Upon a tyrant's head. Ah! had I never seen,
Or known your kindness, what might I have been?
What my enjoyments in my youthful years,
Bereft of all that now my life endears?
And can I e'er these benefits forget?
And can I e'er repay the friendly debt?
No, doubly no;—yet should these rhymings please,
I shall roll on the grass with two-fold ease:
For I have long time been my fancy feeding   80
With hopes that you would one day think the reading
Of my rough verses not an hour misspent;
Should it e'er be so, what a rich content!
Some weeks have pass'd since last I saw the spires
In lucent Thames reflected:—warm desires
To see the sun o'erpeep the eastern dimness,
And morning shadows, streaking into slimness
Across the lawny fields, and pebbly water;
To mark the time as they grow broad, and shorter;
To feel the air that plays about the hills,   90
And sips its freshness from the little rills;
To see high, golden corn wave in the light
When Cynthia smiles upon a summer's night,
And peers among the cloudlets jet and white,
As though she were reclining in a bed
Of bean blossoms, in heaven freshly shed.
No sooner had I stepp'd into these pleasures
Than I began to think of rhymes and measures:

The air that floated by me seem'd to say
'Write! thou wilt never have a better day.' 100
And so I did. When many lines I'd written,
Though with their grace I was not oversmitten,
Yet, as my hand was warm, I thought I'd better
Trust to my feelings, and write you a letter.
Such an attempt required an inspiration
Of a peculiar sort,—a consummation;—
Which, had I felt, these scribblings might have been
Verses from which the soul would never wean:
But many days have passed since last my heart
Was warm'd luxuriously by divine Mozart; 110
By Arne delighted, or by Handel madden'd;
Or by the song of Erin pierc'd and sadden'd:
What time you were before the music sitting,
And the rich notes to each sensation fitting.
Since I have walk'd with you through shady lanes
That freshly terminate in open plains,
And revel'd in a chat that ceased not
When at night-fall among your books we got:
No, nor when supper came, nor after that,—
Nor when reluctantly I took my hat; 120
No, nor till cordially you shook my hand
Mid-way between our homes:—your accents bland
Still sounded in my ears, when I no more
Could hear your footsteps touch the grav'ly floor.
Sometimes I lost them, and then found again;
You chang'd the footpath for the grassy plain.
In those still moments I have wish'd you joys
That well you know to honour:—'Life's very toys
'With him,' said I, 'will take a pleasant charm;
'It cannot be that aught will work him harm.' 130
These thoughts now come o'er me with all their might:—
Again I shake your hand,—friend Charles, good night.

September 1816

TO A YOUNG LADY WHO SENT ME A LAUREL CROWN

Fresh morning gusts have blown away all fear
   From my glad bosom,—now from gloominess
   I mount for ever—not an atom less
Than the proud laurel shall content my bier.
No! by the eternal stars! or why sit here
   In the Sun's eye, and 'gainst my temples press
   Apollo's very leaves, woven to bless
By thy white fingers and thy spirit clear.
Lo! who dares say, 'Do this'? Who dares call down
   My will from its high purpose? Who say, 'Stand,'   **10**
Or 'Go'? This mighty moment I would frown
   On abject Cæsars—not the stoutest band
Of mailed heroes should tear off my crown:
   Yet would I kneel and kiss thy gentle hand!

November 1816

SLEEP AND POETRY

As I lay in my bed slepe full unmete
Was unto me, but why that I ne might
Rest I ne wist, for there n'as erthly wight
[As I suppose] had more of hertis ese
Than I, for I n'ad sicknesse nor disease.
                       Chaucer

What is more gentle than a wind in summer?
What is more soothing than the pretty hummer
That stays one moment in an open flower,
And buzzes cheerily from bower to bower?
What is more tranquil than a musk-rose blowing
In a green island, far from all men's knowing?
More healthful than the leafiness of dales?
More secret than a nest of nightingales?
More serene than Cordelia's countenance?
More full of visions than a high romance?   **10**
What, but thee Sleep? Soft closer of our eyes!

Low murmurer of tender lullabies!
Light hoverer around our happy pillows!
Wreather of poppy buds, and weeping willows!
Silent entangler of a beauty's tresses!
Most happy listener! when the morning blesses
Thee for enlivening all the cheerful eyes
That glance so brightly at the new sun-rise.

But what is higher beyond thought than thee?
Fresher than berries of a mountain tree?   20
More strange, more beautiful, more smooth, more regal,
Than wings of swans, than doves, than dim-seen eagle?
What is it? And to what shall I compare it?
It has a glory, and naught else can share it:
The thought thereof is awful, sweet, and holy,
Chasing away all worldliness and folly;
Coming sometimes like fearful claps of thunder,
Or the low rumblings earth's regions under;
And sometimes like a gentle whispering
Of all the secrets of some wond'rous thing   30
That breathes about us in the vacant air;
So that we look around with prying stare,
Perhaps to see shapes of light, aerial limning,
And catch soft floatings from a faint-heard hymning;
To see the laurel wreath, on high suspended,
That is to crown our name when life is ended.
Sometimes it gives a glory to the voice,
And from the heart up-springs, 'Rejoice! rejoice!'
Sounds which will reach the Framer of all things,
And die away in ardent mutterings.   40

No one who once the glorious sun has seen,
And all the clouds, and felt his bosom clean
For his great Maker's presence, but must know
What 'tis I mean, and feel his being glow:
Therefore no insult will I give his spirit,
By telling what he sees from native merit.

O Poesy! for thee I hold my pen
That am not yet a glorious denizen

Of thy wide heaven—Should I rather kneel
Upon some mountain-top until I feel   50
A glowing splendour round about me hung,
And echo back the voice of thine own tongue?
O Poesy! for thee I grasp my pen
That am not yet a glorious denizen
Of thy wide heaven; yet, to my ardent prayer,
Yield from thy sanctuary some clear air,
Smooth'd for intoxication by the breath
Of flowering bays, that I may die a death
Of luxury, and my young spirit follow
The morning sun-beams to the great Apollo   60
Like a fresh sacrifice; or, if I can bear
The o'erwhelming sweets, 'twill bring to me the fair
Visions of all places: a bowery nook
Will be elysium—an eternal book
Whence I may copy many a lovely saying
About the leaves, and flowers—about the playing
Of nymphs in woods, and fountains; and the shade
Keeping a silence round a sleeping maid;
And many a verse from so strange influence
That we must ever wonder how, and whence   70
It came. Also imaginings will hover
Round my fire-side, and haply there discover
Vistas of solemn beauty, where I'd wander
In happy silence, like the clear Meander
Through its lone vales; and where I found a spot
Of awfuller shade, or an enchanted grot,
Or a green hill o'erspread with chequer'd dress
Of flowers, and fearful from its loveliness,
Write on my tablets all that was permitted,
All that was for our human senses fitted.   80
Then the events of this wide world I'd seize
Like a strong giant, and my spirit teaze
Till at its shoulders it should proudly see
Wings to find out an immortality.

Stop and consider! life is but a day;
A fragile dew-drop on its perilous way
From a tree's summit; a poor Indian's sleep

While his boat hastens to the monstrous steep
Of Montmorenci. Why so sad a moan?
Life is the rose's hope while yet unblown;   90
The reading of an ever-changing tale;
The light uplifting of a maiden's veil;
A pigeon tumbling in clear summer air;
A laughing school-boy, without grief or care,
Riding the springy branches of an elm.

O for ten years, that I may overwhelm
Myself in poesy; so I may do the deed
That my own soul has to itself decreed.
Then will I pass the countries that I see
In long perspective, and continually   100
Taste their pure fountains. First the realm I'll pass
Of Flora, and old Pan: sleep in the grass,
Feed upon apples red, and strawberries,
And choose each pleasure that my fancy sees;
Catch the white-handed nymphs in shady places,
To woo sweet kisses from averted faces,—
Play with their fingers, touch their shoulders white
Into a pretty shrinking with a bite
As hard as lips can make it: till agreed,
A lovely tale of human life we'll read.   110
And one will teach a tame dove how it best
May fan the cool air gently o'er my rest;
Another bending o'er her nimble tread,
Will set a green robe floating round her head,
And still will dance with ever varied ease,
Smiling upon the flowers and the trees:
Another will entice me on, and on
Through almond blossoms and rich cinnamon;
Till in the bosom of a leafy world
We rest in silence, like two gems upcurl'd   120
In the recesses of a pearly shell.

And can I ever bid these joys farewell?
Yes, I must pass them for a nobler life,
Where I may find the agonies, the strife
Of human hearts: for lo! I see afar,

O'ersailing the blue cragginess, a car
And steeds with streamy manes—the charioteer
Looks out upon the winds with glorious fear:
And now the numerous tramplings quiver lightly
Along a huge cloud's ridge; and now with sprightly   130
Wheel downward come they into fresher skies,
Tipt round with silver from the sun's bright eyes.
Still downward with capacious whirl they glide;
And now I see them on the green-hill's side
In breezy rest among the nodding stalks.
The charioteer with wond'rous gesture talks
To the trees and mountains; and there soon appear
Shapes of delight, of mystery, and fear,
Passing along before a dusky space
Made by some mighty oaks: as they would chase   140
Some ever-fleeting music on they sweep.
Lo! how they murmur, laugh, and smile, and weep:
Some with upholden hand and mouth severe;
Some with their faces muffled to the ear
Between their arms; some, clear in youthful bloom,
Go glad and smilingly athwart the gloom;
Some looking back, and some with upward gaze;
Yes, thousands in a thousand different ways
Flit onward—now a lovely wreath of girls
Dancing their sleek hair into tangled curls;   150
And now broad wings. Most awfully intent
The driver of those steeds is forward bent,
And seems to listen: O that I might know
All that he writes with such a hurrying glow.

The visions all are fled—the car is fled
Into the light of heaven, and in their stead
A sense of real things comes doubly strong,
And, like a muddy stream, would bear along
My soul to nothingness: but I will strive
Against all doubtings, and will keep alive   160
The thought of that same chariot, and the strange
Journey it went.
               Is there so small a range
In the present strength of manhood, that the high

Imagination cannot freely fly
As she was wont of old? prepare her steeds,
Paw up against the light, and do strange deeds
Upon the clouds? Has she not shown us all?
From the clear space of ether, to the small
Breath of new buds unfolding? From the meaning
Of Jove's large eye-brow, to the tender greening 170
Of April meadows? Here her altar shone,
E'en in this isle; and who could paragon
The fervid choir that lifted up a noise
Of harmony, to where it aye will poise
Its mighty self of convoluting sound,
Huge as a planet, and like that roll round,
Eternally around a dizzy void?
Ay, in those days the Muses were nigh cloy'd
With honors; nor had any other care
Than to sing out and sooth their wavy hair. 180

Could all this be forgotten? Yes, a schism
Nurtured by foppery and barbarism,
Made great Apollo blush for this his land.
Men were thought wise who could not understand
His glories: with a puling infant's force
They sway'd about upon a rocking horse,
And thought it Pegasus. Ah dismal soul'd!
The winds of heaven blew, the ocean roll'd
Its gathering waves—ye felt it not. The blue
Bared its eternal bosom, and the dew 190
Of summer nights collected still to make
The morning precious: beauty was awake!
Why were ye not awake? But ye were dead
To things ye knew not of,—were closely wed
To musty laws lined out with wretched rule
And compass vile: so that ye taught a school
Of dolts to smooth, inlay, and clip, and fit,
Till, like the certain wands of Jacob's wit,
Their verses tallied. Easy was the task:
A thousand handicraftsmen wore the mask 200
Of Poesy. Ill-fated, impious race!
That blasphemed the bright Lyrist to his face,

And did not know it,—no, they went about,
Holding a poor, decrepid standard out
Mark'd with most flimsy mottos, and in large
The name of one Boileau!

                              O ye whose charge
It is to hover round our pleasant hills!
Whose congregated majesty so fills
My boundly reverence, that I cannot trace
Your hallowed names, in this unholy place,   210
So near those common folk; did not their shames
Affright you? Did our old lamenting Thames
Delight you? Did ye never cluster round
Delicious Avon, with a mournful sound,
And weep? Or did ye wholly bid adieu
To regions where no more the laurel grew?
Or did ye stay to give a welcoming
To some lone spirits who could proudly sing
Their youth away, and die? 'Twas even so:
But let me think away those times of woe: 220
Now 'tis a fairer season; ye have breathed
Rich benedictions o'er us; ye have wreathed
Fresh garlands: for sweet music has been heard
In many places;—some has been upstirr'd
From out its crystal dwelling in a lake,
By a swan's ebon bill; from a thick brake,
Nested and quiet in a valley mild,
Bubbles a pipe; fine sounds are floating wild
About the earth: happy are ye and glad.
These things are doubtless: yet in truth we've had   230
Strange thunders from the potency of song;
Mingled indeed with what is sweet and strong,
From majesty: but in clear truth the themes
Are ugly clubs, the Poets' Polyphemes
Disturbing the grand sea. A drainless shower
Of light is poesy; 'tis the supreme of power;
'Tis might half slumb'ring on its own right arm.
The very archings of her eye-lids charm
A thousand willing agents to obey,
And still she governs with the mildest sway;   240

But strength alone though of the Muses born
Is like a fallen angel: trees uptorn,
Darkness, and worms, and shrouds, and sepulchres
Delight it; for it feeds upon the burrs,
And thorns of life; forgetting the great end
Of poesy, that it should be a friend
To sooth the cares, and lift the thoughts of man.

   Yet I rejoice: a myrtle fairer than
E'er grew in Paphos, from the bitter weeds
Lifts its sweet head into the air, and feeds   250
A silent space with ever sprouting green.
All tenderest birds there find a pleasant screen,
Creep through the shade with jaunty fluttering,
Nibble the little cupped flowers and sing.
Then let us clear away the choking thorns
From round its gentle stem; let the young fawns,
Yeaned in after times, when we are flown,
Find a fresh sward beneath it, overgrown
With simple flowers: let there nothing be
More boisterous than a lover's bended knee;   260
Nought more ungentle than the placid look
Of one who leans upon a closed book;
Nought more untranquil than the grassy slopes
Between two hills. All hail delightful hopes!
As she was wont, th' imagination
Into most lovely labyrinths will be gone,
And they shall be accounted poet kings
Who simply tell the most heart-easing things.
O may these joys be ripe before I die.
Will not some say that I presumptuously   270
Have spoken? that from hastening disgrace
'Twere better far to hide my foolish face?
That whining boyhood should with reverence bow
Ere the dread thunderbolt could reach? How!
If I do hide myself, it sure shall be
In the very fane, the light of Poesy:
If I do fall, at least I will be laid
Beneath the silence of a poplar shade;
And over me the grass shall be smooth shaven;

And there shall be a kind memorial graven.   280
But off Despondence! miserable bane!
They should not know thee, who athirst to gain
A noble end, are thirsty every hour.
What though I am not wealthy in the dower
Of spanning wisdom; though I do not know
The shiftings of the mighty winds that blow
Hither and thither all the changing thoughts
Of man: though no great minist'ring reason sorts
Out the dark mysteries of human souls
To clear conceiving: yet there ever rolls   290
A vast idea before me, and I glean
Therefrom my liberty; thence too I've seen
The end and aim of Poesy. 'Tis clear
As anything most true; as that the year
Is made of the four seasons—manifest
As a large cross, some old cathedral's crest,
Lifted to the white clouds. Therefore should I
Be but the essence of deformity,
A coward, did my very eye-lids wink
At speaking out what I have dared to think.   300
Ah! rather let me like a madman run
Over some precipice; let the hot sun
Melt my Dedalian wings, and drive me down
Convuls'd and headlong! Stay! an inward frown
Of conscience bids me be more calm awhile.
An ocean dim, sprinkled with many an isle,
Spreads awfully before me. How much toil!
How many days! what desperate turmoil!
Ere I can have explored its widenesses.
Ah, what a task! upon my bended knees,   310
I could unsay those—no, impossible!
Impossible!
              For sweet relief I'll dwell
On humbler thoughts, and let this strange assay
Begun in gentleness die so away.
E'en now all tumult from my bosom fades:
I turn full hearted to the friendly aids
That smooth the path of honour; brotherhood,
And friendliness the nurse of mutual good.

The hearty grasp that sends a pleasant sonnet
Into the brain ere one can think upon it;   320
The silence when some rhymes are coming out;
And when they're come, the very pleasant rout:
The message certain to be done to-morrow.
'Tis perhaps as well that it should be to borrow
Some precious book from out its snug retreat,
To cluster round it when we next shall meet.
Scarce can I scribble on; for lovely airs
Are fluttering round the room like doves in pairs;
Many delights of that glad day recalling,
When first my senses caught their tender falling.   330
And with these airs come forms of elegance
Stooping their shoulders o'er a horse's prance,
Careless, and grand—fingers soft and round
Parting luxuriant curls;—and the swift bound
Of Bacchus from his chariot, when his eye
Made Ariadne's cheek look blushingly.
Thus I remember all the pleasant flow
Of words at opening a portfolio.

Things such as these are ever harbingers
To trains of peaceful images: the stirs   340
Of a swan's neck unseen among the rushes:
A linnet starting all about the bushes:
A butterfly, with golden wings broad parted,
Nestling a rose, convuls'd as though it smarted
With over pleasure—many, many more,
Might I indulge at large in all my store
Of luxuries: yet I must not forget
Sleep, quiet with his poppy coronet:
For what there may be worthy in these rhymes
I partly owe to him: and thus, the chimes   350
Of friendly voices had just given place
To as sweet a silence, when I 'gan retrace
The pleasant day, upon a couch at ease.
It was a poet's house who keeps the keys
Of pleasure's temple. Round about were hung
The glorious features of the bards who sung
In other ages—cold and sacred busts

Smiled at each other. Happy he who trusts
To clear Futurity his darling fame!
Then there were fauns and satyrs taking aim   360
At swelling apples with a frisky leap
And reaching fingers, 'mid a luscious heap
Of vine-leaves. Then there rose to view a fane
Of liny marble, and thereto a train
Of nymphs approaching fairly o'er the sward:
One, loveliest, holding her white hand toward
The dazzling sun-rise: two sisters sweet
Bending their graceful figures till they meet
Over the trippings of a little child:
And some are hearing, eagerly, the wild   370
Thrilling liquidity of dewy piping.
See, in another picture, nymphs are wiping
Cherishingly Diana's timorous limbs;—
A fold of lawny mantle dabbling swims
At the bath's edge, and keeps a gentle motion
With the subsiding crystal: as when ocean
Heaves calmly its broad swelling smoothness o'er
Its rocky marge, and balances once more
The patient weeds; that now unshent by foam
Feel all about their undulating home.   380

Sappho's meek head was there half smiling down
At nothing; just as though the earnest frown
Of over thinking had that moment gone
From off her brow, and left her all alone.

Great Alfred's too, with anxious, pitying eyes,
As if he always listened to the sighs
Of the goaded world; and Kosciusko's worn
By horrid suffrance—mightily forlorn.
Petrarch, outstepping from the shady green,
Starts at the sight of Laura; nor can wean   390
His eyes from her sweet face. Most happy they!
For over them was seen a free display
Of out-spread wings, and from between them shone
The face of Poesy: from off her throne
She overlook'd things that I scarce could tell.

The very sense of where I was might well
Keep Sleep aloof: but more than that there came
Thought after thought to nourish up the flame
Within my breast; so that the morning light
Surprised me even from a sleepless night;   400
And up I rose refresh'd, and glad, and gay,
Resolving to begin that very day
These lines; and howsoever they be done,
I leave them as a father does his son.

November–December 1816

DEDICATION
TO LEIGH HUNT, ESQ.

Glory and loveliness have pass'd away;
   For if we wander out in early morn,
   No wreathed incense do we see upborne
Into the east, to meet the smiling day:
No crowd of nymphs soft voic'd and young, and gay,
   In woven baskets bringing ears of corn,
   Roses, and pinks, and violets, to adorn
The shrine of Flora in her early May.
But there are left delights as high as these,
   And I shall ever bless my destiny,   10
That in a time, when under pleasant trees
   Pan is no longer sought, I feel a free,
A leafy luxury, seeing I could please
   With these poor offerings, a man like thee.

February 1817

ON RECEIVING A LAUREL CROWN FROM LEIGH
HUNT

Minutes are flying swiftly, and as yet
   Nothing unearthly has enticed my brain
   Into a delphic Labyrinth—I would fain
Catch an unmortal thought to pay the debt
I owe to the kind Poet who has set

Upon my ambitious head a glorious gain.
Two bending laurel Sprigs—'tis nearly pain
To be conscious of such a Coronet.
Still time is fleeting, and no dream arises
    Gorgeous as I would have it—only I see   **10**
A Trampling down of what the world most prizes
    Turbans and Crowns, and blank regality;
And then I run into most wild surmises
    Of all the many glories that may be.

February 1817

HYMN TO APOLLO

    God of the golden bow,
        And of the golden lyre,
    And of the golden hair,
        And of the golden fire,
            Charioteer
            Of the patient year,
    Where—where slept thine ire,
When like a blank idiot I put on thy wreath,
        Thy laurel, thy glory,
        The light of thy story,   **10**
Or was I a worm—too low crawling, for death?
        O Delphic Apollo!

    The Thunderer grasp'd and grasp'd,
        The Thunderer frown'd and frown'd;
    The eagle's feathery mane
        For wrath became stiffen'd—the sound
            Of breeding thunder
            Went drowsily under,
        Muttering to be unbound.
O why didst thou pity, and for a worm   **20**
        Why touch thy soft lute
        Till the thunder was mute,
Why was not I crush'd—such a pitiful germ?
        O Delphic Apollo!

The Pleiades were up,
   Watching the silent air;
The seeds and roots in the Earth
   Were swelling for summer fare;
     The Ocean, its neighbour,
      Was at its old labour,   30
   When, who—who did dare
To tie, like a madman, thy plant round his brow,
     And grin and look proudly,
     And blaspheme so loudly,
And live for that honour, to stoop to thee now?
     O Delphic Apollo!

February or March 1817

ON SEEING A LOCK OF MILTON'S HAIR

Chief of organic numbers!
   Old Scholar of the Spheres!
Thy spirit never slumbers,
   But rolls about our ears,
For ever, and for ever!
O what a mad endeavour
     Worketh he,
Who to thy sacred and ennobled hearse
Would offer a burnt sacrifice of verse
     And melody.   10

How heavenward thou soundest,
   Live Temple of sweet noise,
And Discord unconfoundest,
   Giving Delight new joys,
And Pleasure nobler pinions!
O, where are thy dominions?
     Lend thine ear
To a young Delian oath,—aye, by thy soul,
By all that from thy mortal lips did roll,
And by the kernel of thine earthly love,   20
Beauty, in things on earth, and things above
     I swear!

When every childish fashion
   Has vanish'd from my rhyme,
Will I, grey-gone in passion,
   Leave to an after-time
     Hymning and harmony
Of thee, and of thy works, and of thy life;
But vain is now the burning and the strife,
Pangs are in vain, until I grow high-rife   30
     With old Philosophy,
And mad with glimpses of futurity!

For many years my offerings must be hush'd;
   When I do speak, I'll think upon this hour,
Because I feel my forehead hot and flush'd,
   Even at the simplest vassal of thy power,—
     A lock of thy bright hair,—
     Sudden it came,
And I was startled, when I caught thy name
     Coupled so unaware;   40
Yet, at the moment, temperate was my blood.
I thought I had beheld it from the flood.

January 1818

THE POET

A Fragment

Where's the Poet? show him! show him,
Muses nine! that I may know him!
'Tis the man who with a man
   Is an equal, be he King,
Or poorest of the beggar-clan,
   Or any other wondrous thing
A man may be 'twixt ape and Plato;
'Tis the man who with a bird,
Wren or Eagle, finds his way to
   All its instincts; he hath heard   10
The Lion's roaring, and can tell
   What his horny throat expresseth,

And to him the Tiger's yell
   Comes articulate and presseth
On his ear like mother-tongue.

October 1818

The Poet and His Public

TO J. H. REYNOLDS
9 April 1818   Teignmouth

—I have not the slightest feel of humility towards the
Public—or to any thing in existence,—but the eternal
Being, the Principle of Beauty,—and the Memory of
great Men—When I am writing for myself for the mere
sake of the Moment's enjoyment, perhaps nature has its
course with me—but a Preface is written to the Public; a
thing I cannot help looking upon as an Enemy, and
which I cannot address without feelings of Hostility—If I
write a Preface in a supple or subdued style, it will not
be in character with me as a public speaker—I wo^d be subdued before my friends, and thank them for subduing me
—but among Multitudes of Men—I have no feel of stooping, I hate the idea of humility to them—
    I never wrote one single Line of Poetry with the least
Shadow of public thought.

This letter acknowledges a favorable notice of *Endymion* in
the *Morning Chronicle,* which his publisher sent to Keats. The
phrase "domestic criticism," meaning self-criticism, contrasts with
public notice such as that which appeared in *Blackwood's* and
the *Quarterly Review,* mentioned here and now notorious for
their hostility toward Keats's work.

TO J. A. HESSEY
8 October 1818   Hampstead

You are very good in sending me the letter from the
Chronicle—and I am very bad in not acknowledging such

a kindness sooner.—pray forgive me—It has so chanced that I have had that paper every day—I have seen today's. I cannot but feel indebted to those Gentlemen who have taken my part—As for the rest, I begin to get a little acquainted with my own strength and weakness.—Praise or blame has but a momentary effect on the man whose love of beauty in the abstract makes him a severe critic on his own Works. My own domestic criticism has given me pain without comparison beyond what Blackwood or the ⟨Edinburgh⟩ Quarterly could possibly inflict. and also when I feel I am right, no external praise can give me such a glow as my own solitary reperception & ratification of what is fine.

———————•—•—•—•———————

The Examiner is another influential journal, this one edited by Keats's friend Leigh Hunt. The letter by Reynolds referred to here was reprinted from a newspaper, *Alfred, West of England Journal.*

TO GEORGE AND GEORGIANA KEATS
14 October 1818   Hampstead

—Reynolds has returned from a six weeks enjoyment in Devonshire, he is well and persuades me to publish my pot of Basil as an answer to the attacks made on me in Blackwood's Magazine and the Quarterly Review. There have been two Letters in my defence in the Chronicle and one in the Examiner, coppied from the Alfred Exeter paper, and written by Reynolds—I do not know who wrote
        Chronicle
those in the ⟨Quarterly⟩—This is a mere matter of the moment—I think I shall be among the English Poets after my death. ⟨The⟩ Even as a Matter of present interest the attempt to crush me in the ⟨Chro⟩ Quarterly has only brought me more into notice and it is a common expression among book men "I wonder the Quarterly should cut its own throat.'

———————•—•—•—•———————

TO B. R. HAYDON
22 December 1818   Hampstead

—I have a little money which may enable me to study and travel three or four years—I never expect to get any thing by my Books: and moreover I wish to avoid publishing —I admire Human Nature but I do not like *Men*—I should like to compose things honourable to Man—but not fingerable over by *Men*.

———·—•—•—·———

TO FANNY BRAWNE
15 (?) July 1819   Shanklin, Isle of Wight

I cannot say when I shall get a volume ready. I have three or four stories half done, but as I cannot write for the mere sake of the press, I am obliged to let them progress or lie still as my fancy chooses. By Christmas perhaps they may appear, but I am not yet sure they ever will. 'Twill be no matter, for Poems are as common as newspapers and I do not see why it is a greater crime in me than in another to let the verses of an half-fledged brain tumble into the reading-rooms and drawing room windows.

———·—•—•—·———

TO JOHN TAYLOR
23 August 1819   Winchester

I feel every confidence that if I choose I may be a popular writer; that I will never be; but for all that I will get a livelihood—I equally dislike the favour of the public with the love of a woman—they are both a cloying treacle to the wings of independence. I shall ever consider them (People) as debtors to me for verses, not myself to them for admiration—which I can do without. I have of late been indulging my spleen by composing a preface *at* them: after all resolving never to write a preface at all. 'There are so many verses,' would I have said to them', give me so much means to buy pleasure with as a relief to my hours of labour—You will observe at the end of this if you put down the Letter 'How a solitarry life engenders pride and egotism!' True: I know it does but this Pride and egotism will enable me to write finer things than any thing else could—so I will indulge it—Just so much as I am hu[m]bled by the genius above my grasp, am I exalted and look with hate and contempt upon the literary world —A Drummer boy who holds out his hand familiarly to a field marshall—that Drummer boy with me is the good word and favour of the public—Who would wish to be among the commonplace crowd of the little-famous— who⟨m⟩ are each individually lost in a throng made up of themselfes? is this worth louting or playing the hypocrite for? To beg suffrages for a seat on the benches of a myriad aristocracy in Letters? This is not wise—I am not a wise man—T is Pride—I will give you a definition of a proud Man—He is a Man who has neither vanity nor wisdom— one fill'd with hatreds cannot be vain—neither can he be wise—

The "xxxxxx" in the next letter means *Reynolds* and reflects Brown's unfortunate habit of editing Keats's letters.

TO CHARLES BROWN
22 September 1819   Winchester

Now I am going to enter on the subject of self. It is quite time I should set myself doing something, and live no longer upon hopes. I have never yet exerted myself. I am getting into an idle minded, vicious way of life, almost content to live upon others. In no period of my life have I acted with any self will, but in throwing up the apothecary-profession. That I do not repent of. Look at x x x x x x: if he was not in the law he would be acquiring, by his abilities, something towards his support. My occupation is entirely literary; I will do so too. I will write, on the liberal side of the question, for whoever will pay me. I have not known yet what it is to be diligent. I purpose living in town in a cheap lodging, and endeavouring, for a beginning, to get the theatricals of some paper.

When I can afford to compose deliberate poems I will. . . .

I shall apply to Hazlitt, who knows the market as well as any one, for something to bring me in a few pounds as soon as possible. I shall not suffer my pride to hinder me. The whisper may go round; I shall not hear it. If I can get an article in the "Edinburg," I will. One must not be delicate.

TO CHATTERTON

O Chatterton! how very sad thy fate!
    Dear child of sorrow—son of misery!
    How soon the film of death obscur'd that eye,
Whence Genius mildly flash'd, and high debate.
How soon that voice, majestic and elate,
    Melted in dying numbers! Oh! how nigh
    Was night to thy fair morning. Thou didst die
A half-blown flow'ret which cold blasts amate.
But this is past: thou art among the stars
    Of highest Heaven: to the rolling spheres   10
Thou sweetly singest: naught thy hymning mars,
    Above the ingrate world and human fears.
On earth the good man base detraction bars
    From thy fair name, and waters it with tears.

1815

TO MY BROTHER GEORGE

Full many a dreary hour have I past,
My brain bewilder'd, and my mind o'ercast
With heaviness; in seasons when I've thought
No spherey strains by me could e'er be caught
From the blue dome, though I to dimness gaze
On the far depth where sheeted lightning plays;
Or, on the wavy grass outstretch'd supinely,
Pry 'mong the stars, to strive to think divinely:
That I should never hear Apollo's song,

Though feathery clouds were floating all along 10
The purple west, and, two bright streaks between,
The golden lyre itself were dimly seen:
That the still murmur of the honey bee
Would never teach a rural song to me:
That the bright glance from beauty's eyelids slanting
Would never make a lay of mine enchanting,
Or warm my breast with ardour to unfold
Some tale of love and arms in time of old.
But there are times, when those that love the bay,
Fly from all sorrowing far, far away; 20
A sudden glow comes on them, naught they see
In water, earth, or air, but poesy.
It has been said, dear George, and true I hold it,
 (For knightly Spenser to Libertas told it,)
That when a Poet is in such a trance,
In air he sees white coursers paw, and prance,
Bestridden of gay knights, in gay apparel,
Who at each other tilt in playful quarrel,
And what we, ignorantly, sheet-lightning call,
Is the swift opening of their wide portal, 30
When the bright warder blows his trumpet clear,
Whose tones reach naught on earth but Poet's ear.
When these enchanted portals open wide,
And through the light the horsemen swiftly glide,
The Poet's eye can reach those golden halls,
And view the glory of their festivals:
Their ladies fair, that in the distance seem
Fit for the silv'ring of a seraph's dream;
Their rich brimm'd goblets, that incessant run
Like the bright spots that move about the sun; 40
And, when upheld, the wine from each bright jar
Pours with the lustre of a falling star.
Yet further off, are dimly seen their bowers,
Of which, no mortal eye can reach the flowers;
And 'tis right just, for well Apollo knows
'Twould make the Poet quarrel with the rose.
All that's reveal'd from that far seat of blisses,
Is, the clear fountains' interchanging kisses,
As gracefully descending, light and thin,
Like silver streaks across a dolphin's fin, 50

When he upswimmeth from the coral caves,
And sports with half his tail above the waves.

These wonders strange he sees, and many more,
Whose head is pregnant with poetic lore.
Should he upon an evening ramble fare
With forehead to the soothing breezes bare,
Would he naught see but the dark, silent blue
With all its diamonds trembling through and through?
Or the coy moon, when in the waviness
Of whitest clouds she does her beauty dress,   60
And staidly paces higher up, and higher,
Like a sweet nun in holy-day attire?
Ah, yes! much more would start into his sight—
The revelries, and mysteries of night:
And should I ever see them, I will tell you
Such tales as needs must with amazement spell you.

These are the living pleasures of the bard:
But richer far posterity's award.
What does he murmur with his latest breath,
While his proud eye looks through the film of death?   70
'What though I leave this dull, and earthly mould,
Yet shall my spirit lofty converse hold
With after times.—The patriot shall feel
My stern alarum, and unsheath his steel;
Or, in the senate thunder out my numbers
To startle princes from their easy slumbers.
The sage will mingle with each moral theme
My happy thoughts sententious; he will teem
With lofty periods when my verses fire him,
And then I'll stoop from heaven to inspire him.   80
Lays have I left of such a dear delight
That maids will sing them on their bridal night.
Gay villagers, upon a morn of May,
When they have tired their gentle limbs with play,
And form'd a snowy circle on the grass,
And plac'd in midst of all that lovely lass
Who chosen is their queen,—with her fine head
Crowned with flowers purple, white, and red:
For there the lilly, and the musk-rose, sighing,

Are emblems true of hapless lovers dying: 90
Between her breasts, that never yet felt trouble,
A bunch of violets full blown, and double,
Serenely sleep:—she from a casket takes
A little book,—and then a joy awakes
About each youthful heart,—with stifled cries,
And rubbing of white hands, and sparkling eyes:
For she's to read a tale of hopes, and fears;
One that I foster'd in my youthful years:
The pearls, that on each glist'ning circlet sleep,
Gush ever and anon with silent creep,   100
Lured by the innocent dimples. To sweet rest
Shall the dear babe, upon its mother's breast,
Be lull'd with songs of mine. Fair world, adieu!
Thy dales, and hills, are fading from my view:
Swiftly I mount, upon wide spreading pinions,
Far from the narrow bounds of thy dominions.
Full joy I feel, while thus I cleave the air,
That my soft verse will charm thy daughters fair,
And warm thy sons!' Ah, my dear friend and brother,
Could I, at once, my mad ambition smother,   110
For tasting joys like these, sure I should be
Happier, and dearer to society.
At times, 'tis true, I've felt relief from pain
When some bright thought has darted through my brain:
Through all that day I've felt a greater pleasure
Than if I'd brought to light a hidden treasure.
As to my sonnets, though none else should heed them,
I feel delighted, still, that you should read them.
Of late, too, I have had much calm enjoyment,
Stretch'd on the grass at my best lov'd employment   120
Of scribbling lines for you. These things I thought
While, in my face, the freshest breeze I caught.
E'en now I'm pillow'd on a bed of flowers
That crowns a lofty clift, which proudly towers
Above the ocean-waves. The stalks, and blades,
Chequer my tablet with their quivering shades.
On one side is a field of drooping oats,
Through which the poppies show their scarlet coats;
So pert and useless, that they bring to mind
The scarlet coats that pester human-kind.   130

And on the other side, outspread, is seen
Ocean's blue mantle streak'd with purple, and green.
Now 'tis I see a canvass'd ship, and now
Mark the bright silver curling round her prow.
I see the lark down-dropping to his nest,
And the broad winged sea-gull never at rest;
For when no more he spreads his feathers free,
His breast is dancing on the restless sea.
Now I direct my eyes into the west,
Which at this moment is in sunbeams drest: 140
Why westward turn? 'Twas but to say adieu!
'Twas but to kiss my hand, dear George, to you!

August 1816

ON FAME

Fame, like a wayward Girl, will still be coy
    To those who woo her with too slavish knees,
But makes surrender to some thoughtless Boy,
    And dotes the more upon a heart at ease;
She is a Gipsey, will not speak to those
    Who have not learnt to be content without her;
A Jilt, whose ear was never whisper'd close,
    Who thinks they scandal her who talk about her;
A very Gipsey is she, Nilus-born,
    Sister-in-law to jealous Potiphar;   10
Ye love-sick Bards, repay her scorn for scorn,
    Ye Artists lovelorn, madmen that ye are!
Make your best bow to her and bid adieu,
Then, if she likes it, she will follow you.

April 1819

VISION AND REVISION: *ENDYMION* AS A TEST CASE

TO J. H. REYNOLDS
18 April 1817   Carisbrooke, Isle of Wight

I shall forthwith begin my Endymion, which I hope I
shall have got some way into by the time you come, when
we will read our verses in a delightful place. . . .

10 May 1817   Margate

I began my Poem about a Fortnight since and have done
some every day except travelling ones—Perhaps I may
have done a good deal for the time but it appears such a
Pin's Point to me that I will not coppy any out—

—————•—•—•—————

In this letter, *Samphire* refers to an aromatic plant that grows
in rocks by the sea. Keats is alluding to *King Lear* (IV, vi, 15),
where Edgar emphasizes the steepness of the Dover cliffs by describing the dangers endured by samphire pickers there. What
"seem like Mice to mine" in Pope are undoubtedly the rhymed
couplets in which he cast his translation of Homer. When Keats
says, "I am now sure of having plenty of it this Summer," he is
referring to envy. Finally, the "G." at the end of the excerpt is
George, his brother.

TO B. R. HAYDON
10 May 1817   Margate

—truth is I have been in such a state of Mind as to read
over my Lines and hate them. I am "one that gathers
Samphire dreadful trade" the Cliff of Poesy Towers above
me—yet when, Tom who meets with some of Pope's
Homer in Plutarch's Lives reads some of those to me they
seem like Mice to mine. I read and write about eight
hours a day. There is an old saying well begun is half
done"—'t is a bad one. I would use instead—Not begun
at all 'till half done" so according to that I have not begun my Poem and consequently (a priori) can say nothing about it. Thank God! I do begin arduously where I
leave off, notwithstanding occasional depressions: and I
hope for the support of a High Power while I clime this
little eminence and especially in my Years of more momentous Labor.

The next passage is from the same letter but written on the
following day, 11 May 1817.

So I now revoke Promise of finishing my Poem by the Autumn which I should have done had I gone on as I have done—but I cannot write while my spirit is fe⟨a⟩vered in a contrary direction and I am now sure of have plenty of it this Summer—At this moment I am in no enviable Situation—I feel that I am not in a Mood to write any to day; and it appears that the lo⟨o⟩ss of it is the beginning of all sorts of irregularities.

. . . You should have heard from me before this—but in the first place I did not like to do so before I had got a little way in the 1ˢᵗ Book and in the next as G. told me you were going to write I delayed till I had hea[r]d from you—

———————

————I went day by day at my Poem for a Month at the end of which time the other day I found my Brain so overwrought that I had neither Rhyme nor reason in it—so was obliged to give up for a few days—I hope soon to be able to resume my Work—I have endeavoured to do so once or twice but to no Purpose—instead of Poetry I have a swimming in my head—And feel all the effects of a Mental Debauch—lowness of Spirits—anxiety to go on without the Power to do so which does not at all tend to my ultimate Progression—However tomorrow I will begin my next Month—This Evening I go to Cantrerbury—having got tired of Margate—I was not right in my head when I came—At Cantʸ I hope the Remembrance of Chaucer will set me forward like a Billiard-Ball—

———————

You will be glad to hear that I have finished my second Book.

———————

The coach that Keats rode to Oxford was named Defiance, and the friend whom he visited was Benjamin Bailey.

10 September 1817   Oxford

When I saw you last I told you of my intention of going to Oxford and 't is now a Week since I disembark'd from his Whipship's Coach the Defiance in this place. I am living in Magdalen Hall on a visit to a young Man with whom I have not been long acquainted, but whom I like very much—we lead very industrious lives he in general⟨s⟩ Studies and I in proceeding at a pretty good rate with a Poem which I hope you will see early in the next year—Perhaps you might like to know what I am writing about —I will tell you—

Many Years ago there was a young handsome Shepherd who fed his flocks on a Mountain's Side called Latmus—he was a very contemplative sort of a Person and lived solitry among the trees and Plains little thinking—that such a beautiful Creature as the Moon was growing mad in Love with him—However so it was; and when he was asleep on the Grass, she used to come down from heaven and admire him excessively from a long time; and at last could not refrain from carying him away in her arms to the top of that high Mountain Latmus while he was a dreaming—but I dare ⟨yo⟩ say have read this and all the other beautiful Tales which have come down from the ancient times of that beautiful Greece. If you have not let me know and I will tell you more at large of others quite as delightful—. . .

I have been writing very hard lately even till an utter incapacity came on, and I feel it now about my head: so you must not mind a little out of the way sayings—though bye the bye where my brain as clear as a bell I think I should have a little propensity thereto. I shall stop here till I have finished the 3rd Book of my Story; which I hope will be accomplish'd in at most three Weeks from to day—

TO JANE AND MARIANE REYNOLDS
14 September 1817   Oxford

I made a little mistake when just now I talked of being far inland: how can that be when Endymion and I are at the bottom of the Sea? Whence I hope to bring him in safety before you leave the Sea Side and if I can so contrive it you shall be greeted by him on the Sands and he shall tell you all his adventures: which at having finished he shall thus proceed. "My dear Ladies, favorites of my gentle Mistress, how ever my friend Keats may have teazed and vexed you believe me he loves you not the less —for instance I am deep in his favor and yet he has been hawling me through the Earth and Sea with unrelenting Perseverence—I know for all this that he is mightily fond of me, by his contriving me all sorts of pleasures—nor is this the least fair Ladies—this one of meeting you on desart shore and greeting you in his Name—He sends you moreover this little scroll"—
"My dear Girls,

I send you per favor of Endymion the assurance of my esteem of you and my utmost wishes for you Health and Pleasure—being ever—Your affectionate Brother. John Keats—

———•—•—•———

TO J. H. REYNOLDS
21 September 1817   Oxford

—I am getting on famous with my third Book—have written 800 lines thereof, and hope to finish it next week— Bailey likes what I have done very much—Believe me, my Dear Reynolds, one of my chief layings-up is the pleasure I shall have in showing it to you. . . .

———•—•—•———

TO B. R. HAYDON
28 September 1817   Oxford

You will be glad to hear that within these last three weeks I have written 1000 lines—which are the third Book of my

Poem. My Ideas with respect to it I assure you are very low—and I would write the subject thoroughly again. but I am tired of it and think the time would be better spent in writing a new Romance which I have in my eye for next summer—Rome was not built in a Day. and all the good I expect from my employment this summer is the fruit of Experience which I hope to gather in my next Poem.

———•◦•———

In the next letter Keats's hope that Apollo was not angered derives from his embarrassment at recalling a night when he and Hunt crowned each other with laurel.

TO BENJAMIN BAILEY
8 October 1817   Hampstead

Haydon says to me Keats dont show your Lines to Hunt on any account or he will have done half for you—so it appears Hunt wishes it to be thought. When he met Reynolds in the Theatre John told him that I was getting on to the completion of 4000 Lines. Ah! says Hunt, had it not been for me they would have been 7000! If he will say this to Reynolds what would he to other People? Haydon received a Letter a little while back on this subject from some Lady—which contains a caution to me through him on this subject—Now is not all this a most paultry thing to think about? You may see the whole of the case by the following extract from a Letter I wrote to George in the spring "As to what you say about "my being a Poet I can retu[r]n no answer but by saying "that the high Idea I have of poetical fame makes me "think I see it towering to high above me. At any rate I "have no ⟨wi⟩ right to talk until Endymion is finished— "it will be a test, a trial of my Powers of Imagination and "chiefly of my invention which is a rare thing indeed—by "which I must make 4000 Lines of one bare circumstance "and fill them with Poetry; and when I consider that this "is a great task, and that when done it will take me but a "dozen paces towards the Temple of Fame—it makes me

"say—God forbid that I should be without such a task!
"I have heard Hunt say and may be asked—why en-
"deavour after a long Poem? To which I should answer—
"Do not the Lovers of Poetry like to have a little Region
"to wander in where they may pick and choose, and in
"which the images are so numerous that many are for-
"gotten and found new in a second Reading: which may
"be food for a Week's stroll in the Summer? Do not they
"like this better than what they can read through before
"Mrs Williams comes down stairs? a Morning work at
"most. Besides a long Poem is a test of Invention which
"I take to be the Polar Star of Poetry, as Fancy is the
"Sails, and Imagination the Rudder. Did our great Poets
"ever write short Pieces? I mean in the shape of Tales—
"This same invention seems i{n}deed of late Years to
"have been forgotten as a Poetical excellence{.} But
"enough of this, I put on no Laurels till I shall have
"finished Endymion, and I hope Apollo is {not} angered
"at my having made a Mockery at him at Hunt's" You
see Bailey how independant my writing has been—Hunts
dissuasion was of no avail—I refused to visit Shelley, that
I might have my own unfetterd scope—and after all I shall
have the Reputation of Hunt's elevé—His corrections
and amputations will by the knowing ones be trased in
the Poem—This is to be sure the vexation of a day—nor
would I say so many Words about it to any but those
whom I know to have my wellfare and Reputation at
Heart—

———•═•═•———

TO BENJAMIN BAILEY
28 October 1817   Hamsptead

I dont suppose I've w[r]itten as many Lines as you have
read Volumes or at least Chapters since I saw you. However, I am in a fair way now to come to a conclusion in
at least three Weeks when I assure you I shall be glad to
dismount for a Month or two—although I'll keep as tight
a reign as possible till then nor suffer myself to sleep. I
will copy for you the opening of the 4 Book—in which
you will see from the Manner I had not an opportunity of

mentioning any Poets, for fear of spoiling the effect of the passage by particularising them!

And from the same letter, written on 30 October:

> . . . You must forgive although I have only written 300 Lines—they would have been five but I have been obliged to go to town.

TO BENJAMIN BAILEY
22 November 1817   Burford Bridge

—My Brother Tom is much Improved—he is going to Devonshire—whither I shall follow him—at present I am just arrived at Dorking to change the Scene—change the Air and give me a spur to wind up my Poem, of which there are wanting 500 Lines.

TO J. H. REYNOLDS
22 November 1817   Burford Bridge

—I like this place very much—There is Hill & Dale and a little River—I went up Box hill this Evening after the Moon—you a' seen the Moon—came down—and wrote some lines. Whenever I am separated from you, and not engaged in a continued Poem—every Letter shall bring you a lyric—but I am too anxious for you to enjoy the whole, to send you a particle. One of the three Books I have with me is Shakespear's Poems: I neer found so many beauties in the sonnets. . . .

He overwhelms a genuine Lover of Poesy with all manner of abuse, talking about—

> "a poets rage
> And stretched metre of an antique song"—

Which by the by will be a capital Motto for my Poem—won't it?—

TO GEORGE AND TOM KEATS
5 January 1818   London

Wells tells me, that you are licking your Chops Tom, in
expectation of my Book coming out; I am sorry to say I
have not began my corrections yet: tomorrow I set out.

———◦—◦—◦———

TO GEORGE AND TOM KEATS
19 January 1818   Hampstead

—I have just finished the revision of my first book, & shall
take it to Taylor's tomorrow—

———◦—◦—◦———

In the next letter "this business" alludes to Haydon's being
commissioned by Taylor to design a frontispiece for *Endymion*.

23 January 1818   Hampstead

My dear Haydon,
I have a complete fellow-feeling with you in this business
— so much so that it would be as well to wait for a choice
out of *Hyperion*— when that Poem is done there will be a
wide range for you—in Endymion I think you may have
many bits of the deep and sentimental cast—the nature
of *Hyperion* will lead me to treat it in a more naked and
grecian Manner—and the march of passion and endeavour
will be undeviating—and one great contrast between them
will be—that the Hero of the written tale being mortal
is led on, like Buonaparte, by circumstance; whereas the
Apollo in Hyperion being a fore-seeing God will shape
his actions like one.

———◦—◦—◦———

TO JOHN TAYLOR
23 January 1818   Hampstead

My dear Taylor,
I have spoken to Haydon about the Drawing—he would
do it with all his Art and Heart too if so I will it—how-

ever he has written thus to me—but I must tell you first, he intends painting a finished picture from the Poem—thus he writes

"When I do any thing for your poem, it must be effectual—an honor to both of us—to hurry up a sketch for the season won't do. I think an engraving from your head, from a Chalk drawing of mine—done with all my might—to which I would put my name, would answer Taylor's Idea more than the other indeed I am sure of it—this I will do & this will be effectual and as I have not done it for any other human being—it will have an effect"

What think you of this? Let me hear—I shall have my second book in readiness forthwith—

Your's most sincerely
John Keats—

TO BENJAMIN BAILEY
23 January 1818   Hampstead

—I have sent my first book to the Press—and this afternoon shall begin preparing the second—

The quote in this letter is from *Richard III*, V, ii, 3.
"Franchesca" is the heroine of Hunt's sentimental verse narrative *The Story of Rimini.*

TO GEORGE AND TOM KEATS
23 January 1818   Hampstead

I have given the 1st book to Taylor; he seemed more than satisfied with it, & to my surprise proposed publishing it in Quarto if Haydon would make a drawing of some event therein, for a Frontispeice. I called on Haydon, he said he would do anything I liked, but said he would rather paint a finished picture, from it, which he seems ⟨to say⟩ eager to do; this in a year or two will be a glorious thing for us; & it will be, for Haydon is struck with the 1st Book. I left Haydon & the next day received a letter from him, proposing to make, as he says, with all his might, a finished chalk sketch of my head, to be engraved in the first style & put at the head of my Poem, saying at the same time he had never done the thing for any human being, & that it must have considerable effect as he will put the name to it—I begin to day to copy my 2nd Book "thus far into the bowels of the Land"—You shall hear whether it will be Quarto or non Quarto, picture or non Picture. Leigh Hunt I showed my 1st Book to, he allows it not much merit as a whole; says it is unnatural & made ten objections to it in the mere skimming over. He says the conversation is unnatural & too high-flown for the Brother & Sister. Says it should be simple forgetting do ye mind, that they are both overshadowed by a Supernatural Power, & of force could not speak like Franchesca in the Rimini. He must first prove that Caliban's poetry is unnatural,—This with me completely overturns his objections—the fact is he & Shelley are hurt & perhaps justly, at my not having showed them the affair officiously & from several hints I have had they appear much disposed to dissect & anatomize, any trip or slip I may have made.—But whose afraid Ay! Tom! demme if I am.

And from the same letter, this portion written on 24 January 1818:

I am in the habit of taking my papers to Dilkes & copying there; so I chat & proceed at the same time. I have been there at my work this evening.

———•—•———

TO J. H. REYNOLDS
3 February 1818   Hampstead

I will call on you at 4 tomorrow, and we will trudge together for it is not the thing to be a stranger in the Land of Harpsicols. I hope also to bring you my 2^{d} book—In the hope that these Scribblings will be some amusement for you this Evening—I remain copying ⟨still⟩ on the Hill

———•—•———

TO JOHN TAYLOR
5 February 1818   London

I have finish'd coppying my Second Book but I want it
for one day to overlook it—

———•••———

TO GEORGE AND TOM KEATS
14 (?) February 1818   Hampstead

—I shall visit you as soon as I have copied my poem all
out, I am now much beforehand with the printer, they
have done none yet, & I am half afraid they will let half
the season by before the printing, I am determined they
shall not trouble me when I have copied it all.—. . . I
saw a sheet of Endymion & have all reason to suppose they
will soon get it done. there shall be nothing wanting on
my part.

———•••———

TO GEORGE AND TOM KEATS
21 February 1818   Hampstead

Taylor says my Poem shall be out in a Month.

———•••———

The line references needed to follow Keats's corrections are
all in Book I of *Endymion* and they run: "soberly," 149; "quiet,"
247; "Ash top," 335; "Dryope," 495. The line "O for a Muse of
fire to ascend!" is Keats's misquotation of the opening line of the
Prologue to Shakespeare's *Henry V*.

TO JOHN TAYLOR
27 February 1818   Hampstead

My dear Taylor,
Your alteration strikes me as being a great improvement—
the page looks much better. And now I will attend to the
Punctuations you speak of—the comma should be at *so-*

berly, and in the other passage the comma should follow *quiet,.* I am extremely indebted to you for this attention and also for your after admonitions—It is a sorry thing for me that any one should have to overcome Prejudices in reading my Verses—that affects me more than any hyper-criticism on any particular Passage. In *Endymion* I have most likely but moved into the Go-cart from the leading strings. In Poetry I have a few Axioms, and you will see how far I am from their Centre. 1st I think Poetry should surprise by a fine excess and not by Singularity—it should strike the Reader as a wording of his own highest thoughts, and appear almost a Remembrance—2nd Its touches of Beauty should never be half way therby making the reader breathless instead of content: the rise, the prog-ress, the setting of imagery should like the Sun come natu-ral natural too him—shine over him and set soberly al-though in magnificence leaving him in the Luxury of twi-light—but it is easier to think what Poetry should be than to write it—and this leads me on to another axiom. That if Poetry comes not as naturally as the Leaves to a tree it had better not come at all. However it may be with me I cannot help looking into new countries with 'O for a Muse of fire to ascend!'—If *Endymion* serves me as a Pioneer perhaps I ought to be content. I have great reason to be content, for thank God I can read and perhaps understand Shakspeare to his depths, and I have I am sure many friends, who, if I fail, will attribute any change in my Life and Temper to Humbleness rather than to Pride —to a cowering under the Wings of great Poets rather than to a Bitterness that I am not appreciated. I am anx-ious to get Endymion printed that I may forget it and proceed. I have coppied the 3rd Book and have begun the 4th. On running my Eye over the Proofs—I saw one Mis-take I will notice it presently and also any others if there be any—There should be no comma in 'the raft branch down sweeping from a tall Ash top'—I have besides made one or two alteration{s} and also altered the 13 Line Page 32 to make sense of it as you will see. I will take care the Printer shall not trip up my Heels—There should be no dash after Dryope in the Line 'Dryope's lone lull-ing of her Child. Remember me to Percy Street.

Your sincere and oblig^d friend
John Keats—

P.S. You shall have a sho[r]t *Preface* in good time—

———•◦•———

TO J. H. REYNOLDS
14 March 1818   Teignmouth

I have copied my fourth Book, and shall write the pref-ace soon. I wish it was all done; for I want to forget it and make my mind free for something new—

———•◦•———

TO TAYLOR AND HESSEY
21 March 1818   Teignmouth

I had no idea of your getting on so fast—I thought of bringing my 4th Book to Town all in good-time for you, especially after the late unfortunate chance.

I did not however for my own sake delay finishing the copy which was done a few days after my arrival here. I send it off to day, and will tell you in a Post script at what time to send for it from the Bull and Mouth or other Inn. You will find the Preface and dedication, and the title Page as I should wish it to stand—for a ramance is a fine thing notwithstanding the circulating Libraries.

———•◦•———

Substituting "Book" for "soul," Keats paraphrases *2 Henry VI* (III, iii, 16) to express his fear of porcupine-critics with their quill-pens. In Shakespeare's time birds were caught in the sticky lime which was spread on twigs to trap them.

Keats borrowed the phrase "to begin from Jove" from Her-rick's "Evensong," line 1.

TO J. H. REYNOLDS
9 April 1818   Teignmouth

—I see swarms of Porcupines with their Quills erect "like lime-twigs set to catch my Winged Book" and I would fright 'em away with a torch—You will say my preface is not much of a Torch. It would have been too insulting "to begin from Jove" and I could not [set] a golden head upon a thing of clay—if there is any fault in the preface it is not affectation: but an undersong of disrespect to the Public.—if I write another preface. it must be done without a thought of those people—I will think about it. If it should not reach you in four—or five days—tell Taylor to publish it without a preface, and let the dedication simply stand "inscribed to the memory of Thomas Chatterton."

———•———

TO J. H. REYNOLDS
10 April 1818   Teignmouth

I am anxious you sho^d find this Preface tolerable. if there is an affectation in it 'tis natural to me.—Do let the Printer's Devil cook it—and 'let me be as the casing air.'

You are too good in this Matter—were I in your state, I am certain I should have no thought but of discontent and illness—I might tho' be taught patience: I had an idea of giving no Preface; however, don't you think this had better go?—O, let it—one should not be too timid of committing faults.

———•———

Here Keats responds to his publisher after receiving an advance copy of *Endymion*.

TO JOHN TAYLOR
24 April 1818   Teignmouth

I think I Did very wrong to leave you to all the trouble of Endymion—but I could not help it then—another time I shall be more bent to all sort of troubles and disagreeables—. . .

And in proportion to my disgust at the task is my sense of your kindness & anxiety—the book pleased me much—it is very free from faults; and although there are one or two words I should wish replaced, I see in many places an improvement greatly to the purpose—

———•◦•———

TO J. A. HESSEY
8 October 1818   Hampstead

—Praise or blame has but a momentary effect on the man whose love of beauty in the abstract makes him a severe critic on his own Works. My own domestic criticism has given me pain without comparison beyond what Blackwood or the ⟨Edinburgh⟩ Quarterly could possibly inflict. and also when I feel I am right, no external praise can give me such a glow as my own solitary reperception & ratification of what is fine. J.S. is perfectly right in regard to the slipshod Endymion. That it is so is no fault of mine.—No!—though it may sound a little paradoxical. It is as good as I had power to make it—by myself—Had I been nervous about its being a perfect piece, & with that view asked advice, & trembled over every page, it would not have been written; for it is not in my nature to fumble—I will write independantly.—I have written independently *without Judgment*—I may write independently *& with judgment* hereafter.—The Genius of Poetry must work out its own salvation in a man: It cannot be matured by law & precept, but by sensation & watchfulness in itself—That which is creative must create itself—In Endymion, I leaped headlong into the Sea, and thereby have become better acquainted with the Soundings, the quicksands, & the rocks, than if I had ⟨stayed⟩ stayed upon the green shore, and piped a silly pipe, and took tea & comfortable advice.—I was never afraid of failure; for I would sooner fail than not be among the greatest—But I am nigh getting into a rant.

ENDYMION: A POETIC ROMANCE

'The stretched metre of an antique song'

PREFACE

Knowing within myself the manner in which this Poem has been produced, it is not without a feeling of regret that I make it public.

What manner I mean, will be quite clear to the reader, who must soon perceive great inexperience, immaturity, and every error denoting a feverish attempt, rather than a deed accomplished. The two first books, and indeed the two last, I feel sensible are not of such completion as to warant their passing the press; nor should they if I thought a year's castigation would do them any good;—it will not: the foundations are too sandy. It is just that this youngster should die away: a sad thought for me, if I had not some hope that while it is dwindling I may be plotting, and fitting myself for verses fit to live.

This may be speaking too presumptuously, and may deserve a punishment: but no feeling man will be forward to inflict it: he will leave me alone, with the conviction that there is not a fiercer hell than the failure in a great object. This is not written with the least atom of purpose to forestall criticisms of course, but from the desire I have to conciliate men who are competent to look, and who do look with a zealous eye, to the honour of English literature.

The imagination of a boy is healthy, and the mature imagination of a man is healthy; but there is a space of life between, in which the soul is in a ferment, the character undecided, the way of life uncertain, the ambition thick-sighted: thence proceeds mawkishness, and all the thousand bitters which those men I speak of must necessarily taste in going over the following pages.

I hope I have not in too late a day touched the beautiful mythology of Greece, and dulled its brightness: for I wish to try once more, before I bid it farewell.

TEIGNMOUTH, *April 10, 1818*

ENDYMION

Book I

A thing of beauty is a joy for ever:
Its loveliness increases; it will never
Pass into nothingness; but still will keep
A bower quiet for us, and a sleep
Full of sweet dreams, and health, and quiet breathing.
Therefore, on every morrow, are we wreathing
A flowery band to bind us to the earth,
Spite of despondence, of the inhuman dearth
Of noble natures, of the gloomy days,
Of all the unhealthy and o'er-darkened ways   10
Made for our searching: yes, in spite of all,
Some shape of beauty moves away the pall
From our dark spirits. Such the sun, the moon,
Trees old, and young, sprouting a shady boon
For simple sheep; and such are daffodils
With the green world they live in; and clear rills
That for themselves a cooling covert make
'Gainst the hot season; the mid forest brake,
Rich with a sprinkling of fair musk-rose blooms:
And such too is the grandeur of the dooms   20
We have imagined for the mighty dead;
All lovely tales that we have heard or read:
An endless fountain of immortal drink,
Pouring unto us from the heaven's brink.

  Nor do we merely feel these essences
For one short hour; no, even as the trees
That whisper round a temple become soon
Dear as the temple's self, so does the moon,
The passion poesy, glories infinite,

Haunt us till they become a cheering light   30
Unto our souls, and bound to us so fast,
That, whether there be shine, or gloom o'ercast,
They alway must be with us, or we die.

Therefore, 'tis with full happiness that I
Will trace the story of Endymion.
The very music of the name has gone
Into my being, and each pleasant scene
Is growing fresh before me as the green
Of our own vallies: so I will begin
Now while I cannot hear the city's din;   40
Now while the early budders are just new,
And run in mazes of the youngest hue
About old forests; while the willow trails
Its delicate amber; and the dairy pails
Bring home increase of milk. And, as the year
Grows lush in juicy stalks, I'll smoothly steer
My little boat, for many quiet hours,
With streams that deepen freshly into bowers.
Many and many a verse I hope to write,
Before the daisies, vermeil rimm'd and white,   50
Hide in deep herbage; and ere yet the bees
Hum about globes of clover and sweet peas,
I must be near the middle of my story.
O may no wintry season, bare and hoary,
See it half finish'd: but let Autumn bold,
With universal tinge of sober gold,
Be all about me when I make an end.
And now at once, adventuresome, I send
My herald thought into a wilderness:
There let its trumpet blow, and quickly dress   60
My uncertain path with green, that I may speed
Easily onward, thorough flowers and weed.
   Upon the sides of Latmos was outspread
A mighty forest; for the moist earth fed
So plenteously all weed-hidden roots
Into o'er-hanging boughs, and precious fruits.
And it had gloomy shades, sequestered deep,
Where no man went; and if from shepherd's keep
A lamb stray'd far a-down those inmost glens,

Never again saw he the happy pens 70
Whither his brethren, bleating with content,
Over the hills at every nightfall went.
Among the shepherds, 'twas believed ever,
That not one fleecy lamb which thus did sever
From the white flock, but pass'd unworried
By angry wolf, or pard with prying head,
Until it came to some unfooted plains
Where fed the herds of Pan: aye great his gains
Who thus one lamb did lose. Paths there were many,
Winding through palmy fern, and rushes fenny, 80
And ivy banks; all leading pleasantly
To a wide lawn, whence one could only see
Stems thronging all around between the swell
Of turf and slanting branches: who could tell
The freshness of the space of heaven above,
Edg'd round with dark tree tops? through which a dove
Would often beat its wings, and often too
A little cloud would move across the blue.

Full in the middle of this pleasantness
There stood a marble altar, with a tress 90
Of flowers budded newly; and the dew
Had taken fairy phantasies to strew
Daisies upon the sacred sward last eve,
And so the dawned light in pomp receive.
For 'twas the morn: Apollo's upward fire
Made every eastern cloud a silvery pyre
Of brightness so unsullied, that therein
A melancholy spirit well might win
Oblivion, and melt out his essence fine
Into the winds: rain-scented eglantine 100
Gave temperate sweets to that well-wooing sun;
The lark was lost in him; cold springs had run
To warm their chilliest bubbles in the grass;
Man's voice was on the mountains; and the mass
Of nature's lives and wonders puls'd tenfold,
To feel this sun-rise and its glories old.

Now while the silent workings of the dawn
Were busiest, into that self-same lawn

All suddenly, with joyful cries, there sped
A troop of little children garlanded;   110
Who gathering round the altar, seem'd to pry
Earnestly round as wishing to espy
Some folk of holiday: nor had they waited
For many moments, ere their ears were sated
With a faint breath of music, which ev'n then
Fill'd out its voice, and died away again.
Within a little space again it gave
Its airy swellings, with a gentle wave,
To light-hung leaves, in smoothest echoes breaking
Through copse-clad vallies,—ere their death, o'ertaking   120
The surgy murmurs of the lonely sea.

  And now, as deep into the wood as we
Might mark a lynx's eye, there glimmered light
Fair faces and a rush of garments white,
Plainer and plainer showing, till at last
Into the widest alley they all past,
Making directly for the woodland altar.
O kindly muse! let not my weak tongue faulter
In telling of this goodly company,
Of their old piety, and of their glee: 130
But let a portion of ethereal dew
Fall on my head, and presently unmew
My soul; that I may dare, in wayfaring,
To stammer where old Chaucer us'd to sing.

  Leading the way, young damsels danced along,
Bearing the burden of a shepherd song;
Each having a white wicker over brimm'd
With April's tender younglings: next, well trimm'd,
A crowd of shepherds with as sunburnt looks
As may be read of in Arcadian books;   140
Such as sat listening round Apollo's pipe,
When the great deity, for earth too ripe,
Let his divinity o'erflowing die
In music, through the vales of Thessaly:
Some idly trail'd their sheep-hooks on the ground,
And some kept up a shrilly mellow sound
With ebon-tipped flutes: close after these,

Now coming from beneath the forest trees,
A venerable priest full soberly,
Begirt with ministring looks: alway his eye   150
Stedfast upon the matted turf he kept,
And after him his sacred vestments swept,
From his right hand there swung a vase, milk-white,
Of mingled wine, out-sparkling generous light;
And in his left he held a basket full
Of all sweet herbs that searching eye could cull:
Wild thyme, and valley-lillies whiter still
Than Leda's love, and cresses from the rill.
His aged head, crowned with beechen wreath,
Seem'd like a poll of ivy in the teeth   160
Of winter hoar. Then came another crowd
Of shepherds, lifting in due time aloud
Their share of the ditty. After them appear'd,
Up-followed by a multitude that rear'd
Their voices to the clouds, a fair wrought car,
Easily rolling so as scarce to mar
The freedom of three steeds of dapple brown:
Who stood therein did seem of great renown
Among the throng. His youth was fully blown,
Showing like Ganymede to manhood grown;   170
And, for those simple times, his garments were
A chieftain king's: beneath his breast, half bare,
Was hung a silver bugle, and between
His nervy knees there lay a boar-spear keen.
A smile was on his countenance; he seem'd,
To common lookers on, like one who dream'd
Of idleness in groves Elysian:
But there were some who feelingly could scan
A lurking trouble in his nether lip,
And see that oftentimes the reins would slip   180
Through his forgotten hands: then would they sigh,
And think of yellow leaves, of owlets' cry,
Of logs piled solemnly.—Ah, well-a-day,
Why should our young Endymion pine away!

    Soon the assembly, in a circle rang'd,
Stood silent round the shrine: each look was chang'd
To sudden veneration: women meek

Beckon'd their sons to silence; while each cheek
Of virgin bloom paled gently for slight fear.
Endymion too, without a forest peer,   190
Stood, wan, and pale, and with an awed face,
Among his brothers of the mountain chace.
In midst of all, the venerable priest
Eyed them with joy from greatest to the least,
And, after lifting up his aged hands,
Thus spake he: 'Men of Latmos! shepherd bands!
Whose care it is to guard a thousand flocks:
Whether descended from beneath the rocks
That overtop your mountains; whether come
From vallies where the pipe is never dumb;   200
Or from your swelling downs, where sweet air stirs
Blue hare-bells lightly, and where prickly furze
Buds lavish gold; or ye, whose precious charge
Nibble their fill at ocean's very marge,
Whose mellow reeds are touch'd with sounds forlorn
By the dim echoes of old Triton's horn:
Mothers and wives! who day by day prepare
The scrip, with needments, for the mountain air;
And all ye gentle girls who foster up
Udderless lambs, and in a little cup   210
Will put choice honey for a favoured youth:
Yea, every one attend! for in good truth
Our vows are wanting to our great god Pan.
Are not our lowing heifers sleeker than
Night-swollen mushrooms? Are not our wide plains
Speckled with countless fleeces? Have not rains
Green'd over April's lap? No howling sad
Sickens our fearful ewes; and we have had
Great bounty from Endymion our lord.
The earth is glad: the merry lark has pour'd   220
His early song against yon breezy sky,
That spreads so clear o'er our solemnity.'

   Thus ending, on the shrine he heap'd a spire
Of teeming sweets, enkindling sacred fire;
Anon he stain'd the thick and spongy sod
With wine, in honour of the shepherd-god.
Now while the earth was drinking it, and while

Bay leaves were crackling in the fragrant pile,
And gummy frankincense was sparkling bright   230
'Neath smothering parsley, and a hazy light
Spread greyly eastward, thus a chorus sang:

'O thou, whose mighty palace roof doth hang
From jagged trunks, and overshadoweth
Eternal whispers, glooms, the birth, life, death
Of unseen flowers in heavy peacefulness;
Who lov'st to see the hamadryads dress
Their ruffled locks where meeting hazels darken;
And through whole solemn hours dost sit, and hearken
The dreary melody of bedded reeds—   240
In desolate places, where dank moisture breeds
The pipy hemlock to strange overgrowth;
Bethinking thee, how melancholy loth
Thou wast to lose fair Syrinx—do thou now,
By thy love's milky brow!
By all the trembling mazes that she ran,
Hear us, great Pan!

'O thou, for whose soul-soothing quiet, turtles
Passion their voices cooingly 'mong myrtles,
What time thou wanderest at eventide
Through sunny meadows, that outskirt the side   250
Of thine enmossed realms: O thou, to whom
Broad leaved fig trees even now foredoom
Their ripen'd fruitage; yellow girted bees
Their golden honeycombs; our village leas
Their fairest blossom'd beans and poppied corn;
The chuckling linnet its five young unborn,
To sing for thee; low creeping strawberries
Their summer coolness; pent up butterflies
Their freckled wings; yea, the fresh budding year
All its completions—be quickly near,   260
By every wind that nods the mountain pine,
O forester divine!

'Thou, to whom every faun and satyr flies
For willing service; whether to surprise
The squatted hare while in half sleeping fit;

Or upward ragged precipices flit
To save poor lambkins from the eagle's maw;
Or by mysterious enticement draw
Bewildered shepherds to their path again;
Or to tread breathless round the frothy main, 270
And gather up all fancifullest shells
For thee to tumble into Naiads' cells,
And, being hidden, laugh at their out-peeping;
Or to delight thee with fantastic leaping,
The while they pelt each other on the crown
With silvery oak apples, and fir cones brown—
By all the echoes that about thee ring,
Hear us, O satyr king!

   'O Hearkener to the loud clapping shears
While ever and anon to his shorn peers 280
A ram goes bleating: Winder of the horn,
When snouted wild-boars routing tender corn
Anger our huntsmen: Breather round our farms,
To keep off mildews, and all weather harms:
Strange ministrant of undescribed sounds,
That come a swooning over hollow grounds,
And wither drearily on barren moors:
Dread opener of the mysterious doors
Leading to universal knowledge—see,
Great son of Dryope, 290
The many that are come to pay their vows
With leaves about their brows!

   'Be still the unimaginable lodge
For solitary thinkings; such as dodge
Conception to the very bourne of heaven,
Then leave the naked brain: be still the leaven,
That spreading in this dull and clodded earth
Gives it a touch ethereal—a new birth:
Be still a symbol of immensity;
A firmament reflected in a sea; 300
An element filling the space between;
An unknown—but no more: we humbly screen
With uplift hands our foreheads, lowly bending,

And giving out a shout most heaven rending,
Conjure thee to receive our humble Pæan,
Upon thy Mount Lycean!'

Even while they brought the burden to a close,
A shout from the whole multitude arose,
That lingered in the air like dying rolls
Of abrupt thunder, when Ionian shoals   310
Of dolphins bob their noses through the brine.
Meantime, on shady levels, mossy fine,
Young companies nimbly began dancing
To the swift treble pipe, and humming string.
Aye, those fair living forms swam heavenly
To tunes forgotten—out of memory:
Fair creatures! whose young children's children bred
Thermopylæ its heroes—not yet dead,
But in old marbles ever beautiful,
High genitors, unconscious did they cull   320
Time's sweet first-fruits—they danc'd to weariness,
And then in quiet circles did they press
The hillock turf, and caught the latter end
Of some strange history, potent to send
A young mind from its bodily tenement.
Or they might watch the quoit-pitchers, intent
On either side; pitying the sad death
Of Hyacinthus, when the cruel breath
Of Zephyr slew him,—Zephyr penitent,
Who now, ere Phœbus mounts the firmament,   330
Fondles the flower amid the sobbing rain.
The archers too, upon a wider plain,
Beside the feathery whizzing of the shaft,
And the dull twanging bowstring, and the raft
Branch down sweeping from a tall ash top,
Call'd up a thousand thoughts to envelope
Those who would watch. Perhaps, the trembling knee
And frantic gape of lonely Niobe,
Poor, lonely Niobe! when her lovely young
Were dead and gone, and her caressing tongue   340
Lay a lost thing upon her paly lip,
And very, very deadliness did nip

Her motherly cheeks. Arous'd from this sad mood
By one, who at a distance loud halloo'd,
Uplifting his strong bow into the air,
Many might after brighter visions stare:
After the Argonauts, in blind amaze
Tossing about on Neptune's restless ways,
Until, from the horizon's vaulted side,
There shot a golden splendour far and wide,   350
Spangling those million poutings of the brine
With quivering ore: 'twas even an awful shine
From the exaltation of Apollo's bow;
A heavenly beacon in their dreary woe.
Who thus were ripe for high contemplating,
Might turn their steps towards the sober ring
Where sat Endymion and the aged priest
'Mong shepherds gone in eld, whose looks increas'd
The silvery setting of their mortal star.
There they discours'd upon the fragile bar   360
That keeps us from our homes ethereal;
And what our duties there: to nightly call
Vesper, the beauty-crest of summer weather;
To summon all the downiest clouds together
For the sun's purple couch; to emulate
In ministring the potent rule of fate
With speed of fire-tail'd exhalations;
To tint her pallid cheek with bloom, who cons
Sweet poesy by moonlight: besides these,
A world of other unguess'd offices.   370
Anon they wander'd, by divine converse,
Into Elysium; vieing to rehearse
Each one his own anticipated bliss.
One felt heart-certain that he could not miss
His quick gone love, among fair blossom'd boughs,
Where every zephyr-sigh pouts, and endows
Her lips with music for the welcoming.
Another wish'd, mid that eternal spring,
To meet his rosy child, with feathery sails,
Sweeping, eye-earnestly, through almond vales: 380
Who, suddenly, should stoop through the smooth wind,
And with the balmiest leaves his temples bind;

And, ever after, through those regions be
His messenger, his little Mercury.
Some were athirst in soul to see again
Their fellow huntsmen o'er the wide champaign
In times long past; to sit with them, and talk
Of all the chances in their earthly walk;
Comparing, joyfully, their plenteous stores
Of happiness, to when upon the moors,   390
Benighted, close they huddled from the cold,
And shar'd their famish'd scrips. Thus all out-told
Their fond imaginations,—saving him
Whose eyelids curtain'd up their jewels dim,
Endymion: yet hourly had he striven
To hide the cankering venom, that had riven
His fainting recollections. Now indeed
His senses had swoon'd off: he did not heed
The sudden silence, or the whispers low,
Or the old eyes dissolving at his woe,   400
Or anxious calls, or close of trembling palms,
Or maiden's sigh, that grief itself embalms:
But in the self-same fixed trance he kept,
Like one who on the earth had never stept.
Aye, even as dead still as a marble man,
Frozen in that old tale Arabian.

Who whispers him so pantingly and close?
Peona, his sweet sister: of all those,
His friends, the dearest. Hushing signs she made,
And breath'd a sister's sorrow to persuade   410
A yielding up, a cradling on her care.
Her eloquence did breathe away the curse:
She led him, like some midnight spirit nurse
Of happy changes in emphatic dreams,
Along a path between two little streams,—
Guarding his forehead, with her round elbow,
From low-grown branches, and his footsteps slow
From stumbling over stumps and hillocks small;
Until they came to where these streamlets fall,
With mingled bubblings and a gentle rush,   420
Into a river, clear, brimful, and flush

With crystal mocking of the trees and sky.
A little shallop, floating there hard by,
Pointed its beak over the fringed bank;
And soon it lightly dipt, and rose, and sank,
And dipt again, with the young couple's weight,—
Peona guiding, through the water straight,
Towards a bowery island opposite;
Which gaining presently, she steered light
Into a shady, fresh, and ripply cove,   430
Where nested was an arbour, overwove
By many a summer's silent fingering;
To whose cool bosom she was used to bring
Her playmates, with their needle broidery,
And minstrel memories of times gone by.

So she was gently glad to see him laid
Under her favourite bower's quiet shade,
On her own couch, new made of flower leaves,
Dried carefully on the cooler side of sheaves
When last the sun his autumn tresses shook,   440
And the tann'd harvesters rich armfuls took.
Soon was he quieted to slumbrous rest:
But, ere it crept upon him, he had prest
Peona's busy hand against his lips,
And still, a sleeping, held her finger-tips
In tender pressure. And as a willow keeps
A patient watch over the stream that creeps
Windingly by it, so the quiet maid
Held her in peace: so that a whispering blade
Of grass, a wailful gnat, a bee bustling   450
Down in the blue-bells, or a wren light rustling
Among sere leaves and twigs, might all be heard.

O magic sleep! O comfortable bird,
That broodest o'er the troubled sea of the mind
Till it is hush'd and smooth! O unconfin'd
Restraint! imprisoned liberty! great key
To golden palaces, strange minstrelsy,
Fountains grotesque, new trees, bespangled caves,
Echoing grottos, full of tumbling waves

And moonlight; aye, to all the mazy world 460
Of silvery enchantment!—who, upfurl'd
Beneath thy drowsy wing a triple hour,
But renovates and lives?—Thus, in the bower,
Endymion was calm'd to life again.
Opening his eyelids with a healthier brain,
He said: 'I feel this thine endearing love
All through my bosom: thou art as a dove
Trembling its closed eyes and sleeked wings
About me; and the pearliest dew not brings
Such morning incense from the fields of May, 470
As do those brighter drops that twinkling stray
From those kind eyes,—the very home and haunt
Of sisterly affection. Can I want
Aught else, aught nearer heaven, than such tears?
Yet dry them up, in bidding hence all fears
That, any longer, I will pass my days
Alone and sad. No, I will once more raise
My voice upon the mountain-heights; once more
Make my horn parley from their foreheads hoar:
Again my trooping hounds their tongues shall loll 480
Around the breathed boar: again I'll poll
The fair-grown yew tree, for a chosen bow:
And, when the pleasant sun is setting low,
Again I'll linger in a sloping mead
To hear the speckled thrushes, and see feed
Our idle sheep. So be thou cheered, sweet,
And, if thy lute is here, softly intreat
My soul to keep in its resolved course.'

    Hereat Peona, in their silver source,
Shut her pure sorrow drops with glad exclaim, 490
And took a lute, from which there pulsing came
A lively prelude, fashioning the way
In which her voice should wander. 'Twas a lay
More subtle cadenced, more forest wild
Than Dryope's lone lulling of her child;
And nothing since has floated in the air
So mournful strange. Surely some influence rare
Went, spiritual, through the damsel's hand;

For still, with Delphic emphasis, she spann'd
The quick invisible strings, even though she saw   500
Endymion's spirit melt away and thaw
Before the deep intoxication.
But soon she came, with sudden burst, upon
Her self-possession—swung the lute aside,
And earnestly said: 'Brother, 'tis vain to hide
That thou dost know of things mysterious,
Immortal, starry; such alone could thus
Weigh down thy nature. Hast thou sinn'd in aught
Offensive to the heavenly power? Caught
A Paphian dove upon a message sent?   510
Thy deathful bow against some deer-herd bent
Sacred to Dian? Haply, thou hast seen
Her naked limbs among the alders green;
And that, alas! is death. No, I can trace
Something more high-perplexing in thy face!"

    Endymion look'd at her, and press'd her hand,
And said, 'Art thou so pale, who wast so bland
And merry in our meadows? How is this?
Tell me thine ailment: tell me all amiss!—
Ah! thou hast been unhappy at the change   520
Wrought suddenly in me. What indeed more strange?
Or more complete to overwhelm surmise?
Ambition is so sluggard: 'tis no prize,
That toiling years would put within my grasp,
That I have sighed for: with so deadly gasp
No man e'er panted for a mortal love.
So all have set my heavier grief above
These things which happen. Rightly have they done:
I, who still saw the horizontal sun
Heave his broad shoulder o'er the edge of the world,   530
Out-facing Lucifer, and then had hurl'd
My spear aloft, as signal for the chace—
I, who, for very sport of heart, would race
With my own steed from Araby; pluck down
A vulture from his towery perching; frown
A lion into growling, loth retire—
To lose, at once, all my toil-breeding fire,

And sink thus low! but I will ease my breast
Of secret grief, here in this bowery nest.

   'This river does not see the naked sky,   540
Till it begins to progress silverly
Around the western border of the wood,
Whence, from a certain spot, its winding flood
Seems at the distance like a crescent moon:
And in that nook, the very pride of June,
Had I been used to pass my weary eves;
The rather for the sun unwilling leaves
So dear a picture of his sovereign power,
And I could witness his most kingly hour,
When he doth tighten up the golden reins,   550
And paces leisurely down amber plains
His snorting four. Now when his chariot last
Its beams against the zodiac-lion cast,
There blossom'd suddenly a magic bed
Of sacred ditamy, and poppies red:
At which I wondered greatly, knowing well
That but one night had wrought this flowery spell;
And, sitting down close by, began to muse
What it might mean. Perhaps, thought I, Morpheus,
In passing here, his owlet pinions shook;   560
Or, it may be, ere matron Night uptook
Her ebon urn, young Mercury, by stealth,
Had dipt his rod in it: such garland wealth
Came not by common growth. Thus on I thought,
Until my head was dizzy and distraught.
Moreover, through the dancing poppies stole
A breeze, most softly lulling to my soul;
And shaping visions all about my sight
Of colours, wings, and bursts of spangly light;
The which became more strange, and strange, and dim,   570
And then were gulph'd in a tumultuous swim:
And then I fell asleep. Ah, can I tell
The enchantment that afterwards befel?
Yet it was but a dream: yet such a dream
That never tongue, although it overteem
With mellow utterance, like a cavern spring,

Could figure out and to conception bring
All I beheld and felt. Methought I lay
Watching the zenith, where the milky way
Among the stars in virgin splendour pours;   580
And travelling my eye, until the doors
Of heaven appear'd to open for my flight,
I became loth and fearful to alight
From such high soaring by a downward glance:
So kept me stedfast in that airy trance,
Spreading imaginary pinions wide.
When, presently, the stars began to glide,
And faint away, before my eager view:
At which I sigh'd that I could not pursue,
And dropt my vision to the horizon's verge;   590
And lo! from opening clouds, I saw emerge
The loveliest moon, that ever silver'd o'er
A shell for Neptune's goblet: she did soar
So passionately bright, my dazzled soul
Commingling with her argent spheres did roll
Through clear and cloudy, even when she went
At last into a dark and vapoury tent—
Whereat, methought, the lidless-eyed train
Of planets all were in the blue again.
To commune with those orbs, once more I rais'd   600
My sight right upward: but it was quite dazed
By a bright something, sailing down apace,
Making me quickly veil my eyes and face:
Again I look'd, and, O ye deities,
Who from Olympus watch our destinies!
Whence that completed form of all completeness?
Whence came that high perfection of all sweetness?
Speak, stubborn earth, and tell me where, O where
Hast thou a symbol of her golden hair?
Not oat-sheaves drooping in the western sun;   610
Not—thy soft hand fair sister! let me shun
Such follying before thee—yet she had,
Indeed, locks bright enough to make me mad;
And they were simply gordian'd up and braided,
Leaving, in naked comeliness, unshaded,
Her pearl round ears, white neck, and orbed brow;

The which were blended in, I know not how,
With such a paradise of lips and eyes,
Blush-tinted cheeks, half smiles, and faintest sighs,
That, when I think thereon, my spirit clings   620
And plays about its fancy, till the stings
Of human neighbourhood envenom all.
Unto what awful power shall I call?
To what high fane?—Ah! see her hovering feet,
More bluely vein'd, more soft, more whitely sweet
Than those of sea-born Venus, when she rose
From out her cradle shell. The wind out-blows
Her scarf into a fluttering pavillion;
'Tis blue, and over-spangled with a million
Of little eyes, as though thou wert to shed,   630
Over the darkest, lushest blue-bell bed,
Handfuls of daisies.'—'Endymion, how strange!
Dream within dream!'—'She took an airy range,
And then, towards me, like a very maid,
Came blushing, waning, willing, and afraid,
And press'd me by the hand: Ah! 'twas too much;
Methought I fainted at the charmed touch,
Yet held my recollections, even as one
Who dives three fathoms where the waters run
Gurgling in beds of coral: for anon,   640
I felt upmounted in that region
Where falling stars dart their artillery forth,
And eagles struggle with the buffeting north
That ballances the heavy meteor-stone;—
Felt too, I was not fearful, nor alone,
But lapp'd and lull'd along the dangerous sky.
Soon, as it seem'd, we left our journeying high,
And straightway into frightful eddies swoop'd;
Such as aye muster where grey time has scoop'd
Huge dens and caverns in a mountain's side;   650
There hollow sounds arous'd me, and I sigh'd
To faint once more by looking on my bliss—
I was distracted; madly did I kiss
The wooing arms which held me, and did give
My eyes at once to death: but 'twas to live,
To take in draughts of life from the gold fount

Of kind and passionate looks; to count, and count
The moments, by some greedy help that seem'd
A second self, that each might be redeem'd
And plunder'd of its load of blessedness.   660
Ah, desperate mortal! I e'en dar'd to press
Her very cheek against my crowned lip,
And, at that moment, felt my body dip
Into a warmer air: a moment more,
Our feet were soft in flowers. There was store
Of newest joys upon that alp. Sometimes
A scent of violets, and blossoming limes,
Loiter'd around us; then of honey cells,
Made delicate from all white-flower bells;
And once, above the edges of our nest,   670
An arch face peep'd,—an Oread as I guess'd.

'Why did I dream that sleep o'er-power'd me
In midst of all this heaven? Why not see,
Far off, the shadows of his pinions dark,
And stare them from me? But no, like a spark
That needs must die, although its little beam
Reflects upon a diamond, my sweet dream
Fell into nothing—into stupid sleep.
And so it was, until a gentle creep,
A careful moving caught my waking ears,   680
And up I started: Ah! my sighs, my tears,
My clenched hands:—for lo! the poppies hung
Dew-dabbled on their stalks, the ouzel sung
A heavy ditty, and the sullen day
Had chidden herald Hesperus away,
With leaden looks: the solitary breeze
Bluster'd, and slept, and its wild self did teaze
With wayward melancholy; and I thought,
Mark me, Peona! that sometimes it brought
Faint fare-thee-wells, and sigh-shrilled adieus!—   690
Away I wander'd—all the pleasant hues
Of heaven and earth had faded: deepest shades
Were deepest dungeons; heaths and sunny glades
Were full of pestilent light; our taintless rills
Seem'd sooty, and o'er-spread with upturn'd gills

Of dying fish; the vermeil rose had blown
In frightful scarlet, and its thorns out-grown
Like spiked aloe. If an innocent bird
Before my heedless footsteps stirr'd, and stirr'd
In little journeys, I beheld in it   700
A disguis'd demon, missioned to knit
My soul with under darkness; to entice
My stumblings down some monstrous precipice:
Therefore I eager followed, and did curse
The disappointment. Time, that aged nurse,
Rock'd me to patience. Now, thank gentle heaven!
These things, with all their comfortings, are given
To my down-sunken hours, and with thee,
Sweet sister, help to stem the ebbing sea
Of weary life.'
                  Thus ended he, and both   710
Sat silent: for the maid was very loth
To answer; feeling well that breathed words
Would all be lost, unheard, and vain as swords
Against the enchased crocodile, or leaps
Of grasshoppers against the sun. She weeps
And wonders; struggles to devise some blame;
To put on such a look as would say, *Shame
On this poor weakness!* but, for all her strife,
She could as soon have crush'd away the life
From a sick dove. At length, to break the pause,   720
She said with trembling chance: 'Is this the cause?
This all? Yet it is strange, and sad, alas!
That one who through this middle earth should pass
Most like a sojourning demi-god, and leave
His name upon the harp-string, should achieve
No higher bard than simple maidenhood,
Singing alone, and fearfully,—how the blood
Left his young cheek; and how he used to stray
He knew not where; and how he would say, *nay,*
If any said 'twas love: and yet 'twas love;   730
What could it be but love? How a ring-dove
Let fall a sprig of yew tree in his path;
And how he died: and then, that love doth scathe
The gentle heart, as northern blasts do roses;

And then the ballad of his sad life closes
With sighs, and an alas!—Endymion!
Be rather in the trumpet's mouth,—anon
Among the winds at large—that all may hearken!
Although, before the crystal heavens darken,
I watch and dote upon the silver lakes   740
Pictur'd in western cloudiness, that takes
The semblance of gold rocks and bright gold sands,
Islands, and creeks, and amber-fretted strands
With horses prancing o'er them, palaces
And towers of amethyst,—would I so teaze
My pleasant days, because I could not mount
Into those regions? The Morphean fount
Of that fine element that visions, dreams,
And fitful whims of sleep are made of, streams
Into its airy channels with so subtle,   750
So thin a breathing, not the spider's shuttle,
Circled a million times within the space
Of a swallow's nest-door, could delay a trace,
A tinting of its quality: how light
Must dreams themselves be; seeing they're more slight
Than the mere nothing that engenders them!
Then wherefore sully the entrusted gem
Of high and noble life with thoughts so sick?
Why pierce high-fronted honour to the quick
For nothing but a dream?' Hereat the youth   760
Look'd up: a conflicting of shame and ruth
Was in his plaited brow: yet, his eyelids
Widened a little, as when Zephyr bids
A little breeze to creep between the fans
Of careless butterflies: amid his pains
He seem'd to taste a drop of manna-dew,
Full palatable; and a colour grew
Upon his cheek, while thus he lifeful spake.

'Peona! ever have I long'd to slake
My thirst for the world's praises: nothing base,   770
No merely slumberous phantasm, could unlace
The stubborn canvas for my voyage prepar'd—
Though now 'tis tatter'd; leaving my bark bar'd

And sullenly drifting: yet my higher hope
Is of too wide, too rainbow-large a scope,
To fret at myriads of earthly wrecks.
Wherein lies happiness? In that which becks
Our ready minds to fellowship divine,
A fellowship with essence; till we shine,
Full alchemiz'd, and free of space. Behold   780
The clear religion of heaven! Fold
A rose leaf round thy finger's taperness,
And soothe thy lips: hist, when the airy stress
Of music's kiss impregnates the free winds,
And with a sympathetic touch unbinds
Æolian magic from their lucid wombs:
Then old songs waken from enclouded tombs;
Old ditties sigh above their father's grave;
Ghosts of melodious prophecyings rave
Round every spot where trod Apollo's foot;   790
Bronze clarions awake, and faintly bruit,
Where long ago a giant battle was;
And, from the turf, a lullaby doth pass
In every place where infant Orpheus slept.
Feel we these things?—that moment have we stept
Into a sort of oneness, and our state
Is like a floating spirit's. But there are
Richer entanglements, enthralments far
More self-destroying, leading, by degrees,
To the chief intensity: the crown of these   800
Is made of love and friendship, and sits high
Upon the forehead of humanity.
All its more ponderous and bulky worth
Is friendship, whence there ever issues forth
A steady splendour; but at the tip-top,
There hangs by unseen film, an orbed drop
Of light, and that is love: its influence,
Thrown in our eyes, genders a novel sense,
At which we start and fret; till in the end,
Melting into its radiance, we blend,   810
Mingle, and so become a part of it,—
Nor with aught else can our souls interknit
So wingedly: when we combine therewith,

Life's self is nourish'd by its proper pith,
And we are nurtured like a pelican brood.
Aye, so delicious is the unsating food,
That men, who might have tower'd in the van
Of all the congregated world, to fan
And winnow from the coming step of time
All chaff of custom, wipe away all slime   820
Left by men-slugs and human serpentry,
Have been content to let occasion die,
Whilst they did sleep in love's elysium.
And, truly, I would rather be struck dumb,
Than speak against this ardent listlessness:
For I have ever thought that it might bless
The world with benefits unknowingly;
As does the nightingale, upperched high,
And cloister'd among cool and bunched leaves—
She sings but to her love, nor e'er conceives   830
How tiptoe Night holds back her dark-grey hood.
Just so may love, although 'tis understood
The mere commingling of passionate breath,
Produce more than our searching witnesseth:
What I know not: but who, of men, can tell
That flowers would bloom, or that green fruit would swell
To melting pulp, that fish would have bright mail,
The earth its dower of river, wood, and vale,
The meadows runnels, runnels pebble-stones,
The seed its harvest, or the lute its tones,   840
Tones ravishment, or ravishment its sweet
If human souls did never kiss and greet?

    'Now, if this earthly love has power to make
Men's being mortal, immortal; to shake
Ambition from their memories, and brim
Their measure of content: what merest whim,
Seems all this poor endeavour after fame,
To one, who keeps within his stedfast aim
A love immortal, an immortal too.
Look not so wilder'd; for these things are true,   850
And never can be born of atomies
That buzz about our slumbers, like brain-flies,

Leaving us fancy-sick. No, no, I'm sure,
My restless spirit never could endure
To brood so long upon one luxury,
Unless it did, though fearfully, espy
A hope beyond the shadow of a dream.
My sayings will the less obscured seem,
When I have told thee how my waking sight
Has made me scruple whether that same night   860
Was pass'd in dreaming. Hearken, sweet Peona!
Beyond the matron-temple of Latona,
Which we should see but for these darkening boughs,
Lies a deep hollow, from whose ragged brows
Bushes and trees do lean all round athwart
And meet so nearly, that with wings outraught,
And spreaded tail, a vulture could not glide
Past them, but he must brush on every side.
Some moulder'd steps lead into this cool cell,
Far as the slabbed margin of a well,   870
Whose patient level peeps its crystal eye
Right upward, through the bushes, to the sky.
Oft have I brought thee flowers, on their stalks set
Like vestal primroses, but dark velvet
Edges them round, and they have golden pits:
'Twas there I got them, from the gaps and slits
In a mossy stone, that sometimes was my seat,
When all above was faint with mid-day heat.
And there in strife no burning thoughts to heed,
I'd bubble up the water through a reed;   880
So reaching back to boy-hood: make me ships
Of moulted feathers, touchwood, alder chips,
With leaves stuck in them; and the Neptune be
Of their petty ocean. Oftener, heavily,
When love-lorn hours had left me less a child,
I sat contemplating the figures wild
Of o'er-head clouds melting the mirror through.
Upon a day, while thus I watch'd, by flew
A cloudy Cupid, with his bow and quiver;
So plainly character'd, no breeze would shiver   890
The happy chance: so happy, I was fain
To follow it upon the open plain,

And, therefore, was just going; when, behold!
A wonder, fair as any I have told—
The same bright face I tasted in my sleep,
Smiling in the clear well. My heart did leap
Through the cool depth.—It moved as if to flee—
I started up, when lo! refreshfully
There came upon my face in plenteous showers
Dew-drops, and dewy buds, and leaves, and flowers,   900
Wrapping all objects from my smothered sight,
Bathing my spirit in a new delight.
Aye, such a breathless honey-feel of bliss
Alone preserved me from the drear abyss
Of death, for the fair form had gone again.
Pleasure is oft a visitant; but pain
Clings cruelly to us, like the gnawing sloth
On the deer's tender haunches: late, and loth,
'Tis scar'd away by slow returning pleasure.
How sickening, how dark the dreadful leisure   910
Of weary days, made deeper exquisite,
By a fore-knowledge of unslumbrous night!
Like sorrow came upon me, heavier still,
Than when I wander'd from the poppy hill:
And a whole age of lingering moments crept
Sluggishly by, ere more contentment swept
Away at once the deadly yellow spleen.
Yes, thrice have I this fair enchantment seen;
Once more been tortured with renewed life.
When last the wintry gusts gave over strife   920
With the conquering sun of spring, and left the skies
Warm and serene, but yet with moistened eyes
In pity of the shatter'd infant buds,—
That time thou didst adorn, with amber studs,
My hunting cap, because I laugh'd and smil'd,
Chatted with thee, and many days exil'd
All torment from my breast;—'twas even then,
Straying about, yet, coop'd up in the den
Of helpless discontent,—hurling my lance
From place to place, and following at chance,   930
At last, by hap, through some young trees it struck,
And, plashing among bedded pebbles, stuck

In the middle of a brook,—whose silver ramble
Down twenty little falls, through reeds and bramble,
Tracing along, it brought me to a cave,
Whence it ran brightly forth, and white did lave
The nether sides of mossy stones and rock,—
'Mong which it gurgled blythe adieus, to mock
Its own sweet grief at parting. Overhead,
Hung a lush screen of drooping weeds, and spread   940
Thick, as to curtain up some wood-nymph's home.
"Ah! impious mortal, whither do I roam?"
Said I, low voic'd: "Ah, whither! 'Tis the grot
"Of Proserpine, when Hell, obscure and hot,
"Doth her resign; and where her tender hands
"She dabbles, on the cool and sluicy sands:
"Or 'tis the cell of Echo, where she sits,
"And babbles thorough silence, till her wits
"Are gone in tender madness, and anon,
"Faints into sleep, with many a dying tone   950
"Of sadness. O that she would take my vows,
"And breathe them sighingly among the boughs,
"To sue her gentle ears for whose fair head,
"Daily, I pluck sweet flowerets from their bed,
"And weave them dyingly—send honey-whispers
"Round every leaf, that all those gentle lispers
"May sigh my love unto her pitying!
"O charitable Echo! hear, and sing
"This ditty to her!—tell her"—so I stay'd
My foolish tongue, and listening, half afraid,   960
Stood stupefied with my own empty folly,
And blushing for the freaks of melancholy.
Salt tears were coming, when I heard my name
Most fondly lipp'd, and then these accents came:
"Endymion! the cave is secreter
"Than the isle of Delos. Echo hence shall stir
"No sighs but sigh-warm kisses, or light noise
"Of thy combing hand, the while it travelling cloys
"And trembles through my labyrinthine hair."
At that oppress'd I hurried in.—Ah! where   970
Are those swift moments? Whither are they fled?
I'll smile no more, Peona; nor will wed

Sorrow the way to death; but patiently
Bear up against it: so farewell, sad sigh;
And come instead demurest meditation,
To occupy me wholly, and to fashion
My pilgrimage for the world's dusky brink.
No more will I count over, link by link,
My chain of grief: no longer strive to find
A half-forgetfulness in mountain wind   980
Blustering about my ears: aye, thou shalt see,
Dearest of sisters, what my life shall be;
What a calm round of hours shall make my days.
There is a paly flame of hope that plays
Where'er I look: but yet, I'll say 'tis naught—
And here I bid it die. Have not I caught,
Already, a more healthy countenance?
By this the sun is setting; we may chance
Meet some of our near-dwellers with my car.'

This said, he rose, faint-smiling like a star   990
Through autumn mists, and took Peona's hand:
They stept into the boat, and launch'd from land.

Book II

O sovereign power of love! O grief! O balm!
All records, saving thine, come cool, and calm,
And shadowy, through the mist of passed years:
For others, good or bad, hatred and tears
Have become indolent; but touching thine,
One sigh doth echo, one poor sob doth pine,
One kiss brings honey-dew from buried days.
The woes of Troy, towers smothering o'er their blaze,
Stiff-holden shields, far-piercing spears, keen blades,
Struggling, and blood, and shrieks—all dimly fades   10
Into some backward corner of the brain:
Yet, in our very souls, we feel amain
The close of Troilus and Cressid sweet.
Hence, pageant history! hence, gilded cheat!
Swart planet in the universe of deeds!
Wide sea, that one continuous murmur breeds

Along the pebbled shore of memory!
Many old rotten-timber'd boats there be
Upon thy vaporous bosom, magnified
To goodly vessels; many a sail of pride, 20
And golden keel'd, is left unlaunch'd and dry.
But wherefore this? What care, though owl did fly
About the great Athenian admiral's mast?
What care, though striding Alexander past
The Indus with his Macedonian numbers?
Though old Ulysses tortured from his slumbers
The glutted Cyclops, what care?—Juliet leaning
Amid her window-flowers,—sighing,—weaning
Tenderly her fancy from its maiden snow,
Doth more avail than these: the silver flow 30
Of Hero's tears, the swoon of Imogen,
Fair Pastorella in the bandit's den,
Are things to brood on with more ardency
Than the death-day of empires. Fearfully
Must such conviction come upon his head,
Who, thus far, discontent, has dared to tread,
Without one muse's smile, or kind behest,
The path of love and poesy. But rest,
In chaffing restlessness, is yet more drear
Than to be crush'd, in striving to uprear 40
Love's standard on the battlements of song.
So once more days and nights aid me along,
Like legion'd soldiers.

                          Brain-sick shepherd prince,
What promise hast thou faithful guarded since
The day of sacrifice? Or, have new sorrows
Come with the constant dawn upon thy morrows?
Alas! 'tis his old grief. For many days,
Has he been wandering in uncertain ways:
Through wilderness, and woods of mossed oaks;
Counting his woe-worn minutes, by the strokes 50
Of the lone woodcutter; and listening still,
Hour after hour, to each lush-leav'd rill.
Now he is sitting by a shady spring,
And elbow-deep with feverous fingering

Stems the upbursting cold: a wild rose tree
Pavillions him in bloom, and he doth see
A bud which snares his fancy: lo! but now
He plucks it, dips its stalk in the water: how!
It swells, it buds, it flowers beneath his sight;
And, in the middle, there is softly pight   60
A golden butterfly; upon whose wings
There must be surely character'd strange things,
For with wide eye he wonders, and smiles oft.

    Lightly this little herald flew aloft,
Follow'd by glad Endymion's clasped hands:
Onward it flies. From languor's sullen bands
His limbs are loos'd, and eager, on he hies
Dazzled to trace it in the sunny skies.
It seem'd he flew, the way so easy was;
And like a new-born spirit did he pass   70
Through the green evening quiet in the sun,
O'er many a heath, through many a woodland dun,
Through buried paths, where sleepy twilight dreams
The summer time away. One track unseams
A wooded cleft, and, far away, the blue
Of ocean fades upon him; then, anew,
He sinks adown a solitary glen,
Where there was never sound of mortal men,
Saving, perhaps, some snow-light cadences
Melting to silence, when upon the breeze   80
Some holy bark let forth an anthem sweet,
To cheer itself to Delphi. Still his feet
Went swift beneath the merry-winged guide,
Until it reach'd a splashing fountain's side
That, near a cavern's mouth, for ever pour'd
Unto the temperate air: then high it soar'd,
And, downward, suddenly began to dip,
As if, athirst with so much toil, 'twould sip
The crystal spout-head: so it did, with touch
Most delicate, as though afraid to smutch   90
Even with mealy gold the waters clear.
But, at that very touch, to disappear
So fairy-quick, was strange! Bewildered,

Endymion sought around, and shook each bed
Of covert flowers in vain; and then he flung
Himself along the grass. What gentle tongue,
What whisperer disturb'd his gloomy rest?
It was a nymph uprisen to the breast
In the fountain's pebbly margin, and she stood
'Mong lilies, like the youngest of the brood.   100
To him her dripping hand she softly kist,
And anxiously began to plait and twist
Her ringlets round her fingers, saying: 'Youth!
Too long, alas, hast thou starv'd on the ruth,
The bitterness of love: too long indeed,
Seeing thou art so gentle. Could I weed
Thy soul of care, by heavens, I would offer
All the bright riches of my crystal coffer
To Amphitrite; all my clear-eyed fish,
Golden, or rainbow-sided, or purplish,   110
Vermilion-tail'd, or finn'd with silvery gauze;
Yea, or my veined pebble-floor, that draws
A virgin light to the deep; my grotto-sands
Tawny and gold, ooz'd slowly from far lands
By my diligent springs; my level lilies, shells,
My charming rod, my potent river spells;
Yes, every thing, even to the pearly cup
Meander gave me,—for I bubbled up
To fainting creatures in a desert wild.
But woe is me, I am but as a child   120
To gladden thee; and all I dare to say,
Is, that I pity thee; that on this day
I've been thy guide; that thou must wander far
In other regions, past the scanty bar
To mortal steps, before thou cans't be ta'en
From every wasting sigh, from every pain,
Into the gentle bosom of thy love.
Why it is thus, one knows in heaven above:
But, a poor Naiad, I guess not. Farewell!
I have a ditty for my hollow cell.'   130

Hereat, she vanished from Endymion's gaze,
Who brooded o'er the water in amaze:

The dashing fount pour'd on, and where its pool
Lay, half asleep, in grass and rushes cool,
Quick waterflies and gnats were sporting still,
And fish were dimpling, as if good nor ill
Had fallen out that hour. The wanderer,
Holding his forehead, to keep off the burr
Of smothering fancies, patiently sat down;
And, while beneath the evening's sleepy frown   140
Glow-worms began to trim their starry lamps,
Thus breath'd he to himself: 'Whoso encamps
To take a fancied city of delight,
O what a wretch is he! and when 'tis his,
After long toil and travelling, to miss
The kernel of his hopes, how more than vile:
Yet, for him there's refreshment even in toil;
Another city doth he set about,
Free from the smallest pebble-bead of doubt
That he will seize on trickling honey-combs: 150
Alas, he finds them dry; and then he foams,
And onward to another city speeds.
But this is human life: the war, the deeds,
The disappointment, the anxiety,
Imagination's struggles, far and nigh,
All human; bearing in themselves this good,
That they are still the air, the subtle food,
To make us feel existence, and to show
How quiet death is. Where soil is men grow,
Whether to weeds or flowers; but for me,   160
There is no depth to strike in: I can see
Naught earthly worth my compassing; so stand
Upon a misty, jutting head of land—
Alone? No, no; and by the Orphean lute,
When mad Eurydice is listening to't;
I'd rather stand upon this misty peak,
With not a thing to sigh for, or to seek,
But the soft shadow of my thrice-seen love,
Than be—I care not what. O meekest dove
Of heaven! O Cynthia, ten-times bright and fair!   170
From thy blue throne, now filling all the air,
Glance but one little beam of temper'd light

Into my bosom, that the dreadful might
And tyranny of love be somewhat scar'd!
Yet do not so, sweet queen; one torment spar'd,
Would give a pang to jealous misery,
Worse than the torment's self: but rather tie
Large wings upon my shoulders, and point out
My love's far dwelling. Though the playful rout
Of Cupids shun thee, too divine art thou,   180
Too keen in beauty, for thy silver prow
Not to have dipp'd in love's most gentle stream.
O be propitious, nor severely deem
My madness impious; for, by all the stars
That tend thy bidding, I do think the bars
That kept my spirit in are burst—that I
Am sailing with thee through the dizzy sky!
How beautiful thou art! The world how deep!
How tremulous dazzlingly the wheels sweep
Around their axle! Then these gleaming reins,   190
How lithe! When this thy chariot attains
Its airy goal, haply some bower veils
Those twilight eyes? Those eyes!—my spirit fails—
Dear goddess, help! or the wide-gaping air
Will gulph me—help!'—At this with madden'd stare,
And lifted hands, and trembling lips he stood;
Like old Deucalion mountain'd o'er the flood,
Or blind Orion hungry for the morn.
And, but from the deep cavern there was borne
A voice, he had been froze to senseless stone;   200
Nor sigh of his, nor plaint, nor passion'd moan
Had more been heard. Thus swell'd it forth: 'Descend,
Young mountaineer! descend where alleys bend
Into the sparry hollows of the world!
Oft hast thou seen bolts of the thunder hurl'd
As from thy threshold; day by day hast been
A little lower than the chilly sheen
Of icy pinnacles, and dipp'dst thine arms
Into the deadening ether that still charms
Their marble being: now, as deep profound   210
As those are high, descend! He ne'er is crown'd
With immortality, who fears to follow

Where airy voices lead: so through the hollow,
The silent mysteries of earth, descend!'

He heard but the last words, nor could contend
One moment in reflection: for he fled
Into the fearful deep, to hide his head
From the clear moon, the trees, and coming madness.

'Twas far too strange, and wonderful for sadness;
Sharpening, by degrees, his appetite   220
To dive into the deepest. Dark, nor light,
The region; nor bright, nor sombre wholly,
But mingled up; a gleaming melancholy;
A dusky empire and its diadems;
One faint eternal eventide of gems.
Aye, millions sparkled on a vein of gold,
Along whose track the prince quick footsteps told,
With all its lines abrupt and angular:
Out-shooting sometimes, like a meteor-star,
Through a vast antre; then the metal woof,   230
Like Vulcan's rainbow, with some monstrous roof
Curves hugely: now, far in the deep abyss,
It seems an angry lightning, and doth hiss
Fancy into belief: anon it leads
Through winding passages, where sameness breeds
Vexing conceptions of some sudden change;
Whether to silver grots, or giant range
Of sapphire columns, or fantastic bridge
Athwart a flood of crystal. On a ridge
Now fareth he, that o'er the vast beneath   240
Towers like an ocean-cliff, and whence he seeth
A hundred waterfalls, whose voices come
But as the murmuring surge. Chilly and numb
His bosom grew, when first he, far away
Descried an orbed diamond, set to fray
Old darkness from his throne: 'twas like the sun
Uprisen o'er chaos: and with such a stun
Came the amazement, that, absorb'd in it,
He saw not fiercer wonders—past the wit
Of any spirit to tell, but one of those   250

Who, when this planet's sphering time doth close,
Will be its high remembrancers: who they?
The mighty ones who have made eternal day
For Greece and England. While astonishment
With deep-drawn sighs was quieting, he went
Into a marble gallery, passing through
A mimic temple, so complete and true
In sacred custom, that he well nigh fear'd
To search it inwards; whence far off appear'd,
Through a long pillar'd vista, a fair shrine,   260
And just beyond, on light tiptoe divine,
A quiver'd Dian. Stepping awfully,
The youth aproach'd; oft turning his veil'd eye
Down sidelong aisles, and into niches old.
And when, more near against the marble cold
He had touch'd his forehead, he began to thread
All courts and passages, where silence dead
Rous'd by his whispering footsteps murmured faint:
And long he travers'd to and fro, to acquaint
Himself with every mystery, and awe;   270
Till, weary, he sat down before the maw
Of a wide outlet, fathomless and dim,
To wild uncertainty and shadows grim.
There, when new wonders ceas'd to float before,
And thoughts of self came on, how crude and sore
The journey homeward to habitual self!
A mad-pursuing of the fog-born elf,
Whose flitting lantern, through rude nettle-briar,
Cheats us into a swamp, into a fire,
Into the bosom of a hated thing.   280

    What misery most drowningly doth sing
In lone Endymion's ear, now he has raught
The goal of consciousness? Ah, 'tis the thought,
The deadly feel of solitude: for lo!
He cannot see the heavens, nor the flow
Of rivers, nor hill-flowers running wild
In pink and purple chequer, nor, up-pil'd,
The cloudy rack slow journeying in the west,
Like herded elephants; nor felt, nor prest

Cool grass, nor tasted the fresh slumberous air;   290
But far from such companionship to wear
An unknown time, surcharg'd with grief, away,
Was now his lot. And must he patient stay,
Tracing fantastic figures with his spear?
'No!' exclaim'd he, 'why should I tarry here?'
No! loudly echoed times innumerable.
At which he straightway started, and 'gan tell
His paces back into the temple's chief;
Warming and glowing strong in the belief
Of help from Dian: so that when again   300
He caught her airy form, thus did he plain,
Moving more near the while: 'O Haunter chaste
Of river sides, and woods, and heathy waste,
Where with thy silver bow and arrows keen
Art thou now forested? O woodland Queen,
What smoothest air thy smoother forehead woos?
Where dost thou listen to the wide halloos
Of thy disparted nymphs? Through what dark tree
Glimmers thy crescent? Wheresoe'er it be,
'Tis in the breath of heaven: thou dost taste   310
Freedom as none can taste it, nor dost waste
Thy loveliness in dismal elements;
But, finding in our green earth sweet contents,
There livest blissfully. Ah, if to thee
It feels Elysian, how rich to me,
An exil'd mortal, sounds its pleasant name!
Within my breast there lives a choking flame—
O let me cool't the zephyr-boughs among!
A homeward fever parches up my tongue—
O let me slake it at the running springs!   320
Upon my ear a noisy nothing rings—
O let me once more hear the linnet's note!
Before mine eyes thick films and shadows float—
O let me 'noint them with the heaven's light!
Dost thou now lave thy feet and ankles white?
O think how sweet to me the freshening sluice!
Dost thou now please thy thirst with berry-juice?
O think how this dry palate would rejoice!
If in soft slumber thou dost hear my voice,

O think how I should love a bed of flowers!— 330
Young goddess! let me see my native bowers!
Deliver me from this rapacious deep!'

Thus ending loudly, as he would o'erleap
His destiny, alert he stood: but when
Obstinate silence came heavily again,
Feeling about for its old couch of space
And airy cradle, lowly bow'd his face
Desponding, o'er the marble floor's cold thrill.
But 'twas not long; for, sweeter than the rill
To its old channel, or a swollen tide 340
To margin sallows, were the leaves he spied,
And flowers, and wreaths, and ready myrtle crowns
Up heaping through the slab: refreshment drowns
Itself, and strives its own delights to hide—
Nor in one spot alone; the floral pride
In a long whispering birth enchanted grew
Before his footsteps; as when heav'd anew
Old ocean rolls a lengthened wave to the shore,
Down whose green back the short-liv'd foam, all hoar,
Bursts gradual, with a wayward indolence. 350

Increasing still in heart, and pleasant sense,
Upon his fairy journey on he hastes;
So anxious for the end, he scarcely wastes
One moment with his hand among the sweets:
Onward he goes—he stops—his bosom beats
As plainly in his ear, as the faint charm
Of which the throbs were born. This still alarm,
This sleepy music, forc'd him walk tiptoe:
For it came more softly than the east could blow
Arion's magic to the Atlantic isles; 360
Or than the west, made jealous by the smiles
Of thron'd Apollo, could breathe back the lyre
To seas Ionian and Tyrian.

O did he ever live, that lonely man,
Who lov'd—and music slew not? 'Tis the pest
Of love, that fairest joys give most unrest;

That things of delicate and tenderest worth
Are swallow'd all, and made a seared dearth,
By one consuming flame: it doth immerse
And suffocate true blessings in a curse.   370
Half-happy, by comparison of bliss,
Is miserable. 'Twas even so with this
Dew-dropping melody, in the Carian's ear;
First heaven, then hell, and then forgotten clear,
Vanish'd in elemental passion.

And down some swart abysm he had gone,
Had not a heavenly guide benignant led
To where thick myrtle branches, 'gainst his head
Brushing, awakened: then the sounds again
Went noiseless as a passing noontide rain   380
Over a bower, where little space he stood;
For as the sunset peeps into a wood
So saw he panting light, and towards it went
Through winding alleys; and lo, wonderment!
Upon soft verdure saw, one here, one there,
Cupids a slumbering on their pinions fair.

After a thousand mazes overgone,
At last, with sudden step, he came upon
A chamber, myrtle wall'd, embowered high,
Full of light, incense, tender minstrelsy,   390
And more of beautiful and strange beside:
For on a silken couch of rosy pride,
In midst of all, there lay a sleeping youth
Of fondest beauty; fonder, in fair sooth,
Than sighs could fathom, or contentment reach:
And coverlids gold-tinted like the peach,
Or ripe October's faded marigolds,
Fell sleek about him in a thousand folds—
Not hiding up an Apollonian curve
Of neck and shoulder, nor the tenting swerve   400
Of knee from knee, nor ankles pointing light;
But rather, giving them to the filled sight
Officiously. Sideway his face repos'd
On one white arm, and tenderly unclos'd,

By tenderest pressure, a faint damask mouth
To slumbery pout; just as the morning south
Disparts a dew-lipp'd rose. Above his head,
Four lilly stalks did their white honours wed
To make a coronal; and round him grew
All tendrils green, of every bloom and hue,   410
Together intertwin'd and trammel'd fresh:
The vine of glossy sprout; the ivy mesh,
Shading its Ethiop berries; and woodbine,
Of velvet leaves and bugle-blooms divine;
Convolvulus in streaked vases flush;
The creeper, mellowing for an autumn blush;
And virgin's bower, trailing airily;
With others of the sisterhood. Hard by,
Stood serene Cupids watching silently.
One, kneeling to a lyre, touch'd the strings,   420
Muffling to death the pathos with his wings;
And, ever and anon, uprose to look
At the youth's slumber; while another took
A willow-bough, distilling odorous dew,
And shook it on his hair; another flew
In through the woven roof, and fluttering-wise
Rain'd violets upon his sleeping eyes.

       At these enchantments, and yet many more,
The breathless Latmian wonder'd o'er and o'er;
Until, impatient in embarrassment,   430
He forthright pass'd, and lightly treading went
To that same feather'd lyrist, who straightway,
Smiling, thus whisper'd: 'Though from upper day
Thou art a wanderer, and thy presence here
Might seem unholy, be of happy cheer!
For 'tis the nicest touch of human honour,
When some ethereal and high-favouring donor
Presents immortal bowers to mortal sense;
As now 'tis done to thee, Endymion. Hence
Was I in no wise startled. So recline   440
Upon these living flowers. Here is wine,
Alive with sparkles—never, I aver,
Since Ariadne was a vintager,

So cool a purple: taste these juicy pears,
Sent me by sad Vertumnus, when his fears
Were high about Pomona: here is cream,
Deepening to richness from a snowy gleam;
Sweeter than that nurse Amalthea skimm'd
For the boy Jupiter: and here, undimm'd
By any touch, a bunch of blooming plums   450
Ready to melt between an infant's gums:
And here is manna pick'd from Syrian trees,
In starlight, by the three Hesperides.
Feast on, and meanwhile I will let thee know
Of all these things around us.' He did so,
Still brooding o'er the cadence of his lyre;
And thus: 'I need not any hearing tire
By telling how the sea-born goddess pin'd
For a mortal youth, and how she strove to bind
Him all in all unto her doting self.   460
Who would not be so prison'd? but, fond elf,
He was content to let her amorous plea
Faint through his careless arms; content to see
An unseiz'd heaven dying at his feet;
Content, O fool! to make a cold retreat,
When on the pleasant grass such love, lovelorn,
Lay sorrowing; when every tear was born
Of diverse passion; when her lips and eyes
Were clos'd in sullen moisture, and quick sighs
Came vex'd and pettish through her nostrils small. 470
Hush! no exclaim—yet, justly mightst thou call
Curses upon his head.—I was half glad,
But my poor mistress went distract and mad,
When the boar tusk'd him: so away she flew
To Jove's high throne, and by her plainings drew
Immortal tear-drops down the thunderer's beard;
Whereon, it was decreed he should be rear'd
Each summer time to life. Lo! this is he,
That same Adonis, safe in the privacy
Of this still region all his winter-sleep.   480
Aye, sleep; for when our love-sick queen did weep
Over his waned corse, the tremulous shower
Heal'd up the wound, and, with a balmy power,

Medicined death to a lengthened drowsiness:
The which she fills with visions, and doth dress
In all this quiet luxury; and hath set
Us young immortals, without any let,
To watch his slumber through. 'Tis well nigh pass'd,
Even to a moment's filling up, and fast
She scuds with summer breezes, to pant through   490
The first long kiss, warm firstling, to renew
Embower'd sports in Cytherea's isle.
Look! how those winged listeners all this while
Stand anxious: see! behold!'—This clamant word
Broke through the careful silence; for they heard
A rustling noise of leaves, and out there flutter'd
Pigeons and doves: Adonis something mutter'd
The while one hand, that erst upon his thigh
Lay dormant, mov'd convuls'd and gradually
Up to his forehead. Then there was a hum   500
Of sudden voices, echoing, 'Come! come!
Arise! awake! Clear summer has forth walk'd
Unto the clover-sward, and she has talk'd
Full soothingly to every nested finch:
Rise, Cupids! or we'll give the blue-bell pinch
To your dimpled arms. Once more sweet life begin!'
At this, from every side they hurried in,
Rubbing their sleepy eyes with lazy wrists,
And doubling over head their little fists
In backward yawns. But all were soon alive: 510
For as delicious wine doth, sparkling, dive
In nectar'd clouds and curls through water fair,
So from the arbour roof down swell'd an air
Odorous and enlivening; making all
To laugh, and play, and sing, and loudly call
For their sweet queen: when lo! the wreathed green
Disparted, and far upward could be seen
Blue heaven, and a silver car, air-borne,
Whose silent wheels, fresh wet from clouds of morn,
Spun off a drizzling dew,—which falling chill   520
On soft Adonis' shoulders, made him still
Nestle and turn uneasily about.
Soon were the white doves plain, with neck stretch'd out,

And silken traces lighten'd in descent;
And soon, returning from love's banishment,
Queen Venus leaning downward open arm'd:
Her shadow fell upon his breast, and charm'd
A tumult to his heart, and a new life
Into his eyes. Ah, miserable strife,
But for her comforting! unhappy sight,   530
But meeting her blue orbs! Who, who can write
Of these first minutes? The unchariest muse
To embracements warm as theirs makes coy excuse.

   O it has ruffled every spirit there,
Saving Love's self, who stands superb to share
The general gladness: awfully he stands;
A sovereign quell is in his waving hands;
No sight can bear the lightning of his bow;
His quiver is mysterious, none can know
What themselves think of it; from forth his eyes   540
There darts strange light of varied hues and dyes:
A scowl is sometimes on his brow, but who
Look full upon it feel anon the blue
Of his fair eyes run liquid through their souls.
Endymion feels it, and no more controls
The burning prayer within him; so, bent low,
He had begun a plaining of his woe.
But Venus, bending forward, said: 'My child,
Favour this gentle youth; his days are wild
With love—he—but alas! too well I see   550
Thou know'st the deepness of his misery.
Ah, smile not so, my son: I tell thee true,
That when through heavy hours I used to rue
The endless sleep of this new-born Adon',
This stranger aye I pitied. For upon
A dreary morning once I fled away
Into the breezy clouds, to weep and pray
For this my love: for vexing Mars had teaz'd
Me even to tears: thence, when a little eas'd,
Down-looking, vacant, through a hazy wood,   560
I saw this youth as he despairing stood:
Those same dark curls blown vagrant in the wind;

Those same full fringed lids a constant blind
Over his sullen eyes: I saw him throw
Himself on wither'd leaves, even as though
Death had come sudden; for no jot he mov'd.
Yet mutter'd wildly, I could hear he lov'd
Some fair immortal, and that his embrace
Had zoned her through the night. There is no trace
Of this in heaven: I have mark'd each cheek,   570
And find it is the vainest thing to seek;
And that of all things 'tis kept secretest.
Endymion! one day thou wilt be blest:
So still obey the guiding hand that fends
Thee safely through these wonders for sweet ends.
'Tis a concealment needful in extreme;
And if I guess'd not so, the sunny beam
Thou shouldst mount up to with me. Now adieu!
Here must we leave thee.'—At these words upflew
The impatient doves, uprose the floating car,   580
Up went the hum celestial. High afar
The Latmian saw them minish into naught;
And, when all were clear vanish'd, still he caught
A vivid lightning from that dreadful bow.
When all was darkened, with Ætnean throe
The earth clos'd—gave a solitary moan—
And left him once again in twilight lone.

He did not rave, he did not stare aghast,
For all those visions were o'ergone, and past,
And he in loneliness: he felt assur'd   590
Of happy times, when all he had endur'd
Would seem a feather to the mighty prize.
So, with unusual gladness, on he hies
Through caves, and palaces of mottled ore,
Gold dome, and crystal wall, and turquois floor,
Black polish'd porticos of awful shade,
And, at the last, a diamond balustrade,
Leading afar past wild magnificence,
Spiral through ruggedest loopholes, and thence
Stretching across a void, then guiding o'er   600
Enormous chasms, where, all foam and roar,

Streams subterranean teaze their granite beds;
Then heighten'd just above the silvery heads
Of a thousand fountains, so that he could dash
The waters with his spear; but at the splash,
Done heedlessly, those spouting columns rose
Sudden a poplar's height, and 'gan to enclose
His diamond path with fretwork, streaming round
Alive, and dazzling cool, and with a sound,
Haply, like dolphin tumults, when sweet shells   610
Welcome the float of Thetis. Long he dwells
On this delight; for, every minute's space,
The streams with changed magic interlace:
Sometimes like delicatest lattices,
Cover'd with crystal vines; then weeping trees.
Moving about as in a gentle wind,
Which, in a wink, to watery gauze refin'd,
Pour'd into shapes of curtain'd canopies,
Spangled, and rich with liquid broideries
Of flowers, peacocks, swans, and naiads fair.   620
Swifter than lightning went these wonders rare;
And then the water, into stubborn streams
Collecting, mimick'd the wrought oaken beams,
Pillars, and frieze, and high fantastic roof,
Of those dusk places in times far aloof
Cathedrals call'd. He bade a loth farewell
To these founts Protean, passing gulph, and dell,
And torrent, and ten thousand jutting shapes,
Half seen through deepest gloom, and griesly gapes,
Blackening on every side, and overhead   630
A vaulted dome like Heaven's, far bespread
With starlight gems: aye, all so huge and strange,
The solitary felt a hurried change
Working within him into something dreary,—
Vex'd like a morning eagle, lost, and weary,
And purblind amid foggy, midnight wolds.
But he revives at once: for who beholds
New sudden things, nor casts his mental slough?
Forth from a rugged arch, in the dusk below,
Came mother Cybele! alone—alone—   640
In sombre chariot; dark foldings thrown

About her majesty, and front death-pale,
With turrets crown'd. Four maned lions hale
The sluggish wheels; solemn their toothed maws,
Their surly eyes brow-hidden, heavy paws
Uplifted drowsily, and nervy tails
Cowering their tawny brushes. Silent sails
This shadowy queen athwart, and faints away
In another gloomy arch.

     Wherefore delay,
Young traveller, in such a mournful place?   650
Art thou wayworn, or canst not further trace
The diamond path? And does it indeed end
Abrupt in middle air? Yet earthward bend
Thy forehead, and to Jupiter cloud-borne
Call ardently! He was indeed wayworn;
Abrupt, in middle air, his way was lost;
To cloud-borne Jove he bowed, and there crost
Towards him a large eagle, 'twixt whose wings,
Without one impious word, himself he flings,
Committed to the darkness and the gloom: 660
Down, down, uncertain to what pleasant doom,
Swift as a fathoming plummet down he fell
Through unknown things; till exhaled asphodel,
And rose, with spicy fannings interbreath'd,
Came swelling forth where little caves were wreath'd
So thick with leaves and mosses, that they seem'd
Large honey-combs of green, and freshly teem'd
With airs delicious. In the greenest nook
The eagle landed him, and farewell took.

 It was a jasmine bower, all bestrown   670
With golden moss. His every sense had grown
Ethereal for pleasure; 'bove his head
Flew a delight half-graspable; his tread
Was Hesperean; to his capable ears
Silence was music from the holy spheres;
A dewy luxury was in his eyes;
The little flowers felt his pleasant sighs
And stirr'd them faintly. Verdant cave and cell
He wander'd through, oft wondering at such swell

Of sudden exaltation: but, 'Alas!'   680
Said he, 'will all this gush of feeling pass
Away in solitude? And must they wane,
Like melodies upon a sandy plain,
Without an echo? Then shall I be left
So sad, so melancholy, so bereft!
Yet still I feel immortal! O my love,
My breath of life, where art thou? High above,
Dancing before the morning gates of heaven?
Or keeping watch among those starry seven,
Old Atlas' children? Art a maid of the waters,   690
One of shell-winding Triton's bright-hair'd daughters?
Or art, impossible! a nymph of Dian's,
Weaving a coronal of tender scions
For very idleness? Where'er thou art,
Methinks it now is at my will to start
Into thine arms; to scare Aurora's train,
And snatch thee from the morning; o'er the main
To scud like a wild bird, and take thee off
From thy sea-foamy cradle; or to doff
Thy shepherd vest, and woo thee mid fresh leaves.   700
No, no, too eagerly my soul deceives
Its powerless self: I know this cannot be.
O let me then by some sweet dreaming flee
To her entrancements: hither, Sleep, awhile!
Hither, most gentle Sleep! and soothing foil
For some few hours the coming solitude.'

    Thus spake he, and that moment felt endued
With power to dream deliciously; so wound
Through a dim passage, searching till he found
The smoothest mossy bed and deepest, where   710
He threw himself, and just into the air
Stretching his indolent arms, he took, O bliss!
A naked waist: 'Fair Cupid, whence is this?'
A well-known voice sigh'd, 'Sweetest, here am I!'
At which soft ravishment, with doting cry
They trembled to each other.—Helicon!
O fountain'd hill! Old Homer's Helicon!
That thou wouldst spout a little streamlet o'er

These sorry pages; then the verse would soar
And sing above this gentle pair, like lark 720
Over his nested young: but all is dark
Around thine aged top, and thy clear fount
Exhales in mists to heaven. Aye, the count
Of mighty Poets is made up; the scroll
Is folded by the Muses; the bright roll
Is in Apollo's hand: our dazed eyes
Have seen a new tinge in the western skies:
The world has done its duty. Yet, oh yet,
Although the sun of poesy is set,
These lovers did embrace, and we must weep 730
That there is no old power left to steep
A quill immortal in their joyous tears.
Long time in silence did their anxious fears
Question that thus it was; long time they lay
Fondling and kissing every doubt away;
Long time ere soft caressing sobs began
To mellow into words, and then there ran
Two bubbling springs of talk from their sweet lips.
'O known Unknown! from whom my being sips
Such darling essence, wherefore may I not 740
Be ever in these arms? in this sweet spot
Pillow my chin for ever? ever press
These toying hands and kiss their smooth excess?
Why not for ever and for ever feel
That breath about my eyes? Ah, thou wilt steal
Away from me again, indeed, indeed—
Thou wilt be gone away, and wilt not heed
My lonely madness. Speak, delicious fair!
Is—is it to be so? No! Who will dare
To pluck thee from me? And, of thine own will, 750
Full well I feel thou wouldst not leave me. Still
Let me entwine thee surer, surer—now
How can we part? Elysium! who art thou?
Who, that thou canst not be for ever here,
Or lift me with thee to some starry sphere?
Enchantress! tell me by this soft embrace,
By the most soft completion of thy face,
Those lips, O slippery blisses, twinkling eyes

And by these tenderest, milky sovereignties—
These tenderest, and by the nectar-wine,   760
The passion'————'O dov'd Ida the divine!
Endymion! dearest! Ah, unhappy me!
His soul will 'scape us—O felicity!
How he does love me! His poor temples beat
To the very tune of love—how sweet, sweet, sweet.
Revive, dear youth, or I shall faint and die;
Revive, or these soft hours will hurry by
In tranced dulness; speak, and let that spell
Affright this lethargy! I cannot quell
Its heavy pressure, and will press at least   770
My lips to thine, that they may richly feast
Until we taste the life of love again.
What! dost thou move? dost kiss? O bliss! O pain!
I love thee, youth, more than I can conceive;
And so long absence from thee doth bereave
My soul of any rest: yet must I hence:
Yet, can I not to starry eminence
Uplift thee; nor for very shame can own
Myself to thee: Ah, dearest, do not groan
Or thou wilt force me from this secrecy,   780
And I must blush in heaven. O that I
Had done't already; that the dreadful smiles
At my lost brightness, my impassion'd wiles,
Had waned from Olympus' solemn height,
And from all serious Gods; that our delight
Was quiet forgotten, save of us alone!
And wherefore so ashamed? 'Tis but to atone
For endless pleasure, by some coward blushes:
Yet must I be a coward!—Horror rushes
Too palpable before me—the sad look   790
Of Jove—Minerva's start—no bosom shook
With awe of purity—no Cupid pinion
In reverence vailed—my crystalline dominion
Half lost, and all old hymns made nullity!
But what is this to love? O I could fly
With thee into the ken of heavenly powers,
So thou wouldst thus, for many sequent hours,
Press me so sweetly. Now I swear at once

That I am wise, that Pallas is a dunce—
Perhaps her love like mine is but unknown—   800
O I do think that I have been alone
In chastity: yes, Pallas has been sighing,
While every eve saw me my hair uptying
With fingers cool as aspen leaves. Sweet love,
I was as vague as solitary dove,
Nor knew that nests were built. Now a soft kiss—
Aye, by that kiss, I vow an endless bliss,
An immortality of passion's thine:
Ere long I will exalt thee to the shine
Of heaven ambrosial; and we will shade   810
Ourselves whole summers by a river glade;
And I will tell thee stories of the sky,
And breathe thee whispers of its minstrelsy.
My happy love will overwing all bounds!
O let me melt into thee; let the sounds
Of our close voices marry at their birth;
Let us entwine hoveringly—O dearth
Of human words! roughness of mortal speech!
Lispings empyrean will I sometime teach
Thine honied tongue—lute-breathings, which I gasp   820
To have thee understand, now while I clasp
Thee thus, and weep for fondness—I am pain'd,
Endymion: woe! woe! is grief contain'd
In the very deeps of pleasure, my sole life?'—
Hereat, with many sobs, her gentle strife
Melted into a languor. He return'd
Entranced vows and tears.

                Ye who have yearn'd
With too much passion, will here stay and pity,
For the mere sake of truth; as 'tis a ditty
Not of these days, but long ago 'twas told   830
By a cavern wind unto a forest old;
And then the forest told it in a dream
To a sleeping lake, whose cool and level gleam
A poet caught as he was journeying
To Phœbus' shrine; and in it he did fling
His weary limbs, bathing an hour's space,

And after, straight in that inspired place
He sang the story up into the air,
Giving it universal freedom. There
Has it been ever sounding for those ears   840
Whose tips are glowing hot. The legend cheers
Yon centinel stars; and he who listens to it
Must surely be self-doom'd or he will rue it:
For quenchless burnings come upon the heart,
Made fiercer by a fear lest any part
Should be engulphed in the eddying wind.
As much as here is penn'd doth always find
A resting place, thus much comes clear and plain;
Anon the strange voice is upon the wane—
And 'tis but echo'd from departing sound,   850
That the fair visitant at last unwound
Her gentle limbs, and left the youth asleep.—
Thus the tradition of the gusty deep.

      Now turn we to our former chroniclers.—
Endymion awoke, that grief of hers
Sweet paining on his ear: he sickly guess'd
How lone he was once more, and sadly press'd
His empty arms together, hung his head,
And most forlorn upon that widow'd bed
Sat silently. Love's madness he had known: 860
Often with more than tortured lion's groan
Moanings had burst from him; but now that rage
Had pass'd away: no longer did he wage
A rough-voic'd war against the dooming stars.
No, he had felt too much for such harsh jars:
The lyre of his soul Æolian tun'd
Forgot all violence, and but commun'd
With melancholy thought: O he had swoon'd
Drunken from pleasure's nipple: and his love
Henceforth was dove-like.—Loth was he to move   870
From the imprinted couch, and when he did,
'Twas with slow, languid paces, and face hid
In muffling hands. So temper'd, out he stray'd
Half seeing visions that might have dismay'd
Alecto's serpents; ravishments more keen

Than Hermes' pipe, when anxious he did lean
Over eclipsing eyes: and at the last
It was a sounding grotto, vaulted, vast,
O'er studded with a thousand, thousand pearls,
And crimson mouthed shells with stubborn curls,   880
Of every shape and size, even to the bulk
In which whales arbour close, to brood and sulk
Against an endless storm. Moreover too,
Fish-semblances, of green and azure hue,
Ready to snort their streams. In this cool wonder
Endymion sat down, and 'gan to ponder
On all his life: his youth, up to the day
When 'mid acclaim, and feasts, and garlands gay,
He stept upon his shepherd throne: the look
Of his white palace in wild forest nook,   890
And all the revels he had lorded there:
Each tender maiden whom he once thought fair,
With every friend and fellow-woodlander—
Pass'd like a dream before him. Then the spur
Of the old bards to mighty deeds: his plans
To nurse the golden age 'mong shepherd clans:
That wondrous night: the great Pan-festival:
His sister's sorrow; and his wanderings all,
Until into the earth's deep maw he rush'd:
Then all its buried magic, till it flush'd   900
High with excessive love. 'And now,' thought he,
'How long must I remain in jeopardy
Of blank amazements that amaze no more?
Now I have tasted her sweet soul to the core
All other depths are shallow: essences,
Once spiritual, are like muddy lees,
Meant but to fertilize my earthly root,
And make my branches lift a golden fruit
Into the bloom of heaven: other light,
Though it be quick and sharp enough to blight   910
The Olympian eagle's vision, is dark,
Dark as the parentage of chaos. Hark!
My silent thoughts are echoing from these shells;
Or they are but the ghosts, the dying swells
Of noises far away?—list!'—Hereupon

He kept an anxious ear. The humming tone
Came louder, and behold, there as he lay,
On either side outgush'd, with misty spray,
A copious spring; and both together dash'd
Swift, mad, fantastic round the rocks and lash'd   920
Among the conchs and shells of the lofty grot,
Leaving a trickling dew. At last they shot
Down from the ceiling's height, pouring a noise
As of some breathless racers whose hopes poize
Upon the last few steps, and with spent force
Along the ground they took a winding course.
Endymion follow'd—for it seem'd that one
Ever pursued, the other strove to shun—
Follow'd their languid mazes, till well nigh
He had left thinking of the mystery,—   930
And was now rapt in tender hoverings
Over the vanish'd bliss. Ah! what is it sings
His dream away? What melodies are these?
They sound as through the whispering of trees,
Not native in such barren vaults. Give ear!

   'O Arethusa, peerless nymph! why fear
Such tenderness as mine! Great Dian, why,
Why didst thou hear her prayer? O that I
Were rippling round her dainty fairness now,
Circling about her waist, and striving how   940
To entice her to a dive! then stealing in
Between her luscious lips and eyelids thin.
O that her shining hair was in the sun,
And I distilling from it thence to run
In amorous rillets down her shrinking form!
To linger on her lilly shoulders, warm
Between her kissing breasts, and every charm
Touch raptur'd!—See how painfully I flow:
Fair maid, be pitiful to my great woe.
Stay, stay thy weary course, and let me lead,   950
A happy wooer, to the flowery mead
Where all that beauty snar'd me.'—'Cruel god,
Desist! or my offended mistress' nod
Will stagnate all thy fountains:—teaze me not

With syren words—Ah, have I really got
Such power to madden thee? And is it true—
Away, away, or I shall dearly rue
My very thoughts: in mercy then away,
Kindest Alpheus, for should I obey
My own dear will, 'twould be a deadly bane.   960
O, Oread-Queen! would that thou hadst a pain
Like this of mine, then would I fearless turn
And be a criminal. Alas, I burn,
I shudder—gentle river, get thee hence.
Alpheus! thou enchanter! every sense
Of mine was once made perfect in these woods.
Fresh breezes, bowery lawns, and innocent floods,
Ripe fruits, and lonely couch, contentment gave;
But ever since I heedlessly did lave
In thy deceitful stream, a panting glow   970
Grew strong within me: wherefore serve me so,
And call it love? Alas, 'twas cruelty.
Not once more did I close my happy eye
Amid the thrushes' song. Away! Avaunt!
O 'twas a cruel thing.'—'Now thou dost taunt
So softly, Arethusa, that I think
If thou wast playing on my shady brink,
Thou wouldst bathe once again. Innocent maid!
Stifle thine heart no more; nor be afraid
Of angry powers: there are deities   980
Will shade us with their wings. Those fitful sighs
'Tis almost death to hear: O let me pour
A dewy balm upon them!—fear no more,
Sweet Arethusa! Dian's self must feel
Sometime these very pangs. Dear maiden, steal
Blushing into my soul, and let us fly
These dreary caverns for the open sky.
I will delight thee all my winding course,
From the green sea up to my hidden source
About Arcadian forests; and will show   990
The channels where my coolest waters flow
Through mossy rocks; where, 'mid exuberant green,
I roam in pleasant darkness, more unseen
Than Saturn in his exile; where I brim

Round flowery islands, and take thence a skim
Of mealy sweets, which myriads of bees
Buzz from their honey'd wings: and thou shouldst please
Thyself to choose the richest, where we might
Be incense-pillow'd every summer night.
Doff all sad fears, thou white deliciousness,   1000
And let us be thus comforted; unless
Thou couldst rejoice to see my hopeless stream
Hurry distracted from Sol's temperate beam,
And pour to death along some hungry sands.'—
'What can I do, Alpheus? Dian stands
Severe before me: persecuting fate!
Unhappy Arethusa! thou wast late
A huntress free in'—At this, sudden fell
Those two sad streams adown a fearful dell.
The Latmian listen'd, but he heard no more,   1010
Save echo, faint repeating o'er and o'er
The name of Arethusa. On the verge
Of that dark gulph he wept, and said: 'I urge
Thee, gentle Goddess of my pilgrimage,
By our eternal hopes, to soothe, to assuage,
If thou art powerful, these lovers' pains;
And make them happy in some happy plains.'

He turn'd—there was a whelming sound—he stept,
There was a cooler light; and so he kept
Towards it by a sandy path, and lo!   1020
More suddenly than doth a moment go,
The visions of the earth were gone and fled—
He saw the giant sea above his head.

Book III

There are who lord it o'er their fellow-men
With most prevailing tinsel: who unpen
Their baaing vanities, to browse away
The comfortable green and juicy hay
From human pastures; or, O torturing fact!
Who, through an idiot blink, will see unpack'd
Fire-branded foxes to sear up and singe

Our gold and ripe-ear'd hopes. With not one tinge
Of sanctuary splendour, not a sight
Able to face an owl's, they still are dight   10
By the blear-eyed nations in empurpled vests,
And crowns, and turbans. With unladen breasts,
Save of blown self-applause, they proudly mount
To their spirit's perch, their being's high account,
Their tiptop nothings, their dull skies, their thrones—
Amid the fierce intoxicating tones
Of trumpets, shoutings, and belabour'd drums,
And sudden cannon. Ah! how all this hums,
In wakeful ears, like uproar past and gone—
Like thunder clouds that spake to Babylon,   20
And set those old Chaldeans to their tasks.—
Are then regalities all gilded masks?
No, there are throned seats unscalable
But by a patient wing, a constant spell,
Or by ethereal things that, unconfin'd,
Can make a ladder of the eternal wind,
And poize about in cloudy thunder-tents
To watch the abysm-birth of elements.
Aye, 'bove the withering of old-lipp'd Fate
A thousand Powers keep religious state,   30
In water, fiery realm, and airy bourne;
And, silent as a consecrated urn,
Hold sphery sessions for a season due.
Yet few of these far majesties, ah, few!
Have bared their operations to this globe—
Few, who with gorgeous pageantry enrobe
Our piece of heaven—whose benevolence
Shakes hand with our own Ceres; every sense
Filling with spiritual sweets to plenitude,
As bees gorge full their cells. And, by the feud   40
'Twixt Nothing and Creation, I here swear,
Eterne Apollo! that thy Sister fair
Is of all these the gentlier-mightiest.
When thy gold breath is misting in the west,
She unobserved steals unto her throne,
And there she sits most meek and most alone;
As if she had not pomp subservient;

As if thine eye, high Poet! was not bent
Towards her with the Muses in thine heart;
As if the ministring stars kept not apart,   50
Waiting for silver-footed messages.
O Moon! the oldest shades 'mong oldest trees
Feel palpitations when thou lookest in:
O Moon! old boughs lisp forth a holier din
The while they feel thine airy fellowship.
Thou dost bless every where, with silver lip
Kissing dead things to life. The sleeping kine,
Couch'd in thy brightness, dream of fields divine:
Innumerable mountains rise, and rise,
Ambitious for the hallowing of thine eyes;   60
And yet thy benediction passeth not
One obscure hiding-place, one little spot
Where pleasure may be sent: the nested wren
Has thy fair face within its tranquil ken,
And from beneath a sheltering ivy leaf
Takes glimpses of thee; thou art a relief
To the poor patient oyster, where it sleeps
Within its pearly house.—The mighty deeps,
The monstrous sea is thine—the myriad sea!
O Moon! far-spooming Ocean bows to thee,   70
And Tellus feels his forehead's cumbrous load.

    Cynthia! where art thou now? What far abode
Of green or silvery bower doth enshrine
Such utmost beauty? Alas, thou dost pine
For one as sorrowful: thy cheek is pale
For one whose cheek is pale: thou dost bewail
His tears, who weeps for thee. Where dost thou sigh?
Ah! surely that light peeps from Vesper's eye,
Or what a thing is love! 'Tis She, but lo!
How chang'd, how full of ache, how gone in woe!   80
She dies at the thinnest cloud; her loveliness
Is wan on Neptune's blue: yet there's a stress
Of love-spangles, just off yon cape of trees,
Dancing upon the waves, as if to please
The curly foam with amorous influence.
O, not so idle: for down-glancing thence

She fathoms eddies, and runs wild about
O'erwhelming water-courses; scaring out
The thorny sharks from hiding-holes, and fright'ning
Their savage eyes with unaccustom'd lightning.   90
Where will the splendour be content to reach?
O love! how potent hast thou been to teach
Strange journeyings! Wherever beauty dwells,
In gulph or aerie, mountains or deep dells,
In light, in gloom, in star or blazing sun,
Thou pointest out the way, and straight 'tis won.
Amid his toil thou gav'st Leander breath;
Thou leddest Orpheus through the gleams of death;
Thou madest Pluto bear thin element;
And now, O winged Chieftain! thou has sent   100
A moon-beam to the deep, deep water-world,
To find Endymion.

                    On gold sand impearl'd
With lilly shells, and pebbles milky white,
Poor Cynthia greeted him, and sooth'd her light
Against his pallid face: he felt the charm
To breathlessness, and suddenly a warm
Of his heart's blood: 'twas very sweet; he stay'd
His wandering steps, and half-entranced laid
His head upon a tuft of straggling weeds,
To taste the gentle moon, and freshening beads,   110
Lash'd from the crystal roof by fishes' tails.
And so he kept, until the rosy veils
Mantling the east, by Aurora's peering hand
Were lifted from the water's breast, and fann'd
Into sweet air; and sober'd morning came
Meekly through billows:—when like taper-flame
Left sudden by a dallying breath of air,
He rose in silence, and once more 'gan fare
Along his fated way.

                    Far had he roam'd,
With nothing save the hollow vast, that foam'd,   120
Above, around, and at his feet; save things
More dead than Morpheus' imaginings:

Old rusted anchors, helmets, breast-plates large
Of gone sea-warriors; brazen beaks and targe;
Rudders that for a hundred years had lost
The sway of human hand; gold vase emboss'd
With long-forgotten story, and wherein
No reveller had ever dipp'd a chin
But those of Saturn's vintage; mouldering scrolls,
Writ in the tongue of heaven, by those souls   130
Who first were on the earth; and sculptures rude
In ponderous stone, developing the mood
Of ancient Nox;—then skeletons of man,
Of beast, behemoth, and leviathan,
And elephant, and eagle, and huge jaw
Of nameless monster. A cold leaden awe
These secrets struck into him; and unless
Dian had chaced away that heaviness,
He might have died: but now, with cheered feel,
He onward kept; wooing these thoughts to steal   140
About the labyrinth in his soul of love.

   'What is there in thee, Moon! that thou shouldst move
My heart so potently? When yet a child
I oft have dried my tears when thou hast smil'd.
Thou seem'dst my sister: hand in hand we went
From eve to morn across the firmament.
No apples would I gather from the tree,
Till thou hadst cool'd their cheeks deliciously:
No tumbling water ever spake romance,
But when my eyes with thine thereon could dance: 150
No woods were green enough, no bower divine,
Until thou liftedst up thine eyelids fine:
In sowing time ne'er would I dibble take,
Or drop a seed, till thou wast wide awake;
And, in the summer tide of blossoming,
No one but thee hath heard me blithly sing
And mesh my dewy flowers all the night.
No melody was like a passing spright
If it went not to solemnize thy reign.
Yes, in my boyhood, every joy and pain   160
By thee were fashion'd to the self-same end;

And as I grew in years, still didst thou blend
With all my ardours: thou wast the deep glen;
Thou wast the mountain-top—the sage's pen—
The poet's harp—the voice of friends—the sun;
Thou wast the river—thou wast glory won;
Thou wast my clarion's blast—thou wast my steed—
My goblet full of wine—my topmost deed:—
Thou wast the charm of women, lovely Moon!
O what a wild and harmonized tune   170
My spirit struck from all the beautiful!
On some bright essence could I lean, and lull
Myself to immortality: I prest
Nature's soft pillow in a wakeful rest.
But, gentle Orb! there came a nearer bliss—
My strange love came—Felicity's abyss!
She came, and thou didst fade, and fade away—
Yet not entirely; no, thy starry sway
Has been an under-passion to this hour.
Now I begin to feel thine orby power   180
Is coming fresh upon me: O be kind,
Keep back thine influence, and do not blind
My sovereign vision.—Dearest love, forgive
That I can think away from thee and live!—
Pardon me, airy planet, that I prize
One thought beyond thine argent luxuries!
How far beyond!' At this a surpris'd start
Frosted the springing verdure of his heart;
For as he lifted up his eyes to swear
How his own goddess was past all things fair,   190
He saw far in the concave green of the sea
An old man sitting calm and peacefully.
Upon a weeded rock this old man sat,
And his white hair was awful, and a mat
Of weeds were cold beneath his cold thin feet;
And, ample as the largest winding-sheet,
A cloak of blue wrapp'd up his aged bones,
O'erwrought with symbols by the deepest groans
Of ambitious magic: every ocean-form
Was woven in with black distinctness; storm,   200
And calm, and whispering, and hideous roar,

Quicksand, and whirlpool, and deserted shore,
Were emblem'd in the woof; with every shape
That skims, or dives, or sleeps, 'twixt cape and cape.
The gulphing whale was like a dot in the spell,
Yet look upon it, and 'twould size and swell
To its huge self; and the minutest fish
Would pass the very hardest gazer's wish,
And show his little eye's anatomy.
Then there was pictur'd the regality   210
Of Neptune; and the sea nymphs round his state,
In beauteous vassalage, look up and wait.
Beside this old man lay a pearly wand,
And in his lap a book, the which he conn'd
So stedfastly, that the new denizen
Had time to keep him in amazed ken,
To mark these shadowings, and stand in awe.

   The old man rais'd his hoary head and saw
The wilder'd stranger—seeming not to see,
His features were so lifeless. Suddenly   220
He woke as from a trance; his snow-white brows
Went arching up, and like two magic ploughs
Furrow'd deep wrinkles in his forehead large,
Which kept as fixedly as rocky marge,
Till round his wither'd lips had gone a smile.
Then up he rose, like one whose tedious toil
Had watch'd for years in forlorn hermitage,
Who had not from mid-life to utmost age
Eas'd in one accent his o'er-burden'd soul,
Even to the trees. He rose: he grasp'd his stole,   230
With convuls'd clenches waving it abroad,
And in a voice of solemn joy, that aw'd
Echo into oblivion, he said:—

   'Thou art the man! Now shall I lay my head
In peace upon my watery pillow: now
Sleep will come smoothly to my weary brow.
O Jove! I shall be young again, be young!
O shell-borne Neptune, I am pierc'd and stung

With new-born life! What shall I do? Where go,
When I have cast this serpent-skin of woe?— 240
I'll swim to the syrens, and one moment listen
Their melodies, and see their long hair glisten;
Anon upon that giant's arm I'll be,
That writhes about the roots of Sicily:
To northern seas I'll in a twinkling sail,
And mount upon the snortings of a whale
To some black cloud; thence down I'll madly sweep
On forked lightning, to the deepest deep,
Where through some sucking pool I will be hurl'd
With rapture to the other side of the world! 250
O, I am full of gladness! Sisters three,
I bow full hearted to your old decree!
Yes, every god be thank'd, and power benign,
For I no more shall wither, droop, and pine.
Thou art the man!' Endymion started back
Dismay'd; and, like a wretch from whom the rack
Tortures hot breath, and speech of agony,
Mutter'd: 'What lonely death am I to die
In this cold region? Will he let me freeze,
And float my brittle limbs o'er polar seas? 260
Or will he touch me with his searing hand,
And leave a black memorial on the sand?
Or tear me piece-meal with a bony saw,
And keep me as a chosen food to draw
His magian fish through hated fire and flame?
O misery of hell! resistless, tame,
Am I to be burnt up? No, I will shout,
Until the gods through heaven's blue look out!—
O Tartarus! but some few days agone
Her soft arms were entwining me, and on 270
Her voice I hung like fruit among green leaves:
Her lips were all my own, and—ah, ripe sheaves
Of happiness! ye on the stubble droop,
But never may be garner'd. I must stoop
My head, and kiss death's foot. Love! love, farewell!
Is there no hope from thee? This horrid spell
Would melt at thy sweet breath.—By Dian's hind

Feeding from her white fingers, on the wind
I see thy streaming hair! and now, by Pan,
I care not for this old mysterious man!'   280

He spake, and walking to that aged form,
Look'd high defiance. Lo! his heart 'gan warm
With pity, for the grey-hair'd creature wept.
Had he then wrong'd a heart where sorrow kept?
Had he, though blindly contumelious, brought
Rheum to kind eyes, a sting to humane thought,
Convulsion to a mouth of many years?
He had in truth; and he was ripe for tears.
The penitent shower fell, as down he knelt
Before that care-worn sage, who trembling felt   290
About his large dark locks, and faultering spake:

'Arise, good youth, for sacred Phœbus' sake!
I know thine inmost bosom, and I feel
A very brother's yearning for thee steal
Into mine own: for why? thou openest
The prison gates that have so long opprest
My weary watching. Though thou know'st it not,
Thou art commission'd to this fated spot
For great enfranchisement. O weep no more;
I am a friend to love, to loves of yore: 300
Aye, hadst thou never lov'd an unknown power,
I had been grieving at this joyous hour.
But even now most miserable old,
I saw thee, and my blood no longer cold
Gave mighty pulses: in this tottering case
Grew a new heart, which at this moment plays
As dancingly as thine. Be not afraid,
For thou shalt hear this secret all display'd,
Now as we speed towards our joyous task.'

So saying, this young soul in age's mask   310
Went forward with the Carian side by side:
Resuming quickly thus: while ocean's tide
Hung swollen at their backs, and jewel'd sands
Took silently their foot-prints.

Now past the midway from mortality,
And so I can prepare without a sigh
To tell thee briefly all my joy and pain.
I was a fisher once, upon this main,
And my boat danc'd in every creek and bay;
Rough billows were my home by night and day,—   320
The sea-gulls not more constant; for I had
No housing from the storm and tempests mad,
But hollow rocks,—and they were palaces
Of silent happiness, of slumberous ease:
Long years of misery have told me so.
Aye, thus it was one thousand years ago.
One thousand years!—Is it then possible
To look so plainly through them? to dispel
A thousand years with backward glance sublime?
To breathe away as 'twere all scummy slime   330
From off a crystal pool, to see its deep,
And one's own image from the bottom peep?
Yes: now I am no longer wretched thrall,
My long captivity and moanings all
Are but a slime, a thin-pervading scum,
The which I breathe away, and thronging come
Like things of yesterday my youthful pleasures.

'I touch'd no lute, I sang not, trod no measures:
I was a lonely youth on desert shores.
My sports were lonely, 'mid continuous roars,   340
And craggy isles, and sea-mew's plaintive cry
Plaining discrepant between sea and sky.
Dolphins were still my playmates; shapes unseen
Would let me feel their scales of gold and green,
Nor be my desolation; and, full oft,
When a dread waterspout had rear'd aloft
Its hungry hugeness, seeming ready ripe
To burst with hoarsest thunderings, and wipe
My life away like a vast sponge of fate,
Some friendly monster, pitying my sad state,   350
Has dived to its foundations, gulph'd it down,
And left me tossing safely. But the crown

Of all my life was utmost quietude:
More did I love to lie in cavern rude,
Keeping in wait whole days for Neptune's voice,
And if it came at last, hark, and rejoice!
There blush'd no summer eve but I would steer
My skiff along green shelving coasts, to hear
The shepherd's pipe come clear from aery steep,
Mingled with ceaseless bleatings of his sheep: 360
And never was a day of summer shine,
But I beheld its birth upon the brine:
For I would watch all night to see unfold
Heaven's gates, and Æthon snort his morning gold
Wide o'er the swelling streams: and constantly
At brim of day-tide, on some grassy lea,
My nets would be spread out, and I at rest.
The poor folk of the sea-country I blest
With daily boon of fish most delicate:
They knew not whence this bounty, and elate   370
Would strew sweet flowers on a sterile beach.

   'Why was I not contented? Wherefore reach
At things which, but for thee, O Latmian!
Had been my dreary death? Fool! I began
To feel distemper'd longings: to desire
The utmost privilege that ocean's sire
Could grant in benediction: to be free
Of all his kingdom. Long in misery
I wasted, ere in one extremest fit
I plung'd for life or death. To interknit   380
One's senses with so dense a breathing stuff
Might seem a work of pain; so not enough
Can I admire how crystal-smooth it felt,
And buoyant round my limbs. At first I dwelt
Whole days and days in sheer astonishment;
Forgetful utterly of self-intent;
Moving but with the mighty ebb and flow.
Then, like a new fledg'd bird that first doth show
His spreaded feathers to the morrow chill,
I tried in fear the pinions of my will.   390
'Twas freedom! and at once I visited

The ceaseless wonders of this ocean-bed.
No need to tell thee of them, for I see
That thou hast been a witness—it must be—
For these I know thou canst not feel a drouth,
By the melancholy corners of that mouth.
So I will in my story straightway pass
To more immediate matter. Woe, alas!
That love should be my bane! Ah, Scylla fair!
Why did poor Glaucus ever—ever dare   400
To sue thee to his heart? Kind stranger-youth!
I lov'd her to the very white of truth,
And she would not conceive it. Timid thing!
She fled me swift as sea-bird on the wing,
Round every isle, and point, and promontory,
From where large Hercules wound up his story
Far as Egyptian Nile. My passion grew
The more, the more I saw her dainty hue
Gleam delicately through the azure clear:
Until 'twas too fierce agony to bear;   410
And in that agony, across my grief
It flash'd, that Circe might find some relief—
Cruel enchantress! So above the water
I rear'd my head, and look'd for Phœbus' daughter.
Æææ's isle was wondering at the moon:—
It seem'd to whirl around me, and a swoon
Left me dead-drifting to that fatal power.

'When I awoke, 'twas in a twilight bower;
Just when the light of morn, with hum of bees,
Stole through its verdurous matting of fresh trees.   420
How sweet, and sweeter! for I heard a lyre,
And over it a sighing voice expire.
It ceased—I caught light footsteps; and anon
The fairest face that morn e'er look'd upon
Push'd through a screen of roses. Starry Jove!
With tears, and smiles, and honey-words she wove
A net whose thraldom was more bliss than all
The range of flower'd Elysium. Thus did fall
The dew of her rich speech: "Ah! Art awake?
"O let me hear thee speak, for Cupid's sake!   430

"I am so oppress'd with joy! Why, I have shed
"An urn of tears, as though thou wert cold dead;
"And now I find thee living, I will pour
"From these devoted eyes their silver store,
"Until exhausted of the latest drop,
"So it will pleasure thee, and force thee stop
"Here, that I too may live: but if beyond
"Such cool and sorrowful offerings, thou art fond
"Of soothing warmth, of dalliance supreme;
"If thou art ripe to taste a long love dream;   440
"If smiles, if dimples, tongues for ardour mute,
"Hang in thy vision like a tempting fruit,
"O let me pluck it for thee." Thus she link'd
Her charming syllables, till indistinct
Their music came to my o'er-sweeten'd soul;
And then she hover'd over me, and stole
So near, that if no nearer it had been
This furrow'd visage thou hadst never seen.

'Young man of Latmos! thus particular
Am I, that thou may'st plainly see how far   450
This fierce temptation went: and thou may'st not
Exclaim, How then, was Scylla quite forgot?

'Who could resist? Who in this universe?
She did so breathe ambrosia; so immerse
My fine existence in a golden clime.
She took me like a child of suckling time,
And cradled me in roses. Thus condemn'd,
The current of my former life was stemm'd,
And to this arbitrary queen of sense
I bow'd a tranced vassal: nor would thence   460
Have mov'd, even though Amphion's harp had woo'd
Me back to Scylla o'er the billows rude.
For as Apollo each eve doth devise
A new appareling for western skies;
So every eve, nay every spendthrift hour
Shed balmy consciousness within that bower.
And I was free of haunts umbrageous;
Could wander in the mazy forest-house

Of squirrels, foxes shy, and antler'd deer,
And birds from coverts innermost and drear   470
Warbling for very joy mellifluous sorrow—
To me new born delights!

                              'Now let me borrow,
For moments few, a temperament as stern
As Pluto's sceptre, that my words not burn
These uttering lips, while I in calm speech tell
How specious heaven was changed to real hell.

  'One morn she left me sleeping: half awake
I sought for her smooth arms and lips, to slake
My greedy thirst with nectarous camel-draughts;
But she was gone. Whereat the barbed shafts   480
Of disappointment stuck in me so sore,
That out I ran and search'd the forest o'er.
Wandering about in pine and cedar gloom
Damp awe assail'd me; for there 'gan to boom
A sound of moan, an agony of sound,
Sepulchral from the distance all around.
Then came a conquering earth-thunder, and rumbled
That fierce complain to silence: while I stumbled
Down a precipitous path, as if impell'd.
I came to a dark valley.—Groanings swell'd   490
Poisonous about my ears, and louder grew,
The nearer I approach'd a flame's gaunt blue,
That glar'd before me through a thorny brake
This fire, like the eye of gordian snake,
Bewitch'd me towards; and I soon was near
A sight too fearful for the feel of fear:
In thicket hid I curs'd the haggard scene—
The banquet of my arms, my arbour queen,
Seated upon an uptorn forest root;
And all around her shapes, wizard and brute,   500
Laughing, and wailing, groveling, serpenting,
Showing tooth, tusk, and venom-bag, and sting!
O such deformities! Old Charon's self,
Should he give up awhile his penny pelf,
And take a dream 'mong rushes Stygian,

It could not be so phantasied. Fierce, wan,
And tyrannizing was the lady's look,
As over them a gnarled staff she shook.
Oft-times upon the sudden she laugh'd out,
And from a basket emptied to the rout   510
Clusters of grapes, the which they raven'd quick
And roar'd for more; with many a hungry lick
About their shaggy jaws. Avenging, slow,
Anon she took a branch of mistletoe,
And emptied on't a black dull-gurgling phial:
Groan'd one and all, as if some piercing trial
Was sharpening for their pitiable bones.
She lifted up the charm: appealing groans
From their poor breasts went sueing to her ear
In vain; remorseless as an infant's bier   520
She whisk'd against their eyes the sooty oil.
Whereat was heard a noise of painful toil,
Increasing gradual to a tempest rage,
Shrieks, yells, and groans of torture-pilgrimage;
Until their grieved bodies 'gan to bloat
And puff from the tail's end to stifled throat:
Then was appalling silence: then a sight
More wildering than all that hoarse affright;
For the whole herd, as by a whirlwind writhen,
Went through the dismal air like one huge Python 530
Antagonizing Boreas,—and so vanish'd.
Yet there was not a breath of wind: she banish'd
These phantoms with a nod. Lo! from the dark
Came waggish fauns, and nymphs, and satyrs stark,
With dancing and loud revelry,—and went
Swifter than centaurs after rapine bent.—
Sighing an elephant appear'd and bow'd
Before the fierce witch, speaking thus aloud
In human accent: "Potent goddess! chief
"Of pains resistless! make my being brief,   540
"Or let me from this heavy prison fly:
"Or give me to the air, or let me die!
"I sue not for my happy crown again;
"I sue not for my phalanx on the plain;
"I sue not for my lone, my widow'd wife;

"I sue not for my ruddy drops of life,
"My children fair, my lovely girls and boys!
"I will forget them; I will pass these joys;
"Ask nought so heavenward, so too—too high:
"Only I pray, as fairest boon, to die,   550
"Or be deliver'd from this cumbrous flesh,
"From this gross, detestable, filthy mesh,
"And merely given to the cold bleak air.
"Have mercy, Goddess! Circe, feel my prayer!"

  'That curst magician's name fell icy numb
Upon my wild conjecturing: truth had come
Naked and sabre-like against my heart.
I saw a fury whetting a death-dart;
And my slain spirit, overwrought with fright,
Fainted away in that dark lair of night.   560
Think, my deliverer, how desolate
My waking must have been! disgust, and hate,
And terrors manifold divided me
A spoil amongst them. I prepar'd to flee
Into the dungeon core of that wild wood:
I fled three days—when lo! before me stood
Glaring the angry witch. O Dis, even now,
A clammy dew is beading on my brow,
At mere remembering her pale laugh, and curse.
"Ha! ha! Sir Dainty! there must be a nurse   570
"Made of rose leaves and thistledown, express,
"To cradle thee my sweet, and lull thee: yes,
"I am too flinty-hard for thy nice touch:
"My tenderest squeeze is but a giant's clutch.
"So, fairy-thing, it shall have lullabies
"Unheard of yet: and it shall still its cries
"Upon some breast more lilly-feminine.
"Oh, no—it shall not pine, and pine, and pine
"More than one pretty, trifling thousand years;
"And then 'twere pity, but fate's gentle shears   580
"Cut short its immortality. Sea-flirt!
"Young dove of the waters! truly I'll not hurt
"One hair of thine: see how I weep and sigh,
"That our heart-broken parting is so nigh.

"And must we part? Ah, yes, it must be so.
"Yet ere thou leavest me in utter woe,
"Let me sob over thee my last adieus,
"And speak a blessing: Mark me! Thou hast thews
"Immortal, for thou art of heavenly race:
"But such a love is mine, that here I chace   590
"Eternally away from thee all bloom
"Of youth, and destine thee towards a tomb.
"Hence shalt thou quickly to the watery vast;
"And there, ere many days be overpast,
"Disabled age shall seize thee; and even then
"Thou shalt not go the way of aged men;
"But live and wither, cripple and still breathe
"Ten hundred years: which gone, I then bequeath
"Thy fragile bones to unknown burial.
"Adieu, sweet love, adieu!"—As shot stars fall,   600
She fled ere I could groan for mercy. Stung
And poison'd was my spirit: despair sung
A war-song of defiance 'gainst all hell.
A hand was at my shoulder to compel
My sullen steps; another 'fore my eyes
Moved on with pointed finger. In this guise
Enforced, at the last by ocean's foam
I found me; by my fresh, my native home.
Its tempering coolness, to my life akin,
Came salutary as I waded in;   610
And, with a blind voluptuous rage, I gave
Battle to the swollen billow-ridge, and drave
Large froth before me, while there yet remain'd
Hale strength, nor from my bones all marrow drain'd.

    'Young lover, I must weep—such hellish spite
With dry cheek who can tell? While thus my might
Proving upon this element, dismay'd,
Upon a dead thing's face my hand I laid;
I look'd—'twas Scylla! Cursed, cursed Circe!
O vulture-witch, hast never heard of mercy?   620
Could not thy harshest vengeance be content,
But thou must nip this tender innocent
Because I lov'd her?—Cold, O cold indeed

Were her fair limbs, and like a common weed
The sea-swell took her hair. Dead as she was
I clung about her waist, nor ceas'd to pass
Fleet as an arrow through unfathom'd brine,
Until there shone a fabric crystalline,
Ribb'd and inlaid with coral, pebble, and pearl.
Headlong I darted; at one eager swirl   630
Gain'd its bright portal, enter'd, and behold!
'Twas vast, and desolate, and icy-cold;
And all around—But wherefore this to thee
Who in few minutes more thyself shalt see?—
I left poor Scylla in a niche and fled.
My fever'd parchings up, my scathing dread
Met palsy half way: soon these limbs became
Gaunt, wither'd, sapless, feeble, cramp'd, and lame.

   'Now let me pass a cruel, cruel space,
Without one hope, without one faintest trace   640
Of mitigation, or redeeming bubble
Of colour'd phantasy; for I fear 'twould trouble
Thy brain to loss of reason: and next tell
How a restoring chance came down to quell
One half of the witch in me.

                    'On a day,
Sitting upon a rock above the spray,
I saw grow up from the horizon's brink
A gallant vessel: soon she seem'd to sink
Away from me again, as though her course
Had been resum'd in spite of hindering force—   650
So vanish'd: and not long, before arose
Dark clouds, and muttering of winds morose.
Old Æolus would stifle his mad spleen,
But could not: therefore all the billows green
Toss'd up the silver spume against the clouds.
The tempest came: I saw that vessel's shrouds
In perilous bustle; while upon the deck
Stood trembling creatures. I beheld the wreck;
The final gulphing; the poor struggling souls:
I heard their cries amid loud thunder-rolls.   660

O they had all been sav'd but crazed eld
Annull'd my vigorous cravings: and thus quell'd
And curb'd, think on't, O Latmian! did I sit
Writhing with pity, and a cursing fit
Against that hell-born Circe. The crew had gone,
By one and one, to pale oblivion;
And I was gazing on the surges prone,
With many a scalding tear and many a groan,
When at my feet emerg'd an old man's hand,
Grasping this scroll, and this same slender wand.   670
I knelt with pain—reach'd out my hand—had grasp'd
These treasures—touch'd the knuckles—they unclasp'd—
I caught a finger: but the downward weight
O'erpowered me—it sank. Then 'gan abate
The storm, and through chill aguish gloom outburst
The comfortable sun. I was athirst
To search the book, and in the warming air
Parted its dripping leaves with eager care.
Strange matters did it treat of, and drew on
My soul page after page, till well-nigh won   680
Into forgetfulness; when, stupefied,
I read these words, and read again, and tried
My eyes against the heavens, and read again.
O what a load of misery and pain
Each Atlas-line bore off!—a shine of hope
Came gold around me, cheering me to cope
Strenuous with hellish tyranny. Attend!
For thou hast brought their promise to an end.

   'In the wide sea there lives a forlorn wretch,
Doom'd with enfeebled carcase to outstretch   690
His loath'd existence through ten centuries,
And then to die alone. Who can devise
A total opposition? No one. So
One million times ocean must ebb and flow,
And he oppressed. Yet he shall not die,
These things accomplish'd:—If he utterly
Scans all the depths of magic, and expounds
The meanings of all motions, shapes and sounds;
If he explores all forms and substances

Straight homeward to their symbol-essences;
He shall not die. Moreover, and in chief,
He must pursue this task of joy and grief
Most piously;—all lovers tempest-tost,
And in the savage overwhelming lost,
He shall deposit side by side, until
Time's creeping shall the dreary space fulfil:
Which done, and all these labours ripened,
A youth, by heavenly power lov'd and led,
Shall stand before him; whom he shall direct
How to consummate all. The youth elect   710
Must do the thing, or both will be destroy'd.'—

'Then,' cried the young Endymion, overjoy'd,
'We are twin brothers in this destiny!
Say, I intreat thee, what achievement high
Is, in this restless world, for me reserv'd.
What! if from thee my wandering feet had swerv'd,
Had we both perish'd?'—'Look!' the sage replied,
'Dost thou not mark a gleaming through the tide,
Of diverse brilliances? 'tis the edifice
I told thee of, where lovely Scylla lies;   720
And where I have enshrined piously
All lovers, whom fell storms have doom'd to die
Throughout my bondage.' Thus discoursing, on
They went till unobscur'd the porches shone;
Which hurryingly they gain'd, and enter'd straight.
Sure never since king Neptune held his state
Was seen such wonder underneath the stars.
Turn to some level plain where haughty Mars
Has legion'd all his battle; and behold
How every soldier, with firm foot, doth hold   730
His even breast: see, many steeled squares,
And rigid ranks of iron—whence who dares
One step? Imagine further, line by line,
These warrior thousands on the field supine:—
So in that crystal place, in silent rows,
Poor lovers lay at rest from joys and woes.—
The stranger from the mountains, breathless, trac'd
Such thousands of shut eyes in order plac'd;

Such ranges of white feet, and patient lips
All ruddy,—for here death no blossom nips. 740
He mark'd their brows and foreheads; saw their hair
Put sleekly on one side with nicest care;
And each one's gentle wrists, with reverence,
Put cross-wise to its heart.

                    'Let us commence,'
Whisper'd the guide, stuttering with joy, 'even now.'
He spake, and, trembling like an aspen-bough,
Began to tear his scroll in pieces small,
Uttering the while some mumblings funeral.
He tore it into pieces small as snow
That drifts unfeather'd when bleak northerns blow; 750
And having done it, took his dark blue cloak
And bound it round Endymion: then struck
His wand against the empty air times nine.—
'What more there is to do, young man, is thine:
But first a little patience; first undo
This tangled thread, and wind it to a clue.
Ah, gentle! 'tis as weak as spider's skein;
And shouldst thou break it—What, is it done so clean?
A power overshadows thee! O, brave!
The spite of hell is tumbling to its grave. 760
Here is a shell; 'tis pearly blank to me,
Nor mark'd with any sign or charactery—
Canst thou read aught? O read for pity's sake!
Olympus! we are safe! Now, Carian, break
This wand against yon lyre on the pedestal.'

   'Twas done: and straight with sudden swell and fall
Sweet music breath'd her soul away, and sigh'd
A lullaby to silence.—'Youth! now strew
These minced leaves on me, and passing through
Those files of dead, scatter the same around, 770
And thou wilt see the issue.'—'Mid the sound
Of flutes and viols, ravishing his heart,
Endymion from Glaucus stood apart,
And scatter'd in his face some fragments light.
How lightning-swift the change! a youthful wight
Smiling beneath a coral diadem,

Out-sparkling sudden like an upturn'd gem,
Appear'd, and, stepping to a beauteous corse,
Kneel'd down beside it, and with tenderest force
Press'd its cold hand, and wept,—and Scylla sigh'd!   780
Endymion, with quick hand, the charm applied—
The nymph arose: he left them to their joy,
And onward went upon his high employ,
Showering those powerful fragments on the dead.
And, as he pass'd, each lifted up its head,
As doth a flower at Apollo's touch.
Death felt it to his inwards: 'twas too much:
Death fell a weeping in his charnel-house.
The Latmian persever'd along, and thus
All were re-animated. There arose   790
A noise of harmony, pulses and throes
Of gladness in the air—while many, who
Had died in mutual arms devout and true,
Sprang to each other madly; and the rest
Felt a high certainty of being blest.
They gaz'd upon Endymion. Enchantment
Grew drunken, and would have its head and bent.
Delicious symphonies, like airy flowers,
Budded, and swell'd, and, full-blown, shed full showers
Of light, soft, unseen leaves of sounds divine.   800
The two deliverers tasted a pure wine
Of happiness, from fairy-press ooz'd out.
Speechless they eyed each other, and about
The fair assembly wander'd to and fro,
Distracted with the richest overflow
Of joy that ever pour'd from heaven.

                                        ——'Away!'
Shouted the new born god; 'Follow, and pay
Our piety to Neptunus supreme!'—
Then Scylla, blushing sweetly from her dream,
They led on first, bent to her meek surprise,   810
Through portal columns of a giant size,
Into the vaulted, boundless emerald.
Joyous all follow'd as the leader call'd,
Down marble steps; pouring as easily
As hour-glass sand,—and fast, as you might see

Swallows obeying the south summer's call,
Or swans upon a gentle waterfall.

Thus went that beautiful multitude, nor far,
Ere from among some rocks of glittering spar,
Just within ken, they saw descending thick   820
Another multitude. Whereat more quick
Moved either host. On a wide sand they met,
And of those numbers every eye was wet;
For each their old love found. A murmuring rose,
Like what was never heard in all the throes
Of wind and waters: 'tis past human wit
To tell; 'tis dizziness to think of it.

This mighty consummation made, the host
Mov'd on for many a league; and gain'd, and lost
Huge sea-marks; vanward swelling in array,   830
And from the rear diminishing away,—
Till a faint dawn surpris'd them. Glaucus cried,
'Behold! behold, the palace of his pride!
God Neptune's palaces!' With noise increas'd,
They shoulder'd on towards that brightening east.
At every onward step proud domes arose
In prospect,—diamond gleams, and golden glows
Of amber 'gainst their faces levelling.
Joyous, and many as the leaves in spring,
Still onward; still the splendour gradual swell'd.   840
Rich opal domes were seen, on high upheld
By jasper pillars, letting through their shafts
A blush of coral. Copious wonder-draughts
Each gazer drank; and deeper drank more near.
For what poor mortals fragment up, as mere
As marble was there lavish, to the vast
Of one fair palace, that far far surpass'd,
Even for common bulk, those olden three,
Memphis, and Babylon, and Nineveh.

As large, as bright, as colour'd as the bow   850
Of Iris, when unfading it doth show
Beyond a silvery shower, was the arch

Through which this Paphian army took its march,
Into the outer courts of Neptune's state:
Whence could be seen, direct, a golden gate,
To which the leaders sped; but not half raught
Ere it burst open swift as fairy thought,
And made those dazzled thousands veil their eyes
Like callow eagles at the first sunrise.
Soon with an eagle nativeness their gaze   860
Ripe from hue-golden swoons took all the blaze,
And then, behold! large Neptune on his throne
Of emerald deep: yet not exalt alone;
At his right hand stood winged Love, and on
His left sat smiling Beauty's paragon.

  Far as the mariner on highest mast
Can see all round upon the calmed vast,
So wide was Neptune's hall: and as the blue
Doth vault the waters, so the waters drew
Their doming curtains, high, magnificent,   870
Aw'd from the throne aloof;—and when storm-rent
Disclos'd the thunder-gloomings in Jove's air;
But sooth'd as now, flash'd sudden everywhere,
Noiseless, sub-marine cloudlets, glittering
Death to a human eye: for there did spring
From natural west, and east, and south, and north,
A light as of four sunsets, blazing forth
A gold-green zenith 'bove the Sea-God's head.
Of lucid depth the floor, and far outspread
As breezeless lake, on which the slim canoe   880
Of feather'd Indian darts about, as through
The delicatest air: air verily,
But for the portraiture of clouds and sky:
This palace floor breath-air,—but for the amaze
Of deep-seen wonders motionless,—and blaze
Of the dome pomp, reflected in extremes,
Globing a golden sphere.

                       They stood in dreams
Till Triton blew his horn. The palace rang;
The Nereids danc'd; the Syrens faintly sang;

And the great Sea-King bow'd his dripping head.   890
Then Love took wing, and from his pinions shed
On all the multitude a nectarous dew.
The ooze-born Goddess beckoned and drew
Fair Scylla and her guides to conference;
And when they reach'd the throned eminence
She kist the sea-nymph's cheek,—who sat her down
A toying with the doves. Then,—'Mighty crown
And sceptre of this kingdom!' Venus said,
'Thy vows were on a time to Nais paid:
Behold!'—Two copious tear-drops instant fell   900
From the God's large eyes; he smil'd delectable,
And over Glaucus held his blessing hands.—
'Endymion! Ah! still wandering in the bands
Of love? Now this is cruel. Since the hour
I met thee in earth's bosom, all my power
Have I put forth to serve thee. What, not yet
Escap'd from dull mortality's harsh net?
A little patience, youth! 'twill not be long,
Or I am skilless quite: an idle tongue,
A humid eye, and steps luxurious,   910
Where these are new and strange, are ominous.
Aye, I have seen these signs in one of heaven,
When others were all blind: and were I given
To utter secrets, haply I might say
Some pleasant words:—but Love will have his day.
So wait awhile expectant. Pr'ythee soon,
Even in the passing of thine honey-moon,
Visit thou my Cythera: thou wilt find
Cupid well-natured, my Adonis kind;
And pray persuade with thee—Ah, I have done,   920
All blisses be upon thee, my sweet son!'—
Thus the fair goddess: While Endymion
Knelt to receive those accents halcyon.

    Meantime a glorious revelry began
Before the Water-Monarch. Nectar ran
In courteous fountains to all cups outreach'd;
And plunder'd vines, teeming exhaustless, pleach'd
New growth about each shell and pendent lyre;

The which, in disentangling for their fire,
Pull'd down fresh foliage and coverture   930
For dainty toying. Cupid, empire-sure,
Flutter'd and laugh'd, and oft-times through the throng
Made a delighted way. Then dance, and song,
And garlanding grew wild; and pleasure reign'd.
In harmless tendril they each other chain'd,
And strove who should be smother'd deepest in
Fresh crush of leaves.

                  O 'tis a very sin
For one so weak to venture his poor verse
In such a place as this. O do not curse,
High Muses! let him hurry to the ending.   940

   All suddenly were silent. A soft blending
Of dulcet instruments came charmingly;
And then a hymn.

               'King of the stormy sea!
Brother of Jove, and co-inheritor
Of elements! Eternally before
Thee the waves awful bow. Fast, stubborn rock,
At thy fear'd trident shrinking, doth unlock
Its deep foundations, hissing into foam.
All mountain-rivers, lost in the wide home
Of thy capacious bosom, ever flow.   950
Thou frownest, and old Æolus thy foe
Skulks to his cavern, 'mid the gruff complaint
Of all his rebels tempests. Dark clouds faint
When, from thy diadem, a silver gleam
Slants over blue dominion. Thy bright team
Gulphs in the morning light, and scuds along
To bring thee nearer to that golden song
Apollo singeth, while his chariot
Waits at the doors of heaven. Thou art not
For scenes like this: an empire stern hast thou;   960
And it hath furrow'd that large front: yet now,
As newly come of heaven, dost thou sit
To blend and interknit

Subdued majesty with this glad time.
O shell-borne King sublime!
We lay our hearts before thee evermore—
We sing, and we adore!

   'Breathe softly, flutes;
Be tender of your strings, ye soothing lutes;
Nor be the trumpet heard! O vain, O vain;   970
Not flowers budding in an April rain,
Nor breath of sleeping dove, nor river's flow,—
No, nor the Æolian twang of Love's own bow,
Can mingle music fit for the soft ear
Of goddess Cytherea!
Yet deign, white Queen of Beauty, thy fair eyes
On our souls' sacrifice.

   'Bright-winged Child!
Who has another care when thou hast smil'd?
Unfortunates on earth, we see at last   980
All death-shadows, and glooms that overcast
Our spirits, fann'd away by thy light pinions.
O sweetest essence! sweetest of all minions!
God of warm pulses, and dishevell'd hair,
And panting bosoms bare!
Dear unseen light in darkness! eclipser
Of light in light! delicious poisoner!
Thy venom'd goblet will we quaff until
We fill—we fill!
And by thy Mother's lips——'

                  Was heard no more   990
For clamour, when the golden palace door
Opened again, and from without, in shone
A new magnificence. On oozy throne
Smooth-moving came Oceanus the old,
To take a latest glimpse at his sheep-fold,
Before he went into his quiet cave
To muse for ever—Then a lucid wave,
Scoop'd from its trembling sisters of mid-sea,
Afloat, and pillowing up the majesty
Of Doris, and the Ægean seer, her spouse—   1000

Next, on a dolphin, clad in laurel boughs,
Theban Amphion leaning on his lute:
His fingers went across it—All were mute
To gaze on Amphitrite, queen of pearls,
And Thetis pearly too.—

                  The palace whirls
Around giddy Endymion; seeing he
Was there far strayed from mortality.
He could not bear it—shut his eyes in vain;
Imagination gave a dizzier pain.
'O I shall die! sweet Venus, be my stay!   1010
Where is my lovely mistress? Well-away!
I die—I hear her voice—I feel my wing—'
At Neptune's feet he sank. A sudden ring
Of Nereids were about him, in kind strife
To usher back his spirit into life:
But still he slept. At last they interwove
Their cradling arms, and purpos'd to convey
Towards a crystal bower far away.

    Lo! while slow carried through the pitying crowd,
To his inward senses these words spake aloud;   1020
Written in star-light on the dark above:
Dearest Endymion! my entire love!
How have I dwelt in fear of fate: 'tis done—
Immortal bliss for me too hast thou won.
Arise then! for the hen-dove shall not hatch
Her ready eggs, before I'll kissing snatch
Thee into endless heaven. Awake! awake!

    The youth at once arose: a placid lake
Came quiet to his eyes; and forest green,
Cooler than all the wonders he had seen,   1030
Lull'd with its simple song his fluttering breast.
How happy once again in grassy nest!

Book IV

Muse of my native land! loftiest Muse!
O first-born on the mountains! by the hues

Of heaven on the spiritual air begot:
Long didst thou sit alone in northern grot,
While yet our England was a wolfish den;
Before our forests heard the talk of men;
Before the first of Druids was a child;—
Long didst thou sit amid our regions wild
Rapt in a deep prophetic solitude.
There came an eastern voice of solemn mood:—   10
Yet wast thou patient. Then sang forth the Nine,
Apollo's garland:—yet didst thou divine
Such home-bred glory, that they cry'd in vain,
'Come hither, Sister of the Island!' Plain
Spake fair Ausonia; and once more she spake
A higher summons:—still didst thou betake
Thee to thy native hopes. O thou hast won
A full accomplishment! The thing is done,
Which undone, these our latter days had risen
On barren souls. Great Muse, thou know'st what prison,   20
Of flesh and bone, curbs, and confines, and frets
Our spirit's wings: despondency besets
Our pillows; and the fresh to-morrow morn
Seems to give forth its light in very scorn
Of our dull, uninspired, snail-paced lives.
Long have I said, how happy he who shrives
To thee! But then I thought on poets gone,
And could not pray:—nor could I now—so on
I move to the end in lowliness of heart.——

   'Ah, woe is me! that I should fondly part   30
From my dear native land! Ah, foolish maid!
Glad was the hour, when, with thee, myriads bade
Adieu to Ganges and their pleasant fields!
To one so friendless the clear freshet yields
A bitter coolness; the ripe grape is sour:
Yet I would have, great gods! but one short hour
Of native air—let me but die at home.'

   Endymion to heaven's airy dome
Was offering up a hecatomb of vows,
When these words reach'd him. Whereupon he bows   40

His head through thorny-green entanglement
Of underwood, and to the sound is bent,
Anxious as hind towards her hidden fawn.

'Is no one near to help me? No fair dawn
Of life from charitable voice? No sweet saying
To set my dull and sadden'd spirit playing?
No hand to toy with mine? No lips so sweet
That I may worship them? No eyelids meet
To twinkle on my bosom? No one dies
Before me, till from these enslaving eyes   50
Redemption sparkles!—I am sad and lost.'

Thou, Carian lord, hadst better have been tost
Into a whirlpool. Vanish into air,
Warm mountaineer! for canst thou only bear
A woman's sigh alone and in distress?
See not her charms! Is Phœbe passionless?
Phœbe is fairer far—O gaze no more:—
Yet if thou wilt behold all beauty's store,
Behold her panting in the forest grass!
Do not those curls of glossy jet surpass   60
For tenderness the arms so idly lain
Amongst them? Feelest not a kindred pain,
To see such lovely eyes in swimming search
After some warm delight, that seems to perch
Dovelike in the dim cell lying beyond
Their upper lids?—Hist!

                              'O for Hermes' wand,
To touch this flower into human shape!
That woodland Hyacinthus could escape
From his green prison, and here kneeling down
Call me his queen, his second life's fair crown!   70
Ah me, how I could love!—My soul doth melt
For the unhappy youth—Love! I have felt
So faint a kindness, such a meek surrender
To what my own full thoughts had made too tender,
That but for tears my life had fled away!—

Ye deaf and senseless minutes of the day,
And thou, old forest, hold ye this for true,
There is no lightning, no authentic dew
But in the eye of love: there's not a sound,
Melodious howsoever, can confound   80
The heavens and earth in one to such a death
As doth the voice of love: there's not a breath
Will mingle kindly with the meadow air,
Till it has panted round, and stolen a share
Of passion from the heart!'—

                        Upon a bough
He leant, wretched. He surely cannot now
Thirst for another love: O impious,
That he can ever dream upon it thus!—
Thought he, 'Why am I not as are the dead,
Since to a woe like this I have been led   90
Through the dark earth, and through the wondrous sea?
Goddess! I love thee not the less: from thee
By Juno's smile I turn not—no, no, no—
While the great waters are at ebb and flow.—
I have a triple soul! O fond pretence—
For both, for both my love is so immense,
I feel my heart is cut for them in twain.'

    And so he groan'd, as one by beauty slain.
The lady's heart beat quick, and he could see
Her gentle bosom heave tumultuously.   100
He sprang from his green covert: there she lay,
Sweet as a muskrose upon new-made hay;
With all her limbs on tremble, and her eyes
Shut softly up alive. To speak he tries.
'Fair damsel, pity me! forgive that I
Thus violate thy bower's sanctity!
O pardon me, for I am full of grief—
Grief born of thee, young angel! fairest thief!
Who stolen hast away the wings wherewith
I was to top the heavens. Dear maid, sith   110
Thou art my executioner, and I feel
Loving and hatred, misery and weal,

Will in a few short hours be nothing to me,
And all my story that much passion slew me;
Do smile upon the evening of my days:
And, for my tortur'd brain begins to craze,
Be thou my nurse; and let me understand
How dying I shall kiss that lilly hand.—
Dost weep for me? Then should I be content.
Scowl on, ye fates! until the firmament   120
Outblackens Erebus, and the full-cavern'd earth
Crumbles into itself. By the cloud girth
Of Jove, those tears have given me a thirst
To meet oblivion.'—As her heart would burst
The maiden sobb'd awhile, and then replied:
'Why must such desolation betide
As that thou speak'st of? Are not these green nooks
Empty of all misfortune? Do the brooks
Utter a gorgon voice? Does yonder thrush,
Schooling its half-fledg'd little ones to brush   130
About the dewy forest, whisper tales?—
Speak not of grief, young stranger, or cold snails
Will slime the rose to night. Though if thou wilt,
Methinks 'twould be a guilt—a very guilt—
Not to companion thee, and sigh away
The light—the dusk—the dark—till break of day!'
'Dear lady,' said Endymion, ''tis past:
I love thee! and my days can never last.
That I may pass in patience still speak:
Let me have music dying, and I seek   140
No more delight—I bid adieu to all.
Didst thou not after other climates call,
And murmur about Indian streams?'—Then she,
Sitting beneath the midmost forest tree,
For pity sang this roundelay——

      'O Sorrow,
      Why dost borrow
The natural hue of health, from vermeil lips?—
      To give maiden blushes
      To the white rose bushes?   150
Or is't thy dewy hand the daisy tips?

'O Sorrow,
       Why dost borrow
The lustrous passion from a falcon-eye?—
       To give the glow-worm light?
       Or, on a moonless night,
To tinge, on syren shores, the salt sea-spry?

       'O Sorrow,
       Why dost borrow
The mellow ditties from a mourning tongue?—   **160**
       To give at evening pale
       Unto the nightingale,
That thou mayst listen the cold dews among?

       'O Sorrow,
       Why dost borrow
Heart's lightness from the merriment of May?—
       A lover would not tread
       A cowslip on the head,
Though he should dance from eve till peep of day—
       Nor any drooping flower   **170**
       Held sacred for thy bower,
Wherever he may sport himself and play.

       'To Sorrow,
       I bade good-morrow,
And thought to leave her far away behind;
       But cheerly, cheerly,
       She loves me dearly;
She is so constant to me, and so kind:
       I would deceive her
       And so leave her,   **180**
But ah! she is so constant and so kind.

'Beneath my palm trees, by the river side,
I sat a weeping: in the whole world wide
There was no one to ask me why I wept,—
       And so I kept
Brimming the water-lily cups with tears
       Cold as my fears.

'Beneath my palm trees, by the river side,
I sat a weeping: what enamour'd bride,
Cheated by shadowy wooer from the clouds,   190
    But hides and shrouds
Beneath dark palm trees by a river side?

'And as I sat, over the light blue hills
There came a noise of revellers: the rills
Into the wide stream came of purple hue—
    'Twas Bacchus and his crew!
The earnest trumpet spake, and silver thrills
From kissing cymbals made a merry din—
    'Twas Bacchus and his kin!
Like to a moving vintage down they came,   200
Crown'd with green leaves, and faces all on flame;
All madly dancing through the pleasant valley,
    To scare thee, Melancholy!
O then, O then, thou wast a simple name!
And I forgot thee, as the berried holly
By shepherds is forgotten, when, in June,
Tall chestnuts keep away the sun and moon:—
    I rush'd into the folly!

'Within his car, aloft, young Bacchus stood,
Trifling his ivy-dart, in dancing mood,   210
    With sidelong laughing;
And little rills of crimson wine imbrued
His plump white arms, and shoulders, enough white
    For Venus' pearly bite:
And near him rode Silenus on his ass,
Pelted with flowers as he on did pass
    Tipsily quaffing.

'Whence came ye, merry Damsels! whence came ye!
So many, and so many, and such glee?
Why have ye left your bowers desolate,   220
    Your lutes and gentler fate?—
"We follow Bacchus! Bacchus on the wing,
    A conquering!
Bacchus, young Bacchus! good or ill betide,

We dance before him thorough kingdoms wide:—
Come hither, lady fair, and joined be
    To our wild minstrelsy!"

'Whence came ye, jolly Satyrs! whence came ye!
So many, and so many, and such glee?
Why have ye left your forest haunts, why left   230
    Your nuts in oak-tree cleft?—
"For wine, for wine we left our kernel tree:
For wine we left our heath, and yellow brooms,
    And cold mushrooms;
For wine we follow Bacchus through the earth;
Great God of breathless cups and chirping mirth!—
Come hither, lady fair, and joined be
    To our mad minstrelsy!"

'Over wide streams and mountains great we went,
And, save when Bacchus kept his ivy tent,   240
Onward the tiger and the leopard pants,
    With Asian elephants:
Onward these myriads—with song and dance,
With zebras striped, and sleek Arabians' prance,
Web-footed alligators, crocodiles,
Bearing upon their scaly backs, in files,
Plump infant laughers mimicking the coil
Of seamen, and stout galley-rowers' toil:
With toying oars and silken sails they glide,
    Nor care for wind and tide.   250

'Mounted on panthers' furs and lions' manes,
From rear to van they scour about the plains;
A three days' journey in a moment done:
And always, at the rising of the sun,
About the wilds they hunt with spear and horn,
    On spleenful unicorn.

'I saw Osirian Egypt kneel adown
    Before the vine-wreath crown!
I saw parch'd Abyssinia rouse and sing
    To the silver cymbals' ring!   260

I saw the whelming vintage hotly pierce
        Old Tartary the fierce!
The kings of Inde their jewel-sceptres vail,
And from their treasures scatter pearled hail;
Great Brahma from his mystic heaven groans,
        And all his priesthood moans;
Before young Bacchus' eye-wink turning pale.—
Into these regions came I following him,
Sick hearted, weary—so I took a whim
To stray away into these forests drear   270
        Alone, without a peer:
And I have told thee all thou mayest hear.
        'Young stranger!
        I've been a ranger
In search of pleasure throughout every clime:
        Alas, 'tis not for me!
        Bewitch'd I sure must be,
To lose in grieving all my maiden prime.

        'Come then, Sorrow!
        Sweetest Sorrow!   280
Like an own babe I nurse thee on my breast:
        I thought to leave thee
        And deceive thee,
But now of all the world I love thee best.

        'There is not one,
        No, no, not one
But thee to comfort a poor lonely maid;
        Thou art her mother,
        And her brother,
Her playmate, and her wooer in the shade.'   290

    O what a sigh she gave in finishing,
And look, quite dead to every worldly thing!
Endymion could not speak, but gazed on her;
And listened to the wind that now did stir
About the crisped oaks full drearily,
Yet with as sweet a softness as might be
Remember'd from its velvet summer song.
At last he said: 'Poor lady, how thus long

Have I been able to endure that voice?
Fair Melody! kind Syren! I've no choice;   300
I must be thy sad servant evermore:
I cannot choose but kneel here and adore.
Alas, I must not think—by Phœbe, no!
Let me not think, soft Angel! shall it be so?
Say, beautifullest, shall I never think?
O thou could'st foster me beyond the brink
Of recollection! make my watchful care
Close up its bloodshot eyes, nor see despair!
Do gently murder half my soul, and I
Shall feel the other half so utterly!—   310
I'm giddy at that cheek so fair and smooth;
O let it blush so ever! let it soothe
My madness! let it mantle rosy-warm
With the tinge of love, panting in safe alarm.—
This cannot be thy hand, and yet it is;
And this is sure thine other softling—this
Thine own fair bosom, and I am so near!
Wilt fall asleep? O let me sip that tear!
And whisper one sweet word that I may know
This is the world—sweet dewy blossom!'—*Woe!*   320
Woe! Woe to that Endymion! Where is he?—
Even these words went echoing dismally
Through the wide forest—a most fearful tone,
Like one repenting in his latest moan;
And while it died away a shade pass'd by,
As of a thunder cloud. When arrows fly
Through the thick branches, poor ring-doves sleek forth
Their timid necks and tremble; so these both
Leant to each other trembling, and sat so
Waiting for some destruction—when lo,   330
Foot-feather'd Mercury appear'd sublime
Beyond the tall tree tops; and in less time
Than shoots the slanted hail-storm, down he dropt
Towards the ground; but rested not, nor stopt
One moment from his home: only the sward
He with his wand light touch'd, and heavenward
Swifter than sight was gone—even before
The teeming earth a sudden witness bore

Of his swift magic. Diving swans appear
Above the crystal circlings white and clear;   340
And catch the cheated eye in wide surprise,
How they can dive in sight and unseen rise—
So from the turf outsprang two steeds jet-black,
Each with large dark blue wings upon his back.
The youth of Caria plac'd the lovely dame
On one, and felt himself in spleen to tame
The other's fierceness. Through the air they flew,
High as the eagles. Like two drops of dew
Exhal'd to Phœbus' lips, away they are gone,
Far from the earth away—unseen, alone,   350
Among cool clouds and winds, but that the free,
The buoyant life of song can floating be
Above their heads, and follow them untir'd.—
Muse of my native land, am I inspir'd?
This is the giddy air, and I must spread
Wide pinions to keep here; nor do I dread
Or height, or depth, or width, or any chance
Precipitous: I have beneath my glance
Those towering horses and their mournful freight.
Could I thus sail, and see, and thus await   360
Fearless for power of thought, without thine aid?—

There is a sleepy dusk, an odorous shade
From some approaching wonder, and behold
Those winged steeds, with snorting nostrils bold
Snuff at its faint extreme, and seem to tire,
Dying to embers from their native fire!

There curl'd a purple mist around them; soon,
It seem'd as when around the pale new moon
Sad Zephyr droops the clouds like weeping willow:
'Twas Sleep slow journeying with head on pillow.   370
For the first time, since he came nigh dead born
From the old womb of night, his cave forlorn
Had he left more forlorn; for the first time,
He felt aloof the day and morning's prime—
Because into his depth Cimmerian
There came a dream, showing how a young man,

Ere a lean bat could plump its wintery skin,
Would at high Jove's empyreal footstool win
An immortality, and how espouse
Jove's daughter, and be reckon'd of his house.   380
Now was he slumbering towards heaven's gate,
That he might at the threshold one hour wait
To hear the marriage melodies, and then
Sink downward to his dusky cave again.
His litter of smooth semilucent mist,
Diversely ting'd with rose and amethyst,
Puzzled those eyes that for the centre sought;
And scarcely for one moment could be caught
His sluggish form reposing motionless.
Those two on winged steeds, with all the stress   390
Of vision search'd for him, as one would look
Athwart the sallows of a river nook
To catch a glance at silver-throated eels,—
Or from old Skiddaw's top, when fog conceals
His rugged forehead in a mantle pale,
With an eye-guess towards some pleasant vale
Descry a favourite hamlet faint and far.

These raven horses, though they foster'd are
Of earth's splenetic fire, dully drop
Their full-vein'd ears, nostrils blood wide, and stop;   400
Upon the spiritless mist have they outspread
Their ample feathers, are in slumber dead,—
And on those pinions, level in mid air,
Endymion sleepeth and the lady fair.
Slowly they sail, slowly as icy isle
Upon a calm sea drifting: and meanwhile
The mournful wanderer dreams. Behold! he walks
On heaven's pavement; brotherly he talks
To divine powers: from his hand full fain
Juno's proud birds are pecking pearly grain: 410
He tries the nerve of Phœbus' golden bow,
And asketh where the golden apples grow:
Upon his arm he braces Pallas' shield,
And strives in vain to unsettle and wield
A Jovian thunderbolt: arch Hebe brings

A full-brimm'd goblet, dances lightly, sings
And tantalizes long; at last he drinks,
And lost in pleasure at her feet he sinks,
Touching with dazzled lips her starlight hand.
He blows a bugle,—an ethereal band   420
Are visible above: the Seasons four,—
Green-kyrtled Spring, flush Summer, golden store
In Autumn's sickle, Winter frosty hoar,
Join dance with shadowy Hours; while still the blast
In swells unmitigated, still doth last
To sway their floating morris. 'Whose is this?
Whose bugle?' he inquires; they smile—'O Dis!
Why is this mortal here? Dost thou not know
Its mistress' lips? Not thou?—'Tis Dian's: lo!
She rises crescented!' He looks, 'tis she,   430
His very goddess: good-bye earth, and sea,
And air, and pains, and care, and suffering;
Good-bye to all but love! Then doth he spring
Towards her, and awakes—and, strange, o'erhead,
Of those same fragrant exhalations bred,
Beheld awake his very dream: the gods
Stood smiling; merry Hebe laughs and nods;
And Phœbe bends towards him crescented.
O state perplexing! On the pinion bed,
Too well awake, he feels the panting side   440
Of his delicious lady. He who died
For soaring too audacious in the sun,
When that same treacherous wax began to run,
Felt not more tongue-tied than Endymion.
His heart leapt up as to its rightful throne,
To that fair shadow'd passion puls'd its way—
Ah, what perplexity! Ah, well a day!
So fond, so beauteous was his bed-fellow,
He could not help but kiss her: then he grew
Awhile forgetful of all beauty save   450
Young Phœbe's, golden hair'd; and so 'gan crave
Forgiveness: yet he turn'd once more to look
At the sweet sleeper,—all his soul was shook,—
She press'd his hand in slumber; so once more
He could not help but kiss her and adore.

At this the shadow wept, melting away.
The Latmian started up: 'Bright goddess, stay!
Search my most hidden breast! By truth's own tongue,
I have no dædale heart: why is it wrung
To desperation? Is there nought for me,   460
Upon the bourne of bliss, but misery?'

    These words awoke the stranger of dark tresses:
Her dawning love-look rapt Endymion blesses
With 'haviour soft. Sleep yawn'd from underneath.
'Thou swan of Ganges, let us no more breathe
This murky phantasm! thou contented seem'st
Pillow'd in lovely idleness, nor dream'st
What horrors may discomfort thee and me.
Ah, shouldst thou die from my heart-treachery!—
Yet did she merely weep—her gentle soul   470
Hath no revenge in it: as it is whole
In tenderness, would I were whole in love!
Can I prize thee, fair maid, all price above,
Even when I feel as true as innocence?
I do, I do.—What is this soul then? Whence
Came it? It does not seem my own, and I
Have no self-passion or identity.
Some fearful end must be: where, where is it?
By Nemesis, I see my spirit flit
Alone about the dark—Forgive me, sweet: 480
Shall we away?' He rous'd the steeds: they beat
Their wings chivalrous into the clear air,
Leaving old Sleep within his vapoury lair.

    The good-night blush of eve was waning slow,
And Vesper, risen star, began to throe
In the dusk heavens silverly, when they
Thus sprang direct towards the Galaxy.
Nor did speed hinder converse soft and strange—
Eternal oaths and vows they interchange,
In such wise, in such temper, so aloof   490
Up in the winds, beneath a starry roof,
So witless of their doom, that verily
'Tis well nigh past man's search their hearts to see;

Whether they wept, or laugh'd, or griev'd, or toy'd—
Most like with joy gone mad, with sorrow cloy'd.

   Full facing their swift flight, from ebon streak,
The moon put forth a little diamond peak,
No bigger than an unobserved star,
Or tiny point of fairy scymetar;
Bright signal that she only stoop'd to tie   500
Her silver sandals, ere deliciously
She bow'd into the heavens her timid head.
Slowly she rose, as though she would have fled,
While to his lady meek the Carian turn'd,
To mark if her dark eyes had yet discern'd
This beauty in its birth—Despair! despair!
He saw her body fading gaunt and spare
In the cold moonshine. Straight he seiz'd her wrist;
It melted from his grasp: her hand he kiss'd,
And, horror! kiss'd his own—he was alone.   510
Her steed a little higher soar'd, and then
Dropt hawkwise to the earth.

                    There lies a den,
Beyond the seeming confines of the space
Made for the soul to wander in and trace
Its own existence, of remotest glooms.
Dark regions are around it, where the tombs
Of buried griefs the spirit sees, but scarce
One hour doth linger weeping, for the pierce
Of new-born woe it feels more inly smart:
And in these regions many a venom'd dart   520
At random flies; they are the proper home
Of every ill: the man is yet to come
Who hath not journeyed in this native hell.
But few have ever felt how calm and well
Sleep may be had in that deep den of all.
There anguish does not sting; nor pleasure pall:
Woe-hurricanes beat ever at the gate,
Yet all is still within and desolate.
Beset with painful gusts, within ye hear
No sound so loud as when on curtain'd bier   530

The death-watch tick is stifled. Enter none
Who strive therefore: on the sudden it is won.
Just when the sufferer begins to burn,
Then it is free to him; and from an urn,
Still fed by melting ice, he takes a draught—
Young Semele such richness never quaft
In her maternal longing! Happy gloom!
Dark Paradise! where pale becomes the bloom
Of health by due; where silence dreariest
Is most articulate; where hopes infest;   540
Where those eyes are the brightest far that keep
Their lids shut longest in a dreamless sleep.
O happy spirit-home! O wondrous soul!
Pregnant with such a den to save the whole
In thine own depth. Hail, gentle Carian!
For, never since thy griefs and woes began,
Hast thou felt so content: a grievous feud
Hath led thee to this Cave of Quietude.
Aye, his lull'd soul was there, although upborne
With dangerous speed: and so he did not mourn   550
Because he knew not whither he was going.
So happy was he, not the aerial blowing
Of trumpets at clear parley from the east
Could rouse from that fine relish, that high feast.
They stung the feather'd horse: with fierce alarm
He flapp'd towards the sound. Alas, no charm
Could lift Endymion's head, or he had view'd
A skyey mask, a pinion'd multitude,—
And silvery was its passing: voices sweet
Warbling the while as if to lull and greet   560
The wanderer in his path. Thus warbled they,
While past the vision went in bright array.

    'Who, who from Dian's feast would be away?
For all the golden bowers of the day
Are empty left? Who, who away would be
From Cynthia's wedding and festivity?
Not Hesperus: lo! upon his silver wings
He leans away for highest heaven and sings,

Snapping his lucid fingers merrily!—
Ah, Zephyrus! art here, and Flora too! 570
Ye tender bibbers of the rain and dew,
Young playmates of the rose and daffodil,
Be careful, ere ye enter in, to fill
     Your baskets high
With fennel green, and balm, and golden pines,
Savory, latter-mint, and columbines,
Cool parsley, basil sweet, and sunny thyme;
Yea, every flower and leaf of every clime,
All gather'd in the dewy morning: hie
     Away! fly, fly!— 580
Crystalline brother of the belt of heaven,
Aquarius! to whom king Jove has given
Two liquid pulse streams 'stead of feather'd wings,
Two fan-like fountains,—thine illuminings
     For Dian play:
Dissolve the frozen purity of air;
Let thy white shoulders silvery and bare
Show cold through water pinions; make more bright
The Star-Queen's crescent on her marriage night:
     Haste, haste away!— 590
Castor has tamed the planet Lion, see!
And of the Bear has Pollux mastery:
A third is in the race! who is the third
Speeding away swift as the eagle bird?
     The ramping Centaur!
The Lion's mane's on end: the Bear how fierce!
The Centaur's arrow ready seems to pierce
Some enemy: far forth his bow is bent
Into the blue of heaven. He'll be shent,
     Pale unrelentor, 600
When he shall hear the wedding lutes a playing.—
Andromeda! sweet woman! why delaying
So timidly among the stars: come hither!
Join this bright throng, and nimbly follow whither
     They all are going.
Danae's Son, before Jove newly bow'd,
Has wept for thee, calling to Jove aloud.

Thee, gentle lady, did he disenthral:
Ye shall for ever live and love, for all
        Thy tears are flowing.—   610
By Daphne's fright, behold Apollo!—'
                                        More
Endymion heard not: down his steed him bore,
Prone to the green head of a misty hill.

    His first touch of the earth went nigh to kill.
'Alas!' said he, 'were I but always borne
Through dangerous winds, had but my footsteps worn
A path in hell, for ever would I bless
Horrors which nourish an uneasiness
For my own sullen conquering: to him
Who lives beyond earth's boundary, grief is dim,   620
Sorrow is but a shadow: now I see
The grass; I feel the solid ground—Ah, me!
It is thy voice—divinest! Where?—who? who
Left thee so quiet on this bed of dew?
Behold upon this happy earth we are;
Let us aye love each other; let us fare
On forest-fruits, and never, never go
Among the abodes of mortals here below,
Or be by phantoms duped. O destiny!
Into a labyrinth now my soul would fly,   630
But with thy beauty will I deaden it.
Where didst thou melt to? By thee will I sit
For ever: let our fate stop here—a kid
I on this spot will offer: Pan will bid
Us live in peace, in love and peace among
His forest wildernesses. I have clung
To nothing, lov'd a nothing, nothing seen
Or felt but a great dream! O I have been
Presumptuous against love, against the sky,
Against all elements, against the tie   640
Of mortals each to each, against the blooms
Of flowers, rush of rivers, and the tombs
Of heroes gone! Against his proper glory
Has my own soul conspired: so my story

Will I to children utter, and repent.
There never liv'd a mortal man, who bent
His appetite beyond his natural sphere,
But starv'd and died. My sweetest Indian, here,
Here will I kneel, for thou redeemed hast
My life from too thin breathing: gone and past   650
Are cloudy phantasms. Caverns lone, farewell!
And air of visions, and the monstrous swell
Of visionary seas! No, never more
Shall airy voices cheat me to the shore
Of tangled wonder, breathless and aghast.
Adieu, my daintiest Dream! although so vast
My love is still for thee. The hour may come
When we shall meet in pure elysium.
On earth I may not love thee; and therefore
Doves will I offer up, and sweetest store   660
All through the teeming year: so thou wilt shine
On me, and on this damsel fair of mine,
And bless our silver lives. My Indian bliss!
My river-lilly bud! one human kiss!
One sigh of real breath—one gentle squeeze,
Warm as a dove's nest among summer trees,
And warm with dew at ooze from living blood!
Whither didst melt? Ah, what of that!—all good
We'll talk about—no more of dreaming.—Now,
Where shall our dwelling be? Under the brow   670
Of some steep mossy hill, where ivy dun
Would hide us up, although spring leaves were none;
And where dark yew trees, as we rustle through,
Will drop their scarlet berry cups of dew?
O thou wouldst joy to live in such a place;
Dusk for our loves, yet light enough to grace
Those gentle limbs on mossy bed reclin'd:
For by one step the blue sky shouldst thou find,
And by another, in deep dell below,
See, through the trees, a little river go   680
All in its mid-day gold and glimmering.
Honey from out the gnarled hive I'll bring,
And apples, wan with sweetness, gather thee,—

Cresses that grow where no man may them see,
And sorrel untorn by the dew-claw'd stag:
Pipes will I fashion of the syrinx flag,
That thou mayst always know whither I roam,
When it shall please thee in our quiet home
To listen and think of love. Still let me speak;
Still let me dive into the joy I seek,—   690
For yet the past doth prison me. The rill,
Thou haply mayst delight in, will I fill
With fairy fishes from the mountain tarn,
And thou shalt feed them from the squirrel's barn.
Its bottom will I strew with amber shells,
And pebbles blue from deep enchanted wells.
Its sides I'll plant with dew-sweet eglantine,
And honeysuckles full of clear bee-wine.
I will entice this crystal rill to trace
Love's silver name upon the meadow's face.   700
I'll kneel to Vesta, for a flame of fire;
And to god Phœbus, for a golden lyre;
To Empress Dian, for a hunting spear;
To Vesper, for a taper silver-clear,
That I may see thy beauty through the night;
To Flora, and a nightingale shall light
Tame on thy finger; to the River-gods,
And they shall bring thee taper fishing-rods
Of gold, and lines of Naiads' long bright tress.
Heaven shield thee for thine utter loveliness!   710
Thy mossy footstool shall the altar be
'Fore which I'll bend, bending, dear love, to thee:
Those lips shall be my Delphos, and shall speak
Laws to my footsteps, colour to my cheek,
Trembling or stedfastness to this same voice,
And of three sweetest pleasurings the choice:
And that affectionate light, those diamond things,
Those eyes, those passions, those supreme pearl springs,
Shall be my grief, or twinkle me to pleasure.
Say, is not bliss within our perfect seisure?   720
O that I could not doubt!'
               The mountaineer

Thus strove by fancies vain and crude to clear
His briar'd path to some tranquillity.
It gave bright gladness to his lady's eye,
And yet the tears she wept were tears of sorrow;
Answering thus, just as the golden morrow
Beam'd upward from the vallies of the east:
'O that the flutter of this heart had ceas'd,
Or the sweet name of love had pass'd away.
Young feather'd tyrant! by a swift decay   730
Wilt thou devote this body to the earth:
And I do think that at my very birth
I lisp'd thy blooming titles inwardly;
For at the first, first dawn and thought of thee,
With uplift hands I blest the stars of heaven.
Art thou not cruel? Ever have I striven
To think thee kind, but ah, it will not do!
When yet a child, I heard that kisses drew
Favour from thee, and so I kisses gave
To the void air, bidding them find out love: 740
But when I came to feel how far above
All fancy, pride, and fickle maidenhood,
All earthly pleasure, all imagin'd good,
Was the warm tremble of a devout kiss,—
Even then, that moment, at the thought of this,
Fainting I fell into a bed of flowers,
And languish'd there three days. Ye milder powers,
Am I not cruelly wrong'd? Believe, believe
Me, dear Endymion, were I to weave
With my own fancies garlands of sweet life,   750
Thou shouldst be one of all. Ah, bitter strife!
I may not be thy love: I am forbidden—
Indeed I am—thwarted, affrighted, chidden,
By things I trembled at, and gorgon wrath.
Twice hast thou ask'd whither I went: henceforth
Ask me no more! I may not utter it,
Nor may I be thy love. We might commit
Ourselves at once to vengeance; we might die;
We might embrace and die: voluptuous thought!
Enlarge not to my hunger, or I'm caught   760

In trammels of perverse deliciousness.
No, no, that shall not be: thee will I bless,
And bid a long adieu.'

The Carian

No word return'd: both lovelorn, silent, wan,
Into the vallies green together went.
Far wandering, they were perforce content
To sit beneath a fair lone beechen tree;
Nor at each other gaz'd, but heavily
Por'd on its hazle cirque of shedded leaves.

Endymion! unhappy! it nigh grieves   770
Me to behold thee thus in last extreme:
Ensky'd ere this, but truly that I deem
Truth the best music in a first-born song.
Thy lute-voic'd brother will I sing ere long,
And thou shalt aid—hast thou not aided me?
Yes, moonlight Emperor! felicity
Has been thy meed for many thousand years;
Yet often have I, on the brink of tears,
Mourn'd as if yet thou wert a forester;—
Forgetting the old tale.

He did not stir   780
His eyes from the dead leaves, or one small pulse
Of joy he might have felt. The spirit culls
Unfaded amaranth, when wild it strays
Through the old garden-ground of boyish days.
A little onward ran the very stream
By which he took his first soft poppy dream;
And on the very bark 'gainst which he leant
A crescent he had carv'd, and round it spent
His skill in little stars. The teeming tree
Had swollen and green'd the pious charactery,   790
But not ta'en out. Why, there was not a slope
Up which he had not fear'd the antelope;
And not a tree, beneath whose rooty shade
He had not with his tamed leopards play'd:
Nor could an arrow light, or javelin,

Fly in the air where his had never been—
And yet he knew it not.

              O treachery!
Why does his lady smile, pleasing her eye
With all his sorrowing? He sees her not.
But who so stares on him? His sister sure!   800
Peona of the woods!—Can she endure—
Impossible—how dearly they embrace!
His lady smiles; delight is in her face;
It is no treachery.

             'Dear brother mine!
Endymion, weep not so! Why shouldst thou pine
When all great Latmos so exalt will be?
Thank the great gods, and look not bitterly;
And speak not one pale word, and sigh no more.
Sure I will not believe thou hast such store
Of grief, to last thee to my kiss again.   810
Thou surely canst not bear a mind in pain,
Come hand in hand with one so beautiful.
Be happy both of you! for I will pull
The flowers of autumn for your coronals.
Pan's holy priest for young Endymion calls;
And when he is restor'd, thou, fairest dame,
Shalt be our queen. Now, is it not a shame
To see ye thus,—not very, very sad?
Perhaps ye are too happy to be glad:
O feel as if it were a common day;   820
Free-voic'd as one who never was away.
No tongue shall ask, whence come ye? but ye shall
Be gods of your own rest imperial.
Not even I, for one whole month, will pry
Into the hours that have pass'd us by,
Since in my arbour I did sing to thee.
O Hermes! on this very night will be
A hymning up to Cynthia, queen of light;
For the soothsayers old saw yesternight
Good visions in the air,—whence will befal,   830
As say these sages, health perpetual

To shepherds and their flocks; and furthermore,
In Dian's face they read the gentle lore:
Therefore for her these vesper-carols are.
Our friends will all be there from nigh and far.
Many upon thy death have ditties made;
And many, even now, their foreheads shade
With cypress, on a day of sacrifice.
New singing for our maids shalt thou devise,
And pluck the sorrow from our huntsmen's brows.   840
Tell me, my lady-queen, how to espouse
This wayward brother to his rightful joys!
His eyes are on thee bent, as thou didst poize
His fate most goddess-like. Help me, I pray,
To lure—Endymion, dear brother, say
What ails thee?' He could bear no more, and so
Bent his soul fiercely like a spiritual bow,
And twang'd it inwardly, and calmly said:
'I would have thee my only friend, sweet maid!
My only visitor! not ignorant though,   850
That those deceptions which for pleasure go
'Mong men, are pleasures real as real may be:
But there are higher ones I may not see,
If impiously an earthly realm I take.
Since I saw thee, I have been wide awake
Night after night, and day by day, until
Of the empyrean I have drunk my fill.
Let it content thee, Sister, seeing me
More happy than betides mortality.
A hermit young, I'll live in mossy cave,   860
Where thou alone shalt come to me, and lave
Thy spirit in the wonders I shall tell.
Through me the shepherd realm shall prosper well;
For to thy tongue will I all health confide.
And, for my sake, let this young maid abide
With thee as a dear sister. Thou alone,
Peona, mayst return to me. I own
This may sound strangely: but when, dearest girl,
Thou seest it for my happiness, no pearl
Will trespass down those cheeks. Companion fair!   870
Wilt be content to dwell with her, to share

This sister's love with me?' Like one resign'd
And bent by circumstance, and thereby blind
In self-commitment, thus that meek unknown:
'Aye, but a buzzing by my ears has flown,
Of jubilee to Dian:—truth I heard?
Well then, I see there is no little bird,
Tender soever, but is Jove's own care,
Long have I sought for rest, and, unaware,
Behold I find it! so exalted too!   880
So after my own heart! I knew, I knew
There was a place untenanted in it:
In that same void white Chastity shall sit,
And monitor me nightly to lone slumber.
With sanest lips I vow me to the number
Of Dian's sisterhood; and, kind lady,
With thy good help, this very night shall see
My future days to her fane consecrate.'

    As feels a dreamer what doth most create
His own particular fright, so these three felt: 890
Or like one who, in after ages, knelt
To Lucifer or Baal, when he'd pine
After a little sleep: or when in mine
Far under-ground, a sleeper meets his friends
Who know him not. Each diligently bends
Towards common thoughts and things for very fear;
Striving their ghastly malady to cheer,
By thinking it a thing of yes and no,
That housewives talk of. But the spirit-blow
Was struck, and all were dreamers. At the last   900
Endymion said: 'Are not our fates all cast?
Why stand we here? Adieu, ye tender pair!
Adieu!' Whereat those maidens, with wild stare,
Walk'd dizzily away. Pained and hot
His eyes went after them, until they got
Near to a cypress grove, whose deadly maw,
In one swift moment, would what then he saw
Engulph for ever. 'Stay!' he cried, 'ah, stay!
Turn, damsels! hist! one word I have to say.
Sweet Indian, I would see thee once again.   910

It is a thing I dote on: so I'd fain,
Peona, ye should hand in hand repair
Into those holy groves, that silent are
Behind great Dian's temple. I'll be yon,
At vesper's earliest twinkle—they are gone—
But once, once, once again—' At this he press'd
His hands against his face, and then did rest
His head upon a mossy hillock green,
And so remain'd as he a corpse had been
All the long day; save when he scantly lifted   920
His eyes abroad, to see how shadows shifted
With the slow move of time,—sluggish and weary
Until the poplar tops, in journey dreary,
Had reach'd the river's brim. Then up he rose,
And, slowly as that very river flows,
Walk'd towards the temple grove with this lament:
'Why such a golden eve? The breeze is sent
Careful and soft, that not a leaf may fall
Before the serene father of them all
Bows down his summer head below the west.   930
Now am I of breath, speech, and speed possest,
But at the setting I must bid adieu
To her for the last time. Night will strew
On the damp grass myriads of lingering leaves,
And with them shall I die; nor much it grieves
To die, when summer dies on the cold sward.
Why, I have been a butterfly, a lord
Of flowers, garlands, love-knots, silly posies,
Groves, meadows, melodies, and arbour roses;
My kingdom's at its death, and just it is   940
That I should die with it: so in all this
We miscall grief, bale, sorrow, heartbreak, woe,
What is there to plain of? By Titan's foe
I am but rightly serv'd.' So saying, he
Tripp'd lightly on, in sort of deathful glee;
Laughing at the clear stream and setting sun,
As though they jests had been: nor had he done
His laugh at nature's holy countenance.
Until that grove appear'd, as if perchance,
And then his tongue with sober seemlihed   950

Gave utterance as he enter'd: 'Ha! I said,
King of the butterflies; but by this gloom,
And by old Rhadamanthus' tongue of doom,
This dusk religion, pomp of solitude,
And the Promethean clay by thief endued,
By old Saturnus' forelock, by his head
Shook with eternal palsy, I did wed
Myself to things of light from infancy;
And thus to be cast out, thus lorn to die,
Is sure enough to make a mortal man   960
Grow impious.' So he inwardly began
On things for which no wording can be found;
Deeper and deeper sinking, until drown'd
Beyond the reach of music: for the choir
Of Cynthia he heard not, though rough briar
Nor muffling thicket interpos'd to dull
The vesper hymn, far swollen, soft and full,
Through the dark pillars of those sylvan aisles.
He saw not the two maidens, nor their smiles,
Wan as primroses gather'd at midnight   970
By chilly finger'd spring. 'Unhappy wight!
Endymion!' said Peona, 'we are here!
What wouldst thou ere we all are laid on bier?'
Then he embrac'd her, and his lady's hand
Press'd, saying: 'Sister, I would have command,
If it were heaven's will, on our sad fate.'
At which that dark-eyed stranger stood elate
And said, in a new voice, but sweet as love,
To Endymion's amaze: 'By Cupid's dove,
And so thou shalt! and by the lilly truth   980
Of my own breast thou shalt, beloved youth!'
And as she spake, into her face there came
Light, as reflected from a silver flame:
Her long black hair swell'd ampler, in display
Full golden; in her eyes a brighter day
Dawn'd blue and full of love. Aye, he beheld
Phœbe, his passion! joyous she upheld
Her lucid bow, continuing thus: 'Drear, drear
Has our delaying been; but foolish fear
Withheld me first; and then decrees of fate;   990

And then 'twas fit that from this mortal state
Thou shouldst, my love, by some unlook'd for change
Be spiritualiz'd. Peona, we shall range
These forests, and to thee they safe shall be
As was thy cradle; hither shalt thou flee
To meet us many a time.' Next Cynthia bright
Peona kiss'd, and bless'd with fair good night:
Her brother kiss'd her too, and knelt adown
Before his goddess, in a blissful swoon.
She gave her fair hands to him, and behold,   1000
Before three swiftest kisses he had told,
They vanish'd far away!—Peona went
Home through the gloomy wood in wonderment.

THE END

AN EXPERIMENT WITH FORM: THE SONNET

In the following letter "rondeau" derives from the French *rond,* or round. Through usage the rondeau has become a 15-line poem in three stanzas wherein the opening words become a refrain. Keats prefaces the excerpt given below with his own modified rondeau, "Bards of Passion and of Mirth."

TO GEORGE AND GEORGIANA KEATS
2 January 1819   Hampstead

These are specimens of a sort of rondeau which I think I shall become partial to—because you have one idea amplified with greater ease and more delight and freedom than in the sonnet—It is my intention to wait a few years before I publish any minor poems—and then I hope to have a volume of some worth—and which those people will realish who cannot bear the burthen of a long poem—In my journal I intend to copy the poems I write the days they are written—

8 March 1819   Hampstead

What Imagination I have I shall enjoy, and greatly, for
I have experienced the satisfaction of having great conceptions without the toil of sonnetteering.

The fable of Andromeda tells of beauty reclaimed. Tied
naked on a rock, vulnerable to one of Neptune's sea monsters, she
is finally rescued by Perseus, who was taken by her fairness.

TO GEORGE AND GEORGIANA KEATS
3 May 1819   Hampstead

I have been endeavouring to discover a better sonnet
stanza than we have. The legitimate does not suit the
language over-well from the pouncing rhymes—the other
kind appears too elegai(a)c—and the couplet at the end
of it has seldom a pleasing effect—I do not pretend to have
succeeded—it will explain itself—

If by dull rhymes our english must be chaind
And, like Andromeda, the Sonnet sweet,
Fetterd in spite of pained Loveliness;
Let us find out, if we must be constrain'd,
Sandals more interwoven & complete
To fit the naked foot of Poesy;
Let us inspect the Lyre & weigh the stress
Of every chord & see what may be gained
By ear industrious & attention meet,
Misers of sound & syllable no less,
Than Midas of his coinage, let us be
Jealous of dead leaves in the bay wreath Crown;
So if we may not let the Muse be free,
She will be bound with Garlands of her own.

ON PEACE
O Peace! and dost thou with thy presence bless
    The dwellings of this war-surrounded Isle;

Soothing with placid brow our late distress,
    Making the triple kingdom brightly smile?
Joyful I hail thy presence; and I hail
    The sweet companions that await on thee;
Complete my joy—let not my first wish fail,
    Let the sweet mountain nymph thy favourite be,
With England's happiness proclaim Europa's Liberty.
O Europe! let not sceptred tyrants see   10
    That thou must shelter in thy former state;
Keep thy chains burst, and boldly say thou art free;
    Give thy kings law—leave not uncurbed the great;
    So with the horrors past thou'lt win thy happier fate!

1814

O SOLITUDE! IF I MUST WITH THEE DWELL

O Solitude! if I must with thee dwell,
    Let it not be among the jumbled heap
    Of murky buildings; climb with me the steep,—
Nature's observatory—whence the dell,
Its flowery slopes, its river's crystal swell,
    May seem a span; let me thy vigils keep
    'Mongst boughs pavillion'd, where the deer's swift leap
Startles the wild bee from the fox-glove bell.
But though I'll gladly trace these scenes with thee,
    Yet the sweet converse of an innocent mind,   10
    Whose words are images of thoughts refin'd,
Is my soul's pleasure; and it sure must be
    Almost the highest bliss of human-kind,
When to thy haunts two kindred spirits flee.

November 1815

TO—

Had I a man's fair form, then might my sighs
    Be echoed swiftly through that ivory shell
    Thine ear, and find thy gentle heart; so well
Would passion arm me for the enterprize:
But ah! I am no knight whose foeman dies;

No cuirass glistens on my bosom's swell;
  I am no happy shepherd of the dell
Whose lips have trembled with a maiden's eyes.
Yet must I dote upon thee,—call thee sweet,
  Sweeter by far than Hybla's honied roses   10
    When steep'd in dew rich to intoxication.
Ah! I will taste that dew, for me 'tis meet,
  And when the moon her pallid face discloses,
    I'll gather some by spells, and incantation.

February 1816

HOW MANY BARDS GILD THE LAPSES OF TIME!

How many bards gild the lapses of time!
  A few of them have ever been the food
  Of my delighted fancy,—I could brood
Over their beauties, earthly, or sublime:
And often, when I sit me down to rhyme,
  These will in throngs before my mind intrude:
  But no confusion, no disturbance rude
Do they occasion; 'tis a pleasing chime.
So the unnumber'd sounds that evening store;
The songs of birds—the whisp'ring of the leaves—   10
  The voice of waters—the great bell that heaves
With solemn sound,—and thousand others more,
  That distance of recognizance bereaves,
Make pleasing music, and not wild uproar.

March 1816

TO ONE WHO HAS BEEN LONG IN CITY PENT

To one who has been long in city pent,
  'Tis very sweet to look into the fair
  And open face of heaven,—to breathe a prayer
Full in the smile of the blue firmament.
Who is more happy, when, with heart's content,
  Fatigued he sinks into some pleasant lair
  Of wavy grass, and reads a debonair

And gentle tale of love and languishment?
Returning home at evening, with an ear
   Catching the notes of Philomel,—an eye   10
Watching the sailing cloudlet's bright career,
   He mourns that day so soon has glided by:
E'en like the passage of an angel's tear
   That falls through the clear ether silently.

June 1816

ON FIRST LOOKING INTO CHAPMAN'S HOMER

Much have I travell'd in the realms of gold,
   And many goodly states and kingdoms seen;
   Round many western islands have I been
Which bards in fealty to Apollo hold.
Oft of one wide expanse had I been told
   That deep-brow'd Homer ruled as his demesne;
   Yet did I never breathe its pure serene
Till I heard Chapman speak out loud and bold:
Then felt I like some watcher of the skies
   When a new planet swims into his ken;   10
Or like stout Cortez when with eagle eyes
   He star'd at the Pacific—and all his men
Look'd at each other with a wild surmise—
   Silent, upon a peak in Darien.

October 1816

TO MY BROTHERS

Small, busy flames play through the fresh laid coals,
   And their faint cracklings o'er our silence creep
   Like whispers of the household gods that keep
A gentle empire o'er fraternal souls.
And while, for rhymes, I search around the poles,
   Your eyes are fix'd, as in poetic sleep,
   Upon the lore so voluble and deep,
That aye at fall of night our care condoles.
This is your birth-day Tom, and I rejoice

That thus it passes smoothly, quietly.   10
Many such eves of gently whisp'ring noise
    May we together pass, and calmly try
What are this world's true joys,—ere the great voice,
    From its fair face, shall bid our spirits fly.

November 18, 1816

KEEN, FITFUL GUSTS ARE WHISP'RING HERE AND THERE

Keen, fitful gusts are whisp'ring here and there
    Among the bushes half leafless, and dry;
    The stars look very cold about the sky,
And I have many miles on foot to fare.
Yet feel I little of the cool bleak air,
    Or of the dead leaves rustling drearily,
    Or of those silver lamps that burn on high,
Or of the distance from home's pleasant lair:
For I am brimfull of the friendliness
    That in a little cottage I have found;   10
Of fair-hair'd Milton's eloquent distress,
    And all his love for gentle Lycid drown'd;
Of lovely Laura in her light green dress,
    And faithful Petrarch gloriously crown'd.

November 1816

ON LEAVING SOME FRIENDS AT AN EARLY HOUR

Give me a golden pen, and let me lean
    On heap'd up flowers, in regions clear, and far;
    Bring me a tablet whiter than a star,
Or hand of hymning angel, when 'tis seen
The silver strings of heavenly harp atween:
    And let there glide by many a pearly car,
    Pink robes, and wavy hair, and diamond jar,
And half discovered wings, and glances keen.
The while let music wander round my ears,
    And as it reaches each delicious ending,   10
        Let me write down a line of glorious tone,
And full of many wonders of the spheres:

For what a height my spirit is contending!
   'Tis not content so soon to be alone.

November 1816

TO G. A. W.

[*Georgiana Augusta Wylie*]

Nymph of the downward smile and sidelong glance,
  In what diviner moments of the day
  Art thou most lovely?—when gone far astray
Into the labyrinths of sweet utterance,
Or when serenely wand'ring in a trance
  Of sober thought?—or when starting away
  With careless robe to meet the morning ray
Thou spar'st the flowers in thy mazy dance?
Haply 'tis when thy ruby lips part sweetly,
  And so remain, because thou listenest: 10
But thou to please wert nurtured so completely
  That I can never tell what mood is best.
I shall as soon pronounce which Grace more neatly
  Trips it before Apollo than the rest.

December 1816

ON THE GRASSHOPPER AND CRICKET

The poetry of earth is never dead:
  When all the birds are faint with the hot sun,
  And hide in cooling trees, a voice will run
From hedge to hedge about the new-mown mead;
That is the Grasshopper's—he takes the lead
  In summer luxury,—he has never done
  With his delights; for when tired out with fun
He rests at ease beneath some pleasant weed.
The poetry of earth is ceasing never:
  On a lone winter evening, when the frost   10
    Has wrought a silence, from the stove there shrills
The Cricket's song, in warmth increasing ever,
  And seems to one in drowsiness half lost,
    The Grasshopper's among some grassy hills.

December 30, 1816

ON THE SEA

It keeps eternal whisperings around
　Desolate shores, and with its mighty swell
　Gluts twice ten thousand Caverns, till the spell
Of Hecate leaves them their old shadowy sound.
Often 'tis in such gentle temper found,
　That scarcely will the very smallest shell
　Be mov'd for days from where it sometime fell,
When last the winds of Heaven were unbound.
Oh ye! who have your eye-balls vex'd and tir'd,
　Feast them upon the wideness of the Sea;　　　　10
　　Oh ye! whose ears are dinn'd with uproar rude,
　Or fed too much with cloying melody—
　　Sit ye near some old Cavern's Mouth and brood,
Until ye start, as if the sea-nymphs quir'd!

April 1817

WHEN I HAVE FEARS THAT I MAY CEASE TO BE

When I have fears that I may cease to be
　Before my pen has glean'd my teeming brain,
Before high-piled books, in charactery,
　Hold like rich garners the full ripen'd grain;
When I behold, upon the night's starr'd face,
　Huge cloudy symbols of a high romance,
And think that I may never live to trace
　Their shadows, with the magic hand of chance;
And when I feel, fair creature of an hour,
　That I shall never look upon thee more,　　　　10
Never have relish in the faery power
　Of unreflecting love;—then on the shore
Of the wide world I stand alone, and think
Till love and fame to nothingness do sink.

January 1818

TO—

Time's sea hath been five years at its slow ebb,
　Long hours have to and fro let creep the sand.
Since I was tangled in thy beauty's web,
　And snared by the ungloving of thine hand.

And yet I never look on midnight sky,
But I behold thine eyes' well memory'd light:
I cannot look upon the rose's dye,
But to thy cheek my soul doth take its flight.
I cannot look on any budding flower,
But my fond ear, in fancy at thy lips   10
And hearkening for a love-sound, doth devour
Its sweets in the wrong sense:—Thou dost eclipse
Every delight with sweet remembering,
And grief unto my darling joys dost bring.

February 1818

WRITTEN IN ANSWER TO A SONNET ENDING THUS:

> Dark eyes are dearer far
> Than those that mock the hyacinthine bell—   By J. H. Reynolds

Blue! 'Tis the life of heaven,—the domain
Of Cynthia,—the wide palace of the sun—
The tent of Hesperus, and all his train,—
The bosomer of clouds, gold, grey and dun.
Blue! 'Tis the life of waters:—Ocean
And all its vassal streams, pools numberless,
May rage, and foam, and fret, but never can
Subside, if not to dark blue nativeness.
Blue! Gentle cousin of the forest-green,
Married to green in all the sweetest flowers,—   10
Forget-me-not,—the Blue bell,—and, that Queen
Of secrecy, the Violet: what strange powers
Hast thou, as a mere shadow! But how great,
When in an Eye thou art, alive with fate!

February 1818

TO SLEEP

O soft embalmer of the still midnight,
Shutting, with careful fingers and benign,
Our gloom-pleas'd eyes, embower'd from the light,
Enshaded in forgetfulness divine:

O soothest Sleep! if so it please thee, close
   In midst of this thine hymn my willing eyes,
Or wait the amen, ere thy poppy throws
   Around my bed its lulling charities.
Then save me, or the passed day will shine
Upon my pillow, breeding many woes,—   10
   Save me from curious Conscience, that still lords
Its strength for darkness, burrowing like a mole;
   Turn the key deftly in the oiled wards,
And seal the hushed Casket of my Soul.

April 1819

ON FAME

'You cannot eat your cake and have it too.'—*Proverb*.

How fever'd is the man, who cannot look
   Upon his mortal days with temperate blood,
Who vexes all the leaves of his life's book,
   And robs his fair name of its maidenhood;
It is as if the rose should pluck herself,
   Or the ripe plum finger its misty bloom,
As if a Naiad, like a meddling elf,
   Should darken her pure grot with muddy gloom,
But the rose leaves herself upon the briar,
   For winds to kiss and grateful bees to feed,   10
And the ripe plum still wears its dim attire,
      The undisturbed lake has crystal space,
      Why then should man, teasing the world for grace
Spoil his salvation for a fierce miscreed?

April 1819

BRIGHT STAR, WOULD I WERE STEDFAST AS THOU ART

Bright star, would I were stedfast as thou art—
   Not in lone splendour hung aloft the night
And watching, with eternal lids apart,
   Like nature's patient, sleepless Eremite,

The moving waters at their priestlike task
  Of pure ablution round earth's human shores,
Or gazing on the new soft-fallen mask
  Of snow upon the mountains and the moors—
No—yet still stedfast, still unchangeable,
  Pillow'd upon my fair love's ripening breast,   10
To feel for ever its soft fall and swell,
  Awake for ever in a sweet unrest,
Still, still to hear her tender-taken breath,
And so live ever—or else swoon to death.

February or late autumn 1819

A COMMERCIAL VENTURE: *OTHO THE GREAT*

TO JOHN TAYLOR
30 January 1818   Hampstead

Argument

My having written that ⟨Passage⟩ will perhaps be of the
greatest Service to me of any thing I ever did—It set
before me at once the gradations of Happines even like
a kind of Pleasure Thermometer—and is my first Step towards the chief Attempt in the Drama—the playing of
different Natures with Joy and Sorrow.

TO C. W. DILKE
31 July 1819   Shanklin, Isle of Wight

—Brown and I are pretty well harnessed again to our dog-
cart. I mean the Tragedy which goes on sinkingly—We
are thinking of introducing an Elephant but have not
historical referance within reach to determine us as to
Otho's Menagerie. When Brown first mention'd this I
took it for a Joke; however he brings such plausible reasons, and discourses so eloquently on the dramatic effect
that I am giving it a serious consideration.

Meleager, or Maleager as Keats spells his name, is best known
in mythology for slaying the fierce Calydonian boar. To have a

figure like Meleager, if one judges by the statue of him at the Vatican Museum, which one scholar thinks Keats had in mind, is to have a body of power and grace. The lover in *Otho the Great* is Ludolph.

TO FANNY BRAWNE
5 August 1819   Shanklin, Isle of Wight

—I leave this minute a scene in our Tragedy and see you (think it not blasphemy) through the mist of Plots speeches, counterplots and counter speeches—The Lover is madder than I am—I am nothing to him—he has a figure like the Statue of Maleager and double distilled fire in his heart.

———•—•—•———

TO BENJAMIN BAILEY
14 August 1819   Winchester

—One of my Ambitions is to make as great a revolution in modern dramatic writing as Kean has done in acting— another to upset the drawling of the blue stocking literary world—if in the course of a few years I do these two things I ought to die content—

———•—•—•———

TO JOHN TAYLOR
23 August 1819   Winchester

—For these three Months Brown has advanced me money: he is not at all flush and I am anxious to get some else-where—We have together been engaged (this I should wish to remain secret) in a Tragedy which I have just finish'd; and from which we hope to share moderate Profits—

———•—•—•———

TO FANNY KEATS
28 August 1819   Winchester

—I have still been hard at work, having completed a Tragedy I think I spoke of to you—But there I fear all

my labour will be thrown away for the present, as I hear
Mr Kean is going to America—. . . Mʳ Brown is copying out our Tragedy of Otho the gre{at} in a superb
style—better than it deserves—there as I said is labour in
vain for the present—I had hoped to give Kean another
opportunity to shine. What can we do now? There is not
another actor of Tragedy in all London or Europe—The
                                      is
Covent Garden Company ⟨are⟩ execrable—Young is the
best among them and he is a ranting, coxcombical taste-
less Actor—A Disgust A Nausea—and yet the very best
after Kean—What a set of barren asses are actors!

———————•◆•◆•———————

TO GEORGE AND GEORGIANA KEATS
17 September 1819   Winchester

Mine I am sure is a tolerable tragedy—it would have been
a bank to me, if just as I had finish'd it I had not heard of
Kean's resolution to go to America. That was the worst
news I could have had. There is no actor can do the principal character besides Kean. At Covent Garden there is a
great chance of its being damn'd. Were it to succeed
even there it would lift me out of the mire. I mean the
mire of a bad reputation which is continually rising
against me. My name with the literary fashionables is
vulgar—I am a weaver boy to them—a Tragedy would lift
me out of this mess. And mess it is as far as it regards our
Pockets—

———————•◆•◆•———————

TO GEORGE AND GEORGIANA KEATS
12 November 1819   Hampstead

Whether I shall at all be set affloat upon the world de-
pends now upon the success of the Tragedy I spoke of.
We have heard nothing from Elliston who is now the
Renter of Drury Lane since the piece was sent in which was
three weeks and more ago. The reason may be that Kean
has not return'd, whose opinion Elliston will partly rely

on. Brown is still very sanguine. The moment I have any certain intelligence concerning it I will let you know.

-----•-•-•-----

Gradus ad Parnassum altissimum means a step toward the top of Parnassus, the home of the Muses.

TO JOHN TAYLOR
17 November 1819   Hampstead

—The little dramatic skill I may as yet have however badly it might show in a Drama would I think be sufficient for a Poem—I wish to diffuse the colouring of St Agnes eve throughout a Poem in which Character and Sentiment would be the figures to such drapery—Two or three such Poems, if God should spare me, written in the course of the next six years, would be a famous gradus ad Parnassum altissimum—I mean they would nerve me up to the writing of a few fine Plays—my greatest ambition—when I do feel ambitious.

-----•-•-•-----

TO JAMES RICE
December 1819   Hampstead

—I suppose Reynolds has given you an account of Brown and Elliston—As he has not rejected our Tragedy I shall not venture to call him directly a fool; but as he wishes to put it off till next season I cant help thinking him little better than a Knave—That it will not be acted this Season is yet uncertain—Perpaps we may give it another furbish and try it at covent Garden. 'T would do one's heart good to see Macready in Ludolph.

-----•-•-•-----

TO FANNY KEATS
20 December 1819   Hampstead

—I have been very busy since I saw you especially the last Week and shall be for some time, in preparing some Poems to come out in the Sp[r]ing and also in hightening the interest of our Tragedy—Of the Tragedy I can give you but news semigood. It is accepted at Drury Lane with a promise of coming out next season: as that will be too long a delay we have determined to get Elliston to bring it out this Season or to transfer it to Covent Garden. This Elliston will not like, as we have every motive to believe that Kean has perceived how suitable the principal Character will be for him. My hopes of success in the literary world are now better than ever—

———•••———

TO GEORGE AND GEORGIANA KEATS
13 January 1820   Hampstead

Not having succeeded at Drury Lane with our Tragedy, we have been making some alterations and are about to try Covent Garden—Brown has just done patching up the Copy, as it is altered—The only reliance I had on it was in Kean's acting—I am *not* affraid it will be damn'd in the Garden—

OTHO THE GREAT

A Tragedy in Five Acts

DRAMATIS PERSONÆ.

OTHO THE GREAT, *Emperor of Germany*
LUDOLPH, *his son*
CONRAD, *Duke of Franconia*
ALBERT, *a Knight, favoured by Otho*
SIGIFRED, *an Officer friend of Ludolph*
THEODORE, ⎱ *Officers*
GONFRED, ⎰
ETHELBERT, *an Abbot*
GERSA, *Prince of Hungary*
An Hungarian Captain
Physician
Page
Nobles, Knights, Attendants, and Soldiers
ERMINIA, *Niece of Otho*
AURANTHE, *Conrad's Sister*
Ladies and Attendants

SCENE. *The Castle of Friedburg, its vicinity,*
and the Hungarian Camp

TIME. *One Day*

OTHO THE GREAT

ACT I

SCENE I. *An Apartment in the Castle. Enter* CONRAD.

CONRAD. So, I am safe emerged from these broils!
   Amid the wreck of thousands I am whole;
   For every crime I have a laurel-wreath,
   For every lie a lordship. Nor yet has
   My ship of fortune furl'd her silken sails,—
   Let her glide on! This danger'd neck is saved,
   By dexterous policy, from the rebel's axe;
   And of my ducal palace not one stone
   Is bruised by the Hungarian petards.
   Toil hard, ye slaves, and from the miser-earth   10
   Bring forth once more my bullion, treasured deep,
   With all my jewel'd salvers, silver and gold,
   And precious goblets that make rich the wine.
   But why do I stand babbling to myself?
   Where is Auranthe? I have news for her
   Shall—

Enter AURANTHE.

AURANTHE. Conrad! what tidings? Good, if I may guess
   From your alert eyes and high-lifted brows.
   What tidings of the battle? Albert? Ludolph? Otho?
CONRAD. You guess aright. And, sister, slurring o'er
   Our by-gone quarrels, I confess my heart   20
   Is beating with a child's anxiety,
   To make our golden fortune known to you.
AURANTHE. So serious?
CONRAD.   Yes, so serious, that before

I utter even the shadow of a hint
Concerning what will make that sin-worn cheek
Blush joyous blood through every lineament,
You must make here a solemn vow to me.

AURANTHE. I prythee, Conrad, do not overact
The hypocrite—what vow would you impose?

CONRAD. Trust me for once,—that you may be assur'd   30
'Tis not confiding in a broken reed,
A poor Court-bankrupt, outwitted and lost,
Revolve these facts in your acutest mood,
In such a mood as now you listen to me:—
A few days since, I was an open rebel
Against the Emperor, had suborn'd his son,
Drawn off his nobles to revolt, and shown
Contented fools causes for discontent
Fresh hatch'd in my ambition's eagle nest—
So thriv'd I as a rebel, and behold   40
Now I am Otho's favourite, his dear friend,
His right hand, his brave Conrad.

AURANTHE.   I confess
You have intrigued with these unsteady times
To admiration; but to be a favourite—

CONRAD. I saw my moment. The Hungarians,
Collected silently in holes and corners,
Appear'd, a sudden host, in the open day.
I should have perish'd in our empire's wreck,
But, calling interest loyalty, swore faith
To most believing Otho; and so help'd   50
His blood-stain'd ensigns to the victory
In yesterday's hard fight, that it has turn'd
The edge of his sharp wrath to eager kindness.

AURANTHE. So far yourself. But what is this to me
More than that I am glad? I gratulate you.

CONRAD. Yes, sister, but it does regard you greatly,
Nearly, momentously,—aye, painfully!
Make me this vow—

AURANTHE.   Concerning whom or what?

CONRAD. Albert!

AURANTHE.   I would inquire somewhat of him:
You had a letter from me touching him?   60

No treason 'gainst his head in deed or word!
Surely you spar'd him at my earnest prayer?
Give me the letter—it should not exist!
CONRAD. At one pernicious charge of the enemy,
    I, for a moment-whiles, was prisoner ta'en
    And rifled,—stuff! the horses' hoofs have minc'd it!
AURANTHE. He is alive?
CONRAD.   He is! but here make oath
    To alienate him from your scheming brain,
    Divorce him from your solitary thoughts,
    And cloud him in such utter banishment,   **70**
    That when his person meets again your eye,
    Your vision shall quite lose its memory,
    And wander past him as through vacancy.
AURANTHE. I'll not be perjured.
CONRAD.   No, nor great, nor mighty;
    You would not wear a crown, or rule a kingdom.
    To you it is indifferent.
AURANTHE.   What means this?
CONRAD. You'll not be perjured! Go to Albert then,
    That camp-mushroom—dishonour of our house.
    Go, page his dusty heels upon a march,
    Furbish his jingling baldric while he sleeps,   **80**
    And share his mouldy ratio in a siege.
    Yet stay,—perhaps a charm may call you back,
    And make the widening circlets of your eyes
    Sparkle with healthy fevers.—The Emperor
    Hath given consent that you should marry Ludolph!
AURANTHE. Can it be, brother? For a golden crown
    With a queen's awful lips I doubly thank you!
    This is to wake in Paradise! Farewell
    Thou clod of yesterday—'twas not myself!
    Not till this moment did I ever feel   **90**
    My spirit's faculties! I'll flatter you
    For this, and be you ever proud of it;
    Thou, Jove-like, struck'dst thy forehead,
    And from the teeming marrow of thy brain
    I spring complete Minerva! But the prince—
    His highness Ludolph—where is he?
CONRAD.   I know not:

When, lackeying my counsel at a beck,
The rebel lords, on bended knees, received
The Emperor's pardon, Ludolph kept aloof,
Sole, in a stiff, fool-hardy, sulky pride; **100**
Yet, for all this, I never saw a father
In such a sickly longing for his son.
We shall soon see him, for the Emperor
He will be here this morning.

AURANTHE.   That I heard
Among the midnight rumours from the camp.

CONRAD. You give up Albert to me?

AURANTHE.   Harm him not!
E'en for his highness Ludolph's sceptry hand,
I would not Albert suffer any wrong.

CONRAD. Have I not laboured, plotted—?

AURANTHE.   See you spare him:
Nor be pathetic, my kind benefactor, **110**
On all the many bounties of your hand,—
'Twas for yourself you laboured—not for me!
Do you not count, when I am queen, to take
Advantage of your chance discoveries
Of my poor secrets, and so hold a rod
Over my life?

CONRAD.   Let not this slave—this villain—
Be cause of feud between us. See! he comes!
Look, woman, look, your Albert is quite safe!
In haste it seems. Now shall I be in the way,
And wish'd with silent curses in my grave, **120**
Or side by side with 'whelmed mariners.

Enter ALBERT.

ALBERT. Fair on your graces fall this early morrow!
So it is like to do, without my prayers,
For your right noble names, like favourite tunes,
Have fall'n full frequent from our Emperor's lips,
High commented with smiles.

AURANTHE.   Noble Albert!

CONRAD (*aside*).   Noble!

AURANTHE. Such salutation argues a glad heart

In our prosperity. We thank you, sir.

ALBERT. Lady! O, would to Heaven your poor servant
Could do you better service than mere words!   130
But I have other greeting than mine own,
From no less man than Otho, who has sent
This ring as pledge of dearest amity;
'Tis chosen I hear from Hymen's jewel'ry,
And you will prize it, lady, I doubt not,
Before all pleasures past, and all to come.
To you great duke—

CONRAD.   To me! What of me, ha?

ALBERT. What pleas'd your grace to say?

CONRAD.   Your message, sir!

ALBERT. You mean not this to me?

CONRAD.   Sister, this way;
For there shall be no 'gentle Alberts' now,   [Aside.
No 'sweet Auranthes!'   141

[Exeunt CONRAD and AURANTHE.

ALBERT (solus). The duke is out of temper; if he knows
More than a brother of a sister ought,
I should not quarrel with his peevishness.
Auranthe—Heaven preserve her always fair!—
Is in the heady, proud, ambitious vein;
I bicker not with her,—bid her farewell!
She has taken flight from me, then let her soar,—
He is a fool who stands at pining gaze!
But for poor Ludolph, he is food for sorrow: 150
No levelling bluster of my licens'd thoughts,
No military swagger of my mind,
Can smother from myself the wrong I've done him,—
Without design, indeed,—yet it is so,—
And opiate for the conscience have I none!   [Exit.

SCENE II. The Court-yard of the Castle.

Martial Music. Enter, from the outer gate, OTHO, Nobles,
    Knights, and Attendants. The Soldiers halt at the gate,
    with Banners in sight.

OTHO. Where is my noble herald?

Enter CONRAD, *from the Castle, attended by two Knights and Servants.* ALBERT *following.*

> Well, hast told
> Auranthe our intent imperial?
> Lest our rent banners, too o' the sudden shown,
> Should fright her silken casements, and dismay
> Her household to our lack of entertainment.
> A victory!

CONRAD.   God save imperial Otho!

OTHO. Aye, Conrad, it will pluck out all grey hairs;
> It is the best physician for the spleen;
> The courtliest inviter to a feast;
> The subtlest excuser of small faults;   10
> And a nice judge in the age and smack of wine.

Enter, from the Castle, AURANTHE, *followed by Pages holding up her robes, and a train of Women. She kneels.*

> Hail my sweet hostess! I do thank the stars,
> Or my good soldiers, or their ladies' eyes,
> That, after such a merry battle fought,
> I can, all safe in body and in soul,
> Kiss your fair hand and lady fortune's too.
> My ring! now, on my life, it doth rejoice
> These lips to feel't on this soft ivory!
> Keep it, my brightest daughter; it may prove
> The little prologue to a line of kings.   20
> I strove against thee and my hot-blood son,
> Dull blockhead that I was to be so blind,
> But now my sight is clear; forgive me, lady.

AURANTHE. My lord, I was a vassal to your frown,
> And now your favour makes me but more humble;
> In wintry winds the simple snow is safe,
> But fadeth at the greeting of the sun:
> Unto thine anger I might well have spoken,
> Taking on me a woman's privilege,
> But this so sudden kindness makes me dumb.   30

OTHO. What need of this? Enough, if you will be
  A potent tutoress to my wayward boy,
  And teach him, what it seems his nurse could not,
  To say, for once, I thank you. Sigifred!
ALBERT. He has not yet return'd, my gracious liege.
OTHO. What then! No tidings of my friendly Arab?
CONRAD. None, mighty Otho.

[*To one of his Knights, who goes out.*

                    Send forth instantly
  An hundred horsemen from my honoured gates,
  To scour the plains and search the cottages.
  Cry a reward, to him who shall first bring   40
  News of that vanished Arabian,
  A full-heap'd helmet of the purest gold.
OTHO. More thanks, good Conrad; for, except my son's,
  There is no face I rather would behold
  Than that same quick-eyed pagan's. By the saints,
  This coming night of banquets must not light
  Her dazzling torches; nor the music breathe
  Smooth, without clashing cymbal, tones of peace
  And in-door melodies; nor the ruddy wine
  Ebb spouting to the lees; if I pledge not,   50
  In my first cup, that Arab!
ALBERT.   Mighty Caesar,
  I wonder not this stranger's victor-deeds
  So hang upon your spirit. Twice in the fight
  It was my chance to meet his olive brow,
  Triumphant in the enemy's shatter'd rhomb;
  And, to say truth, in any Christian arm
  I never saw such prowess.
OTHO.   Did you ever?
  O, 'tis a noble boy!—tut!—what do I say?
  I mean a triple Saladin, whose eyes,
  When in the glorious scuffle they met mine,   60
  Seem'd to say—'Sleep, old man, in safety sleep;
  I am the victory!'
CONRAD.   Pity he's not here.
OTHO. And my son too, pity he is not here.

Lady Auranthe, I would not make you blush,
But can you give a guess where Ludolph is?
Know you not of him?

AURANTHE.   Indeed, my liege, no secret—

OTHO. Nay, nay, without more words, dost know of him?

AURANTHE. I would I were so over-fortunate,
Both for his sake and mine, and to make glad
A father's ears with tidings of his son.   70

OTHO. I see 'tis like to be a tedious day.
Were Theodore and Gonfred and the rest
Sent forth with my commands?

ALBERT.   Aye, my lord.

OTHO. And no news! No news! 'Faith! 'tis very strange
He thus avoids us. Lady, is't not strange?
Will he be truant to you too? It is a shame.

CONRAD. Will't please your highness enter, and accept
The unworthy welcome of your servant's house?
Leaving your cares to one whose diligence
May in few hours make pleasures of them all.   80

OTHO. Not so tedious, Conrad. No, no, no, no,—
I must see Ludolph or the— What's that shout!

VOICES WITHOUT. Huzza! huzza! Long live the Emperor!

OTHER VOICES. Fall back! Away there!

OTHO.   Say, what noise is that?

[ALBERT *advancing from the back of the Stage, whither he had
hastened on hearing the cheers of the soldiery.*

ALBERT. It is young Gersa, the Hungarian prince,
Pick'd like a red stag from the fallow herd
Of prisoners. Poor prince, forlorn he steps,
Slow, in the demure proudness of despair.
If I may judge by his so tragic bearing,
His eye not downcast, and his folded arm,   90
He doth this moment wish himself asleep
Among his fallen captains on yon plains.

Enter GERSA, *in chains, and guarded.*

OTHO. Well said, Sir Albert.

GERSA.   Not a word of greeting,

No welcome to a princely visitor,
Most mighty Otho? Will not my great host
Vouchsafe a syllable, before he bids
His gentlemen conduct me with all care
To some securest lodging?—cold perhaps!

OTHO. What mood is this? Hath fortune touch'd thy brain?

GERSA. O kings and princes of this fev'rous world,   100
What abject things, what mockeries must ye be,
What nerveless minions of safe palaces!
When here, a monarch, whose proud foot is used
To fallen princes' necks, as to his stirrup,
Must needs exclaim that I am mad forsooth,
Because I cannot flatter with bent knees
My conqueror!

OTHO.   Gersa, I think you wrong me:
I think I have a better fame abroad.

GERSA. I prythee mock me not with gentle speech,
But, as a favour, bid me from thy presence;   110
Let me no longer be the wondering food
Of all these eyes; prythee command me hence!

OTHO. Do not mistake me, Gersa. That you may not,
Come, fair Auranthe, try if your soft hands
Can manage those hard rivets to set free
So brave a prince and soldier.

AURANTHE (sets him free).   Welcome task!

GERSA. I am wound up in deep astonishment!
Thank you, fair lady. Otho! emperor!
You rob me of myself; my dignity
Is now your infant; I am a weak child.   120

OTHO. Give me your hand, and let this kindly grasp
Live in our memories.

GERSA.   In mine it will.
I blush to think of my unchasten'd tongue;
But I was haunted by the monstrous ghost
Of all our slain battalions. Sire, reflect,
And pardon you will grant, that, at this hour,
The bruised remnants of our stricken camp
Are huddling undistinguish'd my dear friends,
With common thousands, into shallow graves.

OTHO. Enough, most noble Gersa. You are free   130

To cheer the brave remainder of your host
By your own healing presence, and that too,
Not as their leader merely, but their king;
For, as I hear, your wily enemy,
Who eas'd the crownet from your infant brows,
Bloody Taraxa, is among the dead.

GERSA. Then I retire, so generous Caesar please,
Bearing with me a weight of benefits
Too heavy to be borne.

OTHO.   It is not so;
Still understand me, King of Hungary,   140
Nor judge my open purposes awry.
Though I did hold you high in my esteem
For your self's sake, I do not personate
The stage-play emperor to entrap applause,
To set the silly sort o' the world agape,
And make the politic smile; no, I have heard
How in the Council you condemn'd this war,
Urging the perfidy of broken faith,—
For that I am your friend.

GERSA.   If ever, sire,
You are my enemy, I dare here swear   150
'Twill not be Gersa's fault. Otho, farewell!

OTHO. Will you return, Prince, to our banqueting?

GERSA. As to my father's board I will return.

OTHO. Conrad, with all due ceremony, give
The prince a regal escort to his camp;
Albert, go thou and bear him company.
Gersa, farewell!

GERSA.   All happiness attend you!

OTHO. Return with what good speed you may; for soon
We must consult upon our terms of peace.

[*Exeunt* GERSA *and* ALBERT *with others.*

And thus a marble column do I build   160
To prop my empire's dome. Conrad, in thee
I have another stedfast one, to uphold
The portals of my state; and, for my own
Pre-eminence and safety, I will strive

To keep thy strength upon its pedestal.
For, without thee, this day I might have been
A show-monster about the streets of Prague,
In chains, as just now stood that noble prince:
And then to me no mercy had been shown,
For when the conquer'd lion is once dungeon'd,   170
Who lets him forth again? or dares to give
An old lion sugar-cates of mild reprieve?
Not to thine ear alone I make confession,
But to all here, as, by experience,
I know how the great basement of all power
Is frankness, and a true tongue to the world;
And how intriguing secrecy is proof
Of fear and weakness, and a hollow state.
Conrad, I owe thee much.

CONRAD.   To [kneel and] kiss that hand,
My emperor, is ample recompense,   180
For a mere act of duty.

OTHO.   Thou art wrong;
For what can any man on earth do more?
We will make trial of your house's welcome,
My bright Auranthe!

CONRAD.   How is Friedburg honoured!

Enter ETHELBERT *and six Monks.*

ETHELBERT. The benison of heaven on your head,
Imperial Otho!

OTHO.   Who stays me? Speak! Quick!

ETHELBERT. Pause but one moment, mighty conqueror
Upon the threshold of this house of joy.

OTHO. Pray, do not prose, good Ethelbert, but speak
What is your purpose.   190

ETHELBERT. The restoration of some captive maids,
Devoted to Heaven's pious ministries,
Who, driven forth from their religious cells,
And kept in thraldom by our enemy,
When late this province was a lawless spoil,
Still weep amid the wild Hungarian camp,
Though hemm'd around by thy victorious arms.

OTHO. Demand the holy sisterhood in our name
From Gersa's tents. Farewell, old Ethelbert.
ETHELBERT. The saints will bless you for this pious care.　　　200
OTHO. Daughter, your hand; Ludolph's would fit it best.
CONRAD. Ho! let the music sound!

[*Music.* ETHELBERT *raises his hands, as in benediction of* OTHO.
Exeunt severally. The scene closes on them.

SCENE III. *The Country, with the Castle in the distance.*

Enter LUDOLPH *and* SIGIFRED.

LUDOLPH. You have my secret; let it not be breath'd.
SIGIFRED. Still give me leave to wonder that my Prince
Ludolph and the swift Arab are the same;
Still to rejoice that 'twas a German arm
Death doing in a turban's masquerade.
LUDOLPH. The Emperor must not know it, Sigifred.
SIGIFRED. I prythee, why? What happier hour of time
Could thy pleas'd star point down upon from heaven
With silver index, bidding thee make peace?
LUDOLPH. Still it must not be known, good Sigifred;　　　10
The star may point oblique.
SIGIFRED. 　　　　　　　　　If Otho knew
His son to be that unknown Mussulman
After whose spurring heels he sent me forth,
With one of his well-pleas'd Olympian oaths,
The charters of man's greatness, at this hour
He would be watching round the castle walls,
And, like an anxious warder, strain his sight
For the first glimpse of such a son return'd—
Ludolph, that blast of the Hungarians,
That Saracenic meteor of the fight,　　　20
That silent fury, whose fell scymitar
Kept danger all aloof from Otho's head,
And left him space for wonder.
LUDOLPH. 　　　　　　　　Say no more.
Not as a swordsman would I pardon claim,
But as a son. The bronz'd centurion,

Long toil'd in foreign wars, and whose high deeds
Are shaded in a forest of tall spears,
Known only to his troop, hath greater plea
Of favour with my sire than I can have.

SIGIFRED. My lord, forgive me that I cannot see   30
How this proud temper with clear reason squares.
What made you then, with such an anxious love,
Hover around that life, whose bitter days
You vext with bad revolt? Was't opium,
Or the mad-fumed wine? Nay, do not frown,
I rather would grieve with you than upbraid.

LUDOLPH. I do believe you. No, 'twas not to make
A father his son's debtor, or to heal
His deep heart-sickness for a rebel child.
'Twas done in memory of my boyish days,   40
Poor cancel for his kindness to my youth,
For all his calming of my childish griefs,
And all his smiles upon my merriment.
No, not a thousand foughten fields could sponge
Those days paternal from my memory,
Though now upon my head he heaps disgrace.

SIGIFRED. My Prince, you think too harshly—

LUDOLPH.   Can I so?
Hath he not gall'd my spirit to the quick?
And with a sullen rigour obstinate
Pour'd out a phial of wrath upon my faults?   50
Hunted me as a Tartar does the boar,
Driven me to the very edge o' the world,
And almost put a price upon my head?

SIGIFRED. Remember how he spar'd the rebel lords

LUDOLPH. Yes, yes, I know he hath a noble nature
That cannot trample on the fallen. But his
Is not the only proud heart in his realm.
He hath wrong'd me, and I have done him wrong;
He hath lov'd me, and I have shown him kindness;
We should be almost equal.

SIGIFRED.   Yet, for all this,   60
I would you had appear'd among those lords,
And ta'en his favour.

LUDOLPH.   Ha! till now I thought

My friend had held poor Ludolph's honour dear.
What! would you have me sue before his throne
And kiss the courtier's missal, its silk steps?
Or hug the golden housings of his steed,
Amid a camp, whose steeled swarms I dar'd
But yesterday? And, at the trumpet sound,
Bow like some unknown mercenary's flag,
And lick the soiled grass? No, no, my friend,   **70**
I would not, I, be pardon'd in the heap,
And bless indemnity with all that scum,—
Those men I mean, who on my shoulders propp'd
Their weak rebellion, winning me with lies,
And pitying forsooth my many wrongs;
Poor self-deceived wretches, who must think
Each one himself a king in embryo,
Because some dozen vassals cry'd—my lord!
Cowards, who never knew their little hearts,
Till flurried danger held the mirror up,   **80**
And then they own'd themselves without a blush,
Curling, like spaniels, round my father's feet.
Such things deserted me and are forgiven,
While I, least guilty, am an outcast still,
And will be, for I love such fair disgrace.

SIGIFRED. I know the clear truth; so would Otho see,
For he is just and noble. Fain would I
Be pleader for you—

LUDOLPH.   He'll hear none of it;
You know his temper, hot, proud, obstinate;
Endanger not yourself so uselessly.   **90**
I will encounter his thwart spleen myself,
To-day, at the Duke Conrad's, where he keeps
His crowded state after the victory.
There will I be, a most unwelcome guest,
And parley with him, as a son should do,
Who doubly loathes a father's tyranny;
Tell him how feeble is that tyranny;
How the relationship of father and son
Is no more valid than a silken leash
Where lions tug adverse, if love grow not   **100**
From interchanged love through many years.

Aye, and those turreted Franconian walls,
Like to a jealous casket, hold my pearl—
My fair Auranthe! Yes, I will be there.

SIGIFRED. Be not so rash; wait till his wrath shall pass,
   Until his royal spirit softly ebbs
   Self-influenced; then, in his morning dreams
   He will forgive thee, and awake in grief
   To have not thy good morrow.

LUDOLPH.   Yes, to-day
   I must be there, while her young pulses beat   110
   Among the new-plum'd minions of the war.
   Have you seen her of late? No? Auranthe,
   Franconia's fair sister, 'tis I mean.
   She should be paler for my troublous days—
   And there it is—my father's iron lips
   Have sworn divorcement 'twixt me and my right.

SIGIFRED [aside]. Auranthe! I had hop'd this whim had pass'd.

LUDOLPH. And, Sigifred, with all his love of justice,
   When will he take that grandchild in his arms,
   That, by my love I swear, shall soon be his?   120
   This reconcilement is impossible,
   For see—but who are these?

SIGIFRED.   They are messengers
   From our great emperor; to you, I doubt not,
   For couriers are abroad to seek you out.

Enter THEODORE *and* GONFRED.

THEODORE. Seeing so many vigilant eyes explore
   The province to invite your highness back
   To your high dignities, we are too happy.

GONFRED. We have no eloquence to colour justly
   The emperor's anxious wishes.

LUDOLPH.   Go. I follow you.

[*Exeunt* THEODORE *and* GONFRED.

   I play the prude: it is but venturing—   130
   Why should he be so earnest? Come, my friend,
   Let us to Friedburg castle.

ACT II

Scene I. *An Ante-chamber in the Castle.*

Enter Ludolph *and* Sigifred.

LUDOLPH. No more advices, no more cautioning:
    I leave it all to fate—to any thing!
    I cannot square my conduct to time, place,
    Or circumstance; to me 'tis all a mist!
SIGIFRED. I say no more.
LUDOLPH.   It seems I am to wait
    Here in the ante-room;—that may be a trifle.
    You see now how I dance attendance here,
    Without that tyrant temper, you so blame,
    Snapping the rein. You have medicin'd me
    With good advices; and I here remain,   10
    In this most honourable ante-room,
    Your patient scholar.
SIGIFRED.   Do not wrong me, Prince.
    By Heavens, I'd rather kiss Duke Conrad's slipper,
    When in the morning he doth yawn with pride,
    Than see you humbled but a half-degree!
    Truth is, the Emperor would fain dismiss
    The nobles ere he sees you.

Enter GONFRED, *from the Council-room.*

LUDOLPH.   Well, sir! what?
GONFRED. Great honour to the Prince! The Emperor,
    Hearing that his brave son had re-appeared,
    Instant dismiss'd the Council from his sight,   20
    As Jove fans off the clouds. Even now they pass.
[*Exit.*

Enter the Nobles from the Council-room. They cross the stage,
bowing with respect to LUDOLPH, *he frowning on them.*
CONRAD *follows. Exeunt Nobles.*

LUDOLPH. Not the discoloured poisons of a fen,
    Which he who breathes feels warning of his death,

Could taste so nauseous in the bodily sense,
As these prodigious sycophants disgust
The soul's fine palate.

CONRAD.   Princely Ludolph, hail!
Welcome, thou younger sceptre to the realm!
Strength to thy virgin crownet's golden buds,
That they, against the winter of thy sire,
May burst, and swell, and flourish round thy brows,   30
Maturing to a weighty diadem!
Yet be that hour far off; and may he live,
Who waits for thee, as the chapp'd earth for rain.
Set my life's star! I have lived long enough,
Since under my glad roof, propitiously,
Father and son each other re-possess.

LUDOLPH. Fine wording, Duke! but words could never yet
Forestall the fates; have you not learnt that yet?
Let me look well: your features are the same;
Your gait the same; your hair of the same shade;   40
As one I knew some passed weeks ago,
Who sung far different notes into mine ears.
I have mine own particular comments on 't;
You have your own, perhaps.

CONRAD.   My gracious Prince,
All men may err. In truth I was deceived
In your great father's nature, as you were.
Had I known that of him I have since known,
And what you soon will learn, I would have turn'd
My sword to my own throat, rather than held
Its threatening edge against a good King's quiet: 50
Or with one word fever'd you, gentle Prince,
Who seem'd to me, as rugged times then went,
Indeed too much oppress'd. May I be bold
To tell the Emperor you will haste to him?

LUDOLPH. Your Dukedom's privilege will grant so much.
[*Exit* CONRAD.
He's very close to Otho, Sigifred.
Your hand—I go. Ha! here the thunder comes
Sullen against the wind! If in two angry brows
My safety lies, then Sigifred, I'm safe.

Enter OTHO *and* CONRAD.

OTHO. Will you make Titan play the lackey-page   60
　　To chattering pigmies? I would have you know
　　That such neglect of our high Majesty
　　Annuls all feel of kindred. What is son,—
　　Or friend,—or brother,—or all ties of blood,—
　　When the whole kingdom, centred in ourself,
　　Is rudely slighted? Who am I to wait?
　　By Peter's chair! I have upon my tongue
　　A word to fright the proudest spirit here!—
　　Death!—and slow tortures to the hardy fool,
　　Who dares take such large charter from our smiles!   70
　　Conrad, we would be private. Sigifred!
　　Off! And none pass this way on pain of death!

[*Exeunt* CONRAD *and* SIGIFRED.

LUDOLPH. This was but half expected, my good sire,
　　Yet I am griev'd at it, to the full height,
　　As though my hopes of favour had been whole.
OTHO. How you indulge yourself! What can you hope for?
LUDOLPH. Nothing, my liege; I have to hope for nothing.
　　I come to greet you as a loving son,
　　And then depart, if I may be so free,
　　Seeing that blood of yours in my warm veins   80
　　Has not yet mitigated into milk.
OTHO. What would you, sir?
LUDOLPH.　　　　　　　　　A lenient banishment;
　　So please you let me unmolested pass
　　This Conrad's gates, to the wide air again.
　　I want no more. A rebel wants no more.
OTHO. And shall I let a rebel loose again
　　To muster kites and eagles 'gainst my head?
　　No, obstinate boy, you shall be kept cag'd up,
　　Serv'd with harsh food, with scum for Sunday-drink.
LUDOLPH. Indeed!
OTHO.　　　　　　And chains too heavy for your life: 90
　　I'll choose a gaoler, whose swart monstrous face
　　Shall be a hell to look upon, and she—
LUDOLPH.　　　　　　　　　　　　Ha!
OTHO. Shall be your fair Auranthe.

LUDOLPH.   Amaze! Amaze!

OTHO. To-day you marry her.

LUDOLPH.   This is a sharp jest!

OTHO. No. None at all. When have I said a lie?

LUDOLPH. If I sleep not, I am a waking wretch.

OTHO. Not a word more. Let me embrace my child.

LUDOLPH. I dare not. 'Twould pollute so good a father!
   O heavy crime! that your son's blinded eyes
   Could not see all his parent's love aright,   100
   As now I see it. Be not kind to me—
   Punish me not with favour.

OTHO.   Are you sure,
   Ludolph, you have no saving plea in store?

LUDOLPH. My father, none!

OTHO.   Then you astonish me.

LUDOLPH. No, I have no plea. Disobedience,
   Rebellion, obstinacy, blasphemy,
   Are all my counsellors. If they can make
   My crooked deed show good and plausible,
   Then grant me loving pardon, but not else,
   Good Gods! not else, in any way, my liege!   110

OTHO. You are a most perplexing, noble boy.

LUDOLPH. You not less a perplexing noble father.

OTHO. Well, you shall have free passport through the gates.
   Farewell!

LUDOLPH. Farewell! and by these tears believe,
   And still remember, I repent in pain
   All my misdeeds!

OTHO.   Ludolph, I will! I will!
   But, Ludolph, ere you go, I would enquire
   If you, in all your wandering, ever met
   A certain Arab haunting in these parts.

LUDOLPH. No, my good lord, I cannot say I did.   120

OTHO. Make not your father blind before his time;
   Nor let these arms paternal hunger more
   For an embrace, to dull the appetite
   Of my great love for thee, my supreme child!
   Come near, and let me breathe into thine ear.
   I knew you through disguise. You are the Arab!
   You can't deny it.   [*Embracing him.*

LUDOLPH.   Happiest of days!

OTHO. We'll make it so.

LUDOLPH.   'Stead of one fatted calf
  Ten hecatombs shall bellow out their last,
  Smote 'twixt the horns by the death-stunning mace   130
  Of Mars, and all the soldiery shall feast
  Nobly as Nimrod's masons, when the towers
  Of Nineveh new kiss'd the parted clouds!

OTHO. Large as a God speak out, where all is thine.

LUDOLPH. Aye, father, but the fire in my sad breast
  Is quench'd with inward tears! I must rejoice
  For you, whose wings so shadow over me
  In tender victory, but for myself
  I still must mourn. The fair Auranthe mine!
  Too great a boon! I prythee let me ask   140
  What more than I know of could so have changed
  Your purpose touching her?

OTHO.   At a word, this:
  In no deed did you give me more offence
  Than your rejection of Erminia.
  To my appalling, I saw too good proof
  Of your keen-eyed suspicion,—she is naught!

LUDOLPH. You are convinc'd?

OTHO.   Aye, spite of her sweet looks.
  O, that my brother's daughter should so fall!
  Her fame has pass'd into the grosser lips
  Of soldiers in their cups.

LUDOLPH.   'Tis very sad.   150

OTHO. No more of her. Auranthe—Ludolph, come!
  This marriage be the bond of endless peace!   [*Exeunt.*

SCENE II. *The Entrance of* GERSA's *Tent in the Hungarian Camp.*

Enter ERMINIA.

ERMINIA. Where! where! where shall I find a messenger?
  A trusty soul? A good man in the camp?
  Shall I go myself? Monstrous wickedness!
  O cursed Conrad! devilish Auranthe!

Here is proof palpable as the bright sun!
O for a voice to reach the Emperor's ears!

[*Shouts in the Camp.*

Enter an HUNGARIAN CAPTAIN.

CAPTAIN. Fair prisoner, hear you those joyous shouts?
    The king—aye, now our king,—but still your slave,
    Young Gersa, from a short captivity
    Has just return'd. He bids me say, bright **Dame**,   10
    That even the homage of his ranged chiefs
    Cures not his hot impatience to behold
    Such beauty once again. What ails you, lady?
ERMINIA. Say, is not that a German, yonder? There!
CAPTAIN. Methinks by his stout bearing he should be—
    Yes—'tis one Albert; a brave German knight,
    And much in the emperor's favour.
ERMINIA.   I would fain
    Enquire of friends and kinsfolk; how they fared
    In these rough times. Brave soldier, as you pass
    To royal Gersa with my humble thanks,   20
    Will you send yonder knight to me?
CAPTAIN.   I will.   [*Exit.*
ERMINIA. Yes, he was ever known to be a man
    Frank, open, generous; Albert I may trust.
    O proof! proof! proof! Albert's an honest man;
    Not Ethelbert the monk, if he were here,
    Would I hold more trustworthy. Now!

Enter ALBERT.

ALBERT.   Good Gods!
    Lady Erminia! are you prisoner
    In this beleaguer'd camp? Or are you here
    Of your own will? You pleas'd to send for me.
    By Venus, 'tis a pity I knew not   30
    Your plight before, and, by her Son, I swear
    To do you every service you can ask.
    What would the fairest—?
ERMINIA.   Albert, will you swear?

ALBERT. I have. Well?

ERMINIA.   Albert, you have fame to lose.
  If men, in court and camp, lie not outright,
  You should be, from a thousand, chosen forth
  To do an honest deed. Shall I confide—?

ALBERT. Aye, anything to me, fair creature. Do;
  Dictate my task. Sweet woman,—

ERMINIA.   Truce with that.
  You understand me not; and, in your speech,   40
  I see how far the slander is abroad.
  Without proof could you think me innocent?

ALBERT. Lady, I should rejoice to know you so.

ERMINIA. If you have any pity for a maid,
  Suffering a daily death from evil tongues;
  Any compassion for that Emperor's niece,
  Who, for your bright sword and clear honesty,
  Lifted you from the crowd of common men
  Into the lap of honour;—save me, knight!

ALBERT. How? Make it clear; if it be possible,   50
  I, by the banner of Saint Maurice, swear
  To right you.

ERMINIA.   Possible!—Easy. O my heart!
  This letter's not so soil'd but you may read it:—
  Possible! There—that letter! Read—read it.
                                    [*Gives him a letter.*

ALBERT (*reading*). 'To the Duke Conrad.—Forget the threat
  you made at parting, and I will forget to send the Emperor
  letters and papers of your's I have become possessed of.
  His life is no trifle to me; his death you shall find none to
  yourself.' [*Speaks to himself:*] 'Tis me—my life that's
  pleaded for! [*Reads*] 'He, for his own sake, will be dumb as
  the grave. Erminia has my shame fix'd upon her, sure as a
  wen. We are safe.   AURANTHE.'
  A she-devil! A dragon! I her imp!
  Fire of Hell! Auranthe—lewd demon!
  Where got you this? Where? When?

ERMINIA. I found it in the tent, among some spoils
  Which, being noble, fell to Gersa's lot.
  Come in, and see.   [*They go in and return.*

ALBERT.   Villainy! Villainy!

Conrad's sword, his corslet, and his helm,
And his letter. Caitiff, he shall feel—
ERMINIA. I see you are thunderstruck. Haste, haste away!
ALBERT. O I am tortured by this villainy.
ERMINIA. You needs must be. Carry it swift to Otho;
    Tell him, moreover, I am prisoner
    Here in this camp, where all the sisterhood,
    Forc'd from their quiet cells, are parcell'd out
    For slaves among these Huns. Away! Away!
ALBERT. I am gone.
ERMINIA.   Swift be your steed! Within this hour
    The Emperor will see it.
ALBERT.   Ere I sleep:
    That I can swear.   [*Hurries out.*
GERSA [*without*]. Brave captains! thanks. Enough   80
    Of loyal homage now!

Enter GERSA.

ERMINIA.   Hail, royal Hun!
GERSA. What means this, fair one? Why in such alarm?
    Who was it hurried by me so distract?
    It seem'd you were in deep discourse together;
    Your doctrine has not been so harsh to him
    As to my poor deserts. Come, come, be plain.
    I am no jealous fool to kill you both,
    Or, for such trifles, rob the adorned world
    Of such a beauteous vestal.
ERMINIA.   I grieve, my Lord,
    To hear you condescend to ribald phrase.   90
GERSA. This is too much! Hearken, my lady pure!
ERMINIA. Silence! and hear the magic of a name—
    Erminia! I am she,—the Emperor's niece!
    Prais'd be the Heavens, I now dare own myself!
GERSA. Erminia! Indeed! I've heard of her.
    Prythee, fair lady, what chance brought you here?
ERMINIA. Ask your own soldiers.
GERSA.   And you dare own your name.
    For loveliness you may—and for the rest
    My vein is not censorious.

ERMINIA.   Alas! poor me!
'Tis false indeed.
GERSA.   Indeed you are too fair: 100
The swan, soft leaning on her fledgy breast,
When to the stream she launches, looks not back
With such a tender grace; nor are her wings
So white as your soul is, if that but be
Twin-picture to your face. Erminia!
To-day, for the first day, I am a king,
Yet would I give my unworn crown away
To know you spotless.
ERMINIA.   Trust me one day more,
Generously, without more certain guarantee,
Than this poor face you deign to praise so much;   110
After that, say and do whate'er you please.
If I have any knowledge of you, sir,
I think, nay I am sure, you will grieve much
To hear my story. O be gentle to me,
For I am sick and faint with many wrongs,
Tir'd out, and weary-worn with contumelies.
GERSA. Poor lady!

Enter ETHELBERT.

ERMINIA.   Gentle Prince, 'tis false indeed.
Good morrow, holy father! I have had
Your prayers, though I look'd for you in vain.   120
ETHELBERT. Blessings upon you, daughter! Sure you look
Too cheerful for these foul pernicious days.
Young man, you heard this virgin say 'twas false,—
'Tis false, I say. What! can you not employ
Your temper elsewhere, 'mong these burly tents,
But you must taunt this dove, for she hath lost
The Eagle Otho to beat off assault?
Fie! fie! But I will be her guard myself;
In the Emperor's name. I here demand of you
Herself, and all her sisterhood. She false!
GERSA. Peace! peace, old man! I cannot think she is.   130
ETHELBERT. Whom I have known from her first infancy,
Baptiz'd her in the bosom of the Church,

Watch'd her, as anxious husbandmen the grain,
From the first shoot till the unripe mid-May,
Then to the tender ear of her June days,
Which, lifting sweet abroad its timid green,
Is blighted by the touch of calumny;
You cannot credit such a monstrous tale.

GERSA. I cannot. Take her. Fair Erminia,
   I follow you to Friedburg,—is't not so?   **140**

ERMINIA. Aye, so we purpose.

ETHELBERT.   Daughter, do you so?
   How's this? I marvel! Yet you look not mad.

ERMINIA. I have good news to tell you, Ethelbert.

GERSA. Ho! ho, there! Guards!
   Your blessing, father! Sweet Erminia,
   Believe me, I am well nigh sure—

ERMINIA.   Farewell!
   Short time will show.   *[Enter Chiefs.*
                Yes, father Ethelbert,
   I have news precious as we pass along.

ETHELBERT. Dear daughter, you shall guide me.

ERMINIA.   To no ill.

GERSA. Command an escort to the Friedburg lines.   **150**
                   [Exeunt Chiefs.
   Pray let me lead. Fair lady, forget not
   Gersa, how he believ'd you innocent.
   I follow you to Friedburg with all speed.   *[Exeunt.*

ACT III

SCENE I. *The Country.*

Enter ALBERT.

ALBERT. O that the earth were empty, as when Cain
   Had no perplexity to hide his head!
   Or that the sword of some brave enemy
   Had put a sudden stop to my hot breath,
   And hurl'd me down the illimitable gulph
   Of times past, unremember'd! Better so
   Than thus fast-limed in a cursed snare,

The limbo of a wanton. This the end
Of an aspiring life! My boyhood past
In feud with wolves and bears, when no eye saw   10
The solitary warfare, fought for love
Of honour 'mid the growling wilderness.
My sturdier youth, maturing to the sword,
Won by the syren-trumpets, and the ring
Of shields upon the pavement, when bright-mail'd
Henry the Fowler pass'd the streets of Prague.
Was't to this end I louted and became
The menial of Mars, and held a spear
Sway'd by command, as corn is by the wind?
Is it for this, I now am lifted up   20
By a well-judging Emperor, to see
My honour be my executioner,—
My love of fame, my prided honesty
Put to the torture for confessional?
Then the damn'd crime of blurting to the world
A woman's secret—though a fiend she be,
Too tender of my ignominious life;
But then to wrong the generous Emperor
In such a searching point, were to give up
My soul for foot-ball at Hell's holiday!   30
I must confess,—and cut my throat,—to-day?
To-morrow? Ho! some wine!

Enter SIGIFRED.

SIGIFRED.   A fine humour—
ALBERT. Who goes there? Count Sigifred? Ha! Ha!
SIGIFRED. What, man, do you mistake the hollow sky
  For a throng'd tavern,—and these stubbed trees
  For old serge hangings,—me, your humble friend,
  For a poor waiter? Why, man, how you stare!
  What gipsies have you been carousing with?
  No, no more wine; methinks you've had enough.
ALBERT. You well may laugh and banter. What a fool   40
  An injury may make of a staid man!
  You shall know all anon.
SIGIFRED.   Some tavern brawl?

ALBERT. 'Twas with some people out of common reach;
Revenge is difficult.

SIGIFRED.   I am your friend;
We meet again to-day, and can confer
Upon it. For the present I'm in haste.

ALBERT. Whither?

SIGIFRED.   To fetch King Gersa to the feast.
The Emperor on this marriage is so hot,
Pray Heaven it end not in apoplexy!
The very porters, as I pass'd the doors,   50
Heard his loud laugh, and answer'd in full choir.
I marvel, Albert, you delay so long
From those bright revelries; go, show yourself,
You may be made a duke.

ALBERT.   Aye, very like:
Pray, what day has his Highness fix'd upon?

SIGIFRED. For what?

ALBERT.   The marriage. What else can I mean?

SIGIFRED. To-day! O, I forgot, you could not know;
The news is scarce a minute old with me.

ALBERT. Married to-day! To-day! You did not say so?

SIGIFRED. Now, while I speak to you, their comely heads   60
Are bow'd before the mitre.

ALBERT.   O! monstrous!

SIGIFRED. What is this?

ALBERT.   Nothing, Sigifred. Farewell!
We'll meet upon our subject. Farewell, count!

                                                      [*Exit.*

SIGIFRED. Is this clear-headed Albert? He brain-turn'd!
'Tis as portentous as a meteor.   [*Exit.*

SCENE II. *An Apartment in the Castle.*

Enter, as from Marriage, OTHO, LUDOLPH, AURANTHE, CONRAD,
Nobles, Knights, Ladies, &c. &c. &c. Music.

OTHO. Now, Ludoph! Now, Auranthe! Daughter fair!
What can I find to grace your nuptial day
More than my love, and these wide realms in fee?

LUDOLPH. I have too much.

AURANTHE.   And I, my liege, by far.

LUDOLPH. Auranthe! I have! O, my bride, my love!
    Not all the gaze upon us can restrain
    My eyes, too long poor exiles from thy face,
    From adoration, and my foolish tongue
    From uttering soft responses to the love
    I see in thy mute beauty beaming forth!   10
    Fair creature, bless me with a single word!
    All mine!

AURANTHE. Spare, spare me, my Lord; I swoon else.

LUDOLPH. Soft beauty! by to-morrow I should die,
    Wert thou not mine.   [*They talk apart.*

FIRST LADY.   How deep she has bewitch'd him!

FIRST KNIGHT. Ask you for her recipe for love philtres.

SECOND LADY. They hold the Emperor in admiration.

OTHO. If ever king was happy, that am I!
    What are the cities 'yond the Alps to me,
    The provinces about the Danube's mouth,
    The promise of fair soil beyond the Rhone;   20
    Or routing out of Hyperborean hordes,
    To these fair children, stars of a new age?
    Unless perchance I might rejoice to win
    This little ball of earth, and chuck it them
    To play with!

AURANTHE. Nay, my Lord, I do not know.

LUDOLPH. Let me not famish.

OTHO (*to Conrad*).   Good Franconia.
    You heard what oath I sware, as the sun rose,
    That unless Heaven would send me back my son,
    My Arab,—no soft music should enrich
    The cool wine, kiss'd off with a soldier's smack;   30
    Now all my empire, barter'd for one feast,
    Seems poverty.

CONRAD.   Upon the neighbour-plain
    The heralds have prepar'd a royal lists;
    Your knights, found war-proof in the bloody field,
    Speed to the game.

OTHO.   Well, Ludolph, what say you?

LUDOLPH. My lord!

OTHO.   A tourney?

CONRAD. Or, if 't please you best—

LUDOLPH. I want no more!

FIRST LADY. He soars!

SECOND LADY. Past all reason.

LUDOLPH. Though heaven's choir
  Should in a vast circumference descend
  And sing for my delight, I'd stop my ears!   40
  Though bright Apollo's car stood burning here,
  And he put out an arm to bid me mount,
  His touch an immortality, not I!
  This earth, this palace, this room, Auranthe!

OTHO. This is a little painful; just too much.
  Conrad, if he flames longer in this wise,
  I shall believe in wizard-woven loves
  And old romances; but I'll break the spell.
  Ludolph!

CONRAD. He will be calm, anon.

LUDOLPH. You call'd?

OTHO. Come, come, a little sober sense, Ludolph.   49a

LUDOLPH. Yes, yes, yes, I offend. You must forgive me;   50
  Not being quite recover'd from the stun
  Of your large bounties. A tourney, is it not?

                         [*A senet heard faintly.*

CONRAD. The trumpets reach us.

ETHELBERT [*without*]. On your peril, sirs,
  Detain us!

FIRST VOICE [*without*]. Let not the abbot pass.

SECOND VOICE [*without*]. No,
  On your lives!

FIRST VOICE [*without*]. Holy father, you must not.

ETHELBERT [*without*]. Otho!

OTHO. Who calls on Otho?

ETHELBERT [*without*]. Ethelbert!

OTHO. Let him come in.

Enter ETHELBERT *leading in* ERMINIA.

                  Thou cursed abbot, why
  Hast brought pollution to our holy rites?
  Hast thou no fear of hangman, or the faggot?

Mad Churchman, would'st thou be impaled alive? 59a

LUDOLPH. What portent—what strange prodigy is this? 60

CONRAD. Away!

ETHELBERT.   You, Duke?

ERMINIA.   Albert has surely fail'd me!
    Look at the Emperor's brow upon me bent!

ETHELBERT. A sad delay!

CONRAD.   Away, thou guilty thing!

ETHELBERT. You again, Duke? Justice, most mighty Otho!
    You—go to your sister there and plot again,
    A quick plot, swift as thought to save your heads;
    For lo! the toils are spread around your den,
    The world is all agape to see dragg'd forth
    Two ugly monsters.

LUDOLPH.   What means he, my lord?

CONRAD. I cannot guess.

LUDOLPH.   Best ask your lady sister, 70
    Whether the riddle puzzles her beyond
    The power of utterance.

CONRAD.   Foul barbarian, cease:
    The Princess faints!

LUDOLPH.   Stab him! O, sweetest wife!

                    [*Attendants bear off* AURANTHE.

ERMINIA. Alas!

ETHELBERT.   Your wife?

LUDOLPH.   Aye, Satan! does that yerk ye?

ETHELBERT. Wife! so soon!

LUDOLPH.   Aye, wife! Oh, impudence!
    Thou bitter mischief! Venomous mad priest!
    How dar'st thou lift those beetle brows at me?
    Me—the prince Ludolph, in this presence here,
    Upon my marriage-day, and scandalize
    My joys with such opprobrious surprise? 80
    Wife! Why dost linger on that syllable,
    As if it were some demon's name pronounc'd
    To summon harmful lightning, and make roar
    The sleepy thunder? Hast no sense of fear?
    No ounce of man in thy mortality?
    Tremble! for, at my nod, the sharpen'd axe

Will make thy bold tongue quiver to the roots,
Those grey lids wink, and thou not know it more!
ETHELBERT. O, poor deceived Prince! I pity thee!
    Great Otho! I claim justice—
LUDOLPH.   Thou shalt have 't!   90
    Thine arms from forth a pulpit of hot fire
    Shall sprawl distracted! O that that dull cowl
    Were some most sensitive portion of thy life,
    That I might give it to my hounds to tear!
    Thy girdle some fine zealous-pained nerve
    To girth my saddle! And those devil's beads
    Each one a life, that I might, every day,
    Crush one with Vulcan's hammer!
OTHO.   Peace, my son;
    You far outstrip my spleen in this affair.
    Let us be calm, and hear the abbot's plea   100
    For this intrusion.
LUDOLPH.   I am silent, sire.
OTHO. Conrad, see all depart not wanted here.
                    [Exeunt Knights, Ladies, &c.
    Ludolph, be calm. Ethelbert, peace awhile.
    This mystery demands an audience
    Of a just judge, and that will Otho be.
LUDOLPH. Why has he time to breathe another word?
OTHO. Ludolph, old Ethelbert, be sure, comes not
    To beard us for no cause; he's not the man
    To cry himself up an ambassador
    Without credentials.
LUDOLPH.   I'll chain up myself.   110
OTHO. Old Abbot, stand here forth. Lady Erminia,
    Sit. And now, Abbot! what have you to say?
    Our ear is open. First we here denounce
    Hard penalties against thee, if 't be found
    The cause for which you have disturb'd us here,
    Making our bright hours muddy, be a thing
    Of little moment.
ETHELBERT.   See this innocent!
    Otho! thou father of the people call'd,
    Is her life nothing? Her fair honour nothing?
    Her tears from matins until even-song   120

Nothing? Her burst heart nothing? Emperor!
Is this your gentle niece—the simplest flower
Of the world's herbal—this fair lily blanch'd
Still with the dews of piety, this meek lady
Here sitting like an angel newly-shent,
Who veils its snowy wings and grows all pale,—
Is she nothing?

OTHO.   What more to the purpose, abbot?

LUDOLPH. Whither is he winding?

CONRAD.   No clue yet!

ETHELBERT. You have heard, my Liege, and so, no doubt,
    all here,
Foul, poisonous, malignant whisperings;   130
Nay open speech, rude mockery grown common,
Against the spotless nature and clear fame
Of the princess Erminia, your niece.
I have intruded here thus suddenly,
Because I hold those base weeds, with tight hand,
Which now disfigure her fair growing stem,
Waiting but for your sign to pull them up
By the dark roots, and leave her palpable,
To all men's sight, a Lady, innocent.
The ignominy of that whisper'd tale   140
About a midnight gallant, seen to climb
A window to her chamber neighbour'd near,
I will from her turn off, and put the load
On the right shoulders; on that wretch's head,
Who, by close stratagems, did save herself,
Chiefly by shifting to this lady's room
A rope-ladder for false witness.

LUDOLPH.   Most atrocious!

OTHO. Ethelbert, proceed.

ETHELBERT.   With sad lips I shall:
For, in the healing of one wound, I fear
To make a greater. His young highness here   150
To-day was married.

LUDOLPH.   Good.

ETHELBERT.   Would it were good!
Yet why do I delay to spread abroad
The names of those two vipers, from whose jaws

A deadly breath went forth to taint and blast
This guileless lady?

OTHO.   Abbot, speak their names.

ETHELBERT. A minute first. It cannot be—but may
I ask, great judge, if you to-day have put
A letter by unread?

OTHO.   Does 't end in this?

CONRAD. Out with their names!

ETHELBERT.   Bold sinner, say you so?

LUDOLPH. Out, tedious monk!

OTHO.   Confess, or by the wheel— 160

ETHELBERT. My evidence cannot be far away;
And, though it never come, be on my head
The crime of passing an attaint upon
The slanderers of this virgin.

LUDOLPH.   Speak aloud!

ETHELBERT. Auranthe, and her brother there.

CONRAD.   Amaze!

LUDOLPH. Throw them from the windows!

OTHO. Do what you will!

LUDOLPH.   What shall I do with them?
Something of quick dispatch, for should she hear,
My soft Auranthe, her sweet mercy would
Prevail against my fury. Damned priest! 170
What swift death wilt thou die? As to the lady
I touch her not.

ETHELBERT.   Illustrious Otho, stay!
An ample store of misery thou hast,
Choak not the granary of thy noble mind
With more bad bitter grain, too difficult
A cud for the repentance of a man
Grey-growing. To thee only I appeal,
Not to thy noble son, whose yeasting youth
Will clear itself, and crystal turn again.
A young man's heart, by Heaven's blessing, is 180
A wide world, where a thousand new-born hopes
Empurple fresh the melancholy blood:
But an old man's is narrow, tenantless
Of hopes, and stuff'd with many memories,
Which, being pleasant, ease the heavy pulse—

Painful, clog up and stagnate. Weigh this matter
Even as a miser balances his coin;
And, in the name of mercy, give command
That your knight Albert be brought here before you.
He will expound this riddle; he will show   190
A noon-day proof of bad Auranthe's guilt.
OTHO. Let Albert straight be summon'd.

                    [*Exit one of the Nobles.*
LUDOLPH.   Impossible!
I cannot doubt—I will not—no—to doubt
Is to be ashes!—wither'd up to death!
OTHO. My gentle Ludolph, harbour not a fear;
You do yourself much wrong.
LUDOLPH.   O, wretched dolt!
Now, when my foot is almost on thy neck,
Wilt thou infuriate me? Proof! Thou fool!
Why wilt thou teaze impossibility
With such a thick-skull'd persevering suit?   200
Fanatic obstinacy! Prodigy!
Monster of folly! Ghost of a turn'd brain!
You puzzle me,—you haunt me,—when I dream
Of you my brain will split! Bald sorcerer!
Juggler! May I come near you? On my soul
I know not whether to pity, curse, or laugh.

Enter ALBERT, *and the Nobleman.*

Here, Albert, this old phantom wants a proof!
Give him his proof! A camel's load of proofs!
OTHO. Albert, I speak to you as a man
Whose words once utter'd pass like current gold;   210
And therefore fit to calmly put a close
To this brief tempest. Do you stand possess'd
Of any proof against the honourableness
Of Lady Auranthe, our new-spoused daughter?
ALBERT. You chill me with astonishment. How's this?
My Liege, what proof should I have 'gainst a fame
Impossible of slur?   [OTHO *rises.*
ERMINIA.   O wickedness!

ETHELBERT. Deluded monarch, 'tis a cruel lie.

OTHO. Peace, rebel-priest!

CONRAD.   Insult beyond credence!

ERMINIA. Almost a dream!

LUDOLPH.   We have awaken'd from   220
  A foolish dream that from my brow hath wrung
  A wrathful dew. O folly! why did I
  So act the lion with this silly gnat?
  Let them depart. Lady Erminia!
  I ever griev'd for you, as who did not?
  But now you have, with such a brazen front,
  So most maliciously, so madly striven
  To dazzle the soft moon, when tenderest clouds
  Should be unloop'd around to curtain her;
  I leave you to the desert of the world   230
  Almost with pleasure. Let them be set free
  For me! I take no personal revenge
  More than against a nightmare, which a man
  Forgets in the new dawn.   [*Exit* LUDOLPH.

OTHO. Still in extremes! No, they must not be loose.

ETHELBERT. Albert, I must suspect thee of a crime
  So fiendish—

OTHO.   Fear'st thou not my fury, monk?
  Conrad, be they in your sure custody
  Till we determine some fit punishment.
  It is so mad a deed, I must reflect   240
  And question them in private; for perhaps,
  By patient scrutiny, we may discover
  Whether they merit death, or should be placed
  In care of the physicians.

                    [*Exeunt* OTHO *and Nobles,* ALBERT *following.*

CONRAD. My guards, ho!

ERMINIA.   Albert, wilt thou follow there?
  Wilt thou creep dastardly behind his back,
  And slink away from a weak woman's eye?
  Turn, thou court-Janus! thou forget'st thyself;
  Here is the Duke, waiting with open arms,
[*Enter Guards.*
  To thank thee; here congratulate each other;   250

Wring hands; embrace; and swear how lucky 'twas
That I, by happy chance, hit the right man
Of all the world to trust in.

ALBERT.   Trust! to me!

CONRAD [aside]. He is the sole one in this mystery.

ERMINIA. Well, I give up, and save my prayers for Heaven!
You, who could do this deed, would ne'er relent,
Though, at my words, the hollow prison-vaults
Would groan for pity.

CONRAD.   Manacle them both!

ETHELBERT. I know it—it must be—I see it all!
Albert, thou art the minion!

ERMINIA.   Ah! too plain—   260

CONRAD. Silence! Gag up their mouths! I cannot bear
More of this brawling. That the Emperor
Had plac'd you in some other custody!
Bring them away.   [Exeunt all but ALBERT.

ALBERT. Though my name perish from the book of honour,
Almost before the recent ink is dry,
And be no more remember'd after death,
Than any drummer's in the muster-roll;
Yet shall I season high my sudden fall
With triumph o'er that evil-witted duke!   270
He shall feel what it is to have the hand
Of a man drowning, on his hateful throat.

Enter GERSA *and* SIGIFRED.

GERSA. What discord is at ferment in this house?

SIGIFRED. We are without conjecture; not a soul
We met could answer any certainty.

GERSA. Young Ludolph, like a fiery arrow, shot
By us.

SIGIFRED. The Emperor, with cross'd arms, in thought.

GERSA. In one room music, in another sadness,
Perplexity every where!

ALBERT.   A trifle mere!
Follow; your presences will much avail   280
To tune our jarred spirits. I'll explain.   [Exeunt.

ACT IV

Scene I. AURANTHE's *Apartment.*

AURANTHE *and* CONRAD *discovered.*

CONRAD. Well, well, I know what ugly jeopardy
    We are cag'd in; you need not pester that
    Into my ears. Prythee, let me be spared
    A foolish tongue, that I may bethink me
    Of remedies with some deliberation
    You cannot doubt but 'tis in Albert's power
    To crush or save us?
AURANTHE.   No, I cannot doubt.
    He has, assure yourself, by some strange means,
    My secret; which I ever hid from him,
    Knowing his mawkish honesty.
CONRAD.   Curs'd slave!   10
AURANTHE. Ay, I could almost curse him now myself.
    Wretched impediment! Evil genius!
    A glue upon my wings, that cannot spread,
    When they should span the provinces! A snake,
    A scorpion, sprawling on the first gold step,
    Conducting to the throne, high canopied.
CONRAD. You would not hear my counsel, when his life
    Might have been trodden out, all sure and hush'd;
    Now the dull animal forsooth must be
    Intreated, managed! When can you contrive   20
    The interview he demands?
AURANTHE.   As speedily
    It must be done as my brib'd woman can
    Unseen conduct him to me; but I fear
    'Twill be impossible, while the broad day
    Comes through the panes with persecuting glare.
    Methinks, if 't now were night I could intrigue
    With darkness, bring the stars to second me,
    And settle all this trouble.
CONRAD.   Nonsense! Child!
    See him immediately; why not now?

AURANTHE. Do you forget that even the senseless door-
      posts 30
  Are on the watch and gape through all the house?
  How many whisperers there are about,
  Hungry for evidence to ruin me;
  Men I have spurn'd, and women I have taunted?
  Besides, the foolish prince sends, minute whiles,
  His pages—so they tell me—to enquire
  After my health, entreating, if I please,
  To see me.
CONRAD.   Well, suppose this Albert here;
  What is your power with him?
AURANTHE.   He should be
  My echo, my taught parrot! but I fear 40
  He will be cur enough to bark at me;
  Have his own say; read me some silly creed
  'Bout shame and pity.
CONRAD.   What will you do then?
AURANTHE. What I shall do, I know not: what I would
  Cannot be done; for see, this chamber-floor
  Will not yield to the pick-axe and the spade,—
  Here is no quiet depth of hollow ground.
CONRAD. Sister, you have grown sensible and wise,
  Seconding, ere I speak it, what is now,
  I hope, resolv'd between us.
AURANTHE.   Say, what is 't? 50
CONRAD. You need not be his sexton too: a man
  May carry that with him shall make him die
  Elsewhere,—give that to him; pretend the while
  You will to-morrow succumb to his wishes,
  Be what they may, and send him from the Castle
  On some fool's errand; let his latest groan
  Frighten the wolves!
AURANTHE.   Alas! he must not die!
CONRAD. Would you were both hears'd up in stifling lead!
  Detested—
AURANTHE. Conrad, hold! I would not bear
  The little thunder of your fretful tongue, 60
  Tho' I alone were taken in these toils,
  And you could free me; but remember, sir,

You live alone in my security:
So keep your wits at work, for your own sake,
Not mine, and be more mannerly.

CONRAD.   Thou wasp!
If my domains were emptied of these folk,
And I had thee to starve—

AURANTHE.   O, marvellous!
But Conrad, now be gone; the Host is look'd for;
Cringe to the Emperor, entertain the nobles.
And, do ye mind, above all things, proclaim   70
My sickness, with a brother's sadden'd eye,
Condoling with Prince Ludolph. In fit time
Return to me.

CONRAD.   I leave you to your thoughts.   [*Exit.*

AURANTHE (*sola*). Down, down, proud temper! down,
     Auranthe's pride!
Why do I anger him when I should kneel?
Conrad! Albert! help! help! What can I do?
O wretched woman! lost, wreck'd, swallow'd up,
Accursed, blasted! O, thou golden Crown,
Orbing along the serene firmament
Of a wide empire, like a glowing moon;   80
And thou, bright sceptre! lustrous in my eyes,—
There—as the fabled fair Hesperian tree,
Bearing a fruit more precious! graceful thing,
Delicate, godlike, magic! must I leave
Thee to melt in the visionary air,
Ere, by one grasp, this common hand is made
Imperial? I do not know the time
When I have wept for sorrow; but methinks
I could now sit upon the ground, and shed
Tears, tears of misery. O, the heavy day!   90
How shall I bear my life till Albert comes?
Ludolph! Erminia! Proofs! O heavy day!
Bring me some mourning weeds, that I may 'tire
Myself, as fits one wailing her own death:
Cut off these curls, and brand this lilly hand,
And throw these jewels from my loathing sight,—
Fetch me a missal, and a string of beads,—
A cup of bitter'd water, and a crust,—

I will confess, O holy father!—How!
What is this? Auranthe! thou fool, dolt, 100
Whimpering idiot! up! up! act and quell!
I am safe! Coward! why am I in fear?
Albert! he cannot stickle, chew the cud
In such a fine extreme,—impossible!
Who knocks?   [*Goes to the Door, listens, and opens it.*

Enter ALBERT.

Albert, I have been waiting for you here
With such an aching heart, such swooning throbs
On my poor brain, such cruel—cruel sorrow,
That I should claim your pity! Art not well?
ALBERT. Yes, lady, well.
AURANTHE.   You look not so, alas! 110
But pale, as if you brought some heavy news.
ALBERT. You know full well what makes me look so pale.
AURANTHE. No! Do I? Surely I am still to learn
Some horror; all I know, this present, is
I am near hustled to a dangerous gulph,
Which you can save me from,—and therefore safe,
So trusting in thy love; that should not make
Thee pale, my Albert.
ALBERT.   It does make me freeze.
AURANTHE. Why should it, love?
ALBERT.   You should not ask me that,
But make your own heart monitor, and save 120
Me the great pain of telling. You must know.
AURANTHE. Something has vext you, Albert. There are times
When simplest things put on a sombre cast;
A melancholy mood will haunt a man,
Until most easy matters take the shape
Of unachievable tasks; small rivulets
Then seem impassable.
ALBERT.   Do not cheat yourself
With hope that gloss of words, or suppliant action,
Or tears, or ravings, or self-threaten'd death,
Can alter my resolve.
AURANTHE.   You make me tremble; 130

Not so much at your threats, as at your voice,
Untun'd, and harsh, and barren of all love.

ALBERT. You suffocate me! Stop this devil's parley,
And listen to me; know me once for all.

AURANTHE. I thought I did. Alas! I am deceiv'd.

ALBERT. No, you are not deceiv'd. You took me for
A man detesting all inhuman crime;
And therefore kept from me your demon's plot
Against Erminia. Silent? Be so still;
For ever! Speak no more; but hear my words,   140
Thy fate. Your safety I have bought to-day
By blazoning a lie, which in the dawn
I'll expiate with truth.

AURANTHE.   O cruel traitor!

ALBERT. For I would not set eyes upon thy shame;
I would not see thee dragg'd to death by the hair,
Penanc'd, and taunted on a scaffolding!
To-night, upon the skirts of the blind wood
That blackens northward of these horrid towers,
I wait for you with horses. Choose your fate.
Farewell.

AURANTHE. Albert, you jest; I'm sure you must.   150
You, an ambitious Soldier! I, a Queen,
One who could say,—Here, rule these Provinces!
Take tribute from those cities for thyself!
Empty these armouries, these treasuries,
Muster thy warlike thousands at a nod!
Go! conquer Italy!

ALBERT.   Auranthe, you have made
The whole world chaff to me. Your doom is fix'd.

AURANTHE. Out, villain! dastard!

ALBERT.   Look there to the door!
Who is it?

AURANTHE. Conrad, traitor!

ALBERT.   Let him in.

                                        [Enter CONRAD.
                                                        160
Do not affect amazement, hypocrite,
At seeing me in this chamber.

CONRAD.   Auranthe?

ALBERT. Talk not with eyes, but speak your curses out

Against me, who would sooner crush and grind
A brace of toads, than league with them to oppress
An innocent lady, gull an Emperor,
More generous to me than autumn's sun
To ripening harvests.

AURANTHE.   No more insult, sir!

ALBERT. Aye, clutch your scabbard; but, for prudence sake,
Draw not the sword; 'twould make an uproar, Duke,
You would not hear the end of. At nightfall   **170**
Your lady sister, if I guess aright,
Will leave this busy castle. You had best
Take farewell too of worldly vanities.

CONRAD. Vassal!

ALBERT.   To-morrow, when the Emperor sends
For loving Conrad, see you fawn on him.
Good even!

AURANTHE. You'll be seen!

ALBERT.   See the coast clear then.

AURANTHE [*as he goes*]. Remorseless Albert! Cruel, cruel,
  wretch!   [*She lets him out.*

CONRAD. So, we must lick the dust?

AURANTHE.   I follow him.

CONRAD. How? Where? The plan of your escape?

AURANTHE.   He waits
For me with horses by the forest-side,   **180**
Northward.

CONRAD. Good, good! he dies. You go, say you?

AURANTHE. Perforce.

CONRAD.   Be speedy, darkness! Till that comes,
Fiends keep you company!   [*Exit.*

AURANTHE.   And you! And you!
And all men! Vanish! Oh! Oh! Oh!
      [*Retires to an inner apartment.*

SCENE II. *An Apartment in the Castle.*

Enter LUDOLPH *and* PAGE.

PAGE. Still very sick, my Lord; but now I went
Knowing my duty to so good a Prince;

And there her women in a mournful throng
Stood in the passage whispering: if any
Mov'd 'twas with careful steps and hush'd as death;
They bid me stop.

LUDOLPH.   Good fellow, once again
Make soft enquiry; prythee be not stay'd
By any hindrance, but with gentlest force
Break through her weeping servants, till thou com'st
E'en to her chamber door, and there, fair boy,   10
If with thy mother's milk thou hast suck'd in
Any diviner eloquence; woo her ears
With plaints for me more tender than the voice
Of dying Echo, echoed.

PAGE.   Kindest master!
To know thee sad thus, will unloose my tongue
In mournful syllables. Let but my words reach
Her ears and she shall take them coupled with
Moans from my heart and sighs not counterfeit.
May I speed better!   [*Exit* PAGE.

LUDOLPH.   Auranthe! My Life!
Long have I lov'd thee, yet till now not lov'd: 20
Remembering, as I do, hard-hearted times
When I had heard even of thy death perhaps,
And thoughtless—suffered thee to pass alone
Into Elysium! now I follow thee
A substance or a shadow, wheresoe'er
Thou leadest me,—whether thy white feet press,
With pleasant weight, the amorous-aching earth
Or thro' the air thou pioneerest me,
A shade! Yet sadly I predestinate!
O unbenignest Love, why wilt thou let   30
Darkness steal out upon the sleepy world
So wearily; as if night's chariot wheels
Were clog'd in some thick cloud. O, changeful Love,
Let not her steeds with drowsy-footed pace
Pass the high stars, before sweet embassage
Comes from the pillow'd beauty of that fair
Completion of all delicate nature's wit.
Pout her faint lips anew with rubious health
And with thine infant fingers lift the fringe

Of her sick eyelids; that those eyes may glow 40
With wooing light upon me, ere the Morn
Peers with disrelish, grey, barren, and cold.

Enter GERSA *and Courtiers.*

Otho calls me his Lion—should I blush
To be so tam'd, so——
GERSA.   Do me the courtesy
Gentlemen to pass on.
COURTIER.   We are your servants.
                              [*Exeunt Courtiers.*
LUDOLPH. It seems then, Sir, you have found out the man
You would confer with; me?
GERSA.   If I break not
Too much upon your thoughtful mood, I will
Claim a brief while your patience.
LUDOLPH.   For what cause
Soe'er I shall be honour'd.
GERSA.   I not less. 50
LUDOLPH. What may it be? No trifle can take place
Of such deliberate prologue, serious 'haviour.
But be it what it may I cannot fail
To listen with no common interest—
For though so new your presence is to me,
I have a soldier's friendship for your fame—
Please you explain.
GERSA.   As thus—for, pardon me,
I cannot in plain terms grossly assault
A noble nature; and would faintly sketch
What your quick apprehension will fill up 60
So finely I esteem you.
LUDOLPH.   I attend—
GERSA. Your generous Father, most illustrious Otho,
Sits in the Banquet room among his chiefs—
His wine is bitter, for you are not there—
His eyes are fix'd still on the open doors,
And every passer in he frowns upon
Seeing no Ludolph comes.
LUDOLPH.   I do neglect—

GERSA. And for your absence, may I guess the cause?

LUDOLPH. Stay there! no—guess? more princely you must be—
Than to make guesses at me. 'Tis enough,   70
I'm sorry I can hear no more.

GERSA.   And I
As griev'd to force it on you so abrupt;
Yet one day you must know a grief whose sting
Will sharpen more the longer 'tis conceal'd.

LUDOLPH. Say it at once, sir, dead, dead, is she dead?

GERSA. Mine is a cruel task: she is not dead—
And would for your sake she were innocent—

LUDOLPH. Hungarian! thou amazest me beyond
All scope of thought; convulsest my heart's blood
To deadly churning—Gersa, you are young   80
As I am; let me observe you face to face;
Not grey-brow'd like the poisonous Ethelbert,
No rheumed eyes, no furrowing of age,
No wrinkles where all vices nestle in
Like crannied vermin—no, but fresh and young
And hopeful featur'd. Ha! by heaven you weep
Tears, human tears—Do you repent you then
Of a curs'd torturer's office! Why shouldst join—
Tell me, the league of Devils? Confess—confess
The Lie.—

GERSA. Lie!—but begone all ceremonious points   90
Of honour battailous. I could not turn
My wrath against thee for the orbed world.

LUDOLPH. Your wrath, weak boy? Tremble at mine unless
Retraction follow close upon the heels
Of that late stounding insult: why has my sword
Not done already a sheer judgment on thee?
Despair, or eat thy words. Why, thou wast nigh
Whimpering away my reason: hark ye, Sir,
It is no secret;—that Erminia,
Erminia, Sir, was hidden in your tent;   100
O bless'd asylum! comfortable home!
Begone, I pity thee, thou art a Gull—
Erminia's fresh puppet—

GERSA.   Furious fire!
Thou mak'st me boil as hot as thou canst flame!

And in thy teeth I give thee back the lie!
Thou liest! Thou, Auranthe's fool, a wittol——
LUDOLPH. Look! look at this bright sword;
  There is no part of it to the very hilt
  But shall indulge itself about thine heart—
  Draw—but remember thou must cower thy plumes,   110
  As yesterday the Arab made thee stoop—
GERSA. Patience! not here, I would not spill thy blood
  Here underneath this roof where Otho breathes,
  Thy father—almost mine—
LUDOLPH.   O faltering coward!

Re-enter PAGE.

  Stay, stay, here is one I have half a word with—
  Well—What ails thee, child?
PAGE.   My lord,
LUDOLPH.   What would'st say?
PAGE. They are fled!
LUDOLPH.   They—who?
PAGE.   When anxiously
  I hasten'd back, your grieving messenger,
  I found the stairs all dark, the lamps extinct,
  And not a foot or whisper to be heard.   120
  I thought her dead, and on the lowest step
  Sat listening; when presently came by
  Two muffled up,—one sighing heavily,
  The other cursing low, whose voice I knew
  For the Duke Conrad's. Close I follow'd them
  Thro' the dark ways they chose to the open air;
  And, as I follow'd, heard my lady speak.
LUDOLPH. Thy life answers the truth!
PAGE.   The chamber's empty!
LUDOLPH. As I will be of mercy! So, at last,
  This nail is in my temples!
GERSA.   Be calm in this.   130
LUDOLPH. I am.
GERSA.   And Albert too has disappear'd;
  Ere I met you, I sought him everywhere;
  You would not hearken.

LUDOLPH.   Which way went they, boy?

GERSA. I'll hunt with you.

LUDOLPH.   No, no, no. My senses are
  Still whole. I have surviv'd. My arm is strong—
  My appetite sharp—for revenge! I'll no sharer
  In my feast; my injury is all my own,
  And so is my revenge, my lawful chattels!
  Jackall, lead on: the lion preys tonight,   138a
  Terrier, ferret them out! Burn—burn the witch!
  Trace me their footsteps! Away!   140
                                                          [*Exeunt.*

ACT V

SCENE I. *A part of the Forest.*

Enter CONRAD *and* AURANTHE.

AURANTHE. Go no further; not a step more; thou art
  A master-plague in the midst of miseries.
  Go—I fear thee. I tremble every limb,
  Who never shook before. There's moody death
  In thy resolved looks—Yes, I could kneel
  To pray thee far away. Conrad, go, go—
  There! yonder underneath the boughs I see
  Our horses!

CONRAD. Aye, and the man.

AURANTHE.   Yes, he is there.
  Go, go,—no blood, no blood; go, gentle Conrad!

CONRAD. Farewell!

AURANTHE.   Farewell, for this Heaven pardon you.   10
                                                    [*Exit* AURANTHE.

CONRAD. If he escape me, may I die the death
  In unimagined tortures—or breathe through
  A long life in the foulest sink of the world!
  He dies—'tis well she do not advertise
  The caitiff of the cold steel at his back.

                                                    [*Exit* CONRAD.

Enter LUDOLPH *and* PAGE.

LUDOLPH. Miss'd the way, boy, say not that on your peril!

PAGE. Indeed, indeed I cannot trace them further.

LUDOLPH. Must I stop here? Here solitary die?
   Stifled beneath the thick oppressive shade
   Of these dull boughs,—this oven of dark thickets,—   20
   Silent,—without revenge?—pshaw!—bitter end,—
   A bitter death,—a suffocating death,—
   A gnawing—silent—deadly, quiet death!
   Escap'd?—fled?—vanish'd? melted into air?
   She's gone! I cannot clutch her! no revenge!
   A muffled death, ensnar'd in horrid silence!
   Suck'd to my grave amid a dreamy calm!
   O, where is that illustrious noise of war,
   To smother up this sound of labouring breath,
   This rustle of the trees!

> [AURANTHE *shrieks at a distance.*

PAGE.   My Lord, a noise!   30
   This way—hark!

LUDOLPH.   Yes, yes! A hope! A music!
   A glorious clamour! Now I live again!   [*Exeunt.*

SCENE II. *Another part of the Forest.*

Enter ALBERT (*wounded*).

ALBERT. O for enough life to support me on
   To Otho's feet—

Enter LUDOLPH.

LUDOLPH.   Thrice villainous, stay there!
   Tell me where that detested woman is
   Or this is through thee!

ALBERT.   My good Prince, with me
   The sword has done its worst; not without worst
   Done to another—Conrad has it home—
   I see you know it all—

LUDOLPH.   Where is his sister?

AURANTHE *rushes in.*

AURANTHE.   Albert!

LUDOLPH. Ha! There! there!—He is the paramour!—

There—hug him—dying! O, thou innocence,
Shrine him and comfort him at his last gasp,   10
Kiss down his eyelids! Was he not thy love?
Wilt thou forsake him at his latest hour?
Keep fearful and aloof from his last gaze,
His most uneasy moments, when cold death
Stands with the door ajar to let him in?

ALBERT. O that that door with hollow slam would close
Upon me sudden, for I cannot meet,
In all the unknown chambers of the dead,
Such horrors——

LUDOLPH.   Auranthe! What can he mean?
What horrors? Is it not a joyous time?   20
Am I not married to a paragon
'Of personal beauty and untainted soul?'
A blushing fair-eyed Purity! A Sylph,
Whose snowy timid hand has never sin'd
Beyond a flower pluck'd, white as itself?
Albert, you do insult my Bride—your Mistress—
To talk of horrors on our wedding night.

ALBERT. Alas! poor Prince, I would you knew my heart.
'Tis not so guilty—

LUDOLPH.   Hear you he pleads not guilty—
You are not? or if so what matters it?   30
You have escap'd me,—free as the dusk air—
Hid in the forest—safe from my revenge;
I cannot catch you—You should laugh at me,
Poor cheated Ludolph,—make the forest hiss
With jeers at me—You tremble; faint at once,
You will come to again. O Cockatrice,
I have you. Whither wander those fair eyes
To entice the Devil to your help, that he
May change you to a Spider, so to crawl
Into some cranny to escape my wrath?   40

ALBERT. Sometimes the counsel of a dying man
Doth operate quietly when his breath is gone—
Disjoin those hands—part—part, do not destroy
Each other—forget her—our miseries
Are equal shar'd, and mercy is—

LUDOLPH.   A boon

When one can compass it. Auranthe, try
Your oratory—your breath is not so hitch'd—
Aye, stare for help—   [ALBERT *groans and dies.*
                There goes a spotted soul
Howling in vain along the hollow night—
Hear him—he calls you—Sweet Auranthe, come!   50
AURANTHE. Kill me.
LUDOLPH.   No! What? upon our marriage-night!
The earth would shudder at so foul a deed—
A fair Bride, a sweet Bride, an innocent Bride!
No, we must revel it, as 'tis in use
In times of delicate brilliant ceremony:
Come, let me lead you to our halls again—
Nay, linger not—make no resistance, sweet—
Will you—Ah wretch, thou canst not, for I have
The strength of twenty lions 'gainst a lamb—
Now one adieu for Albert—come away.—   60
                                        [*Exeunt.*

SCENE III. *An inner Court of the Castle.*

Enter SIGIFRED, GONFRED, *and* THEODORE *meeting.*

THEODORE. Was ever such a night?
SIGIFRED.   What horrors more?
Things unbeliev'd one hour, so strange they are,
The next hour stamps with credit.
THEODORE.   Your last news?
GONFRED. After the Page's story of the death
Of Albert and Duke Conrad?
SIGIFRED.   And the return
Of Ludolph with the Princess.
GONFRED.   No more, save
Prince Gersa's freeing Abbot Ethelbert,
And the sweet lady, fair Erminia,
From prison.
THEODORE. Where are they now? hast yet heard?
GONFRED. With the sad Emperor they are closeted;   10
I saw the three pass slowly up the stairs,
The lady weeping, the old Abbot cowl'd.

SIGIFRED. What next?

THEODORE.   I ache to think on't.

GONFRED.   'Tis with fate.

THEODORE. One while these proud towers are hush'd as death.

GONFRED. The next our poor Prince fills the arched rooms
   With ghastly ravings.

SIGIFRED.   I do fear his brain.

GONFRED. I will see more. Bear you so stout a heart?

                              [*Exeunt into the Castle.*

SCENE IV. *A Cabinet, opening towards a Terrace.*

OTHO, ERMINIA, ETHELBERT, *and a Physician, discovered.*

OTHO. O, my poor Boy! my Son! my Son! my Ludolph!
   Have ye no comfort for me, ye Physicians
   Of the weak Body and Soul?

ETHELBERT.   'Tis not the Medicine
   Either of heaven or earth can cure unless
   Fit time be chosen to administer—

OTHO. A kind forbearance, holy Abbot—come
   Erminia, here sit by me, gentle Girl;
   Give me thy hand—hast thou forgiven me?

ERMINIA. Would I were with the saints to pray for you!

OTHO. Why will ye keep me from my darling child?　　　　10

PHYSICIAN. Forgive me, but he must not see thy face—

OTHO. Is then a father's countenance a Gorgon?
   Hath it not comfort in it? Would it not
   Console my poor Boy, cheer him, heal his spirits?
   Let me embrace him, let me speak to him—
   I will—who hinders me? Who's Emperor?

PHYSICIAN. You may not, Sire—'twould overwhelm him quite,
   He is so full of grief and passionate wrath,
   Too heavy a sigh would kill him—or do worse.
   He must be sav'd by fine contrivances—　　　　20
   And most especially we must keep clear
   Out of his sight a Father whom he loves—
   His heart is full, it can contain no more,
   And do its ruddy office.

ETHELBERT.   Sage advice;

We must endeavour how to ease and slacken
The tight-wound energies of his despair,
Not make them tenser—

OTHO.   Enough! I hear, I hear.
Yet you were about to advise more—I listen.

ETHELBERT. This learned doctor will agree with me,
That not in the smallest point should he be thwarted   30
Or gainsaid by one word—his very motions,
Nods, becks and hints, should be obey'd with care,
Even on the moment: so his troubled mind
May cure itself—

PHYSICIAN.   There is no other means.

OTHO. Open the door: let's hear if all is quiet—

PHYSICIAN. Beseech you, Sire, forbear.

ERMINIA.   Do, do.

ORTHO.   I command!
Open it straight—Sh!—quiet—my lost Boy!
My miserable Child!

LUDOLPH (indistinctly without). Fill, full,—
My goblet—here's a health!

ERMINIA.   O, close the door!

OTHO. Let, let me hear his voice; this cannot last—   40
And fain would I catch up his dying words
Though my own knell they be—this cannot last—
O let me catch his voice—for lo! I hear
This silence whisper me that he is dead!
It is so. Gersa?

Enter GERSA

PHYSICIAN.   Say, how fares the prince?

GERSA. More calm—his features are less wild and flush'd—
Once he complain'd of weariness—

PHYSICIAN.   Indeed!
'Tis good—'tis good—let him but fall asleep,
That saves him.

OTHO.   Gersa, watch him like a child—
Ward him from harm—and bring me better news—   50

PHYSICIAN. Humour him to the height. I fear to go;
For should he catch a glimpse of my dull garb,

It might affright him—fill him with suspicion
That we believe him sick, which must not be—
GERSA. I will invent what soothing means I can.

[*Exit* GERSA.

PHYSICIAN. This should cheer up your Highness—weariness
Is a good symptom and most favourable—
It gives me pleasant hopes. Please you walk forth
Onto the Terrace; the refreshing air
Will blow one half of your sad doubts away.   60

[*Exeunt.*

SCENE V. *A Banqueting Hall, brilliantly illuminated, and set
forth with all costly magnificence, with Supper-tables, laden
with services of Gold and Silver. A door in the back scene,
guarded by two Soldiers. Lords, Ladies, Knights, Gentlemen,
&c. whispering sadly, and ranging themselves; part entering
and part discovered.*

FIRST KNIGHT. Grievously are we tantaliz'd, one and all—
Sway'd here and there, commanded to and fro
As though we were the shadows of a dream
And link'd to a sleeping fancy. What do we here?
GONFRED. I am no Seer—you know we must obey
The prince from A to Z—though it should be
To set the place in flames. I pray hast heard
Where the most wicked Princess is?
FIRST KNIGHT.   There, Sir,
In the next room—have you remark'd those two
Stout soldiers posted at the door?
GONFRED.   For what?   10

[*They whisper.*

FIRST LADY. How ghast a train!
SECOND LADY. Sure this should be some splendid burial.
FIRST LADY. What fearful whispering! See, see,—Gersa there!

Enter GERSA.

GERSA. Put on your brightest looks; smile if you can;
Behave as all were happy; keep your eyes
From the least watch upon him; if he speaks

To any one, answer collectedly,
Without surprise, his questions, howe'er strange.
Do this to the utmost,—though, alas! with me
The remedy grows hopeless! Here he comes,— 20
Observe what I have said,—show no surprise.

Enter LUDOLPH, *followed by* SIGIFRED *and* PAGE.

LUDOLPH. A splendid company! rare beauties here!
  I should have Orphean lips, and Plato's fancy,
  Amphion's utterance, toned with his lyre,
  Or the deep key of Jove's sonorous mouth,
  To give fit salutation. Methought I heard,
  As I came in, some whispers,—what of that?
  'Tis natural men should whisper; at the kiss
  Of Psyche given by Love, there was a buzz
  Among the gods!—and silence is as natural. 30
  These draperies are fine, and, being a mortal,
  I should desire no better; yet, in truth,
  There must be some superior costliness,
  Some wider-domed high magnificence!
  I would have, as a mortal I may not,
  Hanging of heaven's clouds, purple and gold,
  Slung from the spheres; gauzes of silver mist,
  Loop'd up with cords of twisted wreathed light,
  And tassell'd round with weeping meteors!
  These pendent lamps and chandeliers are bright 40
  As earthly fires from dull dross can be cleansed;
  Yet could my eyes drink up intenser beams
  Undazzled,—this is darkness,—when I close
  These lids, I see far fiercer brilliances,—
  Skies full of splendid moons, and shooting stars,
  And spouting exhalations, diamond fires,
  And panting fountains quivering with deep glows!
  Yes—this is dark—is it not dark?
SIGIFRED.   My Lord,
  'Tis late; the lights of festival are ever
  Quench'd in the morn.
LUDOLPH.   'Tis not to-morrow then? 50
SIGIFRED. 'Tis early dawn.

GERSA.   Indeed full time we slept;
  Say you so, Prince?
LUDOLPH.   I say I quarrell'd with you;
  We did not tilt each other,—that's a blessing,—
  Good gods! no innocent blood upon my head!
SIGIFRED. Retire, Gersa!
LUDOLPH.   There should be three more here:
  For two of them, they stay away perhaps,
  Being gloomy-minded, haters of fair revels,—
  They know their own thoughts best.
                              As for the third,
  Deep blue eyes—semi-shaded in white lids,
  Finish'd with lashes fine for more soft shade,   60
  Completed by her twin-arch'd ebon brows—
  White temples of exactest elegance,
  Of even mould felicitous and smooth—
  Cheeks fashion'd tenderly on either side,
  So perfect, so divine that our poor eyes
  Are dazzled with the sweet proportioning,
  And wonder that 'tis so,—the magic chance!
  Her nostrils, small, fragrant, faery-delicate;
  Her lips—I swear no human bones e'er wore
  So taking a disguise—you shall behold her!   70
  We'll have her presently; aye, you shall see her,
  And wonder at her, friends, she is so fair—
  She is the world's chief Jewel, and by heaven
  She's mine by right of marriage—she is mine!
  Patience, good people, in fit time I send
  A Summoner—she will obey my call,
  Being a wife most mild and dutiful.
  First I would hear what music is prepared
  To herald and receive her—let me hear!
SIGIFRED. Bid the musicians soothe him tenderly.   80
                              [A soft strain of Music.
LUDOLPH. Ye have none better—no—I am content;
  'Tis a rich sobbing melody, with reliefs
  Full and majestic; it is well enough,
  And will be sweeter, when ye see her pace
  Sweeping into this presence, glisten'd o'er
  With emptied caskets, and her train upheld

By ladies, habited in robes of lawn,
Sprinkled with golden crescents; (others bright
In silks, with spangles shower'd,) and bow'd to
By Duchesses and pearled Margravines—   90
Sad, that the fairest creature of the earth—
I pray you mind me not—'tis sad, I say,
That the extremest beauty of the world
Should so entrench herself away from me,
Behind a barrier of engender'd guilt!

SECOND LADY. Ah! what a moan!

FIRST KNIGHT.   Most piteous indeed!

LUDOLPH. She shall be brought before this company,
And then—then—

FIRST LADY.   He muses.

GERSA.   O, Fortune, where will this end?

SIGIFRED. I guess his purpose! Indeed he must not have
That pestilence brought in,—that cannot be,   100
There we must stop him.

GERSA.   I am lost! Hush, hush!
He is about to rave again.

LUDOLPH. A barrier of guilt! I was the fool.
She was the cheater! Who's the cheater now,
And who the fool? The entrapp'd, the caged fool,
The bird-lim'd raven? She shall croak to death
Secure! Methinks I have her in my fist,
To crush her with my heel! Wait, wait! I marvel
My father keeps away: good friend, ah! Sigifred!
Do bring him to me—and Erminia   110
I fain would see before I sleep—and [holy] Ethelbert,
That he may bless me, as I know he will
Though I have curs'd him.

SIGIFRED.   Rather suffer me
To lead you to them—

LUDOLPH.   No, excuse me, no—
The day is not quite done—go bring them hither.

[*Exit* SIGIFRED.

Certes, a father's smile should, like sun light,
Slant on my sheafed harvest of ripe bliss—
Besides, I thirst to pledge my lovely Bride
In a deep goblet: let me see—what wine?

The strong Iberian juice, or mellow Greek?   120
Or pale Calabrian? Or the Tuscan grape?
Or of old Ætna's pulpy wine presses,
Black stain'd with the fat vintage, as it were
The purple slaughter-house, where Bacchus' self
Prick'd his own swollen veins? Where is my Page?

PAGE.   Here, here!

LUDOLPH. Be ready to obey me; anon thou shalt
Bear a soft message for me—for the hour
Draws near when I must make a winding up
Of bridal Mysteries—a fine-spun vengeance!
Carve it on my Tomb, that when I rest beneath   130
Men shall confess—This Prince was gull'd and cheated,
But from the ashes of disgrace he rose
More than a fiery Dragon—and did burn
His ignominy up in purging fires—
Did I not send, Sir, but a moment past,
For my Father?

GERSA.   You did.

LUDOLPH.   Perhaps 'twould be
Much better he came not.

GERSA.   He enters now!

Enter OTHO, ERMINIA, ETHELBERT, SIGIFRED, *and Physician.*

LUDOLPH. O thou good Man, against whose sacred head
I was a mad conspirator, chiefly too
For the sake of my fair newly wedded wife,   140
Now to be punish'd, do not look so sad!
Those charitable eyes will thaw my heart,
Those tears will wash away a just resolve,
A verdict ten times sworn! Awake—awake—
Put on a judge's brow, and use a tongue
Made iron-stern by habit! Thou shalt see
A deed to be applauded, 'scribed in gold!
Join a loud voice to mine, and so denounce
What I alone will execute!

OTHO.   Dear son,
What is it? By your father's love, I sue   150
That it be nothing merciless!

LUDOLPH.   To that demon?
  Not so! No! She is in temple-stall
  Being garnish'd for the sacrifice, and I,
  The Priest of Justice, will immolate her
  Upon the altar of wrath! She stings me through!—
  Even as the worm doth feed upon the nut,
  So she, a scorpion, preys upon my brain!
  I feel her gnawing here! Let her but vanish,
  Then, father, I will lead your legions forth,
  Compact in steeled squares, and speared files,   160
  And bid our trumpets speak a fell rebuke
  To nations drows'd in peace!
ORTHO.   To-morrow, Son,
  Be your word law—forget to-day—
LUDOLPH.   I will
  When I have finish'd it—now! now! I'm pight,
  Tight-footed for the deed!
ERMINIA.   Alas! Alas!
LUDOLPH. What Angel's voice is that? Erminia!
  Ah! gentlest creature, whose sweet innocence
  Was almost murder'd; I am penitent,
  Wilt thou forgive me? And thou, holy Man,
  Good Ethelbert, shall I die in peace with you?   170
ERMINIA. Die, my lord!
LUDOLPH.   I feel it possible.
OTHO.   Physician?
PHYSICIAN. I fear me he is past my skill.
OTHO.   Not so!
LUDOLPH. I see it, I see it—I have been wandering—
  Half-mad—not right here—I forget my purpose.
  Bestir, bestir, Auranthe! ha! ha! ha!
  Youngster! Page! go bid them drag her to me!
  Obey! This shall finish it!   [Draws a dagger
OTHO.   O my Son! my Son!
SIGIFRED. This must not be—stop there!
LUDOLPH.   Am I obey'd?
  A little talk with her—no harm—haste! haste!

                                          [Exit Page.
  Set her before me—never fear I can strike.   180

SEVERAL VOICES. My Lord! My Lord!
GERSA.   Good Prince!
LUDOLPH. Why do ye trouble me? out—out—out away!
   There she is! take that! and that! no, no—
   That's not well done—Where is she?

[*The doors open. Enter* PAGE. *Several women are seen grouped about* AURANTHE *in the inner room*

PAGE. Alas! My Lord, my Lord! they cannot move her!
   Her arms are stiff,—her fingers clench'd and cold—
LUDOLPH. She's dead!   [*Staggers and falls into their arms.*
ETHELBERT.   Take away the dagger.
GERSA.   Softly; so!
OTHO. Thank God for that!
SIGIFRED.   I fear it could not harm him.
GERSA. No!—brief be his anguish!
LUDOLPH. She's gone—I am content—Nobles, good night!   190
   We are all weary—faint—set ope the doors—
   I will to bed!—To-morrow—   [*Dies.*

                   THE CURTAIN FALLS.

AMONG THE ENGLISH POETS

TO J. H. REYNOLDS
3 February 1818   Hampstead

Modern poets differ from the Elizabethans in this. Each of the moderns like an Elector of Hanover governs his petty state, & knows how many straws are swept daily from the Causeways in all his dominions & has a continual itching that all the Housewives should have their coppers
                              Emperors of vast
well scoured: the antients were ⟨Emperors of large⟩ Provinces, they had only heard of the remote ones and scarcely cared to visit them.—I will cut all this—I will have no more of Wordsworth or Hunt in particular—

TO J. H. REYNOLDS
11 July 1818   Maybole, Scotland

I am approaching Burns's Cottage very fast—We have made continual enquiries from the time we saw his Tomb at Dumfries—his name of course is known all about—his great reputation among the ⟨Plotting⟩ plodding people is "that he wrote a good MONY sensible things"—One of the pleasantest means of annulling self is approaching such a shrine as the Cottage of Burns—we need not think of his misery —that is all gone—bad luck to it—I shall look upon it hereafter with unmixed pleasure as I do upon my Stratford on ⟨and⟩ Avon day with Bailey—I shall fill this sheet for you in the Bardies Country. . . .

———•—•—•———

TO GEORGE AND GEORGIANA KEATS
19 February 1819   Hampstead

. . . they are very shallow people who take every thing literal A Man's life of any worth is a continual allegory —and very few eyes can see the Mystery of his life—a life like the scriptures, figurative—which such people can no more make out than they can the hebrew Bible. Lord Byron cuts a figure—but he is not figurative—Shakspeare led a life of Allegory; his works are the comments on it—

———•—•—•———

TO GEORGE AND GEORGIANA KEATS
20 September 1819   Winchester

You speak of Lord Byron and me—There is this great difference between us. He describes what he sees—I describe what I imagine—Mine is the hardest task. You see the immense difference—

———•—•—•———

TO J. H. REYNOLDS
21 September 1819   Winchester

I always somehow associate Chatterton with autumn. He is the purest writer in the English Language. He has no French idiom, or particles like Chaucer⟨s⟩—'tis genuine

English Idiom in English words. I have given up Hyperion
—there were too many Miltonic inversions in it—Miltonic verse cannot be written but in an artful or rather
artist's humour. I wish to give myself up to other sensations. English ought to be kept up.

———•—•—•———

TO GEORGE AND GEORGIANA KEATS
24 September 1819   Winchester

In the course of a few months I shall be as good an
Italian Scholar as I am a french one—I am reading Ariosto
at present: not manageing more than six or eight stanzas
at a time. When I have done this language so as to be
able to read it tolerably well—I shall set myself to get
complete in latin and there my learning must stop. I do
not think of venturing upon Greek. I would not go even
so far if I were not persuaded of the power the knowledge
of any language gives one. the fact is I like to be acquainted with foreign languages. . . .

—I shall never become attach'd to a foreign idiom so
as to put it into my writings. The Paradise lost though so
fine in itself is a curruption of our Language—it should
be kept as it is unique—a curiosity. a beautiful and grand
Curiosity. The most remarkable Production of the world
—A northern dialect accommodating itself to greek and
latin inversions and intonations. The purest english I
think—or what ought to be the purest—is Chatterton's—
The Language had existed long enough to be entirely un-
corrupted of Chaucer's gallicisms and still the old words
are used—Chatterton's language is entirely northern—I
prefer the native music of it to Milton's cut by feet I have
but lately stood on my guard against Milton. Life to him
would be death to me. Miltonic verse cannot be written
but it the vein of art—I wish to devote myself to another
sensation—

———•—•—•———

Though not a close friend, Shelley upon hearing that Keats
was gravely ill invited him to Italy. This is Keats's reply. He de-

clines, but in so doing graciously alludes to two of Shelley's poetic dramas, *The Cenci* and *Prometheus Unbound*. The passage "load every rift" is from Spenser's *The Faerie Queene,* II, vii, 28, line 5.

16 August 1820   Hampstead

My dear Shelley,
I am very much gratified that you, in a foreign country, and with a mind almost over occupied, should write to me in the strain of the Letter beside me. If I do not take advantage of your invitation it will be prevented by a circumstance I have very much at heart to prophesy—There is no doubt that an english winter would put an end to me, and do so in a lingering hateful manner, therefore I must either voyage or journey to Italy as a soldier marches up to a battery. My nerves at present are the worst part of me, yet they feel soothed when I think that come what extreme may, I shall not be destined to remain in one spot long enough to take a hatred of any four particular bed-posts. I am glad you take any pleasure in my poor Poem;—which I would willingly take the trouble to unwrite, if possible, did I care so much as I have done about Reputation. I received a copy of the Cenci, as from yourself from Hunt. There is only one part of it I am judge of; the Poetry, and dramatic effect, which by many spirits now a days is considered the mammon. A modern work it is said must have a purpose, which may be the God—*an artist* must serve Mammon—he must have "self concentration" selfishness perhaps. You I am sure will forgive me for sincerely remarking that you might curb your magnanimity and be more of an artist, and 'load every rift' of your subject with ore. The thought of such discipline must fall like cold chains upon you, who perhaps never sat with your wings furl'd for six Months together. And is not this extraordina[r]y talk for the writer of Endymion? whose mind was like a pack of scattered cards— I am pick'd up and sorted to a pip. My Imagination is a Monastry and I am its Monk—you must explain my

metap^{cs} to yourself. I am in expectation of Prometheus every day. Could I have my own wish for its interest effected you would have it still in manuscript—or be but now putting an end to the second act. I remember you advising me not to publish my first-blights, on Hampstead heath—I am returning advice upon your hands. Most of the Poems in the volume I send you have been written above two years, and would never have been publish'd but from a hope of gain; so you see I am inclined enough to take your advice now. I must exp[r]ess once more my deep sense of your kindness, adding my sincere thanks and respects for Mrs Shelley. In the hope of soon seeing you {I} remain

most sincerely {yours,}
John Keats—

TO GEORGE AND GEORGIANA KEATS
14 October 1818   Hampstead

—This is a mere matter of the moment—I think I shall be among the English Poets after my death.

TO BYRON

Byron! how sweetly sad thy melody!
   Attuning still the soul to tenderness,
   As if soft Pity, with unusual stress,
Had touch'd her plaintive lute, and thou, being by,
Hadst caught the tones, nor suffer'd them to die.
   O'ershading sorrow doth not make thee less
   Delightful: thou thy griefs dost dress
With a bright halo, shining beamily,
As when a cloud the golden moon doth veil,
   Its sides are ting'd with a resplendent glow,   10
Through the dark robe oft amber rays prevail,
   And like fair veins in sable marble flow;
Still warble, dying swan! still tell the tale,
   The enchanting tale, the tale of pleasing woe.
December 1814

OH HOW I LOVE, ON A FAIR SUMMER'S EVE

Oh how I love, on a fair summer's eve,
    When streams of light pour down the golden west,
    And on the balmy zephyrs tranquil rest
The silver clouds, far—far away to leave
All meaner thoughts, and take a sweet reprieve
    From little cares; to find, with easy quest,
    A fragrant wild, with Nature's beauty drest,
And there into delight my soul deceive.
There warm my breast with patriotic lore,
    Musing on Milton's fate—on Sydney's bier—   10
        Till their stern forms before my mind arise:
Perhaps on wing of Poesy upsoar,
    Full often dropping a delicious tear,
        When some melodious sorrow spells mine eyes.
Early summer 1816

ADDRESSED TO HAYDON

Highmindedness, a jealousy for good,
    A loving-kindness for the great man's fame,
    Dwells here and there with people of no name,
In noisome alley, and in pathless wood:
And where we think the truth least understood,
    Oft may be found a 'singleness of aim,'
    That ought to frighten into hooded shame
A money-mong'ring, pitiable brood.
How glorious this affection for the cause
    Of stedfast genius, toiling gallantly!   10
What when a stout unbending champion awes
    Envy, and Malice to their native sty?
Unnumber'd souls breathe out a still applause,
    Proud to behold him in his country's eye.
October (?) 1816

ADDRESSED TO THE SAME

Great spirits now on earth are sojourning;
    He of the cloud, the cataract, the lake,

Who on Helvellyn's summit, wide awake,
Catches his freshness from Archangel's wing:
He of the rose, the violet, the spring,
    The social smile, the chain for Freedom's sake:
    And lo!—whose stedfastness would never take
A meaner sound than Raphael's whispering.
And other spirits there are standing apart
    Upon the forehead of the age to come;   **10**
These, these will give the world another heart,
    And other pulses. Hear ye not the hum
Of mighty workings?——
    Listen awhile ye nations, and be dumb.
November 1816

HAPPY IS ENGLAND! I COULD BE CONTENT

Happy is England! I could be content
    To see no other verdure than its own;
    To feel no other breezes than are blown
Through its tall woods with high romances blent:
Yet do I sometimes feel a languishment
    For skies Italian, and an inward groan
    To sit upon an Alp as on a throne,
And half forget what world or worldling meant.
Happy is England, sweet her artless daughters;
    Enough their simple loveliness for me,   **10**
      Enough their whitest arms in silence clinging:
    Yet do I often warmly burn to see
      Beauties of deeper glance, and hear their singing,
And float with them about the summer waters.
December 1816

LINES ON THE MERMAID TAVERN

Souls of Poets dead and gone,
What Elysium have ye known,
Happy field or mossy cavern,
Choicer than the Mermaid Tavern?
Have ye tippled drink more fine
Than mine host's Canary wine?

Or are fruits of Paradise
Sweeter than those dainty pies
Of venison? O generous food!
Drest as though bold Robin Hood   10
Would, with his maid Marian,
Sup and bowse from horn and can.

    I have heard that on a day
Mine host's sign-board flew away,
Nobody knew whither, till
An astrologer's old quill
To a sheepskin gave the story,
Said he saw you in your glory,
Underneath a new old sign
Sipping beverage divine,   20
And pledging with contented smack
The Mermaid in the Zodiac.

    Souls of Poets dead and gone,
What Elysium have ye known,
Happy field or mossy cavern,
Choicer than the Mermaid Tavern?
February 3, 1818

SPENSER! A JEALOUS HONOURER OF THINE

Spenser! a jealous honourer of thine,
    A forester deep in thy midmost trees,
Did last eve ask my promise to refine
    Some English that might strive thine ear to please.
But Elfin Poet 'tis impossible
    For an inhabitant of wintry earth
To rise like Phœbus with a golden quell
    Fire-wing'd and make a morning in his mirth.
It is impossible to escape from toil
    O' the sudden and receive thy spiriting: 10
The flower must drink the nature of the soil
    Before it can put forth its blossoming:
Be with me in the summer days and I
Will for thine honour and his pleasure try.
February 5, 1818

SONNET WRITTEN IN THE COTTAGE WHERE BURNS WAS BORN

This mortal body of a thousand days
    Now fills, O Burns, a space in thine own room,
Where thou didst dream alone on budded bays,
    Happy and thoughtless of thy day of doom!
My pulse is warm with thine own Barley-bree,
    My head is light with pledging a great soul,
My eyes are wandering, and I cannot see,
    Fancy is dead and drunken at its goal;
Yet can I stamp my foot upon thy floor,
    Yet can I ope thy window-sash to find   10
The meadow thou hast tramped o'er and o'er,—
    Yet can I think of thee till thought is blind,—
Yet can I gulp a bumper to thy name,—
O smile among the shades, for this is fame!
July 11, 1818

ODE

Bards of Passion and of Mirth,
Ye have left your souls on earth!
Have ye souls in heaven too,
Double lived in regions new?
Yes, and those of heaven commune
With the spheres of sun and moon;
With the noise of fountains wond'rous,
And the parle of voices thund'rous;
With the whisper of heaven's trees
And one another, in soft ease   10
Seated on Elysian lawns
Brows'd by none but Dian's fawns;
Underneath large blue-bells tented,
Where the daisies are rose-scented,
And the rose herself has got
Perfume which on earth is not;
Where the nightingale doth sing
Not a senseless, tranced thing,
But divine melodious truth;

Philosophic numbers smooth; 20
Tales and golden histories
Of heaven and its mysteries.

Thus ye live on high, and then
On the earth ye live again;
And the souls ye left behind you
Teach us, here, the way to find you,
Where your other souls are joying,
Never slumber'd, never cloying.
Here, your earth-born souls still speak
To mortals, of their little week; 30
Of their sorrows and delights;
Of their passions and their spites;
Of their glory and their shame;
What doth strengthen and what maim.
Thus ye teach us, every day,
Wisdom, though fled far away.

Bards of Passion and of Mirth,
Ye have left your souls on earth!
Ye have souls in heaven too,
Double-lived in regions new! 40

December 1818

KEATS'S CORRESPONDENTS

BENJAMIN BAILEY

Bailey was a student at Oxford preparing for ordination in the Church of England when Keats met him at Reynolds' in the spring of 1817. He invited Keats to spend September of that year at Oxford, thus providing the poet with a congenial atmosphere for composing the entire third book of *Endymion*. As a university man and a professed Christian, Bailey forced Keats to reevaluate his position—and to take a stand where he had none—on theological and philosophical questions. Consequently, the letters to Bailey are more carefully reasoned than those to any of Keats's other correspondents. They also give us our most extended view of Keats's religious attitudes.

FANNY BRAWNE

Keats met Frances or Fanny Brawne shortly after returning in August 1818, from his walking trip through Scotland. In December he described her to his brother George as "beautiful and elegant, graceful, silly, fashionable and strange." In April 1819, or shortly after, Fanny—along with her mother, sister, and brother—moved into half of the duplex house in Hampstead named Wentworth Place. At this time Keats and Charles Brown shared the other half. Keats and Fanny became engaged in fall of 1819, but the poet offered to release her from her promise the next year when his death was imminent.

CHARLES BROWN

The Scotsman Charles Brown brought out Keats's large capacity for fun. When the poet met him late in summer of 1817, Brown was a sometime merchant (bankrupted) and a sometime playwright (author of a comic opera, *Narensky; or, The Road to Yaroslaf*) living frugally in his half of a house, Wentworth Place in Hampstead. Keats and Brown became close friends the next summer when they made a walking tour of Scotland together. When the poet's brother Tom died in December 1818, Brown insisted that Keats move into Wentworth Place with him. When funds were low the following year, he suggested to Keats that they collaborate on a stage tragedy to make money. Their play, *Otho the Great,* was written but not produced. (For a discussion of its composition see pp. 360–364.)

CHARLES COWDEN CLARKE

Clarke, only eight years Keats's senior, was the master's son and assistant at Enfield School, which the poet attended from 1803 to 1811. In the four years following, when he was apprenticed to the surgeon Thomas Hammond, Keats would often visit Enfield to learn from Clarke about the major English poets and the standard forms of English verse. Clarke also introduced Keats to the poetry and journalism of Leigh Hunt, and in October 1816, to the man himself—the young poet's first important contact with the London literary world.

CHARLES WENTWORTH DILKE

Dilke owned half of Wentworth Place, Charles Brown the other half. He and his wife Maria were fond of the Keats brothers and frequently entertained them. The Dilkes moved out of the house in April 1819, renting it to the Brawnes, who were so important to Keats in his last years.

BENJAMIN ROBERT HAYDON

Keats met Haydon the painter through Leigh Hunt in October 1816. Hunt and Haydon were temperamental and ideological opposites. Hunt's irreverent skepticism often roused the more ortho-dox Haydon to fury; Hunt's penchant for the coy and diminutive was the antithesis to Haydon's penchant for the doggedly grand. When Keats broke with Hunt the following March, Haydon seemed most likely to succeed him as the poet's mentor. Haydon had then just emerged from a long struggle to persuade the British government to buy the Parthenon statuary, since known as the Elgin Marbles. He took Keats to see these imposing specimens of Greek genius the first week of March 1817—soon after the laurel-crowning episode at Hunt's and possibly the same day that Keats's first volume of poetry was published. Haydon, then, made Keats aware of an aesthetic grandeur he had not before comprehended. Moreover, he introduced him to important new subject matter, ancient Greek art, which Keats treated most spectacularly in the *Ode on a Grecian Urn.*

LEIGH HUNT
Hunt attracted the young Keats on two counts: as poet and as politi-cal hero. The editor of an outspoken liberal newspaper, the *Examiner,* Hunt was imprisoned for his frank attack on the personal morals of the Prince Regent. Keats wrote a sonnet to commemorate Hunt's release from prison on February 2, 1815, and his first published verse was the sonnet "O Solitude!" printed in the *Examiner* on May 5, 1816. Keats finally met Hunt through Charles Cowden Clarke in October 1816. By then the young poet had already absorbed much of the manner of the older poet. Hunt accepted Keats into his circle and he helped him toward the publication of his first volume, *Poems,* which appeared in March 1817. Hunt's influence on Keats and their friendship waned rapidly thereafter. *Endymion,* begun in April 1817, was in one sense an effort on Keats's part to declare his independence from his former mentor.

GEORGE KEATS, TOM KEATS, FANNY KEATS
The poet was the oldest of the four Keats children, his brother George the next oldest, and his sister Fanny the youngest. Their father died in 1804 when the poet was eight; their mother, in 1810 when the poet was fourteen. Keats was separated from his brothers and sister during most of his adolescence, when he was in training to become a surgeon. Fanny went to live with their

guardian, Richard Abbey, who often made it difficult for the poet to visit her. George, and later Tom, worked for a time in Abbey's London office. It was not until the poet reached legal maturity and had given up the surgical profession (October–November 1816) that the three brothers could share lodgings together—first in Cheapside in the city and later in Well Walk, Hampstead. George reached legal maturity in February 1818. He married Georgiana Wylie in May of that year and emigrated to America in June. One benefit of this separation to Keats's readers is the series of long, running letters, extraordinarily rich in personal and literary detail, that the poet wrote to the new world. When George left for America, Tom Keats was already suffering from an advanced case of tuberculosis. He died under the poet's care on December 1, 1818.

JOHN HAMILTON REYNOLDS

Keats met Reynolds through Leigh Hunt in October 1816. They were both poets (at the time of their meeting, Reynolds already had three volumes of verse in print). They were about the same age, and both came to react against Hunt's influence. The two young men agreed so well that they planned to collaborate in rendering a group of Boccaccio's tales in English verse. But Keats's "Isabella," finished in April, 1818, was the only result of the plan, for Reynolds shortly abandoned poetry for a legal career. If their project came to little, their friendship came to much. Besides giving Keats invaluable encouragement on the craft of verse, Reynolds drew from him some of the most penetrating remarks on poetry that his letters contain. Above all, Reynolds introduced Keats to his own circle of friends. These included Benjamin Bailey, Charles Brown, Charles Wentworth Dilke, the publishers Taylor and Hessey, and their legal counsel Richard Woodhouse.

JOHN TAYLOR and JAMES AUGUSTUS HESSEY

When Keats broke with Hunt, he also broke with Hunt's associates, the Ollier brothers, who had published his first volume of poetry. The other two volumes published during his lifetime were done by John Taylor and James Augustus Hessey, with whom Keats established an almost ideal author-publisher relationship. Taylor and Hessey believed (rightly, of course) that the young poet had genius. They treated him tactfully and made money available to him for living expenses and for his voyage to Italy. It is no wonder, then, that besides the humdrum business customarily transacted between an author and his publishers, Keats's letters to these men exhibit a warm friendship and a lively interest in poetry.

RICHARD WOODHOUSE

Woodhouse, the legal advisor to Taylor and Hessey, was if anything even more devoted than they were to Keats. A discriminating collector of the poet's works, he once (unknown to Keats) put a sum of fifty pounds at his disposal.

NOTES TO THE POEMS

Written on the Day That Mr. Leigh Hunt Left Prison
Leigh Hunt finished his two-year sentence for libeling the Prince Regent on February 2, 1815.

To Kosciusko
Thaddeus Kosciusko (1746–1817) was a Polish patriot who fought against tyranny. The measure of Keats's admiration for the Polish hero is the comparison to Alfred (849–899), England's pre-eminent scholar, soldier, law-giver, and ruler. Kosciusko and Alfred are paired again in *Sleep and Poetry* (ll. 385–388).

Written in Disgust of Vulgar Superstition
The celebrated kingdom of Lydia was in Asia Minor and flourished from roughly 800 B.C. to 550 B.C. The musical style associated with its airs was delicate and soft, qualities opposite to the strident toll of church bells.

Read me a lesson, Muse, and speak it loud
Ben Nevis, a mountain in west Scotland, is the highest peak in Great Britain.

Lamia
The story of the poem comes from Robert Burton's *The Anatomy of Melancholy* (1621), the celebrated psychological treatise on

religious and love repressions. Burton calls "one Menippus Lycius, a young man twenty-five years of age," "a philosopher . . . able to moderate his passions, though not this of love." Apollonius is a senior philosopher. Lamia is what her name signifies in Greek, "a fabulous monster" with a woman's body.

ll. 1–5. Legend regards the fairy broods over which Oberon reigned as successors to the nymphs and satyrs, deities of woods and fields. So Oberon's driving the older spirits from the woods dates the poem's action in classical time.

l. 7. Hermes is the Greek name for Mercury, the wing-capped, wing-footed messenger of Jove (l. 10), known as much for his sexual expeditions as his official missions. Keats catches him off-duty.

l. 15. Tritons are sea deities generally pictured as half-man, half-fish.

l. 46. *Couchant* derives from the French *coucher*, to lie. *Cirque* means coiled. *Gordian* in l. 47 emphasizes the tangled intricacy of Lamia's position by suggesting the knot King Gordius tied.

l. 57. *Wannish:* dark, gloomy, black (from the Old English *wann*).

l. 58. Ariadne received a crown of seven stars from Bacchus, who loved her after she was abandoned by Theseus, to whom she was devoted. The tiara memorialized the princess in the form of a constellation. Like most of the details about Lamia, Ariadne's tiara hints of both beauty and tragedy.

l. 63. Proserpine resided in Sicily amid the splendid vistas and meadows of Enna before Pluto, taken by her beauty, carried her to Hades. Though made queen of the lower region, she yearned for her earthly habitat.

l. 81. Lethe is a river in Hades famed for its power to create forgetfulness of the past. Hermes is called the star of the waters of oblivion because one of his duties was to conduct the dead to Hades.

l. 103. Silenus was Bacchus' foster-father. Fat, jolly, usually wearing a floral headpiece, and always drunk, he can be found with satyrs and fauns, lesser debauchees frequently referred to as Sileni.

l. 115. Circe's head represents the enchantress' power to lure with a venomous potion and to transform her victims, as she did when Ulysses' companions were changed into swine.

l. 133. The Caduceus was described earlier in l. 89 as Hermes' "serpent rod." The attribute of his heraldic station, the rod was Apollo's gift in return for the lyre received from Hermes. The

Caduceus possesses many powers, that of transformation being the one Keats uses here.

l. 174. Cenchreae (Keats's spelling is his own) is a harbor on the isthmus of Corinth.

l. 179. Cleone is a village between Corinth and Argos, an ancient capital whose most famous ruler was Agamemnon.

l. 198. *Unshent:* not marred (*shent* means disgraced, lost, ruined).

l. 207. Nereids were sea nymphs, handmaids to Neptune, with power to calm or ruffle the water. Thetis (l. 208) was one of these fifty sea creatures.

l. 212. Mulciber is commonly known by his first name, Vulcan. He presided over fire and was the patron of artists working in iron and metal.

l. 248. Orpheus went to Hades to retrieve his beloved Eurydice from Pluto. Having moved the underworld with his song, the singer was on his way to success; but he could not control his desire to look back at her. In doing so he violated the cunning pact he entered with Pluto, which forbade that glance, and thereby lost her a second time. The analogous look on Lycius' face foretells, as did much of Lamia's appearance, disaster.

l. 265. The Pleiades were seven sisters. Like Ariadne, they became a stellar constellation after death. All except Merope were courted by immortals, and Keats may have Merope in mind since she married a mortal, a Corinthian like Lycius. Significantly, that misalliance tarnished Merope's luster, making her star the dimmest.

l. 320. Though Venus had many suitors, she remained partial to Adonis. When he died of a boar's bite, the goddess changed him into a flower (an anemone). Proserpine revived him with the understanding that Adonis spend half the year with her, half with Venus. His life cycle corresponds to that of the seasons, and the festival in his honor began with a lamentation and ended with joy as Adonis returned to life again.

l. 329. Peris are from Persian mythology and are represented as benevolent genii endowed with grace and beauty.

l. 333. Pyrrha symbolizes renewal and new life. During her life all mankind was destroyed by a flood. Pyrrha and her husband, Deucalion, saved themselves in a boat. The stones Pyrrha threw at the bidding of an oracle became women, those Deucalion threw became men; and the human race was restored.

386–387. *Sounds Aeolian* are those made by the wind over which Aeolus is god. The door hinges resemble a wind-harp responding to air currents.

Part II

48. Lycius is referring to the star Venus, called Lucifer as a morning star, Hesperus as an evening star. Of all the fixed stars, Venus is the brightest when in fullest phase. It orbits between Mercury and the Earth, a relationship analogous to the temperaments of Lamia and Hermes.

137. *Fret* is used in its architectural sense—to adorn with interlaced work.

151. *To gaze amain:* to look with full force, vehemently.

185. *Libbard:* a variant of leopard.

187. Ceres, the goddess of corn and harvests, was associated with the cornucopia overflowing with the earth's fruits.

217. *Osier:* a willow used in basketwork.

224. *Adder's tongue:* a fern resembling a snake's tongue.

226. The *thyrsus* is Bacchus' staff covered with vine leaves, emblems of intoxication.

245. The meaning of *pledge* is explained by Lycius' taking a cup (l. 241) and glancing at Apollonius. The gesture is a toast assuring fidelity.

l. 301. A *perceant* eye penetrates sharply.

Ode on Melancholy
l. 1. *Lethe:* the river of forgetfulness in hell.
ll. 2–5. Wolf's-bane, nightshade, and yew-berries are all poisons.
l. 4. *Proserpine:* the goddess and queen of the underworld.
l. 7. *Psyche:* the soul, conventionally represented as a butterfly.

Ode on Indolence
l. 10. Phidias (c. 500–432 B.C.) was the Greek sculptor who supervised all civic projects in the arts during Pericles' rule in Athens. Because of the impressive scale of his work the effect of mentioning Phidias is to diminish the figures on the vase.

I stood tip-toe upon a little hill
ll. 24–25. Mercury, as messenger of the gods, had winged heels.
l. 98. *sorrel:* any of a variety of low-growing, fleshy-leaved plants.

l. 116. *O Maker of sweet poets:* the moon, called variously in this poem *Cynthia* (ll. 204, 239) and *Diana* (l. 197). Keats capitalized on the myth that the moon-goddess was the twin sister of the sun-god Apollo by making her equally with him the inspirer of poets.

ll. 141–150. Keats briefly sketches here the story of how Cupid and Psyche fell in love, were separated, and finally reunited in heaven after Psyche was made a goddess.

ll. 157–162. *Lemprière's Classical Dictionary,* Keats's own reference book for mythological information, gives the following entry on Syrinx: "a nymph of Arcadia, daughter of the river Ladon. Pan became enamoured of her, and attempted to offer her violence; but Syrinx escaped, and at her own request was changed by the gods into a reed. . . . The god made himself a pipe with the reeds, into which his favorite nymph had been changed." This incident is alluded to in ll. 238–243 of *Endymion,* Book I.

l. 164. *Narcissus:* a handsome youth who was so enamoured of his own beauty that he gazed for hours at his reflection in the water and at last destroyed himself in frustration.

ll. 179–180. The poet who told these stories was Ovid, in Book III of his *Metamorphoses.* "Echo's bale" or woe came as a result of her unrequited love for Narcissus.

On Leigh Hunt's Poem "The Story of Rimini"

l. 6. *Hesperus:* Venus as the evening star.

To J. H. Reynolds, Esq.

l. 7. Medieval battle garb suits Voltaire no less well than do witch eyes and a cherub's mouth.

l. 11. This Brutus is Junius Brutus Booth (1796–1852), actor. *so so:* tipsy, unsteady.

l. 16. *tushes:* tusks.

l. 26. The Enchanted Castle is a painting by the French landscapist Claude (1600–1682). Biographers agree that Keats probably did not see Claude's original but an engraving of it by François Vivarès (1709–1780) and William Woollett (1735–1785).

l. 29. Urganda was a character in *Amadis of Gaul,* a fifteenth-century romance.

l. 42. *Santon of Chaldee:* a soothsaying hermit of Chaldea, the Asian country whose capital was Babylon.

l. 44. Cuthbert was a seventh-century English monk.

l. 46. Lapland is a center of witchcraft, the rites of which are resided over by Hecate, the goddess of sorcery. In *Paradise Lost* (II, 662–666) she dances with Lapland witches:

> *Nor uglier follow the night-hag, when, called*
> *In secret, riding through the air she comes,*
> *Lured with the smell of infant blood, to dance*
> *With Lapland witches, while the laboring moon*
> *Eclipses at their charms. . . .*

l. 61. *Postern-gate:* back gate.

l. 108. *Kamtschatcan:* Kamchatka is a peninsula in northeast Russia. From the sea and travel literature Keats read the place acquired associations of remoteness and wildness.

To Homer

l. 2. The Cyclades are islands in the Aegean Sea that circle Delos.

Fancy

l. 16. *ingle:* hearth, flame, blaze.

l. 34. *dewy sward:* dewy turf.

ll. 81–82. Proserpine was Ceres' daughter; Pluto, the "God of Torment," carried her off to the underworld.

ll. 85–89. Hebe, a daughter of Jupiter and Juno, was the goddess of youth with the power to rejuvenate others. She was made cup-bearer to all the gods by Juno. While pouring nectar at a grand festival, Hebe struck an indecent posture and was dismissed by Jupiter. Hebe is pictured as a virgin arrayed in flowers and beautiful garments.

l. 85. *zone:* girdle.

The Eve of St. Agnes

St. Agnes Eve is January 20 when, as the legend goes and Keats explains (ll. 46–54), a virgin will dream of a prospective lover through the saint's intercession if the girl ritualistically prepares herself. *Agnes* means chastity and purity. The lover's name, Porphyro, derives from the Greek for purple, the color Keats uses (l. 138, "purple riot") to show the intensity of the youth's passion.

l. 71. The innocent lamb is part of the "ceremonies due." In l. 115 Porphyro refers to "the holy loom" which nuns use to weave a cloth of lambs' wool for the altar.

l. 126. *Mickle:* a great quantity of, or much.

l. 171. Merlin was the soothsayer in the Arthurian romances.

l. 188. *Amain:* in full force, exceedingly.

l. 218. *warm gules:* soft red lights.

l. 241. *swart Paynims:* dark pagans.

l. 257. *Morphean amulet:* sleep-inducing charm. Morpheus is the god of sleep.

ll. 262–270. As with the sleeping virgin, there are special ceremonies required of the dream hero. This stanza recounts Porphyro's setting forth a rare feast, dates from Fez (l. 269), a sacred Islamic city in Morocco, and delicacies from comparably exotic places.

l. 277. *eremite:* hermit.

l. 292. Alain Chartier, a medieval French poet, wrote the poem, translated, "The Lady Without Pity." The title was borrowed for Keats's ballad.

l. 325. *flaw-blown:* blown in violent blast, gust-blown.

l. 344. *Haggard* was the name for a wild female hawk and has come to signify the qualities of that bird—wild, intractable, untamed.

l. 349. *Rhenish:* Rhine wine; *mead:* liquor made by fermenting honey and water.

l. 366. *owns:* recognizes.

l. 377. *Ave* means "hail," the prayer being the "Hail Mary."

The Eve of Saint Mark

April 24 is the eve of Saint Mark's feast. His principal shrine is the cathedral in Venice. Because this poem was never finished, the reader can only conjecture how Keats might have used the passage he concocted in Middle English. One guess is that he would have played the drab English town against a world of imagination evoked by legend and far-off places.

l. 12. *aguish:* from an outdated medical term (*ague*) meaning either fever or chill.

l. 33. *Moses' breastplate:* God prescribed to Moses in precise detail the breastplate that his brother Aaron was to wear as high priest. See Exodus 28:15–30.

ll. 33–34. The vision of the seven candlesticks occurs in the first chapter of Revelations. "I saw seven golden candlesticks; And in the midst of the seven candlesticks one like unto the Son of man" (Revelations 1:12–13).

l. 35. Saint Mark's symbol in Christian iconography is the winged lion.

ll. 36–38. The Ark of the Covenant was the sacred chest of ancient

Israel, containing the tablets of the ten commandments. It was surmounted by two golden cherubim between whose wings God was believed to be present. The specifications for the Ark are precisely set forth in Exodus 25:10–22.

The story of the golden mice is to be found in I Samuel 5–6. The Philistines had captured the Ark from the Israelites and as a result met with ill fortune. They determined therefore to return it with an offering of reparation that included five golden mice.

l. 40. *Minster-square:* a monastery or the church of a monastery. The word came to be used, as it is here, for a cathedral or any large church. See also l. 60, *minster-gate.*

l. 81. *Avadavat:* an Indian bird.

l. 93. *eremite:* hermit. Keats is referring here to the monk who copied the book that Bertha is reading.

ll. 98a–p. These lettered lines were first published in 1906 and editors have customarily inserted them at this point in the poem.

Ode To Fanny
l. 40. *blow-ball:* dandelion head.

Ode To a Nightingale
l. 2. *hemlock:* a poisonous potion made of hemlock, an herb.

l. 4. *Lethe:* the waters of oblivion and forgetfulness.

l. 16. *Hippocrene:* the Muses' sacred fountain.

l. 37. *Fays:* fairies, here stars.

l. 51. *Darkling:* in darkness, in the dark.

l. 66. The *Book of Ruth* tells of a woman who suffers alienation from her own people because of fidelity to her mother-in-law. Ruth must live by gleaning wheat, for which Keats gives the more generic name *corn* (l. 67), which in Britain denotes grain.

Ode on a Grecian Urn
l. 7. Tempe, a valley in Greece, and Arcadia represent perfect contentment in classical tradition.

l. 41. *Attic:* from Attica or Athens, its people, or its culture.

Hyperion
This fragmentary epic, like *Ode to Psyche* and *To Autumn*, treats that critical moment of change when an old order is about to give way to a new. Here the process centers on divine succession, the younger gods displacing their predecessors.

A review of the theogony shaping the poem will clarify Keats's intention. In the beginning was Chaos. From empty darkness emerge Uranus, the Sky (whom Keats calls Coelus), and Tithea, the Earth. The marriage of the most ancient of gods produced the Titans (Ceus, Creus, Hyperion, Mnemosyne, Cottus, Phoebe, Briareus, Thetis, Saturn, and Gyges). As in many stories of paternity, the father Uranus was vexed by the unruly behavior of his offspring. In anger he confined them in the bosom of the earth. The punishment seemed unjust to Tithea so she urged her sons to avenge the wrong. Saturn was brave enough to lead the conspiracy. Hiding with a sickle, he sprang on his father, mutilated him, and freed the Titans from captivity. Uranus' throne vacated, Saturn ruled.

The agreement under which Saturn took power forbade him to raise any sons. Each male child was a threat to Titan supremacy, as Saturn was to Uranus'. To prevent deposition Saturn devoured his sons as they were born. Rhea, his wife, like Tithea, resented Saturn's cruelty. She wanted her sons to live. She hid three of them (Zeus or Jupiter, Neptune, and Pluto) and gave Saturn stones instead, which satisfied his infanticidal hunger. Zeus, the most important of the three, was secretly raised in Crete.

The cycle of filial insurrection repeated itself. Zeus and his brothers warred against the Titans. The struggle took ten years before Zeus triumphed. *Hyperion* takes up the contest between the Olympians and the Titans just before its resolution. All the Titans except Hyperion, the sun god, have fallen; and the day of the King of Day is darkening. His fall and Apollo's succession to solar power mark the movement of *Hyperion*.

The theogonic background of *Hyperion* is complicated. The reader wanting to flesh out the details should consult Hesiod's *Works and Days* and Ovid's *Metamorphoses* (Book I).

Book I

l. 13. *Naiad:* a minor deity who presided over rivers and springs. ll. 26–33. The goddess is Thea, Hyperion's spouse. The Egyptian context underscores her great power, now checked, and her enigmatic beauty. Achilles (l. 29) was the bravest Greek in the Trojan war. Ixion's wheel (l. 30) represents the eternal punishment through endless motion which Jupiter imposed on Ixion for seducing Juno. l. 181. Aurora, a daughter of Hyperion and Thea, was the goddess of dawn. Usually described in a rose-colored chariot, she also opens the eastern gates of day with rosy fingers.

l. 246. Tellus is synonymous with Earth, Tithea.

l. 307. Coelus is synonymous with Sky, Uranus.

Book II

l. 4. Cybele was Saturn's wife. She is identified as Ops later in l. 113.

l. 20. Typhon was a giant with a hundred serpentine heads and a warring disposition to match them. Dolor is Keats's addition to the Titan family. Porphyrion was another giant born of the sky and earth.

l. 44. Iäpetus was a Titan. The Greeks regarded him as the father of all mankind.

l. 53. Keats changes Asia's father, who was Oceanus. One scholar suggests that Keats identified Caf with the Caucasus, the immense mountains between the Euxine and Caspian seas.

l. 60. *Oxus:* a large river flowing into the east part of the Caspian.

l. 66. *Enceladus:* the most powerful giant to oppose Jupiter.

l. 74. Phorcus was a sea god who married his sister Ceto, the mother of the dragons Keats mentions, the Gorgons.

l. 75. Oceanus and Tethys, his wife, were the greatest sea gods. Clymene (l. 76) is one of their daughters.

l. 77. Themis was a daughter of Sky and Earth and the first to whom men built temples.

l. 371. Numidia was a country in northern Africa whose men were known as great warriors.

ll. 374–378. Memnon was an Ethiopian king. After he was killed in combat, the Ethiopians built a statue in his honor. The statue had the marvelous property of uttering a melody every sunrise. The sound was compared to the breaking of a harp string when taut. At sunset the melody was sorrowful. The sounds emitted by the statue were affected by the rays of the sun on it.

Book III

l. 10. Delphi, a town on the southwest side of Parnassus, was Apollo's sanctuary and the home of a widely celebrated oracle.

l. 12. Doris was a Greek country known for the simple but strong qualities of style in its arts.

l. 24. Delos was the pivotal island among the Cyclades group. It was Apollo's birthplace, with an altar to him regarded as one of the seven wonders of the world.

ll. 31–32. Apollo's mother was Latona; his twin-sister, Diana.

l. 82. The Titaness Mnemosyne bore the nine muses.

To George Felton Mathew

Mathew, an aspiring but ungifted poet, was a friend to Keats during his stay at Guy's Hospital, London, where he studied medicine (October 1815 to July 1816). The poem was sent as a letter to Mathew in November 1815.

l. 5. The brother poets were Francis Beaumont (c. 1584–1616) and John Fletcher (1579–1625), so called because of the disputable claim of their joint authorship of some fifty plays.

l. 18. "Lydian airs" comes from Milton's *L'Allegro* (l. 136). The music of the kingdom of Lydia (Asia Minor) was known for its languorous sensuality. Milton's passage (ll. 135–140) runs:

> And ever against eating cares
> Lap me in soft Lydian airs,
> Married to immortal verse
> Such as the meeting soul may pierce
> In notes, with many a winding bout
> Of linked sweetness long drawn out. . . .

l. 69. Sir William Wallace (c. 1270–1305) is a national Scottish hero who doggedly drove the English from Scotland and for the moment secured order under a rule admired for its vigor and wisdom.

l. 75. A phrase from *The Faerie Queene* (I, iii, stanza 4).

On Seeing the Elgin Marbles

The Marbles are sculptures—friezes and statues—that decorated the Parthenon at Athens. They were named for the diplomat Lord Elgin who received permission from the Turks to remove them to England (1806) where the government eventually brought them (1816).

On Sitting Down to Read *King Lear* Once Again

l. 2. *Syren:* a sea nymph whose melodious voice totally captivates its hearers.

l. 9. *Albion:* old Celtic for England. The Celtic atmosphere of these lines (the oak groves, l. 11, were the place of Druidic worship) corresponds to *Lear's* setting.

l. 14. *Phoenix:* the bird which immolates itself and rises revitalized from its own ashes.

Isabella: or, the Pot of Basil

Boccaccio's *Decameron* (Day IV, Novel 5) provides the model from which the poem was adapted. Keats alters the setting from Sicilian Messina to Tuscan Florence and reduces the number of brothers from three to two, but for the most part he stays close to the original story of intrigue generated from furtive love, class separation, and fraternal cruelty.

l. 2. *palmer:* wandering pilgrim. As a mark of his pilgrimage to the Holy Land, the devout carried a palm leaf or palm branch.

l. 95. Theseus' spouse was Ariadne, daughter of the Cretan king, Minos. Ariadne did all for love of Theseus. Taken by him to the island of Naxos and abandoned there, she hanged herself in despair.

l. 99. Dido, queen of Carthage, was like Ariadne in that she killed herself after she was abandoned by her lover, Aeneas, who left her to found Rome. Vergil tells the story in Book IV of the *Aeneid.*

l. 150. *ghittern:* (gittern or cithern) a guitarlike instrument, strung with wire and played with a hard plectrum.

l. 229. *widow's weed:* mourning apparel.

l. 262. *Hinnom's vale:* a valley in ancient Jerusalem where the Israelites sacrificed their children to the god Moloch. See 2 Chronicles 28:3.

l. 393. Perseus' sword decapitated the Gorgon Medusa.

l. 442. Melpomene was the muse of tragedy.

l. 451. *Baälites of pelf:* worshipers of stolen property.

On Visiting the Tomb of Burns

l. 1. The town is Dumfries, Scotland.

l. 9. Minos, son of Jupiter, was king of Crete. Known for his wise rule in life, he was given in death the office of assigning the places the dead occupy and the punishment they are to endure.

The Fall of Hyperion

Keats put *Hyperion* aside in the spring of 1819; in August he approached the Titan story from a fresh direction and worked on the new version, *The Fall of Hyperion,* into September, along with *Lamia* and *Otho.* The word *Fall* in the later title suggests the difference in approach. *Hyperion* leaves off with Apollo's undergoing with Mnemosyne those lessons in grief and doubt that are preparatory to his achieving godhead. The action implies that what was to follow would have concerned that assumption of new powers of truth and inspiration. The *Fall* refocuses on the old god's impending end. The new emphasis is psychological and tragic rather than narrative. The subtitle, *A Dream,* gives the poem's frame, a strategy that goes closer to the psychology of disaster, announcing a special flexibility of form. The dreamer and controlling consciousness of the *Fall* is a poet who witnesses the fall of the earliest god of poetry and is thereby instructed in the values of art and life. The teacher here is once again Mnemosyne, the priestess of memory who bore the muses. In this poem, however, she goes under her Roman name Moneta. There is a stylistic change from the old to the new *Hyperion* that accords with Keats's new exploration. The grand, epic manner of the earlier poem is replaced by a lyrical idiom expressing the mental responses of the poet-witness.

The theogony bearing on the poem is given in a note to Canto I. *Hyperion,* p. xxx.

l. 21. *plantain:* a plant with broad flat leaves spreading close to the ground.

l. 35. The fabled horn, a cornucopia, was associated with Amalthea, daughter of a Cretan king. She fed Jupiter with goat's milk and was memorialized as a constellation. The horn was passed on to the nymphs with the power to answer any of their desires.

l. 48. *Caliphat:* the office of a Mohammedan chief.

l. 75. *that place the moth could not corrupt.* Biblical allusions in Keats's poetry are somewhat rare. This one comes from Matthew 6:19: "Lay not up for yourselves treasures upon earth, where moth and rust doth corrupt, and where thieves break through and steal."

l. 103. *Maian:* May.

l. 203. Pythia was Apollo's priestess at Delphi. Seated over a subterranean hole emitting sulphureous vapors which inspired the Pythia (there came to be several), the priestess frequently went into convulsions when delivering her oracles.

l. 208. Hector was the most valiant and fearless of the Trojan chiefs.

His name has come to signify a blustering bully, pushy and boast-
ful.

l. 463. Cf. The last line of Dante's inscription on the gate of hell
(*Inferno*, III, 9): ". . . leave all hope, you who enter." A Dan-
tesque atmosphere pervades *The Fall of Hyperion*, and a comparison
with the *Commedia*'s atmosphere would profit the reader. Moneta's
function, for instance, parallels Vergil's and Beatrice's. Her epithet,
Shade of Memory, echoes Dante's use of "shade" for dark, lost
spirit. The narrator's swoon, the instructive nature of his journey,
and the suitability of punishment to offense are problems uniting
both poems at the center of intention and execution.

Ode To Psyche

Cupid, the god of love, was enamoured of Psyche, a mortal. After
bitter trials Jupiter made Psyche (which means soul) a goddess.
Keats makes much of her late deification.

l. 4. *soft-conched ear: conched* means shell-shaped.

l. 14. *Tyrian:* royal purple.

l. 20. *aurorean:* dawnlike.

l. 26. *Phoebe's sapphire-region'd star:* the moon.

l. 27. *Vesper:* Venus as the evening star.

l. 37. *too late for the fond believing lyre:* too late for foolish and
devout poets to sing (her) praises.

l. 41. *lucent fans:* shining wings.

Ode to Apollo

l. 14. *Maro:* Vergil.

l. 34. *Æolian lyre:* a box fitted with strings which emit sound when
played upon by the wind.

l. 36. Tasso is a sixteenth-century Italian poet.

To Charles Cowden Clarke

l. 27. *Helicon:* a mountain in Greece, considered one of the haunts
of Apollo and the Muses. Hippocrene, the spring of poetic inspiration, flowed from Mount Helicon, and the two—as here—are
often linked.

l. 29. *Baiæ's shore:* the site of a luxurious resort of the early Roman
emperors, located about ten miles west of Naples.

l. 30. *Tasso:* sixteenth-century Italian poet whose major work was
the epic *Gerusalemme Liberata,* which dealt with the conquest of
Jerusalem by the crusaders.

l. 31. *Armida's bowers:* Armida is a character in Tasso's *Gerusalemme Liberata*. The episode alluded to by Keats occurs in Canto XVI, where this Saracen enchantress lures the Christian warrior Rinaldo into her sumptuous gardens.

l. 33. *Mulla's stream:* the river that ran near Spenser's home, Kilcolman Castle, in the south of Ireland. Spenser celebrated this stream in his poetry, most notably in *Colin Clout's Come Home Again,* where he relates the myth about the Mulla's love affair with the Bregog, another local river.

ll. 35, 36, 37. *Belphoebe, Una, Archimago:* characters in Spenser's *The Faerie Queene*. Belphoebe, one of a pair of twins, was conceived by the sun and raised by the goddess Diana, whose virginal way of life she followed. (See *The Faerie Queene,* III, vi and IV, vii and viii.) Una and Archimago are adversaries in Book I of Spenser's poem, where Una represents supernatural truth and Archimago, diabolical falsehood.

l. 40. *Titania:* queen of the fairies in Shakespeare's *A Midsummer Night's Dream*.

l. 41. *Urania:* the muse of astronomy.

l. 44. *Libertas:* Leigh Hunt, "wrong'd" because he was imprisoned for his outspoken journalism.

l. 63. *Atlas:* the giant who in classical mythology supported the heavens on his shoulders.

l. 68. *Clio:* the muse of history.

ll. 70–71. *Alfred, Tell, Brutus:* Alfred the Great, ninth-century Saxon king; William Tell, Swiss patriot famous for shooting the apple from his son's head rather than submit to tyranny; and Marcus Junius Brutus, Roman statesman of the first century B.C., who killed Julius Caesar in the name of Roman liberty.

l. 111. *Arne:* Thomas Augustine Arne, eighteenth-century English composer.

Sleep and Poetry

l. 9. *Cordelia:* King Lear's youngest daughter in Shakespeare's play.

l. 74. *Meander:* a river in Asia Minor, fabled for its winding course.

l. 89. *Montmorenci:* a river in the Canadian province of Quebec.

ll. 181–182. *a schism / Nurtured by foppery and barbarism:* Keats refers here and throughout the verse paragraph that follows to the neoclassical age in English poetry, during which order and regularity (the "musty laws" of l. 195) replaced Elizabethan exuberance.

l. 187. *Pegasus:* a winged horse symbolizing poetic inspiration.

l. 198. *the certain wands of Jacob's wit.* In Chapter 30 of Genesis, Jacob makes a bargain with his father-in-law Laban by which all dark or speckled animals in Laban's flocks will become his. Laban plays unfairly by removing the speckled animals from the rest, thereby insuring that their coloring will not spread to the young of the flock at large. Jacob, however, outwits his father-in-law by setting up peeled branches (Keats's "wands') in front of the watering troughs. By a kind of natural magic the stripes on the branches produce speckled offspring in all the animals who drink. The improbability and arbitrariness of the scheme make it an appropriate metaphor for Keats to apply to the rigid and equally arbitrary practices of the neoclassical poets.

l. 202. *Lyrist:* Apollo.

l. 206. *Boileau:* seventeenth-century French poet whose *L'Art Poétique* was a manifesto of the neoclassical ideals in literature that Keats abhorred. Particular scorn is implied by having English poets marching under the banner of a foreigner.

ll. 233–234. In Book IX of the *Odyssey* the Cyclops, Polyphemus, hurls stones (not clubs) at Odysseus and his men as they flee in ships.

l. 249. *Paphos:* the site of a splendid shrine to Venus.

l. 303. *Dedalian wings:* Dedalus fashioned wings from feathers and wax for himself and his son Icarus to effect their escape from King Minos of Crete. The sun melted the wax of Icarus' wings, and he fell into the sea.

ll. 335–336. *Bacchus . . . Ariadne.* Bacchus fell in love with Ariadne after she had been abandoned by her former lover, Theseus, on the island of Naxos.

l. 381. Sappho is a Greek poetess who wrote about 600 B.C.

Dedication to Leigh Hunt, Esq.

With this sonnet Keats dedicated the *Poems* of 1817 to Hunt.

l. 8; l. 12. *Flora . . . Pan:* here, as in *Sleep and Poetry* (l. 102), Keats links these two classical deities, who represent to him a carefree enjoyment of natural beauty. Flora was the goddess of flowers and gardens; Pan, the god of shepherds, huntsmen, and country folk.

Hymn To Apollo

l. 25. *Pleiades:* a cluster of stars in the constellation Taurus.

On Seeing a Lock of Milton's Hair

l. 18. *Delian oath:* an oath to Apollo, who was born on the island of Delos.

To My Brother George

l. 24. *Libertas:* Leigh Hunt.

l. 128. *scarlet coats:* the uniform worn by British soldiers.

On Fame ("Fame, like a wayward Girl")

l. 9. *Nilus-born:* Egyptian.

l. 10. *Potiphar:* (Genesis 39) the Egyptian official in whose house Joseph served as chief steward. Potiphar's wife tried unsuccessfully to seduce Joseph. Keats's substitution of "sister-in-law" for wife seems to be whimsy.

Endymion

A few introductions are in order at the start of *Endymion*, if only to avoid awkwardness later. Endymion, the hero, has several names. Because he lived on Mount Latmos, he is often called the "Latmian" or simply the "mountaineer." Because Caria in Asia Minor was his native land, he is also known as the "Carian." His beloved, the moon goddess, Diana (sometimes abbreviated as Dian to fit the meter), goes under the names of Cynthia and Phœbe as well. Her twin-brother Apollo, god of poetry and healing, is frequently heard from as Phœbus.

Book I

The opening book of *Endymion* divides into two main parts. The first is concerned with a pastoral festival in which the hero appears as a shepherd leading his people in their rustic observances honoring Pan, god of shepherds. The *Hymn to Pan* (ll. 232–306) is the high point of this section. Its movement announces the principal theme of Book I, the ascent from earthly sights to heavenly vision, from Pan as the god of all physical nature to Pan the "Dread opener of the mysterious doors" (l. 288) leading beyond, "to the very bourne of heaven" (l. 295). The second part of Book I, comprising the hero's debate with his sister Peona (l. 507 to the end), recapitulates this movement. Against Peona's earthbound criticism that he is too much occupied with things of heaven, Endymion emphatically defends himself in the "fellowship with ssence" passage, beginning with l. 777. The passage, a central one in all of Keats's work, actually vindicates the imagination as the power by which the mind rises out of its self-confinement to seek and embrace a larger world. In context this is Endymion's way of rejecting Peona's advice and of setting his course toward the highest form of love.

l. 140. *Arcadia:* a province in the Greek Peloponnesus and one of Pan's favorite haunts. The name is closely linked to the pastoral tradition in literature and almost automatically evokes the idealized existence of its shepherd inhabitants.

l. 141–144. *Apollo's pipe . . . Thessaly.* Like Pan, Apollo served among his other roles as a shepherd god. In the mythological episode alluded to here he took refuge with Admetus, king of Thessaly, and tended the king's flocks in order to escape the wrath of his father Jupiter.

l. 170. *Ganymede:* a boy so handsome that Jupiter, king of the gods, fell in love with him. To suggest how attractive Endymion was, Keats compares him with Ganymede grown to manhood, implying that Jupiter's favorite could only have improved with age.

l. 236. *hamadryads:* tree nymphs.

l. 243. *Syrinx:* a nymph who caught Pan's fancy. She escaped him by being changed into a reed, only to be cut down by the unwitting god as he was gathering materials for a flute.

l. 263. Fauns and satyrs were woodland deities, part man and part goat. Like Pan, their chief, they were known for their unrelenting pursuit of nymphs.

l. 272. *Naiads:* nymphs of rivers, springs, and fountains.

l. 290. *Dryope:* Pan's mother.

l. 306. Mount Lycaeus was a center of worship to Pan.

l. 510. *Paphian dove.* "Paphian" refers to Venus, to whom the dove was sacred, just as the deer in the next lines were sacred to Diana.

l. 531. *Lucifer:* not to be confused with the Biblical Satan, this Lucifer is the planet Venus when it rises as the morning star before sunrise.

l. 555. *sacred ditamy and poppies red:* plants sacred to Diana. Ditamy, more commonly spelled *dittany,* is a variety of mint.

l. 559. *Morpheus:* the god of dreams.

l. 563. Mercury's rod, the caduceus, had the power of inducing sleep.

l. 671. *Oread:* a mountain nymph. Oreads were sacred to Diana.

l. 862. *Latona:* mother of Diana and Apollo.

Book II

In this book the love pangs that torment Endymion and Diana find parallels in two other mythological love stories, that of Venus and Adonis and that of Alpheus and Arethusa. Venus and Diana, both goddesses, each fell in love with a young mortal and had to endure a long parting. After being killed by a wild boar Adonis could wake from his death sleep only during the warm months of the year. But whereas Venus' separation from Adonis was beyond the control of either, Diana's separation from Endymion was not. Diana held off, knowing that as the goddess of chastity she had a reputation to maintain among the immortals, and she feared their ridicule.

In the traditional telling the nymph Arethusa was loathe to yield to Alpheus' importunity and begged Diana to rescue her. The goddess changed Arethusa into a fountain, which turned out to be of little help, for Alpheus was a river-god and continued to pursue the reluctant nymph by taking his natural form as a flowing stream. Keats concocted his own version of this myth. Not coyness—but fear of offending Diana, to whom she is bound by a vow of chastity —keeps Arethusa from enjoying a love that she desires.

l. 23. *the great Athenian admiral:* Themistocles, whose fleet destroyed the superior forces of the Persians under Xerxes at Salamis in the year 480 B.C.

l. 24. *striding Alexander:* Alexander the Great, who first ruled over Macedonia but went on to conquer most of the world known to the ancients as far east as India (hence the reference to the Indus River in the next line).

ll. 26–27. In Book IX of the *Odyssey,* Ulysses put out the single eye of his captor, the Cyclops, as that giant slept after gorging on Ulysses' men.

l. 31. *Hero:* the heroine of Marlowe's poem, *Hero and Leander.*

l. 31. *Imogen:* Shakespeare's heroine in *Cymbeline.*

l. 32. *Pastorella:* the beloved of Calidore in Book VI of Spenser's *The Faerie Queene.*

l. 109. *Amphitrite:* the wife of the chief sea-god, Poseidon or Neptune.

l. 118. *Meander:* the son of Oceanus, Neptune's predecessor as sea-god when the Titans ruled the world.

l. 262. *A quiver'd Dian:* a statue of Diana holding a quiver of arrows, one of her emblems as goddess of the hunt.

l. 359–363. *the east could blow / Arion's magic . . . To seas Ionian and Tyrian.* Arion, son of Neptune, was a lyrist whose song was so winning that once it brought dolphins to rescue him after he had been put overboard by some envious sailors. The event occurred in the eastern Mediterranean, and the *east* of l. 359 must refer to the wind that would sweep Arion's music westward toward the Atlantic. Conversely, the throne of Apollo, another supreme musician, would be in the west, requiring a breeze out of that quarter to carry his melodies to the Ionian and Tyrian seas, which lie at the opposite or eastern end of the Mediterranean.

l. 492. *Cytherea:* an island associated with Venus. The pigeons and doves mentioned in l. 497 were her sacred birds.

l. 611. *Thetis:* the chief of the Nereids or sea-nymphs and the mother of Homer's hero Achilles. Ovid mentions in Book XI of the *Metamorphoses* that she rode on a dolphin, a detail that Keats may have had in mind in writing his description of her.

l. 627. *founts Protean. Protean* refers to Proteus, a sea-god whose name has become synonymous with shape-changing. Hence the play of water in these fountains was ever varied.

l. 691. *Triton:* the son of Neptune and Amphitrite. He served as his father's herald, blowing into (or "winding") a shell as if it were a horn.

l. 716. *Helicon:* a mountain in Greece, sacred to the muses. From it flowed Hippocrene, a fountain whose waters bestowed poetic inspiration.

l. 791. *Minerva:* the Roman name for the goddess of wisdom, called Pallas Athena (ll. 799, 802) by the Greeks. Because of her perpetual celibacy Minerva was a standard for sobriety in conduct.

Book III

Except for the first two hundred odd lines, which are given over to praise of Cynthia, Book III is taken up with the single story of Glaucus and Scylla, which can be found in Books XIII and XIV of Ovid's *Metamorphoses*. Keats has added his own twists. In Ovid, Circe transformed Scylla into the monster whose name, paired with Charybdis, has become proverbial as one of two equally gruesome alternatives. Keats's Circe, however, simply puts Scylla into a deathlike trance (l. 618) from which she can be revived at length by the efforts of a certain youth—Endymion, of course. Glaucus can achieve a happy, if long-delayed, union with Scylla only if he reclaims the bodies of all lovers lost at sea; Endymion can advance his suit by helping Glaucus. In Keats's hands, therefore, the myth becomes an object-lesson in the need to sympathize with others in their sufferings.

l. 38. *Ceres:* an earth goddess who presides over grain and harvests. As such, she should be contrasted with Cynthia, a heavenly deity.

l. 71. *Tellus:* Mother Earth herself, one of the oldest of the classical deities.

l. 97. *Leander:* the lover of Hero, whose "toil" was to swim the Hellespont nightly to meet his beloved.

l. 98. Orpheus, by the sheer enchantment of his song, gained admission to the underworld to bring back his beloved Eurydice.

l. 99. *Pluto:* god of the underworld, who rose to the "thin element" or air above to win a wife for himself.

l. 133. *Nox:* Latin for "night." She is one of the oldest deities and was held responsible for whatever was terrible and unexplained in human life.

l. 269. *Tartarus:* the lowest region of hell where the most wicked of mankind are punished.

l. 503. *Charon:* boatman on the river Styx, which lies at the entrance to hell. His charge to ferry the dead across the river was a penny. Keats's meaning is that if Charon were to take time off and fall asleep among the rushes on the bank, even he could not dream of monsters to equal those mentioned here.

l. 567. *Dis:* another name for the god of the underworld, more commonly known as Hades or Pluto.

ll. 850–854. *the bow / Of Iris . . . this Paphian army . . . Neptune's state:* three elegant circumlocutions. The first refers to the rainbow; the second, to the troupe of lovers (*Paphian* refers to Venus, goddess of love); the third, to the sea.

l. 889. *Syrens:* traditionally, a group of sea-nymphs who lured passing sailors to their death by the enchantment of their song. Here they are harmless enough.

l. 893. *ooze-born Goddess:* Venus, who merits inclusion in this company of sea-deities because she was born from the ocean's foam.

l. 899. *Nais:* the mother of Glaucus.

l. 951. *Æolus:* god of the winds. The adjectival form of his name commonly appears in the phrase "Aeolian harp," a frame with strings which produces a kind of music when played upon by the wind. See l. 973.

l. 1000. *the Ægean seer:* Nereus, a sea-god and prophet whose principal habitation was in the Aegean Sea. He and his wife Doris were both children of Oceanus. They had fifty daughters, the Nereids or sea-nymphs (l. 1014), among whose number was Thetis (l. 1005), the mother of Homer's hero Achilles.

Book IV
The last is the most confusing and controversial of the four books of *Endymion*. It introduces a major character, the Indian maiden. In falling in love with her Endymion complicates his dilemma, for he is now torn among three allegiances: those to the moon, the Indian maiden, and the ideal woman who has appeared in his dreams. The three turn out at length to be one and the same, and the hero is free to love without hindrance.

The allegorical meaning of these events becomes more intelligible when seen in light of the ideas discussed in "The Poet and Reality." Endymion's aspiration to love the moon and the dream woman parallel the reaching of the imagination toward any ideal or truth beyond immediate experience. At the same time the world of experience cannot be ignored. Its pain presses in as insistently as the plight of the Indian maiden. Keats's point is that we need not make a choice between the two; paradoxically, the way to the ideal is through immersion in the real world and not in a flight from it. Endymion wins the moon-goddess by wooing the Indian maiden.

ll. 11–12. *the Nine, / Apollo's garland:* the nine muses, who, like Apollo, inspired literary creation.

l. 15. *Ausonia:* one of the ancient names for Italy.

l. 66. *Hermes' wand.* Hermes or Mercury reputedly had the power to raise the dead with his rod, the caduceus. The Indian maiden wishes for such a wand to change one of the woodland plants into a man.

l. 68. *Hyacinthus:* a youth whom Apollo unintentionally killed in a game of quoits. The god then changed his favorite into the flower that bears his name.

l. 121. *Erebus:* a deity of the underworld whose name is often (as here) used to signify a region of darkness in hell.

l. 145. *roundelay:* a simple song with a refrain.

l. 196. *Bacchus and his crew:* the god of wine attended by his customary entourage, the Satyrs, who were goatlike men much given to drunken revels. One of Bacchus' most celebrated feats was his triumphant expedition to the East, which is recounted in the passage following. Wherever he went, throngs capitulated to the genial god's easy rule. Since Bacchus—especially under his other name, Dionysus—was the god of poetry as well as the god of wine, Keats might be referring here to the historical movement of human culture from its center in the ancient East toward Greece.

l. 215. *Silenus:* Bacchus' tutor, the oldest and wisest of the Satyrs.

l. 257. *Osirian Egypt* refers to Egypt in the ancient times when Osiris was its principal deity.

l. 259. *Abyssinia:* the country that is now called Ethiopia.

l. 262. *Tartary:* a large undefined area in central Asia, named for the nomadic Tartars, a tribe proverbial for their savagery.

l. 265. *Brahma:* the supreme divine principle in Hinduism.

l. 375. *Cimmerian:* dark or dismal. The Cimerii were a nation who lived in caves and constant gloominess.

l. 394. *Skiddaw:* a mountain in the lake district of England.

l. 415. *Hebe:* the cup-bearer of the gods.

l. 427. *Dis:* Pluto, god of the underworld.

ll. 441–442. *He who died / For soaring too audacious:* Icarus, whose father Dedalus fashioned wings of wax and feathers to enable the two of them to escape from the labyrinth in which they were imprisoned on the island of Crete. Against his father's warning Icarus flew too high, and the sun melted his wings thus causing his death. The adjective *dædale* (l. 459) derives from Dedalus' name and signifies cunning or crafty.

l. 536. *Semele:* the mother of Bacchus.

l. 567. *Hesperus:* the evening star, which ordinarily appears low in the western sky at sunset. For this celebration, however, he moves towards the zenith and stays up late into the night.

l. 570. *Zephyrus . . . and Flora:* the god of the west wind and the goddess of flowers, who are married to each other.

l. 582. *Aquarius:* the water-bearer, the first of several constellations to appear in the heavens in this passage. The others are Gemini or the twins, *Castor* (l. 591) and Pollux (l. 592); Leo, the *Lion* (l. 591); Ursa Major, the *Bear* (l. 592); Sagittarius, the *Centaur* (l. 595), customarily pictured with an arrow poised for shooting; *Andromeda* (l. 602) and her lover and rescuer Perseus, *Danae's Son* (l. 606).

l. 611. *Daphne:* a reluctant nymph pursued by Apollo and changed into a laurel tree.

l. 701. *Vesta:* goddess of the hearth and fire. In ancient times a flame was kept constantly burning at her shrine.

l. 713. *Delphos:* the shrine where Apollo gave his most authoritative oracles.

l. 953. *Rhadamanthus:* a judge in hell.

l. 955. *Promethean clay:* man. Prometheus was supposed to have made the first man and woman from clay, which he animated with the fire that he stole from heaven.

To—

Robert Gittings, Keats's latest biographer, suggests that the sonnet was addressed to "a lively dark-haired girl called Mary Frogley," who was part of the Mathew circle the poet associated with while studying medicine. Mr. Bate notes that Mary Frogley "seems to have had something of a crush" on the poet.

l. 10. Hybla is a Sicilian mountain noted for its abundance of fragrant flowers and honey.

To one who has been long in city pent

l. 1. The first line echoes Milton's "As one who long in populous city pent" (*Paradise Lost,* IX, 445).

l. 10. Philomel is poetic for nightingale.

On First Looking into Chapman's Homer

George Chapman (c. 1559–1634) not only translated Homer but wrote sacred verse and plays.

l. 6. *demesne:* domain.

l. 7. *serene:* expanse of clear sky.

l. 14. Darien is the Isthmus of Panama where Balboa, not Cortez, first stared at the Pacific.

To My Brothers

l. 9. Tom was seventeen on November 18, 1816.

Keen, fitful gusts are whisp'ring here and there

The "little cottage" in line 10 locates the origin of the friendly spirit as Leigh Hunt's place in Hampstead, where Keats visited shortly before writing the sonnet in November 1816.

ll. 11–12. Milton's "eloquent distress" for "Lycid" was expressed in his famous pastoral elegy for Edward King, *Lycidas.*

To G. A. W

Georgiana Augusta Wylie became the poet's sister-in-law, Mrs. George Keats.

l. 13. There were three Graces: Aglaia, Thalia, Euphrosyne.

On the Sea

l. 4. Hecate was synonymous with Proserpine, queen of hell. Hecate presided over enchantment and magic and had power over earth and heaven, land and sea.

To—

The occasion of this sonnet was the poet's casually seeing a woman at Vauxhall in February 1818.

Written in Answer to a Sonnet Ending Thus

l. 2. Cynthia was the surname of Diana, moon goddess, after her birthplace, Mount Cynthus.

l. 3. Hesperus was the name applied to the evening star (Venus).

Otho the Great

ACT I, Scene 1.

l. 9. *petards:* bombs. Shakespeare made this a household word through the phrase "hoist with his own petar" (meaning "blown up by his own bomb") from *Hamlet,* III, iv, 207.

l. 80. *baldric:* a belt worn over the shoulder, across the breast, and under the opposite arm, used to carry such instruments as swords and knives.

l. 81. *ratio:* ration (of food).

ll. 93–95. *Jove-like . . . complete Minerva.* In the myth Minerva was born fully grown and completely armed from the head of her father Jove.

l. 134. *Hymen:* the god of marriage.

ACT I, Scene 2.

l. 59. *Saladin:* sultan of Egypt and Syria (born 1138, died 1193) who drove the crusaders out of Jerusalem and effectively ended their power in Palestine. Keats is committing an anachronism here, for Otho lived (912–973) two centuries before Saladin. He wanted the name of a well-known infidel, however, and Saladin served that purpose.

l. 172. *sugar-cates.* Cates are choice foods or delicacies.

ACT I, Scene 3.
l. 11. *oblique:* slanted, but by extension perverse, sinister, or unfavorable.
l. 12. *Mussulman:* a Moslem.
l. 20. *Saracenic:* the adjectival form of *Saracen.* The word can apply generically to any of the Moslems who opposed the crusaders.
l. 21. *scymitar:* a curved sword used by the Turks and Arabs.
l. 51. *Tartar:* a generic name for the Mongolian and Turkic tribes who invaded the region around Asia Minor in the middle ages.
l. 66. *housings:* saddlecloths.
l. 100. *adverse:* acting against each other or in a contrary direction.

ACT II, Scene 1.
l. 60. *Titan.* The Titans, who are dealt with at length in *Hyperion,* were a race of giant gods. Keats uses this allusion to create contrast with the pigmies of the next line.
l. 67. *By Peter's chair.* The chair of Saint Peter is the symbol of the Pope's authority and infallibility.
l. 87. *kites:* hawklike birds.
l. 129. *hecatombs.* A hecatomb is the slaughter of a hundred oxen or cattle at the same time.
ll. 132–133. According to the Bible Nimrod was "a mighty hunter before the Lord." "The beginning of his kingdom was Babel," and he "builded Nineveh" (Genesis 10:9, 10, 11). Keats may be telescoping his allusions here, since the towers that "kiss'd the parted clouds" would refer more properly to Babel than to Nineveh.

ACT II, Scene 2.
Last line in the letter. *Wen:* a growth or cyst.
l. 101. *fledgy:* feathery.

ACT III, Scene 1.
l. 7. *fast-limed in a cursed snare.* This refers to the old practice of smearing a sticky substance called "bird lime" on the twigs of trees. The birds, unable to free themselves, were thus easy prey. The image is common in Shakespeare, whom Keats probably had in mind.

ACT III, Scene 2.
l. 21. *Hyperborean:* refers to a mythical region beyond the north wind. Thus, the word has the sense of "from the north."

l. 59. *Hast thou no fear of hangman, or the faggot?* "The faggot" is a synecdoche for burning at the stake.

l. 98. Vulcan was the god of fire and smiths.

l. 108. *beard:* to seize a man by the beard, therefore to defy him openly.

l. 123. *herbal:* a book cataloguing and describing plants.

l. 125. *an angel newly-shent. Shent* means rebuked, put down, or even ruined. In this context it should probably be paraphrased as "fallen."

l. 163. *attaint:* disgrace, stain on one's honor.

l. 248. *court-Janus.* Janus is a two-faced god. Courtiers are proverbial for their flattery. By this phrase, then, Erminia is accusing Albert of falsely reversing himself to placate the king.

ACT IV, Scene 1.

l. 51. *You need not be his sexton.* A sexton digs graves. This phrase means, then: "You need not dig his grave" or "You will not necessarily be the cause of his death."

l. 82. *the fabled fair Hesperian tree.* Hesperus, the personification of the West, had three daughters, the Hesperides, whose task was to guard a miraculous tree bearing golden apples. The tree was located in an inaccessible garden beyond the Straits of Gibraltar, the western limit of the world known to the ancients.

ACT IV, Scene 2.

l. 14. *dying Echo.* The nymph Echo pined away for love of Narcissus until only her voice was left.

l. 35. *embassage:* the message of an ambassador.

l. 91. *battailous:* pertaining to battle.

l. 106. *wittol:* a man who knows of his wife's infidelity and yet accepts it.

ACT V, Scene 1.

l. 15. *caitiff:* a captive or prisoner.

ACT V, Scene 2.

l. 36. *Cockatrice:* a mythic serpent with a fatal glance.

ACT V, Scene 4.

l. 12. *Gorgon:* one of the three sisters in Greek mythology who had snakes for hair and who were so horrid that anyone looking at them was turned to stone.

ACT V, Scene 5.
l. 23. Orpheus' song was so moving that it gained him admittance to the underworld and the release of his beloved Eurydice from the kingdom of the dead.
l. 24. Amphion built the walls of Thebes with his lyre.
l. 90. *Margravines:* the wives of margraves, who were military governors of the marches or border provinces of feudal Germany.

Oh how I love, on a fair summer's eve
l. 10. *Sydney:* the sixteenth-century English poet, Sir Philip Sidney.

Addressed to the Same
The "same" in the title is Haydon, Keats's painter friend. The sonnet was probably written soon after Keats's meeting with Haydon and Leigh Hunt, before his enthusiasm for the latter had cooled.
l. 2. *He of the cloud:* Wordsworth. The imagery of this line and the next refers to the subjects of Wordsworth's nature poetry.
l. 3. *Helvellyn:* a mountain in the Lake District of northwest England, the area in which Wordsworth lived and about which he wrote.
l. 5. *He of the rose:* Leigh Hunt.
l. 7. *[He] whose stedfastness:* Haydon.

Lines on the Mermaid Tavern
This poem (as well as *Bards of Passion and of Mirth*) is a rondeau. For a description of this form and of Keats's attitude toward it, see p. xxx. The Mermaid Tavern was the haunt of Ben Jonson and other literary lights of the Elizabethan age—including, possibly, Shakespeare.
l. 12. *bowse:* drink heartily.

Sonnet Written in the Cottage Where Burns Was Born
Keats and Brown visited Burns' birthplace on July 11, 1818.
l. 5. *Barley-bree: Bree* is Scottish for broth or liquor. Keats mentioned in a letter that he and Brown drank some whiskey at Burns' cottage.

INDEX

First lines of poetry are italicized.

1 2 3 4 5 6 7 8 9 10 11 12 13 14 15 16 17 18 19 20 21 22 23 24 25   80 79 78 77 76 75 74 73 72 71